Electoral Dynamics in Indonesia

D1610929

Electoral Dynamics in Indonesia

Money Politics, Patronage and Clientelism at the Grassroots

Edited by

Edward Aspinall and Mada Sukmajati

NUS PRESS
SINGAPORE

Published by:

NUS Press
National University of Singapore
AS3-01-02, 3 Arts Link
Singapore 117569
Fax: (65) 6774-0652
E-mail: nusbooks@nus.edu.sg
Website: http://nuspress.nus.edu.sg

ISBN 978-981-4722-04-9 (Paper)

National Library Board, Singapore Cataloguing-in-Publication Data

Names: Aspinall, Edward, editor. | Sukmajati, Mada, 1976- editor. | NUS Press,
    publisher.
Title: Electoral dynamics in Indonesia: money politics, patronage and clientelism
    at the grassroots / edited by Edward Aspinall and Mada Sukmajati.
Description: Singapore: NUS Press, National University of Singapore, [2016]
Identifiers: OCN 928277967 | ISBN 978-981-4722-04-9 (paperback)
Subjects: LCSH: Elections--Indonesia. | Political campaigns--Indonesia. |
    Indonesia--Politics and government.
Classification: LCC JQ778 | DDC 324.959804--dc23

Cover image: Voting day in Jakarta, 2014 (Photograph by Eduardo Ramirez).

Typeset by: International Typesetters Pte Ltd
Printed by: Markono Print Media Pte Ltd

Contents

List of Maps, Tables and Figures

MAPS

TABLES

FIGURES

Acknowledgements

This book is the product of intensive research collaboration. For one month in the lead up to Indonesia's national legislative elections on 9 April 2014, and for a short time following them, 50 researchers located in 20 provinces around Indonesia interviewed candidates and campaigners, observed campaign events and, where possible, "shadowed" candidates and campaigners as they interacted with voters. In total, our team conducted over 1,500 interviews, and recorded observations of hundreds of separate campaign events. Brought together through a joint research project coordinated by the Coral Bell School of Asia Pacific Affairs at the Australian National University (ANU) and the Politics and Government Research Center (PolGov) at the University of Gadjah Mada (UGM), these 50 researchers all participated in a training workshop on research goals and methods prior to the commencement of the campaign period. Most of those whose analyses are presented in this book also participated in a meeting two months after the election, where we identified common patterns and worked through first drafts of the chapters presented here. Our goals were simple: to identify the chief mechanisms that Indonesian legislative candidates used to appeal to voters in the 2014 elections, especially but not exclusively focusing on their use of patronage and clientelist networks, and to seek to identify both common patterns and regional, party or other specificities from the mass of observations we had compiled.

Of the chapters in this book, all but one (Chapter 23 by Cillian Nolan) were authored by participants in this collaborative research project. Our major thanks, therefore, go to the project researchers, not all of whose reports could be published here. They gave up their time, in many cases leaving behind teaching or other responsibilities, to participate in the research, but also contributed their analytical skills, as well as invaluable local knowledge and insights. All but Chapters 1, 18, 20 and 23 were translated from Indonesian by Edward Aspinall. We are particularly pleased to be bringing to an international readership the works of a large number of Indonesian researchers whose insights on electoral politics might not otherwise be accessible to readers outside the country. An Indonesian language version of this book, with some difference in chapters, was published in 2014 (Edward Aspinall and Mada Sukmajati, eds., *Politik Uang di Indonesia: Patronase dan Klientelisme pada Pemilu Legislatif*, Yogyakarta: PolGov, Universitas Gadjah Mada, 2014).

The initial inspiration and framework for the book is a four-country study of "money politics" across Southeast Asia, comparing Malaysia, Indonesia, Thailand and the Philippines. This larger study is funded by the Centre for Democratic Institutions (CDI) at the Australian National University and the Australian Research Council (through grant DP140103114). We thank the Chief Investigators in this project, Meredith Weiss, Allen Hicken, Paul Hutchcroft and Marcus Mietzner (Edward Aspinall is a fifth chief investigator) for the intellectual inspiration and framework we used in designing this project and book. As well as the present volume, a companion volume on Malaysia has already been published (Meredith L. Weiss, ed., *Electoral Dynamics in Malaysia: Findings from the Grassroots*, Singapore: Institute of Southeast Asian Studies, 2013), and we plan to produce similar books on elections in Thailand and the Philippines.

Funding for the research encapsulated in this book was also provided by CDI and the ARC, with supplementary funding provided by PolGov. We are very grateful to these institutions, especially CDI which has been very supportive of this research from the start. The ARC has also supported parts of Edward Aspinall's research for this project through grants DP120103181 and FT120100742. Institutional support for the research project was primarily provided by a secretariat consisting of staff at PolGov, UGM, who organised the workshops, coordinated the finances and other logistics, and oversaw data collection and compilation. We are especially thankful to Rangga Herdi Seno Prakoso, Melathi Hingar and Desi Rahmawati who provided exceptional administrative support, as well as to members of academic staff, especially Miftah Adhi Ikhsanto and the head of PolGov, Professor Purwo Santoso. Additional administrative support was provided by staff at the Coral Bell School of Asia Pacific Affairs, notably Beverley Williams and Daniel Stiegel.

Among our academic colleagues, special thanks must be given to Mulyadi Sumarto at UGM, who played an important role in helping to design and manage this research during its early stages, and whose prior work on clientelism in Indonesian social welfare programmes was one source of intellectual inspiration. We also thank colleagues who participated in the workshops either as trainers or in helping to review and comment on research papers: Burhannudin Muhtadi, Kuskridho Ambardi, Ari Dwipayana, Amalinda Savarini, Muhammad Najib, Marcus Mietzner and Meredith Weiss.

We also thank the two anonymous reviewers of the volume for NUS Press, Paul Kratoska, Peter Schoppert and Qua Lena at NUS Press as well as Dayaneetha De Silva for her expert copyediting and Janelle Caiger for proofreading. Amit Prasad prepared the index.

Glossary and Abbreviations

abangan	syncretic Muslims; nominal or less observant Muslims (usually in contrast to *santri*)
adat	custom, tradition; customary or traditional law
aliran	stream, used to distinguish between various currents of Indonesian Islam and/or affiliated organisations and political parties
arisan	informal communal savings system
aspiration funds	see *dana aspirasi*
basis	electoral base
bingkisan	a gift in the form of a parcel
blusukan	impromptu meet-the-people style campaigning; small-scale getting-to-know-the-candidate session
bom	bomb; distribution of cash to voters on voting day (also dawn attack, *eksekusi*)
botoh	gambling boss
BPS	Badan Pusat Statistik (Central Bureau of Statistics)
buah tangan	mementoes or souvenirs; gifts given by candidates on house-to-house visits
bupati	district head; regent (head of rural district or *kabupaten*)
camat	subdistrict head
dana aspirasi	aspiration funds; constituency development funds made accessible to incumbent legislators for discretionary spending in their electoral districts. Also called *jasmas*

dapil	*daerah pemilihan*, electoral district
dawn attack	*serangan fajar*
dayah	Islamic boarding school (Aceh), *pesantren*
DKM	Dewan Kemakmuran Masjid (mosque welfare councils)
DKPP	Dewan Kehormatan Penyelenggara Pemilu (General Election Honour Council)
DPR	Dewan Perwakilan Rakyat (People's Representative Council), the Indonesian parliament
DPRA	Dewan Perwakilan Rakyat Aceh (Aceh People's Representative Assembly), Aceh's provincial parliament
DPRD	Dewan Perwakilan Rakyat Daerah (Regional People's Representative Council), regional legislature at provincial or district/municipality level
DPRD I	Regional legislature at provincial level
DPRD II	Regional legislature at district/municipality level
DPRP	Dewan Perwakilan Rakyat Papua (Papuan People's Representative Council), Papua's provincial parliament
dukun	shaman or spiritual healer
dusun	hamlet
eksekusi	execution; the distribution of envelopes with cash to voters close to or on voting day (also dawn attack, *bom*)
fam	clan (predominantly Eastern Indonesia)
figur	figure; the personal qualities of a candidate, usually implying a combination of a candidate's wealth, charisma, reputation and politico-business network
FSPMI	Federasi Serikat Pekerja Metal Indonesia (Indonesian Federation of Metalworkers' Unions)
GAM	Gerakan Aceh Merdeka (Free Aceh Movement)

Gerindra	Partai Gerakan Indonesia Raya (Greater Indonesia Movement Party)
GKS	Gereja Kristen Sumba (Christian Church of Sumba)
GMIM	Gereja Masehi Injili di Minahasa (Christian Evangelical Church in Minahasa)
GMIT	Gereja Masehi Injili di Timor (Christian Evangelical Church in Timor)
Golkar	Golongan Karya; successor to the regime party in the New Order period
hadith	sayings and deeds of the Prophet
Hanura	Partai Hati Nurani Rakyat (People's Conscience Party)
haram	prohibited under Islamic law
HKTI	Himpunan Kerukunan Tani Indonesia (Indonesian Farmers Harmony Association)
HSS	Hulu Sungai Selatan (South Hulu Sungai)
HST	Hulu Sungai Tengah (Central Hulu Sungai)
INTI	Perhimpunan Indonesia Tionghoa (Indonesian Association of Chinese)
jasmas	*jaring aspirasi masyarakat* (lit. "net the community's aspirations"); programme for disbursement of aspiration funds (*dana aspirasi*)
kabupaten	rural district
kader	cadre; in a success team, a grassroots vote broker
karang taruna	neighbourhood youth group
kecamatan	subdistrict
kelurahan	precinct, urban equivalent of a rural village or *desa*
kepala suku	clan chief (Papua)
korcam	*koordinator kecamatan*, district coordinator of a success team

kordes	*koordinator desa*, village coordinator of a success team
korlap	*koordinator lapangan*, field coordinator of a success team; a grassroots vote broker (also *kader*; *sabet*)
kota	town, urban district, municipality
KPA	Komite Peralihan Aceh (Aceh Transitional Committee), organisation for former GAM combatants
KPK	Komisi Pemberantasan Korupsi (Corruption Eradication Commission)
KPPA	Komite Pemenangan Partai Aceh (Aceh Party Victory Committee)
KPPS	Kelompok Penyelenggara Pemungutan Suara (polling booth committee)
KPU	Komisi Pemilihan Umum (General Elections Commission)
KUBE	*kelompok usaha bersama* (cooperative business group), small-scale enterprise
kyai	Islamic scholar
LSI	Lembaga Survei Indonesia (Indonesian Survey Institute)
madrasah	Islamic school
main uang	play the money; engage in money politics
majelis taklim	Islamic study group; also *kelompok pengajian*
massa mengambang	floating masses; a term for uncommitted voters
meunasah	Islamic prayer hall (Aceh)
MUI	Majelis Ulama Indonesia (Indonesian Ulama Council)
musholla	Islamic prayer hall
musyawarah	deliberations or discussions
Nasdem	Partai Nasional Demokrat (National Democrat Party)
noken system	voting system in Papua highlands, supposed to involve voters openly

xviGlossary and Abbreviations

	indicating their vote by way of a traditional bag or *noken*; in practice often proxy or bloc voting by brokers without the participation of voters
NTT	Nusa Tenggara Timur (East Nusa Tenggara)
NU	Nahdlatul Ulama; traditionalist Islamic organisation
paguyuban	an informal association (often ethnic in character)
PAN	Partai Amanat Nasional (National Mandate Party), party associated with Muhammadiyah
Panwaslu	Panitia Pengawas Pemilu (Elections Supervisory Committee)
PBB	Partai Bintang Bulan (Moon Star Party), an Islamist Party
PDS	Partai Damai Sejahtera (Peace and Justice Party), a Christian Party
PDI-P	Partai Demokrasi Indonesia-Perjuangan (Indonesian Democracy Party of Struggle)
pengajian	Islamic study sessions
penggelembungan suara	vote inflation, usually through bribery of polling booth officials
peranakan	native-born, assimilated (Indonesian Chinese)
pesantren	Islamic boarding school
PKB	Partai Kebangkitan Nasional (National Awakening Party), party informally associated with Nahdlatul Ulama
PKK	Pembinaan Kesejahteraan Keluarga (Family Welfare Guidance), community-level women's welfare groups
PKPI	Partai Keadilan dan Persatuan Indonesia (Indonesian Justice and Unity Party)
PKS	Partai Keadilan Sejahtera (Prosperous Justice Party), an Islamist party

PMII	Pergerakan Mahasiswa Islam Indonesia (Islamic Student Movement of Indonesia), NU-affiliated student organisation
PNA	Partai Nasional Aceh
politik uang	money politics
PPIP	Proyek Perbaikan Infrastruktur Pedesaan (Village Infrastructure Improvement Projects)
PPK	Panitia Pemilihan Kecamatan (Subdistrict Election Committee)
PPP	Partai Persatuan Pembangunan (United Development Party), an Islamist Party
PPS	Panitia Pemungutan Suara (Village-level Voting Committee)
PR	proportional representation
preman	gangster, street tough
program	(used by candidates) for small-scale economic development projects using public funds
PUK	Pimpinan Unit Kerja (Workplace Leadership Unit)
punya massa	"has a mass"; (a candidate or broker who) has a following
putra daerah	local son (indigenous inhabitant of an area)
reformasi	reformation, the post-Suharto era
rejeki	fortune or material benefit from God; used by some to describe cash payments to voters
relawan	volunteers, (vote) brokers
RT	*rukun tetangga*, subneighbourhoods, the lowest level of community administration in Indonesia, usually incorporating a few dozen households
rukun	informal organisations of a particular lineage, village or region (Minahasa)
RW	*rukun warga*, neighbourhoods, the second lowest level of community administration in Indonesia, comprising several RT

sabet	Jv., to whip; grassroots vote broker, also *korlap/kader*
sangu	Jv., pocket money; term for payment used in vote buying
santri	devout Muslims; religious student
serangan fajar	dawn attack; cash payments to voters on morning of the polls, or the preceding evening or days
shariah	Islamic law
silaturahmi	ties of friendship, Islamic fellowship
sosialisasi	socialisation; promotion of the candidate
success team	a vote brokerage network, election campaign organisation
tandem	collaboration between candidates running at different levels (district, provincial and/or national) for campaigning and sometimes vote-buying purposes
tim sukses	success team; also *tim relawan, tim kemenangan*. A vote brokerage network or election campaign organisation
tokoh	figure or leader; *tokoh masyarakat*, community leader; *ketokohan* reputation as a leader
uang es	"ice money"; one of many terms for small cash payments distributed to voters during campaigning (*uang cendol, uang lelah, uang makan, uang pulsa, uang pinang, uang saksi, uang sayur, uang transport*); also *sangu*
ustad, ustadzah	male, female preachers
wani piro?	"How much are you brave enough to pay?". Standard response: *piro-piro wani* "as brave as you want", as much money as you can
zakat	annual Muslim religious tax, tithe

Currency Conversion Table

In 2014 at the time of the election, the US$ to rupiah exchange rate was 11,000 rupiah to one US dollar.

Commonly used figures in this book:

Rp (Indonesian rupiah)	US$
Rp 10,000	= $0.90
Rp 20,000	= $1.80
Rp 50,000	= $4.40
Rp 100,000	= $8.90
Rp 500,000	= $44
Rp 1 million	= $89
Rp 100 million	= $8,900
Rp 500 million	= $44,000
Rp 1 billion	= $89,000
Rp 5 billion	= $440,000

Map of Indonesia

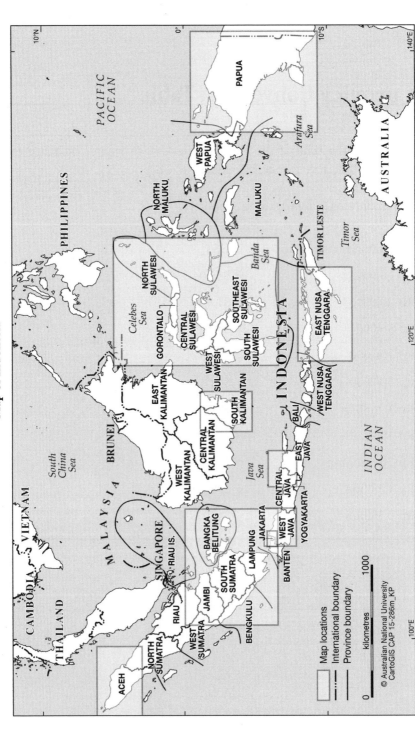

chapter **1**

Patronage and Clientelism in Indonesian Electoral Politics

Edward Aspinall and Mada Sukmajati

How do Indonesian politicians win elections? What appeals do they use to convince voters, and what sorts of networks, machines and organisations do they rely upon in order to reach out to them? In particular, to what extent do candidates win voters' support by distributing cash, goods and other benefits, and to what extent are these strategies supplemented (or replaced) by other appeals, whether they be programmatic, charismatic or identity-based? This book sets out to answer these questions by way of a series of local case studies of grassroots electioneering across Indonesia in the lead-up to the 2014 legislative elections. Many other studies of Indonesian elections have surveyed national trends and patterns in voting and party performance.[1] In this book, we look at elections up

---

[1] See, for example, Aris Ananta, Evi Nurvidya Arifin and Leo Suryadinata, *Indonesian Electoral Behaviour: A Statistical Perspective* (Singapore: ISEAS, 2004); Dwight Y. King, *Half-hearted Reform: Electoral Institutions and the Struggle for Democracy in Indonesia* (Westport, CT: Praeger, 2003); Saiful Mujani, R. William Liddle and Kuskridho Ambardi, *Kuasa Rakyat: Analisis Tentang Perilaku Memilih dalam Pemilihan Legislatif dan Presiden Indonesia pasca-Orde Baru* [People Power: An Analysis of Voting Behaviour in Legislative and Presidential Elections in Post-New Order Indonesia's Legislative and Presidential Elections] (Jakarta: Mizan, 2012);

close, studying interactions between candidates, campaign workers and voters in their home towns, neighbourhoods and villages.

For many commentators and participants, the legislative elections of 2014 were the "money politics" election. Jimly Asshiddiqie, the head of the chief body with oversight functions over Indonesia's electoral commissions, described money politics as being the most "massive" it had ever been in 2014; observers from Indonesia Corruption Watch described the 2014 election as the most "brutal" ever,[2] and one Islamic leader colourfully talked of the elections as "capitalistic, cannibalistic, and corrupt".[3] In the weeks that followed the 9 April poll, the consensus view that developed in the media was that candidates had distributed cash payments to voters, handed out goods, and bribed electoral officials at levels that had never previously been witnessed in Indonesia's electoral history. Losing candidates who said that they had not distributed cash to voters, such as the famous Golkar politician Nurul Arifin, publicly regretted their decisions.[4]

The term "money politics" has been widely used to describe such practices since Indonesia's new democratic era began in the late 1990s. Although it is in common usage, the term is imprecise, and covers a wide range of phenomena. In the early years of the democratic transition,

---

Marcus Mietzner, *Money, Power, and Ideology: Political Parties in Post-Authoritarian Indonesia* (Singapore: NUS Press, 2013).

[2] "Jimly: Politik Uang Terjadi Masif, Pemilu 2014 Bisa Lebih Buruk" [Jimly: Money Politics Massive, 2014 Election Might Be Worst Yet], *Detiknews*, 17 Apr. 2014, available at: http://news.detik.com/berita/2558272/jimly-politik-uang-terjadi-masif-pemilu-2014-bisa-lebih-buruk; Sjafri Ali, "ICW: Politik Uang Harus Diundangkan sebagai Tindak Pidana Korupsi" [ICW: Legislation Should Treat Money Politics as Part of the Crime of Corruption"], *Pikiran Rakyat*, 14 May 2014, available at: http://www.pikiran-rakyat.com/nasional/2014/05/14/281428/icw-politik-uang-harus-diundangkan-sebagai-tindak-pidana-korupsi.

[3] "Kapitalistik, Kanibal, dan Korupsi Hiasi Pemilu 2014" [Capitalism, Cannibalism, and Corruption Decorate the 2014 Election], *Waspada*, 7 May 2014.

[4] Muhammad Muhyiddin, "Nurul Arifin Menyesal Tak Sebar Duit Saat Pemilu" [Nurul Arifin Regrets Not Distributing Cash during the Election], *Tempo*, 8 Nov. 2014, available at: http://nasional.tempo.co/read/news/2014/11/08/078620560/nurul-arifin-menyesal-tak-sebar-duit-saat-pemilu.

people often described bribery *within* legislative bodies—for example, in elections to choose governors, mayors or district heads (a procedure that was replaced by direct popular elections in 2005)—as a form of money politics. Others have used the term when discussing vote buying within party congresses, or political corruption more broadly, such as when legislators skim money from government projects or receive kickbacks from businesspeople. Over the last decade, however, usage of the term has tended to narrow. When people talk about money politics now, more often than not they are referring to the practice of distributing cash (and sometimes goods) to voters during general elections.

Rather than using the vague term "money politics" to guide our analysis in this book, we instead draw on terms that are widely used in the comparative literature on electoral politics across the world. Our key concerns are with *patronage* and *clientelism*. As with many social science terms, the meanings of these words are themselves contested; indeed, some scholars treat them as synonyms.[5] So it is important to be clear from the start about what we mean when using them in this book.

We define *patronage*, following Martin Shefter, as "a divisible benefit that politicians distribute to individual voters, campaign workers, or contributors in exchange for political support".[6] Patronage thus includes cash, goods, services and other economic benefits (such as jobs or contracts) that politicians distribute to supporters or potential supporters. Such gifts can be distributed to individuals (an envelope containing cash, for example) or to groups (a new football pitch in a particular neighbourhood), a distinction we return to below. Patronage might be derived from private funds (in vote buying, for example) or from public

[5] See, for example, Herbert Kitschelt and Steven I. Wilkinson, eds., *Patrons, Clients, and Policies: Patterns of Democratic Accountability and Political Competition* (Cambridge: Cambridge University Press, 2007), p. 7.

[6] Martin Shefter, *Political Parties and the State: The American Historical Experience* (Princeton, NJ: Princeton University Press, 1994), p. 283n3; see also Paul Hutchcroft, "Linking Capital and Countryside: Patronage and Clientelism in Japan, Thailand and the Philippines", in *Clientelism, Social Policy and the Quality of Democracy*, ed. Diego Abente Brun and Larry Diamond (Baltimore, MD: Johns Hopkins University Press, 2014), pp. 176–7, whose work we are especially indebted to in drawing the distinction between the two concepts.

sources (in pork barrel projects). We distinguish, however, patronage from programmatic goods, which are benefits that a person receives by belonging to a broad social category targeted by a general government programme—for example, healthcare cards offering free treatment to poor households. We elaborate more on this distinction, and on the varieties of patronage, below.

If patronage refers to the material or other benefits that might be distributed by a politician to a voter or supporter, *clientelism*, by contrast, refers to the nature of the relationship between them. Clientelism is, as Paul Hutchcroft explains, a *"personalistic relationship of power"* within which a material benefit (patronage) is exchanged for political support.[7] Hutchcroft, drawing on earlier works, especially by James C. Scott, emphasises that clientelistic relationships are face-to-face ones.[8] As Allen Hicken explains, most definitions of clientelism require at least three components: contingency or reciprocity, in which the "delivery of a good or service on the part of both the patron and client is in direct response to a delivery of a reciprocal benefit by the other party" (typically, a material resource exchanged for a vote or other form of political support); hierarchy, emphasising the unequal power relations between the patron and the client; and iteration, implying that the clientelistic exchange is never one-off, but part of an ongoing relationship.[9] As we shall explore later in this chapter, not all patronage is distributed by way of relationships that are truly clientelistic. For example, a candidate might distribute goods to voters whom he or she has never met before and might never meet again; in such a case the relationship is not iterative, and the element of reciprocity will often also be absent because many recipients will not feel obliged to repay the candidate with a vote. Indonesian candidates use various voter mobilisation structures in order to get around these problems, and we introduce them below.

---

[7] Hutchcroft, "Linking Capital and Countryside", p. 177; emphasis in original.

[8] James C. Scott, "Patron–Client Politics and Political Change in Southeast Asia", *American Political Science Review* 66, 1 (1972): 91–113.

[9] Allen D. Hicken, "Clientelism", *Annual Review of Political Science* 14, 1 (2011): 291.

Right from the start, however, we wish to make two of the main findings of this book very clear. First, *all* our authors found that patronage distribution was central to the campaign strategies of the vast majority of candidates in Indonesia's 2014 legislative elections. Some of the studies (especially on Bekasi in Chapter 11 and South Kalimantan in Chapter 18) do focus on candidates who deliberately resisted, with varying success, the pull of money politics. However, when conducting field research during the 2014 general elections it was simply impossible to avoid the centrality of patronage politics. Indeed, it was commonplace for candidates, early in a research interview, to bemoan the "transactional" or "materialistic" expectations of voters and, unprompted, to begin detailing the methods they were using to meet those expectations. We wish to be absolutely clear on this score: our findings demonstrate that patronage distribution is *the* central mode of political campaigning in Indonesian legislative elections. Second, across this large and diverse archipelago, the vast majority of candidates relied on informal networks of vote brokers—usually called "success teams" (*tim sukses*) but going under a variety of names—to reach out to voters. To be sure, a few candidates relied on party machines, but this was far from being the dominant pattern; most candidates developed informal clientelistic structures to mobilise voters, though they often faced great challenges in making these structures work effectively for them.

For the remainder of this introductory chapter, we do five things. First, we briefly explain the research setting in terms of the existing literature on patronage and clientelism in Indonesian politics, and the research goals and design underpinning this book. Second, we set the scene by explaining the institutional framework of the 2014 legislative elections. Part of this involves describing Indonesia's major parties, but the focus is the electoral system. Since 2009 Indonesia has adopted a fully open-list proportional representation (PR) system in its legislative elections. As we shall see, this system is widely blamed by political candidates and voters alike for increasing pressures for patronage politics. Third, we elaborate on the forms of patronage that were distributed during this election, distinguishing varieties such as vote buying, club goods and pork barrel spending in terms of the types of benefit conferred, the identities of the recipients targeted, and the source of funds drawn upon. Fourth, we discuss clientelistic relationships in the context of the organisational structures candidates used, especially the roles of vote brokers organised through success teams, political parties and social networks. Fifth, we note some of the patterns of variation in patronage politics across Indonesia indicated by the chapters, link these variations to themes in the wider literature on clientelism, point out some limitations of the book and highlight future research agendas.

SETTING, SCOPE AND GOALS OF THIS BOOK

The literature on post-Suharto politics is, of course, full of references to patronage, clientelism and money politics; indeed, these ideas have been the central focus of several excellent studies. Typically, however, the main concerns of this literature have been different from those that motivate this book. Often, the primary concern has been to identify patronage politics as a force of cohesion holding important elements of the political system together. Thus, for example, both Dan Slater and Kuskridho Ambardi write of the cartelisation of Indonesian party politics in ways that emphasise the distribution of material resources within and between parties.[10] In his riposte to this literature, to the extent that he deals with patronage, Marcus Mietzner likewise focuses primarily on party financing, the alleged oligarchic capture of parties, and the weakness of state subsidies for parties, rather than on how parties and candidates distribute economic resources to voters or supporters.[11] Other studies focus on the role of patronage *inside* political parties.[12]

---

[10] Dan Slater, "Indonesia's Accountability Trap: Party Cartels and Presidential Power after Democratic Transition", *Indonesia* 78 (2004): 61–92; Kuskridho Ambardi, *Mengungkap Politik Kartel: Studi tentang Sistem Kepartaian di Indonesia Era Reformasi* [Uncovering the Politics of Cartels: A Study of Indonesia's Party System in the Reform Era] (Jakarta: Kepustakaan Populer Gramedia, 2009).

[11] Mietzner, *Money, Power, and Ideology.*

[12] Dirk Tomsa, *Party Politics and Democratization in Indonesia: Golkar in the Post-Suharto Era* (London and New York: Routledge, 2008).

The so-called "oligarchy literature", in which Richard Robison and Vedi Hadiz, as well as Jeffrey Winters, argue that extremely wealthy actors dominate Indonesia's democracy, also emphasises the role of patronage as a political glue, even if these scholars devote relatively little attention to detailing the mechanisms through which such rule is exercised.[13] Similarly, much of the recent abundant work on local government and local executive government elections has discussed money politics, identifying what might be called a money politics syndrome consisting of corruption, illicit fundraising and informal relationships linking local bureaucratic, political and business elites.[14] Michael Buehler's work on the importance of personal networks in local government head elections deserves particular note.[15] Studies on political parties and national electoral competition, by contrast, have tended to emphasise factors such as party machines and candidate appeal.[16] Often, works on electoral politics touch on clientelism and patronage insofar as

---

[13] Richard Robison and Vedi R. Hadiz, *Reorganising Power in Indonesia: The Politics of Oligarchy in an Age of Markets* (London: RoutledgeCurzon, 2004); Richard Robison and Vedi R. Hadiz, "The Political Economy of Oligarchy and the Reorganisation of Power in Indonesia", *Indonesia* 96 (2013): 35–57; Jeffrey Winters, *Oligarchy* (Cambridge: Cambridge University Press, 2011); Jeffrey Winters, "Oligarchy and Democracy in Indonesia", *Indonesia* 96 (2013): 11–33.

[14] Vedi R. Hadiz, *Localising Power in Post-Authoritarian Indonesia: A Southeast Asia Perspective* (Stanford, CA: Stanford University Press, 2010); Syarif Hidayat, "*Pilkada*, Money Politics and the Dangers of 'Informal Governance' Practices", in *Deepening Democracy in Indonesia?: Direct Elections for Local Leaders (Pilkada)*, ed. Maribeth Erb and Priyambudi Sulistiyanto (Singapore: ISEAS, 2009), pp. 125–46; Nankyung Choi, "Democracy and Patrimonial Politics in Local Indonesia", *Indonesia* 88 (2009): 131–64; Nankyung Choi, *Local Politics in Indonesia: Pathways to Power* (London: Routledge, 2011).

[15] Michael Buehler, "The Rising Importance of Personal Networks in Indonesian Local Politics: An Analysis of the District Government Head Elections in South Sulawesi in 2005", in Erb and Sulistiyanto, *Deepening Democracy*, pp. 267–85.

[16] Mujani, Liddle and Ambardi, *Kuasa Rakyat*.

they intersect with other phenomena: for example, Ryan Tans analyses the different sorts of coalitions that are mobilised in local executive government head elections in regional Indonesia, comparing them on several dimensions, including their distinctive relations to patronage politics; Nathan Allen and Dirk Tomsa similarly look at the *effects* of clientelistic arrangements on party system fragmentation.[17]

This summary only mentions part of the large literature on money politics in Indonesia, but is enough to indicate that this literature is wide-ranging. However, although such literature frequently *asserts* that patronage and clientelistic exchange are commonplace in electoral politics, we have hitherto lacked detailed analyses of the *mechanisms* through which patronage and clientelism work. This book, therefore, has a particular aim: it focuses on election campaigning, specifically on how relationships between candidates and voters are oiled by patronage and shaped by clientelism. Thus, our book deals little with some other concerns, including how elected representatives behave once in office, or even how they raise their campaign funds. Instead, our aim is to examine closely the varied forms of patronage that candidates distribute to voters, and the mechanisms, networks and techniques that they use while doing so. Only a few works have investigated such issues in Indonesia, and mostly not in much detail.[18] As a result, the Indonesian

---

[17] Ryan Tans, *Mobilizing Resources, Building Coalitions: Local Power in Indonesia* (East-West Center Policy Studies No. 64, Honolulu, 2012); Nathan W. Allen, "From Patronage Machine to Partisan Melee: Subnational Corruption and the Evolution of the Indonesian Party System", *Pacific Affairs* 87, 1 (2014): 221–45; Dirk Tomsa, "Party System Fragmentation in Indonesia: The Subnational Dimension", *Journal of East Asian Studies* 14, 2 (2014): 249–78.

[18] See, for example, Edward Aspinall, "Parliament and Patronage", *Journal of Democracy* 25, 4 (2014): 96–110; Edward Aspinall, "When Brokers Betray: Clientelism, Social Networks, and Electoral Politics in Indonesia", *Critical Asian Studies* 46, 4 (2014): 545–70; Samuel Clark and Blair Palmer, "Peaceful Pilkada, Dubious Democracy: Aceh's Post-Conflict Elections and their Implications" (Indonesian Social Development Paper no. 11, World Bank, Jakarta, 2008); Ulla Fionna, "Vote-buying in Indonesia's 2014 Elections: The Other Side of the Coin", *ISEAS Perspective* No. 35, 2014, available at http://www.iseas.edu.sg/documents/publication/ISEAS_Perspective_2014_35-Vote-buying_in_Indonesia%27s_2014_

literature is rather sparse on certain topics when compared to other Southeast Asian countries; there are, for example, several detailed studies of the mechanics of vote buying in Thailand.[19] For the first time, this volume contains several chapters (13, 14, 15, 16) that explain exactly how vote buying works in Indonesia.

The researchers who contributed chapters to this book set out to closely observe election campaigning in a large number of locations across Indonesia, focusing especially on the appeals that candidates used and the organisations they relied upon to reach out to voters. Because we were interested in the effects of various social, political and economic factors on patronage and clientelism, we chose diverse case study sites, including urban (Jakarta, Medan) and peri-urban (Bekasi, Tangerang, Bandung) settings, and rural locations including those reliant on rice production (Central and East Java), plantations (South Sumatra) and mining (South Sumatra, Southeast Sulawesi). Some sites were largely mono-ethnic (for example, Central Java, Bireuen, Aceh); others were highly ethnically diverse (for example, Medan, Bangka Belitung, North Sulawesi, East Nusa Tenggara, the Aceh highlands). Many were predominantly Islamic; others (North Sulawesi, East Nusa Tenggara, Papua) were home to non-Muslim majorities. Some of the majority Islamic areas were dominated by devout or *santri* Muslims; some had large populations of the syncretic or *abangan* Muslims of Java (Madiun, Central Java, Cirebon). Meanwhile, because we were also interested in the effects of constituency size on candidate strategies, some chapters focus on races for seats in the lowest rural district (*kabupaten*) or urban municipality (*kota*) DPRDs, often singling out just one or two electoral districts or ranging more freely through an entire *kabupaten*

Elections.pdf; Achmad Uzair Fauzan, "Winning the Villages", *Inside Indonesia* 97 (July–Sept. 2009), available at http://www.insideindonesia.org/feature-editions/winning-the-villages.

[19] For example, William A. Callahan and Duncan McCargo, "Vote-Buying in Thailand's Northeast: The July 1995 General Elections", *Asian Survey* 36, 4 (1996): 376–92; Anyarat Chattharakul, "Thai Electoral Campaigning: Vote-Canvassing Networks and Hybrid Voting", *Journal of Current Southeast Asian Affairs* 29, 4 (2010): 67–95.

or *kota*. Some chapters focus on provincial and national races; others compare campaigning across all three levels in one locale.

Each author strove to develop a general picture of campaign dynamics in their chosen electoral district, but also, in writing the chapter, to zoom in on one or two major thematic issues that were particularly significant there (thus, for example, Chapter 10 on Jakarta focuses equally on the role of constituency service and Islamic party candidates; Chapter 15 on Blora provides an explanation of vote buying, but also discusses brokerage and women candidates). Accordingly, the book chapters not only provide insights into local election dynamics in diverse social settings but also focus on varied aspects of campaign organisation and strategy, sometimes with more than one key topic covered in a single chapter, and with similar themes picked up in a large number of chapters. It thus would have been difficult to group the chapters thematically and we opted for a more simple geographic arrangement for the book, progressing from West to East across the archipelago. Some readers will doubtless find it more convenient to range across the volume, seeking out themes and issues that match their particular concerns.

Most of the field research fell into two main categories: first, interviews with political candidates and campaigners, with each researcher interviewing on average 30 such informants; and, second, direct observation of campaign events and, where possible, "shadowing" of candidates and campaigners. Most of the authors became personally close to certain candidates and campaign workers, and observed their campaign efforts at first hand. As a result, we believe they have been able to write analyses of aspects of campaign strategy, organisation and execution—such as vote buying—with a granularity that has hitherto largely been absent in the literature on election campaigning in Indonesia.

We should also stress that the researchers were not concerned with patronage and clientelism to the exclusion of other appeals or organisational forms. Rather, our goal was to open-mindedly locate and assess these phenomena within the broader universe of methods that candidates could or did use: where candidates relied equally, or more, on programmatic promises, party loyalties, ethnic appeals and the like, it was the researchers' responsibility to record and analyse these phenomena. We used the same basic approach as researchers who wrote for a companion volume on Malaysia, with the chapters in that book detailing significant non-patronage-based campaigning in that country.[20] As already noted, however, we found that patronage distribution and clientelistic organisation were by far the dominant modes of election campaigning across Indonesia, and far more prominent than in neighbouring Malaysia. Apart from this core finding, readers will discover as they progress through the book that we found considerable variety in many aspects of electoral dynamics across Indonesia.

THE INSTITUTIONAL FRAMEWORK: ELECTORAL RULES AND POLITICAL PARTIES

Indonesian legislative elections are massive affairs.[21] In 2014, candidates were running for seats in legislative assemblies at three levels: the national-level Dewan Perwakilan Rakyat (DPR, People's Representative Council); 33 province-level Dewan Perwakilan Rakyat Daerah (DPRD, Regional People's Representative Councils); and DPRDs in 497 *kabupaten* and *kota*.[22] In total, 19,699 seats were contested in these bodies. All were in multi-member constituencies, or electoral districts (*daerah pemilihan, dapil*). A single electoral district for the DPR could contain more than three million voters. District DPRD constituencies, however, could be tiny, especially in remote districts, with just a few thousand voters. The tenor of election campaigning in such constituencies

---

[20] Meredith Weiss, ed., *Electoral Dynamics in Malaysia: Findings from the Grassroots* (Singapore: ISEAS, 2013).

[21] Parts of some of the paragraphs in this section are modified from Aspinall, "Parliament and Patronage".

[22] In addition to the DPR and DPRDs, candidates were also running for the 136-seat Regional Representative Council (DPD). The members are non-party candidates, with each province acting as a single electoral district. Because this body lacks lawmaking powers and, consequently, weight in Indonesia's national politics, participants in the research project leading to this book agreed it would not be a focus of our research, and the book does not deal with DPD races.

was concomitantly more intimate. All DPR and DPRD candidates had to be nominated by registered political parties. With 12 national parties fielding candidates, plus 3 local parties in Aceh province, an estimated 180,000 candidates were competing.[23]

The growing importance of patronage, including vote buying, in Indonesia's legislative election can largely be traced to Indonesia's adoption in 2009 of an open-list form of PR to elect the national parliament and regional assemblies. In open-list systems, voters in multi-member districts can vote either for an individual candidate or for a party. The number of seats that each party wins in a district is in proportion to the combined votes for the party and all its individual candidates there. In Indonesia, given that there are many parties (12 nationally and an additional 3 local parties in Aceh), and that each electoral district has between 3 and 10 seats in the national legislature, and 3 and 12 seats in the provincial and district legislatures, even the bigger parties usually win no more than 1 or 2 seats in an electoral district—or, more rarely, 3. The candidate (or candidates) with the highest individual vote total(s) on the party list then claim the party's seat(s) in the electoral district. This system creates a strong incentive for individual candidates to devote their resources to campaigning for themselves rather than for their party, and even to compete vigorously against fellow candidates from their own party.

This system is itself a product of legal change over the last 15 years. In the first post-Suharto election in 1999, Indonesia had a fully closed-list PR system in which the individual winner(s) of a party's seat(s) in an electoral district was determined by their place(s) on the party's list on the ballot paper (though in practice party leaders sometimes disregarded the list order in allocating seats after the election). In 2004, a semi-open system was adopted, allowing voters to choose either a party or an individual candidate; candidates could be elected outside of their order on the party list only if they obtained an individual vote equal to or above the full party quota needed to attain a seat. Only two DPR candidates met this requirement. A more open system was planned for the 2009 elections whereby an individual candidate would

---

[23] Thanks for help from Kevin Evans in arriving at this estimate.

need to receive only 30 per cent of the party quota in order to secure election independent of the party list. The Constitutional Court annulled this system, however, and replaced it with fully open-list PR not long before the election that year.

At that time, there was a sudden change in the tenor of campaigning, with candidates suddenly having a much stronger incentive to compete against their party colleagues. But if the 2009 elections were a sudden learning experience, by 2014 everybody involved was fully aware of how the system operated, and most candidates were prepared for it. In practice, this meant candidates often had a very good idea in advance of how many seats their party would win in the electoral district where they were competing. They also knew, therefore, that the real competition was to win enough individual votes to defeat rivals on their own party list, and so win one of the party's allocated seats in that district. Certainly, the overwhelming majority of candidates we encountered on the campaign trail, when asked who their main competitors were, nominated candidates from their own party.

The connection to patronage is clear: when candidates are running against candidates whose party identity—and therefore platform and official ideology—are the same, they face a strong incentive to differentiate themselves in other ways. Offering "concrete" (a word we heard often from candidates) benefits to their constituents was one way to do this. We should stress, however, that it was not the only way candidates could differentiate themselves: another response was to create personal campaign teams and make other efforts to promote their individual name recognition and generate a sense of personal connection with voters. Indonesia is far from unique in these regards. It is widely recognised that systems favouring a personal vote encourage vote buying and other forms of patronage politics.[24] But patronage is not the only possible strategy that candidates can adopt in such systems; Hicken notes that candidates chasing personal votes can also rely on "name and fame".[25]

---

[24] Allen D. Hicken, "How Do Rules and Institutions Encourage Vote Buying?", in *Elections for Sale: The Causes and Consequences of Vote Buying*, ed. Frederic C. Schaffer (Boulder, CO: Lynne Reinner, 2008), pp. 47–60.

[25] Ibid., p. 50.

It is clear that patronage *delivered to voters* in Indonesia's legislative elections has become more important, along with the shift toward candidate-centred voting. Mass individualised vote buying was much rarer in 2004 than in 2014. To the extent that patronage and clientelism were crucial in the 2004 elections, "they played a larger role *within* the political parties, rather than as the chief mechanism binding ordinary voters to parties".[26] For example, wealthy candidates often purchased high positions on party lists by bribing party officials, giving themselves a greater chance of being elected.

It should also be noted, however, that as well as the change to legislative elections, another change in a parallel electoral system has also helped inculcate the culture of vote buying in Indonesian elections. We speak here of direct elections for local government heads (governors in the provinces, district heads or *bupati* in *kabupaten* and *walikota* or mayors in *kota*). Prior to 2005 these individuals were elected by local legislatures (DPRDs), accompanied by frequent reports of rampant vote buying *within* these bodies.[27] The shift to popular elections for such positions from 2005 shifted the locus of patronage politics to the broader electorate. Thus, in 2014 when we asked legislative candidates to reflect on electoral history in their home region, they often pointed to a particular gubernatorial, *bupati* or mayoral election in recent times as marking the point at which mass vote buying had become part of the local political repertoire.

It should also be noted that Indonesia's open-list PR system does encourage certain forms of cooperation between candidates: the fact that races occur concurrently at three levels (national, provincial and district) means that candidates from the different levels are not competing against each other for votes. Because *kabupaten* and *kota* electoral districts

---

[26] Edward Aspinall, "Elections and the Normalization of Politics in Indonesia", *South East Asia Research* 13, 2 (2005): 144–5.

[27] Nankyung Choi, "Local Elections and Party Politics in Post-Reformasi Indonesia: A View from Yogyakarta", *Contemporary Southeast Asia* 26, 2 (2004): 280–301; Vedi R. Hadiz, "Power and Politics in North Sumatra: the Uncompleted *Reformasi*", in *Local Power and Politics in Indonesia: Democratisation and Decentralisation*, ed. Edward Aspinall and Greg Fealy (Singapore: ISEAS, 2003), pp. 119–31.

(*dapil*) are nested inside provincial electoral districts, which are in turn nested inside national electoral districts (the exception to this general rule is Java, where national and provincial electoral districts share the same boundaries), it is relatively easy for candidates running at different levels to coordinate their efforts in the hope of maximising their individual chances of success. As is touched upon in several of our chapters, a DPR candidate will often form an alliance with one (in Java) or more (outside Java) provincial candidates and several district candidates, sharing costs, holding joint events and generally promoting each other's candidacy, often including collaboration in vote buying. These deals are generally called "tandem", and are mostly organised on an ad hoc basis between individual candidates, usually (though not always) running in the same party.

Another element of the institutional structure requiring explanation is the party system. Non-party candidates are unable to stand in Indonesia's legislative elections; only persons nominated by a nationally registered party (or, in Aceh province, by a local party) can do so. To register in 2014, a national party had to show, among other things, that it had functioning branches in all provinces, 75 per cent of districts and, within those districts, 50 per cent of subdistricts; it also had to show that in those districts it had a membership of at least 1,000 people or 1/1000th of the population of the relevant districts.[28] Though 46 national parties tried to register for the 2014 election, only 12 were allowed to run (down from 38 in 2009, 24 in 2004, and 48 in 1999). The goal of the registration requirements (and similar though less demanding provisions in earlier elections) was to prevent local or regionalist parties from competing for power and thus encouraging "disintegrative" pressures. The only exception was Aceh province, where in 2014 three local parties also competed for provincial and district seats (this exception was a result of the 2005 peace agreement that ended Aceh's armed conflict by enticing Gerakan Aceh Merdeka (GAM, Free Aceh Movement) members to give up their guerrilla struggle and transform themselves into a

---

[28] Article 8, Law No. 8 of 2012 on General Elections of Members of the People's Representative Council, Regional Representative Council, and Regional People's Representative Councils (henceforth the General Elections Law No. 8 of 2012).

political party).[29] In terms of parties, therefore, Indonesian legislative elections exhibit a high degree of national uniformity. To be sure, there are obvious national patterns: for example, Islamic parties do badly in majority Christian or Hindu areas. But unlike in some countries where regionalist parties are important, in Indonesia candidates compete all around the country using the same parties (with the partial exception of Aceh), even if these parties must then adapt to local cultural structures.

There is already a large literature on Indonesia's parties and party system.[30] It is possible to categorise the parties in various ways. For example, as Mietzner argues, identity cleavages still play an important role in the party system.[31] One key division, though it is blurring, is between parties based on sociocultural identities and catch-all parties. The first group includes several parties that are rooted in segments of the Islamic community. Partai Kebangkitan Bangsa (PKB, National Awakening Party) draws on the "traditionalist" Islamic community which is concentrated in certain rural parts of the country, notably East Java, and centred on the organisation Nahdlatul Ulama; Partai Amanat Nasional (PAN, National Mandate Party) is based on the "modernist" and more urban organisation, Muhammadiyah. Both of these parties, though drawing on these respective social bases, style themselves as pluralist in orientation. At the more Islamist end of the spectrum, Partai Keadilan Sejahtera (PKS, Prosperous Justice Party) was founded by a core of Muslim Brotherhood-inspired campus activists, and is known for a trademark constituency-service style of election campaigning, including the provision of free medical services.[32] Partai

---

[29] Edward Aspinall, *The Helsinki Peace Agreement: A More Promising Basis for Peace in Aceh?* (East-West Center Policy Studies No. 20, Washington, DC, 2005).

[30] Mietzner, *Money, Power, and Ideology*; Leonard Sebastian, ed., "Special Focus: Political Parties and Democracy in Indonesia", *South East Asia Research* 20, 4 (2012): 463–568; Sunny Tanuwidjaja, "Political Islam and Islamic Parties in Indonesia: Critically Assessing the Evidence of Islam's Political Decline", *Contemporary Southeast Asia* 32, 1 (2010): 29–49; Andreas Ufen, "Political Parties in Post-Suharto Indonesia: Between Politik Aliran and 'Philippinisation'" (GIGA Working Paper No. 37, GIGA Institute of Asian Studies, Hamburg, 2006).

[31] Mietzner, *Money, Power, and Ideology*, p. 220.

[32] Michael Buehler, "Revisiting the Inclusion–Moderation Thesis in the Context of

Persatuan Pembangunan (PPP, United Development Party) promotes itself as the "big house of the Islamic community". In contrast, Partai Demokrasi Indonesia-Perjuangan (PDI-P, Indonesian Democratic Party of Struggle) styles itself as "nationalist" and has a strong following in areas inhabited by less religiously observant Muslims, and by minorities such as Hindus in Bali and Christians elsewhere. It can also be counted on to consistently and vigorously promote pluralism and minority rights in national policy debates.

A second broad category consists of catch-all parties which are not strongly rooted in any particular cultural constituency. Golkar, the former electoral vehicle of Suharto's New Order regime, is the most venerable. Founded in the 1960s, and consistently Indonesia's second-largest party in elections since 1999 (except in 2004 when it held first place), Golkar has always defined its mission in developmentalist terms and tried to transcend the socioreligious divides that mark Indonesian society (though, in fact, it has a social base of its own, among bureaucrats and businesspeople). It is also the quintessential Indonesian patronage machine.[33] An increasingly important subcategory is "presidentialist parties": parties that were created by or for major political figures, all of them tycoons or ex-generals, who harbour presidential ambitions. The most important such party in recent history has been Partai Demokrat, ex-president Susilo Bambang Yudhoyono's personal vehicle since 2004. Four such parties (Demokrat, Gerindra, Hanura, Nasdem) are now represented in the DPR, with their combined vote share increasing from 9 per cent in 2004, to 30 per cent in 2009 and 34 per cent in 2014. All four presidentialist parties can trace their origins to Golkar, in that they were founded by individuals who were either former Golkar members or who came from social groups (such as former military men) associated with Golkar. Viewed another way, in 2014, almost 50 per cent of the vote was won by Golkar

---

Decentralized Institutions: The Behavior of Indonesia's Prosperous Justice Party in National and Local Politics", *Party Politics* 9, 2 (2012): 210–29; Yon Machmudi, *Islamising Indonesia: The Rise of Jemaah Tarbiyah and the Prosperous Justice Party (PKS)* (Canberra: ANU ePress, 2008).

[33] Tomsa, *Party Politics and Democratization*.

and its successor parties. Given that these parties are especially strongly reliant on personalist appeals and patronage delivery, their growing prominence is itself a telling sign of the gradually changing shape of Indonesia's party system.

All the parties, however, are little differentiated in programmatic terms (except on issues concerning the place of religion in national life). There is, for example, little of the left–right cleavage on matters of economic policy, the role of markets and redistribution that is visible in many countries. In part, this lack of programmatic distinctiveness is a product of the over-sized "rainbow coalitions" that have drawn most major parties into post-Suharto cabinets;[34] it is also a product of the role played by the DPR commissions, bodies where negotiations over lawmaking take place, typically involving horse-trading between parties that are notionally part of both government *and* opposition.[35] But programmatic vagueness is also a sign of Indonesia's patronage-oriented polity in which legislators are more interested in the legislatures' budgeting processes than lawmaking, hoping to access social programmes, development projects and other forms of state spending that they can turn into sources of campaign funding or political largesse for their supporters.

Of course, this patronage orientation does not mean that parties have not tried to develop and promote distinctive brands. On the contrary, in 2014 the major parties ran vigorous national campaigns featuring slick advertising and media strategies. Mostly these campaigns concentrated on promoting either socially resonant party images, or a party's leader and presidential candidate (the presidential election took place on 9 July, three months after the legislative poll). Examples in the first category included PDI-P's television advertisements stressing pluralist themes and PKB promotions restating the party's roots in

[34] Dan Slater, "Unbuilding Blocs: Indonesia's Accountability Deficit in Historical Perspective", *Critical Asian Studies* 46, 2 (2014): 287–315.

[35] Stephen Sherlock, "The Parliament in Indonesia's Decade of Democracy: People's Forum or Chamber of Cronies?", in *Problems of Democratisation in Indonesia: Elections, Institutions, and Society*, ed. Edward Aspinall and Marcus Mietzner (Singapore: ISEAS, 2010), pp. 160–78.

the traditionalist Islamic community. The most vigorous presidential-style campaign was waged by Gerindra (Partai Gerakan Indonesia Raya, Greater Indonesian Movement Party), whose advertisements all featured party leader Prabowo Subianto, and borrowed heavily from the nationalist imagery of Indonesia's early postcolonial era. Prabowo presented himself as an outsider and vigorously condemned Indonesia's political elite for its corruption and ineffectualness.[36] Equally important was the PDI-P's campaign promoting its—ultimately successful—presidential candidate, Joko Widodo, known as Jokowi.[37] Despite the looming presidential contest, no single policy issue prompted vigorous debate between party leaders during the legislative campaign. Moreover, even candidates running for parties promoting their own presidential candidates still faced the same pressures as everybody else to increase their personal vote, and hence to run grassroots campaigns and distribute patronage.

VARIETIES OF PATRONAGE

As already noted, we define patronage as a divisible benefit exchanged for political support. We should stress, however, that the element of *exchange* that is central here is often highly problematic in practice. When political candidates distribute gifts or payments to voters they frequently cannot be confident about how the recipients will respond. In fact, this is one of the major problems of patronage politics for its practitioners: where there is a secret ballot, "Prospective vote buyers typically have no guarantees that voters who accept shall dutifully reciprocate on election day."[38] Voters may view the benefits they receive in varied ways: some may think they are bound to repay the giver

---

[36] Edward Aspinall, "Oligarchic Populism: Prabowo Subianto's Challenge to Indonesian Democracy", *Indonesia* 99 (2015): 1–28.

[37] Marcus Mietzner, "How Jokowi Won and Democracy Survived", *Journal of Democracy* 25, 4 (2014): 111–26.

[38] Frederic C. Schaffer and Andreas Schedler, "What is Vote Buying?", in Schaffer, *Elections for Sale*, p. 19.

with support; others may think of the gift as a non-binding goodwill gesture; others might take offence. Politicians often try to get around these problems by presenting their patronage in ways that accord with local cultural values—for example, by packaging their gifts as religiously sanctioned charity or presenting them as embodying the sort of social generosity that any wealthy and respectable figure should engage in. They thus try to activate social norms about gratitude and personal obligation in order to encourage voters to reciprocate. They also try to develop ongoing clientelistic relationships with recipients, or approach them via trusted intermediaries or brokers with whom the voters have close personal relationships, something we turn to in the next section.

Many of our chapter authors explore these issues within the cultural context and meanings of patronage. At this point, it is worth bearing them in mind as background to the following summary of the chief varieties of patronage politics encountered in Indonesia. This section also doubles as an introduction to the terminology used consistently throughout the book.

Vote Buying

In this book, we identify vote buying with a rather narrow set of behaviours: the systematic distribution of cash payments and/or goods to voters in the few days leading up to the election with the implicit expectation that recipients will repay with their vote.[39] In Indonesia, though a variety of terms are used for this practice, a universally recognised expression is *serangan fajar*—"dawn attack", a term that is drawn from Indonesia's revolutionary history and that originally reflected the fact that payments were sometimes distributed just after the dawn prayer on voting day. As several chapters show, some candidates in Indonesia were highly systematic in their vote-buying efforts, mobilising large teams to draw up lists of voters and deliver cash payments to

---

[39] Unlike some other literature, for example, Lisa Björkman, "'You Can't Buy a Vote': Meanings of Money in a Mumbai Election", *American Ethnologist* 41, 4 (2014): 617–34.

them. In particular, our four chapters (14, 15, 16 and 17) on rural East and Central Java electoral constituencies include studies of vote buying that provide a level of detail that has hitherto been absent in the Indonesian literature, partly reflecting what appeared to be a greater intensity—and social legitimacy—of vote buying in these parts of Java than in most other locations. Several other chapters, including those on South Sumatra (6), Cirebon (13), Southeast Sulawesi (20) and Jayapura (22), also touch on vote buying, but in somewhat less detail; the chapter on South Kalimantan (18) includes a series of studies of candidates who *refused* to engage in the practice. In itself these vote-buying efforts are a huge research topic. Some of the most interesting and controversial issues touched upon in this volume, and raised in broader comparative literature, include the tendency of brokerage structures to leak funds and candidates' efforts to prevent this, and the targeting of recipients, especially the question of whether candidates target party loyalists or swing voters.[40] We also hope that this volume will contribute to debates on how vote-buying patterns differ across regions with varying socioeconomic and political profiles, and constituency size, and how these payments are understood and appreciated by the recipients (see Noor Rohman's analysis on Pati, Central Java, Chapter 14).

Individual Gifts

Candidates also delivered a huge variety of individual gifts to voters, as illustrated in many of the chapters. Typically, candidates presented such gifts when they met voters, either on house-to-house visits or at campaign events, with the gift being presented as a sort of social lubricant, keepsake or memento. Sometimes these gifts were distributed by campaign teams, and in such cases they could be hard to distinguish from systematic vote buying. The most common gifts consisted of several categories: small items (such as calendars and key chains) bearing the candidate's name and image; foodstuffs (rice, sugar, cooking oil, instant noodles); and small

---

[40] Aspinall, "When Brokers Betray"; Simeon Nichter, "Vote Buying or Turnout Buying? Machine Politics and the Secret Ballot", *American Political Science Review* 102, 1 (2008): 19–31.

items of clothing and other household items, especially those with a religious meaning (headscarves, prayer robes, prayer mats) or minor household items (crockery, plastic ware). The possibilities were virtually endless, and almost any small or inexpensive item could be provided to individuals: Chapter 5 provides an example of a candidate who based his strategy around the distribution of potted plants. Another all but ubiquitous practice which should be specially noted was the provision of free food, drinks, cigarettes and other consumables—ranging from modest snacks to lavish feasts—at meetings attended by candidates and voters. It will be immediately obvious that the distinction between such gifts and vote buying can be blurred; even so, most candidates drew a sharp line between the two practices and did not consider gift giving to be part of money politics. (The critical difference in their minds was that vote buying was usually carried out systematically, with meticulously compiled voter lists and the aim of reaching a set target of voters.)

Services and Activities

As well as cash and material objects, candidates often provided a variety of activities and services. Typical activities include campaign-events-cum-community-celebrations where candidates promoted themselves while also appearing as supporters of community engagement. Such activities included sports competitions, community parties, chess or dominoes tournaments, prayer meetings, cooking demonstrations, singing meetings, bird whistling competitions, fishing contests—again, the list is all but endless. Many candidates also funded community services: free medical check-ups and treatment were once a PKS trademark, but have now been mimicked by many candidates from other parties. Also common was the provision of free ambulances, alongside similar services such as rubbish collection. Another striking feature of the 2014 election was the frequency with which candidates provided free health and death/disability insurance to voters; in fact, the Hanura (Partai Hati Nurani Rakyat, People's Conscience Party) and Nasdem (Partai Nasional Demokrat, National Democrats) parties did this as a matter of policy. Finally, many candidates also provided personalised assistance to constituents who needed to access government services, such as a government health or scholarship programme. Interestingly, the region where we found community service to be the most prominent was also the most urban and developed electoral constituency in our sample—Jakarta—a place where retail vote buying was also particularly low (Chapter 10). At the same time, Jakarta was far from being the only place where this practice occurred: Rudi Rohi in his analysis of East Nusa Tenggara (Chapter 21), Indonesia's poorest province in terms of per capita income, describes one candidate who positioned himself as a broker distributing access to a national scholarship scheme for poor students.

Club Goods

We define club goods as patronage that is provided for the collective benefit of bounded social groups rather than for individuals. The vast majority of examples encountered in the Indonesian case fit into two subcategories: donations to community associations, and donations to communities living in a particular urban precinct, village or other location. A huge variety of formal and informal institutions exist at the grassroots in Indonesia: religious groups, sports clubs, youth associations, women's groups, farmers' cooperatives and so on. It was extremely common for candidates to visit such groups and provide them with collectively beneficial gifts such as religious paraphernalia, sports equipment, musical instruments, sound systems, kitchen utensils, marquees and farming equipment. Likewise, candidates often donated funds to build, renovate or repair community infrastructure: for example, a house of worship, road, bridge or drainage canal, or to provide street lighting, village water wells, and connections to the electricity grid. Again, few candidates considered club goods as proscribed money politics precisely because, they said, such gifts provide public benefit. In order to deliver club goods, and in order to try to ensure that the beneficiaries repaid them with votes, candidates generally relied on the mediation of leaders of the relevant communities as vote brokers. One of the chief research issues here is therefore how and why candidates choose between individualised patronage strategies and club goods: it was common for candidates to view the distribution of club goods as legally and morally more supportable, but also as a less reliable strategy, unless strong support from community leaders could be locked in. This argument is developed particularly strongly in Ahmad Zainul Hamdi's chapter on brokerage and club goods in East Java (Chapter 17).

Pork Barrel Projects

So far, we have been describing inducements that were distributed to voters mostly in advance of casting their ballots, and which were primarily funded privately, whether by the candidate personally or by a private donor (though the ultimate source of such funds is often corrupt extraction from the state budget). A slightly different form of patronage covered in this book is pork barrel projects, which we define as geographically targeted and publicly funded benefits in repayment of, or expectation of, political support. As we shall see, many candidates promised to provide publically funded "programmes" or "projects" to their constituents—typically club goods consisting of small-scale infrastructure projects, or benefits to community groups, especially for income-generating activities. Incumbents often relied on track records of having delivered such benefits when campaigning for re-election. In many district and provincial parliaments there are special funds available for legislators for this purpose. These are often known by the term *dana aspirasi* (aspiration funds), with the idea being that individual legislators respond to their constituents' "aspirations" by providing them with government projects. Similar funds are found in many countries, and are generally known as constituency development funds.[41] What makes us view these projects as a form of patronage is the element of contingency involved: legislators typically delivered these projects in the hope or expectation that they would be repaid with votes. As we shall see (Chapters 7, 12 and 16), incumbents standing for re-election also often cultivated the beneficiaries of these projects as clients, drawing them into their campaign teams.

This list summarises only the most prominent forms of patronage encountered during our research and discussed in the following pages.

---

[41] Albert van Zyl, "What is Wrong with Constituency Development Funds?", International Budget Partnership, Budget Brief 10 (2010), available at http://www.internationalbudget.org/publications/brief10/.

There were also payments and other benefits provided by candidates not to voters but to their active supporters, most commonly in the form of payments to success team members, but also of more clientelistic and ongoing rewards to them, such as jobs or favoured treatment in the allocation of government projects. Special note should also be made of the interplay between patronage and electoral fraud. Electoral fraud is often considered to be an *alternative* to vote buying or patronage, but our research suggests that it might also be considered as being part of the same continuum.[42] Certainly, we encountered many instances in which candidates were able to choose between investing their money in buying votes from individual voters (retail vote buying) or buying them from election officials, who in return for payment could switch votes between individual candidates within the same party or even between parties during the vote tabulation process (an action that might be called wholesale vote buying, or even vote trading, as opposed to the retail vote buying embodied in the "dawn attack").[43] Each method had its own costs and benefits; in particular, buying votes from election officials tended to be more reliable, but also more expensive. Unfortunately, this topic was not planned as a major focus of this research from the start, because we believed it would have required researchers to focus on election administrators rather than candidates, and though it is touched upon in several chapters (see especially Chapter 23) it is not explored in detail. It needs to be marked as a future research priority.

A few more notes are in order. First, we should stress that we draw a sharp distinction between patronage and programmatic goods. In any election, political parties or candidates will make promises of new policies that will provide material benefits to particular classes of person if enacted: a new fertiliser subsidy for farmers, a pension increase for

---

[42] See, for example, Fabrice Lehoucq, "When Does a Market for Votes Emerge?", in Schaffer, *Elections for Sale*, pp. 33–45.

[43] Mohammad Najib, "Keterlibatan Penyelenggara Pemilu dalam *Vote Trading*" [The Involvement of Election Organisers in Vote Trading], in *Politik Uang di Indonesia: Patronase dan Klientelisme pada Pemilu Legislatif 2014* [Money Politics in Indonesia: Patronage and Clientelism in the 2014 Legislative Election], ed. Edward Aspinall and Mada Sukmajati (Yogyakarta: PolGov, Universitas Gadjah Mada, 2014), pp. 511–36.

the elderly, a new scholarship for poor children and so on. Following Susan Stokes, we classify such redistribution as being programmatic when three criteria are satisfied: (i) the goals of the programme are "a matter of public debate"; (ii) those "objectives shape the official, codified criteria for distribution of the program or resource"; and (iii) those criteria then "shape the actual distribution of the program or good".[44] For this reason, we categorise aspiration funds and other pork barrel projects as forms of patronage because politicians typically deliver projects, not to the communities that most accorded with official criteria (for example, the poorest communities in a district), but to where they have in the past and are likely in the future to get most votes. There are also many examples of clientelistic distribution of government programmes in this book which occur when a programme is established with open and public criteria, but whose actual delivery is shaped by political affiliations and payback. An example of this is when a politician facilitates access for a voter's son or daughter to a government scholarship programme that should be open to all, with an expectation of repayment in the form of a vote. We should stress, however, that our research team hardly encountered truly programmatic politics during their observations of grassroots campaigning—for example, we rarely observed candidates who spent much time explaining their parties' welfare, health or other policies to constituents. Indeed, when candidates used the Indonesian term *program*, they were usually referring to pork barrel projects of various sorts, as Rubaidi explains (Chapter 16).

Second, we should again stress that we are not exclusively concerned with patronage in this book, but also look at other sorts of appeals, such as those based on the personal charisma of a candidate, or group identity. We are particularly concerned with how such appeals may *overlap* with, or present themselves as *alternatives* to, patronage. For example, as we shall see, identity appeals—especially those based on shared religion, ethnicity and region—are commonplace in grassroots

---

[44] Susan C. Stokes, "Pork, by Any Other Name … Building a Conceptual Scheme of Distributive Politics", paper presented at American Political Science Association Annual Meeting, Toronto, 3–6 Sept. 2009, p. 10, available at: http://ssrn.com/abstract=1449057.

election campaigning in Indonesia. But do they *reinforce* communal appeals, as when a candidate originating from a certain group is assumed to direct patronage toward members of that group (this is the contention of Kanchan Chandra's study of patronage politics in India[45]), or can patronage also be used to reach out *across* identity lines and so counter an identity disadvantage (as when a Christian candidate provides patronage goods to Muslim voters in a majority Islamic district)? Similarly, almost all candidates will say that what really counts under the open-list PR system is *figur* or *ketokohan*—both terms that can be roughly translated as the personal reputation of a candidate. But to what extent is that reputation built on a candidate's track record of providing patronage to voters in their district? Several studies in this book suggest that this is often central.

We should also note a striking absence in this book: relatively few of our authors encountered violence, or the threat of it, as an important factor in grassroots election campaigning. The chief exceptions are noted in the chapters on Bireuen, Aceh (Chapter 2) and East Nusa Tenggara (Chapter 21). The relative absence of violence is at first sight a surprising finding, given the prevalence of thuggish paramilitaries in contemporary Indonesia, and given the evidence we have of violence in some electoral settings in the country.[46] Moreover, violence and intimidation are frequently closely related to patronage politics, in part because both arise during situations of highly unequal personalised power relations, in part because patronage politicians need methods to ensure that the recipients of patronage actually deliver on their promises of political support, and will be more likely to do so if they fear violent retaliation. Accordingly, violence has featured as a significant part of the electoral repertoire in other patronage polities in Southeast Asia,

[45] Kanchan Chandra, *Why Ethnic Parties Succeed: Patronage and Ethnic Head Counts in India* (Cambridge: Cambridge University Press, 2004).

[46] Ian Wilson, *The Politics of Protection Rackets in Post-New Order Indonesia: Coercive Capital, Authority and Street Politics* (London: Routledge, 2015); Mohammad Zulfan Tadjoeddin, *Explaining Collective Violence in Contemporary Indonesia: From Conflict to Cooperation* (Houndmills: Palgrave Macmillan, 2014), pp. 153–74.

notably the Philippines and Thailand. Buehler suggests that there is little inter-candidate violence in Indonesian elections partly because the power-sharing logic that operates at the local level, and the multiplicity of elected offices, reduces the winner-takes-all dynamic that encourages violence in Thai and Philippine elections.[47] At this point we can do little more than note the relatively peaceable nature of legislative elections in Indonesia as a topic for future research.

Finally, a point should be made about the legal situation. At first blush, the vast majority of transactions this study is concerned with would appear to be technically illegal. Article 86 (1) j of the 2012 elections law prohibits "promising or giving money or other materials" to community members for electoral purposes.[48] However, various technical points make such provisions difficult to enforce, including the fact that the prohibitions apply only to candidates and registered campaign team members, whereas it is often members of informal and unregistered success teams who distribute cash and goods. Reports of the alleged offence also have to be submitted to the election supervisory body within seven days, accompanied by sufficient evidence. As a result, it is very difficult to successfully prosecute instances of money politics. This helps explain why so many of the activities we study in this book took place relatively openly. As mentioned, many practitioners viewed only vote buying in the narrowest sense—the distribution of individual cash payments in the few days leading to the election—as a form of morally dubious and legally impermissible money politics. They frequently stated that gift giving, providing club goods and other forms of patronage were perfectly legitimate.

CLIENTELISM AND VOTER MOBILISATION NETWORKS

As well as studying patronage in all its forms, a second aim of this volume is to analyse the networks that legislative candidates used to

---

[47] Buehler, "The Rising Importance of Personal Networks".
[48] Article 86 (1) j, General Elections Law No. 8 of 2012.

reach out to and mobilise voters in the 2014 elections. In Indonesia, we found candidates using vote brokerage networks resembling those found in many countries. Grassroots brokers played the essential role in these structures. These brokers were typically formal or informal community leaders or ordinary community members who worked on the candidate's behalf, persuading their neighbours or associates to vote for the candidate, and often delivering cash payments or goods on his or her behalf.

Before we describe these brokerage networks, we should explain why they are important. One reason is obvious. All candidates, especially in large constituencies, found it impossible to interact personally with enough voters sufficiently frequently to win their votes; hence, they needed agents who would work on their behalf, organising their campaigns and delivering information to voters. Also, in many respects, the networks found in Indonesia were like the organisational structures found in elections everywhere. For example, there was often a degree of specialisation in these teams: better resourced DPR candidates, for example, would have team members who handled media relations or ran social media campaigns.

Additional factors, however, make vote brokerage networks especially salient in patronage democracies. As already mentioned, politicians using patronage face a major "reciprocity problem": how do they ensure that beneficiaries of their munificence will repay them with their votes? The comparative literature identifies this as a critical issue in patronage politics everywhere, but it is not merely a theoretical problem; as some of our chapters illustrate, it is something that many candidates in Indonesia worried about deeply.[49] Many of them feared that they would make donations to community groups, or deliver cash to individual voters, but get few votes in return, wasting their money without winning a seat. Brokers are one way to get around this problem: if the payment or gift is delivered, not by a politician with whom the recipient has no ongoing relationship, but by a person whom he or she knows and trusts, it is more likely to elicit feelings of gratitude and obligation. The broker will also be able to monitor and urge compliance with the "deal":

---

[49] E.g. Schaffer and Schedler, "What is Vote Buying?", pp. 18–28.

for instance, he or she will be more likely to know if the recipient is having second thoughts about the candidate.[50]

We have also mentioned that one way of making patronage delivery more reliable is to embed it in relationships that are truly clientelistic insofar as they involve, not simply one-off material exchange, but ongoing mutual benefit between unequal partners. As we shall see in several chapters, candidates often rewarded their success team members not only (or mostly) with cash payments but also with promises of future employment, contracts or other benefits. Such structures were often filled with individuals who had received benefits from the candidate in the past. This is also one reason that candidates were keen to recruit formal and informal community leaders (*tokoh masyarakat*) into their campaign structures, precisely because voters would often be in similar relationships of dependence with those leaders.

With these preliminary thoughts in mind, let us mention the three basic varieties of vote brokerage networks that are used in Indonesia and discussed in this book.

Success Teams

These are the most common form of brokerage structure used by candidates. Almost every serious candidate in the 2014 legislative elections had a success team, though such teams also went by other names (alternatives included *tim pemenangan* "victory team", *tim keluarga*, "family team" and *tim relawan*, "volunteer team"). Teams also varied greatly in size: teams supporting rich DPR candidates could have literally thousands of members; poor district candidates might have only a handful. A critical feature of success teams was that they were *personal*, having the function of promoting the campaign of an individual candidate, although cooperation with other candidates, especially via tandem arrangements, was common. Another key feature

---

[50] Susan C. Stokes, Thad Dunning, Marcelo Nazareno and Valeria Brusco, *Brokers, Voters, and Clientelism: The Puzzle of Distributive Politics* (New York: Cambridge University Press, 2013); Wang Chin-Sou and Charles Kurzman, "The Logistics: How to Buy Votes", in Schaffer, *Elections for Sale*, pp. 61–78.

Fig. 1.1 Typical Success Team Structure for a DPRD II Candidate

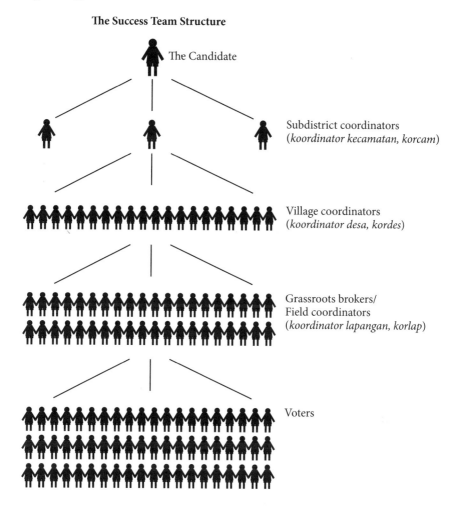

The Success Team Structure

The Candidate

Subdistrict coordinators
(*koordinator kecamatan, korcam*)

Village coordinators
(*koordinator desa, kordes*)

Grassroots brokers/
Field coordinators
(*koordinator lapangan, korlap*)

Voters

was their pyramidal and territorial structure. A typical success team for a DPRD II member would incorporate a core team of advisors and assistants who worked directly with the candidate, helping to plan and coordinate the campaign, and lower down, a series of subdistrict coordinators (*koordinator kecamatan, korcam*), village coordinators (*koordinator desa, kordes*) and then, finally, the grassroots brokers or "field coordinators" (*koordinator lapangan, korlap*) who interacted directly with voters (again, a variety of names were used for all these positions) (see Fig. 1.1).

Individuals occupying nodal points in the pyramid were typically in charge of recruiting the individuals below them, often targeting their friends, neighbours, business associates, relatives or other associates. The ultimate goal was to be able to connect the candidate, at the apex of the pyramid, to the individual voters at the household level, and to do so by way of brokers who had intimate relationships with those individuals.

This structure was used by most candidates, but it was especially critical for candidates engaged in vote buying, because it was the neighbourhood-level brokers who drew up lists of voters willing to vote for the candidate, passed those lists upward through the team structure, made the payments, and then ensured that recipients went to the polling booth on voting day. As we shall see in several chapters, however, the same problems of compliance that bedevil relationships between candidates and voters also afflicted these teams, and candidates were often very concerned about embezzlement, indolence and defection by their brokers, problems which often made these teams much less reliable at delivering the vote than was hoped for.[51]

Social Network Machines

As well as using territorially organised success teams, candidates often also tried to gain endorsement of influential community leaders, with the goal that these leaders would then mobilise their social networks into supporting the candidate. These community leaders often headed formal institutions, such as low-level community government units like villages, hamlets, *rukun warga* (RW, neighbourhoods) or *rukun tetangga* (RT, subneighbourhoods), or they might be the leaders of formal associations, such as religious groups, ethnic organisations or sports clubs. Equally commonly, however, they were informal leaders, such as religious figures, village elders, heads of kinship groups, *adat* (customary) leaders, or simply people whose opinion was valued in

---

[51] See also Aspinall, "When Brokers Betray"; Stokes et al., *Brokers, Voters, and Clientelism*; Wang and Kurzman, "The Logistics", pp. 68–70.

their neighbourhood. The key point is that such people had a following (*punya massa*, "has a mass" or "a following", was the widely used Indonesian term), whose support candidates hoped could be gained through the leader's mediation and endorsement. In other words, candidates frequently tried to piggyback on existing social networks and, as Rohi argues in his chapter on East Nusa Tenggara (21), tried to make use of the social trust generated within such networks for electoral purposes. Sometimes, candidates would do so by drawing the community leaders into their territorially based success teams, but often they would simply augment the success team with community leaders-cum-brokers (whose followings were in any case often spread through more than one neighbourhood or village and thus did not always match well with the success team format). We can thus think of brokerage structures using two separate routes to reach voters: the territorially organised success team (or party) route and the social network route, though they often overlapped.

Reliance on such community leaders was typically connected with distribution of club goods: when candidates recruited community leaders they often provided their organisation, institution, network or following with a collective benefit. Thus, a village head supports a candidate and the candidate builds a new road in the village; a religious leader joins a success team and his church is repaired; the head of a housewives' group joins and her group receives a donation of cooking equipment; and so on. Though most candidates sought out such leaders because of their social influence, in fact reciprocity problems often occurred in this form of vote brokerage too: a community leader might receive a club good, urge his or her supporters to vote for the giver, but then fail to deliver. Thus, some candidates preferred individual vote-buying to relying on community leaders who promised to deliver vote banks, but with everything riding on those leaders' social influence.

Parties

As already noted, parties played a surprisingly minimal role in organising most candidates' grassroots campaigns. This does not mean, however, that they were not involved at all: often, one particular candidate who occupied a senior leadership position in the local party structure would be able to dominate it and effectively turn the local party branch into a personal success team, using it to promote his or her personal campaign (of course, to the detriment of other individuals on the party list in that electoral district). Party structures thus tended to be associated with the strongest candidates (see Chapter 12 on Bandung for one discussion). More commonly, however, the local party branches would be riven with factionalism and individual candidates would be able to rely on the support of individual branches, leaders or party cadres and bring them into their own success teams. Thus, the success teams described above were often partly populated by party cadres. It should be noted, however, that the role of the party organisation varied by party: PKS, for example, was by far the most systematically organised and we found higher levels of cooperation between PKS candidates than between candidates from any other party. For example, PKS was quite effective at doing something that several parties attempted but generally failed to achieve: dividing the territory of a single electoral district up between the party's various candidates, and allocating each zone to a different candidate to avoid their competing directly for the same voters. At the other end of the spectrum, the catch-all and presidentialist parties were all but indistinguishable at the grassroots, and in interviews candidates for these parties often discussed their campaign strategies without referring at all to their party identities or structures.

PATTERNS OF PATRONAGE AND FUTURE RESEARCH AGENDAS

This book presents a series of sketches of how grassroots campaigning worked, along with discussions of the varied forms of patronage politics and clientelism used by candidates across a wide range of geographic and social settings in Indonesia's 2014 legislative elections. Though we are not able to present definitive answers to many of the key questions in the study of patronage politics, such as those regarding causation and variation, some of the patterns that readers will notice as they read the book are suggestive of such answers and point toward future research. For example, it is a widely shared view in the field that clientelistic politics tends to decline as economic development increases.[52] Readers will also notice that relatively wealthy and more urban provinces—the strongest example is Jakarta—seem less susceptible to patronage politics, especially in the form of individualised vote buying. Rurality is also sometimes considered to be a facilitating factor in patronage politics because the more static and intimate social relationships found in rural villages, compared with in urban precincts, allow for more effective penetration by clientelistic networks;[53] it is striking that the most intense vote buying we detected took place in rural districts of Java. In even less developed and isolated rural settings where traditional authority figures and social structures continue to wield considerable influence, electoral patterns tend to be more broker-centred, with local notables being able to deliver blocs of votes in their communities (even, in highland Papua, dispensing with the need for voting altogether, as Chapter 23 demonstrates).

As for institutional structures, in addition to the intensification of vote buying that has occurred as Indonesia has moved toward an electoral system emphasising the personal vote, other aspects of our findings also connect with wider debates. For example, increased constituency size is sometimes seen as reducing patronage politics:[54] it was one of our consistent findings that candidates running vote-buying efforts in the district-level DPRDs, where they typically had to win the votes of just a few thousand, or even a few hundred, voters consistently spent several times more per head than did their counterparts running in the much more populous national or provincial constituencies.

This book is far from being the last word on the topics of money politics, patronage and clientelism in Indonesia. Many of the

---

[52] Kitschelt and Wilkinson, *Patrons, Clients, and Policies*, pp. 24–8; Stokes et al., *Brokers, Voters, and Clientelism*, pp. 152–71.

[53] See, for example, Hicken, "How Do Rules and Institutions Encourage Vote Buying?", pp. 55–6; Stokes et al., *Brokers, Voters, and Clientelism*, pp. 219–21.

[54] For example, Gary W. Cox, *The Efficient Secret: The Cabinet and the Development of Political Parties in Victorian England* (New York: Cambridge University Press, 1987), p. 57; Hicken, "How Do Rules and Institutions Encourage Vote Buying?", pp. 56–7; Susan C. Stokes, "Is Vote Buying Undemocratic?", in Schaffer, *Elections for Sale*, pp. 86–7; Stokes et al., *Brokers, Voters, and Clientelism*, pp. 214–6.

topics we introduce in this volume await more systematic analysis. Moreover, legislative elections are just one variety of election. Other elections deserve equal scrutiny: village head elections (preliminary investigations suggest that vote buying is widespread at this level, and the payments are even higher than in district DPRD elections); direct elections of local government heads (though there have been many excellent studies of these elections,[55] few have focused on patronage distribution in as much detail as the current volume), and presidential elections.

Some members of the team who authored chapters in this volume conducted follow-up research on the campaigning for Indonesia's July 2014 presidential election, in the same locations where they studied the legislative election. It should be noted, in keeping with the comments about constituency size above, that these researchers found much less patronage politics and vote buying in the 2014 presidential elections than they did in the legislative elections. Where payments and gifts were made in the presidential election, they tended to be directed toward community leaders and other brokers rather than to ordinary voters.

Another point to stress is that this volume focuses on the *distribution* end of clientelist politics—specifically, the nexus connecting candidates, brokers and voters during campaigning. Many topics related to patronage politics fall outside this focus yet deserve more systematic research. These include candidate fundraising (an issue which has already received attention)[56] and also the ways by which successful candidates reward their supporters at other points of the electoral cycle.

Likewise, we have little to say about the *effects* that the patterns of electoral mobilisation we describe in the volume have on wider political phenomena, such as policymaking, economic redistribution or the quality of governance. These effects can be severe; as Hicken puts it, "clientelism has the potential to reverse the standard accountability

---

[55] See especially Erb and Sulistiyanto, *Deepening Democracy*.

[56] Marcus Mietzner, "Party Financing in Post-Soeharto Indonesia: Between State Subsidies and Political Corruption", *Contemporary Southeast Asia* 29, 2 (2007): 238–63; Ambardi, *Mengungkap Politik Kartel*.

relationship that is central to democratic theory".[57] Even so, we avoided these topics because the Indonesian literature is full of generalisations on the effects of patronage politics yet lacking in careful analyses of the mechanisms that supposedly generate them. This does not mean, however, that these topics are unimportant; on the contrary, they are critical. For example, one observation that was made repeatedly by political candidates during our research was that their reliance on costly money politics generates enormous pressures on victorious candidates to recoup their campaign investments by way of corruption. In this context, it is worth noting the assessment released by the non-governmental organisation KontraS that, of the 560 DPR members elected in 2014, 160 were suspected of involvement in corruption, including 63 who had been interrogated by law enforcement agencies, 16 who had been charged and 5 who had been convicted.[58] The connection between patronage collection and distribution is just one of many matters that require more systematic future research. It is in a spirit of contributing to an ongoing inquiry that we offer this book to readers.

---

[57] Hicken, "Clientelism", p. 302.

[58] "KontraS: Ratusan Anggota DPR Miliki Rekam Jejak Buruk" [KontraS: Hundreds of DPR Members Have a Bad Record], *Detiknews*, 14 Oct. 2014, available at: http://news.detik.com/berita/2718402/kontras-ratusan-anggota-dpr-miliki-rekam-jejak-buruk.

Map of Aceh and Medan

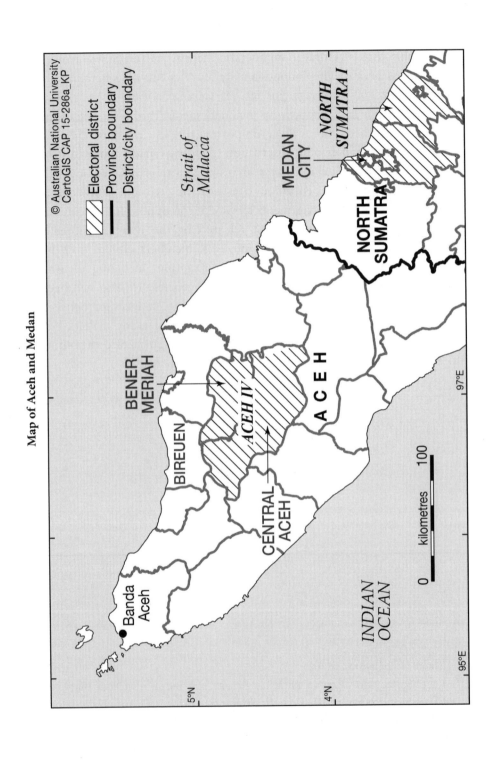

chapter **2**

Bireuen, Aceh: The Aftermath of Post-conflict Politics and the Decline of Partai Aceh

Rizkika Lhena Darwin

Aceh, Indonesia's westernmost province, has a party system that differs from the rest of Indonesia. When representatives of the Indonesian government and Gerakan Aceh Merdeka (GAM, Free Aceh Movement) signed the Helsinki Memorandum of Understanding (Helsinki MoU) in 2005, ending 32 years of separatist conflict in the territory, they included a provision that allowed the establishment of local parties in Aceh. This provision was critical to achieving peace, because the guerrillas of GAM needed a pathway to peacefully compete for power in the province, in a context where national regulations required parties to show they had party structures throughout Indonesia if they wanted to run in elections. The Helsinki MoU provision was enshrined in the 2006 Law on the Government of Aceh, allowing local parties registered in Aceh alone to run alongside national parties for seats in the district and provincial parliaments in the province (only national parties can run for seats in the DPR).[1]

---

[1] *Undang-Undang Republik Indonesia Nomor 11 Tahun 2006 Tentang Pemerintahan Aceh* [Law No. 11 of 2006 on the Government of Aceh].

In the 2009 election, six local parties ran, but it was Partai Aceh, established by former leaders and supporters of GAM, that emerged as dominant, winning 47 per cent of the popular vote at the provincial level, and gaining 33 of the 69 seats in the provincial parliament, the Dewan Perwakilan Rakyat Aceh (DPRA, Aceh People's Representative Assembly). It also won a plurality in 16 of the province's 23 district parliaments, including 7 where it attained a majority.[2] In the post-MoU period, former GAM leaders have also dominated local executive government elections in the province, taking the governorship in the 2006 and 2012 elections, and also winning about half of the district head (*bupati*) positions. Aceh's politics have been dominated by the ex-combatants and by their main party, in a way that is highly unusual in Indonesia.

Yet the 2014 election showed the first signs of Partai Aceh's electoral tide turning. At the provincial level, the party gained only 35 per cent of the vote, and 29 out of 81 DPRA seats. Its vote plunged in many district parliaments, including in areas that had been GAM bases in the conflict years and Partai Aceh strongholds in 2009. One such district is Bireuen, on the east coast of Aceh. Here the drop was especially dramatic: in 2009 Partai Aceh won 67 per cent of the district vote, and 25 of the 35 seats in the district parliament; in 2014 this fell to 32.5 per cent and 13 of the 40 seats.

This chapter focuses on explaining how and why the Partai Aceh vote declined in Bireuen in 2014, by surveying the main strategies and structures used by its candidates and by candidates from other parties. This study finds growing convergence between Partai Aceh and mainstream parties, with patronage politics becoming more influential than ideology, and Partai Aceh adapting to the techniques of patronage distribution. This declining distinctiveness of Partai Aceh—plus growing popular disappointment with its rule—suggest that electoral politics in Aceh are starting to resemble patterns in other parts of Indonesia.

---

[2] Blair Palmer, "Services Rendered: Peace, Patronage and Post-conflict Elections in Aceh", in *Problems of Democratisation in Indonesia: Elections, Institutions and Society*, ed. Edward Aspinall and Marcus Mietzner (Singapore: ISEAS, 2010), p. 291; Shane J. Barter, "The Free Aceh Elections? The 2009 Legislative Contests in Aceh", *Indonesia* 91 (2011): 113–30.

BACKGROUND: BIREUEN AND POST-CONFLICT POLITICS

Bireuen, which was established as a separate district (*kabupaten*) in 2000 when it was split off from North Aceh, was one of GAM's major bases during the years of separatist conflict, especially in its final and most violent phase between 1999 and 2005. Many of the movement's most famous fighters were based here, and the conflict had severe effects on the local population: a 2006 survey conducted by a team from the Harvard Medical School found 85 per cent of randomly selected respondents in Bireuen had experienced combat; 66 per cent reported having had a family member or friend killed.[3] GAM was deeply embedded in the structures of local village communities, with the result that, when security forces used violence against it, civilians often suffered badly.

When peace came to Aceh, the district continued to be regarded as a GAM stronghold. The Komite Peralihan Aceh (KPA, Aceh Transitional Committee), the organisation set up for GAM ex-combatants, continued to dominate at the village level and played a major role in establishing a predatory political economy of construction contracting and security services throughout the district.[4] This grassroots strength was the foundation of a strong showing for Partai Aceh in the 2009 election in Bireuen, when it won 25 out of 35 seats in the district parliament, one of the strongest majorities in any local parliament in post-Suharto Indonesia. Politicians linked to GAM also dominated the local government. Nurdin Abdul Rahman, a former academic and a member of the GAM negotiating team in Helsinki, won as district head by a landslide in an election in 2007. He later had a falling out with former combatants, including those in Partai Aceh, and was defeated by Partai Aceh nominee Ruslan Daud, who won a first-round victory with almost 50 per cent of the vote in 2012.

---

[3] Byron J. Good, Mary-Jo DelVecchio Good, Jesse Grayman and Matthew Lakoma, *Psychosocial Needs Assessment of Communities Affected by the Conflict in the Districts of Pidie, Bireuen and Aceh Utara* (Jakarta: Ministry of Health, 2006), p. 3.

[4] Edward Aspinall, *Islam and Nation: Separatist Rebellion in Aceh, Indonesia* (Stanford, CA: Stanford University Press, 2009).

Table 2.1
Bireuen District Parliament Seats, 2009 and 2014

	2009	2014
Local parties		
Partai Aceh	25	13
Partai Bersatu Aceh	1	–
Partai Nasional Aceh	–	5
Partai Daulat Aceh	–	1
National parties		
Partai Demokrat	4	2
PPP	2	4
PAN	2	3
PKS	1	4
Golkar	–	4
Nasdem	–	3
Gerindra	–	1
Total	*35*	*40*

Despite its previous dominance, Partai Aceh's vote plunged in the 2014 legislative election, with its seats in the district parliament dropping by almost half, to 13. Seats won by national parties more than doubled, from 9 to 21, while a new local party, Partai Nasional Aceh (PNA, Aceh National Party) took five seats (Table 2.1). The number of incumbents returned was also very low: only 6 of the 25 Partai Aceh legislators first elected in 2009 were re-elected and only 2 other incumbents (one from PAN, National Mandate Party, the other from Partai Demokrat) retained their seats. How can we account for this dramatic change in the composition of the local parliament?

PARTAI ACEH'S COMPETITORS: DISTRIBUTIVE POLITICS AND CLIENTELIST NETWORKS

One way to explain the decline of Partai Aceh is to look at strategies used by its competitors. In the lead-up to the April 2014 election in Bireuen, it was obvious that candidates from both national and local parties relied on patronage distribution and clientelist networks in order to attract votes. In short, candidates in Bireuen used strategies that were not far different from those found in other parts of Indonesia, as described in many chapters of this book.

Most candidates stressed that the key to political success was their ability to build personal relationships with voters. Most did this by door-to-door campaigning. Candidates typically stated that their efforts began with their most intimate social acquaintances. As one PAN candidate explained:

> I use a family approach (*pendekatan kekeluargaan*) with my constituents, maximising my connections to my relatives and close family. When we meet with constituents, that kind of approach is much more effective than putting up billboards on the roads. And when I visit constituents, I don't forget to bring headscarves as souvenirs as a way to get close to the women; they really like headscarves.[5]

This practice of providing voters with mementoes (*buah tangan*) during door-to-door campaigning was very common. The gifts included prayer mats, sugar, rice and other minor items. Candidates often described such gifts as one way to build *silaturahmi* (ties of friendship; a concept explored by Caroline Paskarina in Chapter 12). As one candidate put it, "headscarves and blouses function to build emotional ties with the voters".[6] Some candidates packaged their gift-giving in religious terminology; for example, a PKS candidate distributed cash and rice—which he rather inventively described as *zakat* (the religious tax paid annually to help the less fortunate)—as well as mobile telephone vouchers:

> This sort of method is more effective. *Zakat* is at the same time a religious good deed and a means to attract the support of constituents. In my view, spending money on public campaigns is wasteful and ineffective. It's better just to give the money to our constituents.[7]

Candidates also used existing social institutions to ingratiate themselves with constituents. In Acehnese society three kinds of institutions were particularly amenable for this purpose: coffee shops, which are an important site of male socialisation in both urban and rural Aceh; mosques and *meunasah* (prayer halls); and Islamic boarding

---

[5] Interview, Munzir Mustafa, PAN candidate, 13 Mar. 2014.
[6] Interview, Dwi Syahrinal, 27 Mar. 2014.
[7] Confidential interview, 13 Mar. 2014.

schools (known as *dayah* in Aceh, *pesantren* elsewhere in Indonesia). Male and female candidates from both national and local parties used these public spaces for their campaigning. A candidate from PDI-P was typical:

> I use a system of approaching people directly in the coffee shops and the *meunasah*, because I think going house to house is ineffective. And if you organise a meeting and bring together people in some place, then the candidate has to give out transport money and souvenirs. So the coffee shops are more effective, because I don't have to pay those who want to drink coffee with me. At most I only have to pay for their coffee and food. And I often also go to the *meunasah* and mosques to show myself to the community.[8]

Candidates often moved from *meunasah* to *meunasah* at prayer times and, after prayer had finished, chatted to members of the congregations about their candidacy. This approach had the added benefit of helping to create an image of piety for the candidate, an advantage in deeply religious Aceh. Many candidates also gave donations to *meunasah* as part of their campaign strategies. For example, one Golkar candidate I observed gave cattle to be slaughtered and consumed during celebrations of the Prophet Muhammad's birthday.

The practice of making donations to *dayah* was also commonplace. One Golkar candidate donated cement, sand and bricks to a *dayah*, in the hope of winning support from its *teungku* (religious scholars) and students. I witnessed another candidate, also from Golkar, receive a telephone call from someone requesting donations of Qurans to a *dayah*, and him acceding to the request (though, not, he assured me, because he was a candidate, but simply because he was charitable). Meanwhile, coffee shops were important, not as a respected institution where a candidate could build his or her religious reputation, but simply as a convenient location to meet community members and develop a reputation as someone who interacted easily with ordinary people.

As well as one-on-one and informal interactions, many candidates also used small meetings, involving a few dozen individuals, usually called *musyawarah* (deliberations or discussions) with community

---

[8] Confidential interview, 20 Mar. 2014.

members. Often, the candidate invited residents from one or two villages to attend such a meeting, typically in the candidate's own house or in a party office (it was generally only locally powerful Partai Aceh candidates who held their meetings in village *meunasah*, which were public facilities not supposed to be used for campaigning purposes). Typically, at such meetings, candidates would introduce themselves and say something about their party and its programme. Those attending would then use the opportunity to make requests of the candidate. At one meeting I attended, residents sought assistance for housing construction for poor residents, submitted proposals for financial assistance for home industry projects and asked for infrastructure such as roads and bridges. Candidates responded by promising to fulfil these requests should they be elected; they were assisted in doing so because members of the Bireuen district parliament have access to "aspiration funds" of approximately Rp 500 million annually. (Aspiration funds are a form of constituency development fund that can be allocated for community projects at the legislator's discretion.) Such meetings typically ended with the distribution of small payments (typically around Rp 20,000) of "transport money" and "souvenirs", such as headscarves, to those attending.

Only three parties held large open-air campaign rallies in Bireuen: Partai Aceh, PNA (a local party that had split off from Partai Aceh following an internal dispute, and was its main rival) and Partai Persatuan Pembangunan (PPP, United Development Party), an Islamic party with a history of electoral strength in Aceh. These were among the only campaign events with a strong programmatic element; speakers at the PPP rally emphasised the party's role in supporting implementation of Islamic law, or shariah, an element of Aceh's special autonomy. PNA, by contrast, reflected on its origins as a party backed by former Aceh governor Irwandi Yusuf (2006–12), with its speakers emphasising various welfare programmes introduced under his tenure, notably a local health insurance scheme, scholarship programmes, a village cash transfer scheme and assistance for *dayah*.[9] Speakers at the Partai Aceh

---

[9] On Irwandi Yusuf and PNA, see International Crisis Group (ICG), "Indonesia: Averting Election Violence in Aceh", Asia Program Briefing 135 (Jakarta/Brussels: ICG, 2012).

rally—the largest held in Bireuen—stressed more ideological themes (see below). Despite their more programmatic and ideological themes, most participants at these events received cash payments of Rp 15,000 to Rp 30,000 as "transport money", usually distributed by village-level party coordinators after participants had returned home to their villages.

To organise their campaigns and connect them with voters, most candidates established personal success teams. The size and reach of these teams, however, varied greatly according to the candidate's financial resources. Candidates without significant financial resources often relied on only a handful of close friends or family members. Wealthier candidates could establish teams with pyramidal structures covering several subdistricts (there were between two and four subdistricts in each electoral constituency) and include village teams as well. Some only established a few village-level teams; others relied on a single team—or tried to—to cover the whole constituency. For example, one PAN candidate explained:

> I have formed six success teams to help me win, covering the whole electoral constituency. I run one team directly and five are run by people I trust. They have chosen members who are their relatives and close friends to help them campaign for my victory. So I don't have a team in each village, just those six teams to cover the whole electoral district.[10]

Typically, candidates paid for the services of their team members by providing them with modest operational costs. Candidates also offered to reward team members should they be successful, by promising them access to aspiration fund projects, for example, to help their women supporters with funds to establish home industries. Some team members also profited because they were asked to distribute cash to voters and were paid for doing this.

It was difficult to obtain a clear picture of the extent of retail vote buying in Bireuen because most candidates and success team members were unwilling to discuss this practice. I believe it was widespread, though not universal, and very often disguised as the distribution of

---

[10] Interview, Munzir Mustafa, 13 Mar. 2014.

"transport money". Candidates who engaged in the practice typically relied on their success team members to distribute the cash. As one of the few such team members (working for a Gerindra candidate) who was prepared to talk about his experiences explained:

> Pak Alex [not his real name] is distributing his envelopes through me as the intermediary. I give them to people who we can confirm will support him. The envelopes won't contain much, just between [Rp] 20,000 to 50,000. This village is a PPP base area, so to get access here you have to give goods or money in order to soften the hearts of the people.[11]

For some parties, the party machinery played a prominent role in campaigning. This was especially the case for local parties. For example, PNA had a Bapilu (Election Victory Agency) that organised campaigning on behalf of all the party's candidates in the district. Partai Damai Aceh, a party based on the *ulama* and *dayah* networks, also organised joint success teams for all of its candidates running in particular electoral districts, with the costs shared between the candidates.[12] Among the national parties, PKS also coordinated its candidates' campaigns closely. PKS also had an enthusiastic group of party cadres who, as in other parts of Indonesia, carried out free health checks for voters and blood donation drives (at these events attendees were also provided with gifts, such as drinking glasses, mortars-and-pestles, spices, prayer books and snacks). Candidates from all parties who occupied party leadership posts tended to be able to mobilise party cadres to support them. The general pattern, however, among the national parties was for candidate-centred success teams to dominate.

PARTAI ACEH: FROM IDEOLOGY TO PATRONAGE

The political context had changed dramatically in Aceh between 2009 and 2014. In 2009, post-conflict politics were in their infancy, and Partai Aceh had just been formed. Many people voted for the party

---

[11] Confidential interview, 1 Apr. 2014.
[12] Interview, Sartika Handayani Sari, 14 Mar. 2014.

because they sympathised with GAM's Acehnese nationalist outlook, or because they wanted to support the peace process that had then been under way for just a few years.[13] By 2014, the party had long been the dominant force in local politics, and many former supporters were becoming disappointed with its performance. Partai Aceh leaders themselves sensed a mood shift. As one incumbent legislator in the Bireuen district parliament explained:

> Our challenges are very big in 2014, whereas in 2009 Aceh had just ended its conflict. In 2009, it was like this: even an ashtray could get elected to parliament—if that ashtray had been involved in the GAM struggle.[14]

In 2014 Partai Aceh still had three main advantages. These advantages related to ideology, organisation and government support. First, in ideological terms, the party still drew strongly upon its history of struggle against the Indonesian state, its claims to represent Acehnese identity, and its role in ending the Aceh conflict. As in 2009, Partai Aceh campaigners and candidates tried hard to depict the party as the only legitimate representative of the Acehnese, underscoring its role—as GAM's successor—in bringing and safeguarding peace in Aceh. One Partai Aceh candidate stressed that this was the party's central message:

> The discourse of Acehnese identity, the Helsinki MoU and the struggle—these are the main things I bring to the campaign. My slogan is "To struggle for the Helsinki MoU". And [I tell voters] Partai Aceh arose as a result of the blood that was shed by our martyrs. The party arose as a result of the Helsinki MoU. And the guns of our ex-combatants were exchanged for the formation of Partai Aceh. Other parties just need to get 50 people together to form a party, and they can do it straight away. That's very different from us. It's only the Partai Aceh who can take Aceh's problems to the international community, because it was Partai Aceh who created the peace agreement.[15]

---

[13] Palmer, "Services Rendered"; Barter, "The Free Aceh Elections?".

[14] Interview, Abdul Gani Isa, Partai Aceh incumbent in Bireuen district parliament, 17 Mar. 2014.

[15] Ibid.

As in the past, these historical claims were a powerful message for many voters.

A second strength was organisational: Partai Aceh possessed a political machine far surpassing those possessed by its rivals. Growing directly out of the structure of the old insurgency, the party itself had functioning structures down to the village level, as well as the parallel structure of GAM's paramilitary wing, the KPA, which also extended to the villages. Institutionally, KPA supported Partai Aceh without differentiating between individual candidates. However, individual KPA members, including its leaders, were free to join individual candidates' success teams, so long as they were from Partai Aceh.[16] The party also had its own election campaign body, Komite Pemenangan Partai Aceh (KPPA, Partai Aceh Victory Committee), which coordinated individual campaigns, promoted the party and organised joint events. Partai Aceh candidates and cadres tended to emphasise the role of this coordinating body in interviews. Critically, the KPA was still a formidable repressive apparatus with the power to pressure voters, directly or indirectly. This was recognised as an important factor in the 2009 legislative election, and in local government head elections in Aceh;[17] I personally witnessed KPA people pressuring voters at polling booths on voting day, by approaching them and openly asking them to support Partai Aceh.

However, many Partai Aceh candidates did not rely just on these bodies. They also established their own individual success teams, typically drawing in not only individuals with KPA and Partai Aceh backgrounds but also others. Thus, both Partai Aceh and KPA were riddled with personalist networks around individual candidates, each seeking not only to promote the party but also to promote their own campaigns. Moreover, stronger Partai Aceh candidates were also able to draw on other informal and informal institutions, such as the village government, which itself often overlapped with GAM networks. Thus, one Partai Aceh incumbent explained:

---

[16] Interview, Muhammad, 20 Mar. 2014.

[17] International Crisis Group, "Indonesia: How GAM Won in Aceh", Asia Briefing 61 (Jakarta/Brussels: ICG, 2007).

The most effective campaign method is via your success team, apart
from the candidate himself going down to the villages personally.
Another effective method is to bring on board the village apparatus.
Lots of village officials have come to me and offered to help me,
including *geusyik* [the Acehnese term for village heads], members of
the *tuha peut* [council of village elders] and village youth leaders.
These are the networks that help my campaign.[18]

Just as with candidates from other parties, however, these structures
functioned as mechanisms for patronage distribution. As a member of
the above candidate's success team explained:

> The success team formed by Ahmad [not his real name] accommodates
> all the demands made by the community, both during the campaign
> period and afterwards, after he is elected. For example, if a community
> needs football or volleyball equipment, we give it. Now it's *maulid* [the
> celebration of the Prophet's birthday], so we give away lots of drinking
> water. We give what the communities request.[19]

And just like candidates from the national parties, the more
established Partai Aceh candidates compensated their success team
members with modest cash payments, and with promises to help them
further should they be elected.

A third advantage Partai Aceh candidates had was that they received
full support from local governments, at the provincial, district and village
levels—all of which were dominated by their party and its sympathisers.
In part, this support came in the form of programmatic mobilisation.
Thus, at a large Partai Aceh rally in Bireuen on 5 April 2014, Partai
Aceh head and deputy governor of Aceh, Muzakkir Manaf, promised
that the Aceh government would continue various health and welfare
programmes if the party won. The district head of Bireuen, Ruslan
Daud, was even more specific: "If Partai Aceh wins, motorcycles will
be provided as official vehicles for *tengku imum* (village imams) in 609
villages, there will be distribution of rice to the poor, and we will build
1,000 homes for poor residents."[20]

---

[18] Confidential interview, 17 Mar. 2014
[19] Confidential interview, 20 Mar. 2014.
[20] Field notes, 5 Apr. 2014.

More important, however, was the mobilisation of the government apparatus (officially supposed to be neutral) in favour of the party. The *bupati* himself officiated at the launch of various village-level projects during the campaign period, and even on election day itself presided over the transfer of Rp 20 million for the construction of one *meunasah*, which was itself being used as a polling booth, and all the polling booth officials were in attendance. There were also credible reports that the *bupati* organised a closed meeting in which village officials were ordered to support Partai Aceh,[21] as well as reports that pressure was exerted on local officials to intervene in the vote counting and tabulation process in order to favour the party. Though such reports are hard to verify, one speaker at a Partai Aceh campaign hinted very strongly that this was on the cards: "We ask for everybody's prayers that lots of people will not participate in the election, even that nobody at all should participate—so that all their votes can go to Partai Aceh."[22] The implication of this statement was that the unmarked ballot papers of citizens who failed to vote would somehow be added to the vote tally of Partai Aceh candidates.

These factors certainly provided Partai Aceh candidates with real advantages in 2014 in Bireuen. However, the most striking element of their campaigning was how they were beginning to adapt themselves to the patronage-based and transactional strategies used by candidates from mainstream national parties. This process of adaptation was overt. As one Partai Aceh candidate explained:

> Another challenge is that lots of other candidates are approaching the people by going door to door and giving out souvenirs. So my team and I are also approaching people door to door. And I've developed a programme of giving out souvenirs, too, but it depends on what our opponents' movements are. If our political opponent gives foodstuffs, we will give out similar packets, but ones that are greater in value than our opponent's.[23]

---

[21] Field notes, 8 Apr. 2014.

[22] Field notes, 30 Mar. 2014.

[23] Field notes, 8 Apr. 2014.

As a result of such adaptation, wealthy Partai Aceh candidates differed little from wealthy national party candidates in their capacity—or propensity—to distribute cash or goods to voters. They differed from their national party rivals mostly in having the additional organisational and financial resources mentioned above, plus the backing of local government. Likewise, Partai Aceh candidates who were incumbents—like those from other parties—not only distributed patronage during the campaign period but also relied heavily on their distribution of aspiration fund projects in previous years, campaigning strongly in areas which had benefitted from their largesse. Thus, though the ideological component of Partai Aceh campaigning persisted, it was also transforming into a patronage-based party.

CONCLUSION

How, then, are we to explain the decline in the Partai Aceh vote in Bireuen, and by extension in the rest of Aceh, in 2014? We cannot point to any single factor, but rather to an amalgam. One core factor was the split in Partai Aceh ranks that led to the formation of PNA as a competitor local party. This split originated in the conflict over the gubernatorial succession in 2012, when Partai Aceh decided not to back incumbent Irwandi Yusuf, despite his GAM origins.[24] Many former Partai Aceh members, including ex-combatants, shifted to PNA. PNA campaigners tried to counter Partai Aceh's historical claims with near-identical claims of their own: at one PNA rally I witnessed PNA leader and former Sabang mayor, Munawar Liza Zainal describe PNA as a "party mandated by the Helsinki MoU". They also directly attacked Partai Aceh and told voters not to trust its promises. Thus, at the same rally, another PNA speaker reminded voters that the *bupati* had made the promise to provide *tengku imum* with motorbikes—as mentioned above—during his own election campaign in 2012, but had still not delivered, telling his audience to "ask them what they give once they already sit in the government".[25]

---

[24] ICG, "Indonesia: Averting Election Violence in Aceh".
[25] Field notes, 4 Apr. 2014.

This points to an obvious second factor: growing public distrust in, and disappointment with, Partai Aceh, leading to the growing ineffectiveness of its ideological and historical claims. More voters were starting to judge the party in pragmatic terms, rather than in terms of their sympathy for GAM and its struggle. Partai Aceh leaders themselves recognised this trend, seeing it as a result of the fact that they had not managed to get the central government to implement all elements of the Helsinki MoU. At the grassroots, such disappointment was more likely to manifest itself in grumbles about the party's inability to address poverty and other social problems, as well as in resentment at the access to resources obviously being enjoyed by many former combatants.[26] Many ordinary people believed that the Partai Aceh struggle had transformed into a struggle for nice houses, luxury cars and economic privileges for its own leaders and cadres.

Such disappointments fed the voters' pragmatism: if Partai Aceh leaders were motivated by materialistic concerns, why shouldn't they adopt the same attitude? Thus, many voters viewed the election as a time to secure material rewards rather than ideological goals. Partai Aceh leaders saw this change and adapted to it. Though they still had by far the strongest party machine, and they still made Acehnese nationalist appeals, Partai Aceh candidates also established personal success teams and distributed patronage. In other words, they started to compete with the mainstream parties on their own terms, while candidates from those parties were themselves becoming more assertive. In short, Acehnese electoral politics was undergoing a process of normalisation, shifting from the highly ideological nature of the early post-conflict phase, and coming to resemble political dynamics in other parts of Indonesia. Patronage was replacing ideology as the main political currency.

---

[26] Edward Aspinall, "Combatants to Contractors: The Political Economy of Peace in Aceh", *Indonesia* 87 (2009): 1–34.

chapter **3**

Bener Meriah, Aceh: Money Politics and Ethnicity in a New Electoral District

Teuku Muhammad Jafar Sulaiman

For the residents of the highlands districts (*kabupaten*) of Bener Meriah and Central Aceh, the 2014 legislative election was very different from previous elections. In 2009, these two districts had been combined with the district of Bireuen, on Aceh's eastern coast, to form one electoral district in the province's parliamentary elections. In 2014 Bener Meriah and Central Aceh were reconstituted into a single electoral district (Aceh IV). The formation of this separate electoral district had for some time been a goal of local ethnic Gayo politicians. The Gayo, a group indigenous to Aceh's highlands, live predominantly in these two districts, where they form a majority. Most local candidates and campaigners said that this change of electoral boundaries greatly enhanced ethnopolitical sentiment in the highlands in the approach to the 2014 election. With Gayo voters now a majority, Gayo politicians had more opportunities to represent their own region in the provincial parliament in the capital, Banda Aceh, and promote its developmental catch-up with other parts of Aceh. As one such candidate explained, "primordialism became an important factor, ethnicity became an important factor, in the election of members of the legislature for the first time in 2014 in this electoral district".[1]

---

[1] Interview, Hendra Budian, Golkar candidate, 22 Mar. 2014.

In 2009, when Central Aceh and Bener Meriah were combined with Bireuen, it was difficult for Gayo candidates to be elected because they faced competition from candidates whose voter base was in Bireuen, where the population of 406,000 was more than that of Central Aceh and Bener Meriah combined (183,000 and 129,000 respectively).[2] Bireuen is a strongly ethnically Acehnese district where Partai Aceh—the successor party to Gerakan Aceh Merdeka (GAM)—was very strong (see Chapter 2).

In the 2014 election, Gayo candidates competing for seats in their new majority Gayo constituency mobilised ethnic appeals. Many of them openly called on candidates to *pilih singkite* ("vote for one of our own", in the Gayo language). Likewise, many called on voters to spurn *caleg impor* ("imported candidates"), a term widely used to describe both non-Gayo and ethnic Gayo candidates residing outside the two highlands districts.

But there was more to this election than ethnicity. From interviews with candidates and campaign workers, and observations of electioneering, it was also obvious that patronage politics was endemic in the new electoral district. Some candidates or their success team members engaged in vote buying, making direct cash payments to voters. There was also much distribution of club goods to communities, such as donations to community associations, assistance for houses of worship, and grants to farmers' groups. Promises of pork barrel projects for particular villages were also common, with some candidates even producing formal, written "political contracts" with community representatives—typically, village heads—promising to provide their community with funds or amenities. Village heads often played key brokerage roles: candidates tried to win them over with promises of village welfare, in exchange for which they were expected to deliver community votes en bloc.

This chapter investigates the combination of ethnic and patronage politics in the 2014 legislative election in Aceh electoral district IV. The focus is on the competition for provincial parliamentary seats, rather

---

[2] These population figures are for 2013: Badan Pusat Statistik Aceh, *Aceh dalam Angka 2013* [Aceh in Figures 2013] (Banda Aceh: BPS, 2013), p. 40.

than for seats in the district legislatures or national parliament. This focus was chosen because it was at the provincial level that the electoral boundaries changed in such a way as to create a new ethnic majority, and a goal of the research was to focus precisely on the effects of this ethnic shift. Most of the research was carried out in Bener Meriah, with supplementary research in Central Aceh. I investigate both the relative importance of patronage and ethnic identity politics, and the relationship between them. Accordingly, the chapter is divided into three sections: a background section explaining the local context, a section on ethnic strategies used by candidates, followed by a discussion of patronage. The chapter concludes by arguing that, although ethnic mobilisation featured in the campaigning, patronage politics was dominant, with both aspects reinforcing each other.

BACKGROUND: A NEW ELECTORAL DISTRICT FOR THE GAYO HIGHLANDS

Bener Meriah and Central Aceh districts together constitute the heart of the Aceh highlands, and the home of the Gayo people. Bener Meriah is the newest district in Aceh province, having been formed in 2004, after it was split off from Central Aceh. Central Aceh is still the dominant highland district, hosting the largest town in the region, Takengon, on the shore of a large crater lake, Laut Tawar. Both districts have an agricultural economy. The mountainous setting is ideal for cultivating cool climate crops, notably coffee, which has been grown here since Dutch times. There is also much smallholder production of vegetables. Both districts are heavily forested: 59 per cent of Central Aceh and 37 per cent of Bener Meriah are classified as protected forest areas (*hutan lindung*).

Ethnically, both districts are quite heterogeneous (but both districts are overwhelmingly Muslim). In Bener Meriah, about 40 per cent are Gayo, 30 per cent are Javanese (there is a long history of Javanese migration to the area dating to the Dutch colonial period), and about 25 per cent ethnic Acehnese originating from Aceh's coastal areas. In Central Aceh, about 75 per cent of the population are Gayo with the remainder made up of migrants, mostly Javanese and Acehnese. In both districts, a scattering of other migrants, such as Chinese, Balinese, Minangkabau and Arabs live in the towns. Overall, the Gayo represent an absolute majority in the new electoral district.

The Gayo, as well as being characterised by a strongly Islamic identity (a factor they share in common with ethnic Acehnese) also have a strong sense of their own separate ethnic identity, signified by numerous symbolic markers, including the Gayo language and various cultural traditions such as *didong*, a genre which combines dance and vocals and is usually performed on major Islamic holidays or at weddings, circumcisions, harvests and other major events, and *tari guel*, another dance often used for welcoming guests and at weddings.[3] In recent times, Gayo identity has also been emphasised in contrast with Acehnese identity as a result of the separatist war that ran sporadically between the late 1970s and 2005 in Aceh.[4] Many residents of the central highlands, including Gayo, were engaged in violent conflict with GAM guerrillas after it tried to establish itself in the highlands from the late 1990s. In this part of Aceh, the separatist conflict at times resembled an interethnic war. As a result, many Gayo came to support moves to establish a separate highlands province (Aceh Leuser Antara)—which is strongly opposed by many ethnic Acehnese, including supporters of Partai Aceh.[5] During the course of that conflict, many Gayo came to identify with Indonesian national symbols rather than Acehnese ones, which explains why most prominent Gayo candidates in 2014 ran through national, rather than local, political parties.

In this context, local and Gayo representation in the Aceh provincial parliament became a source of considerable discontent in the highlands. In 2009 only one person with origins in either Bener Meriah or Central

3 On the Gayo, see John R. Bowen, *Sumatran Politics and Poetics: Gayo History, 1900–1989* (New Haven, CT: Yale University Press, 1991) and *Muslims through Discourse: Religion and Ritual in Gayo Society* (Princeton, NJ: Princeton University Press, 1993).

4 Edward Aspinall, *Islam and Nation: Separatist Rebellion in Aceh, Indonesia* (Stanford, CA: Stanford University Press, 2009).

5 Stefan Ehrentraut, "Dividing Aceh? Minorities, Partition Movements and State-Reform in Aceh Province" (ARI Working Paper Series 137, Asia Research Institute, National University of Singapore, 2010).

Aceh was elected in the constituency that then included Bireuen: this was Ilham Ilyas Leubee, the son of a famous GAM founder, who was elected representing Partai Aceh.[6] The others were all ethnic Acehnese: seven from Bireuen, and two from the provincial capital, Banda Aceh. According to Ligadinsyah, a prominent former GAM leader and Partai Nasional Aceh (PNA) candidate—who was Gayo—this result set the scene for ethnic mobilisation in 2014:

> The late Ilham was the only representative from the Gayo lands, whereas all the others were from outside. This composition had the effect of reducing the people's representation in the Gayo region. The legislators only paid attention to Bireuen, which was their voter base. So, we learned from 2009 ... "Gayo versus non-Gayo" sentiment would rise to the surface in 2014.[7]

An underlying view shared by many local politicians and ordinary citizens was that the lack of local Gayo representation in Banda Aceh resulted in the provincial government's neglect of Central Aceh and Bener Meriah. Another candidate argued that these districts were "left far behind by other regions" in Aceh because they lacked representation.[8]

Such attitudes led to considerable lobbying of the electoral authorities by Gayo politicians and community leaders for the electoral boundaries to be redrawn. A group of nine people took the case to the Constitutional Court, and the national Electoral Commission intervened to increase the total number of provincial electoral districts from eight to ten, making room for the new highlands constituency. The result was the new Aceh electoral district IV, consisting only of Central Aceh and Bener Meriah, with its reduced representation of six rather than ten seats in the Dewan Perwakilan Rakyat Aceh (DPRA, provincial parliament).

---

[6] Ilham Ilyas Leube was renominated in electoral district IV in 2014, with the top position on the Partai Aceh slate, but he died after the candidate list was issued. Even so, he attracted about 6,000 votes. Note also that in July 2013 one other ethnic Gayo entered the Aceh parliament representing the constituency: this happened when PAN replaced one of its members, an Acehnese from Bireuen, with Ismaniar, a Gayo.

[7] Interview, Ligadinsyah, 1 Apr. 2014.

[8] Interview, Sri Wahyuni, Partai Nasdem district candidate, 17 Apr. 2014.

PILIH SINGKITE: IDENTITY POLITICS IN A NEW ELECTORAL DISTRICT

With this background in mind, it is not surprising that Gayo political representation became a major theme in the contest for provincial parliamentary seats in the highlands in 2014. As an example, and to set the scene, consider the following extract from the *Lintas Gayo* website, an online media source that is widely read in the highlands:

> In the past, the Gayo highlands were in the same electoral district as Bireuen, but in 2014 following a long struggle the General Election Commission finally decided to make Central Aceh and Bener Meriah into an electoral district of their own: electoral district IV. There are 93 candidates running [for legislative seats], many of whom are the best sons and daughters of Bener Meriah and Central Aceh. But some parties have also smuggled in "outsiders" as candidates. All Gayo voters should take note of this, and remember our experiences up to now, when we have been together with Bireuen as an electoral district. Many of our candidates were thus unable to give voice to, or struggle for, the aspirations of this central region. Of course, we greatly hope that in the 2014 election, the representatives of the Gayo that are sent to the DPRA will be the best sons of the Gayo—people who want and are able to voice the aspirations of the Gayo community. We say this with good reason, of course, because this central region of Aceh very much needs greater attention in the future. We are still a region that gets virtually nothing from the development pie. We lag behind other districts and towns of Aceh. Hopefully, the voters will not make the wrong choices. If we once more fail this year to place the best candidates in the DPRA, don't hope that the central region will be able to make progress. Our conditions will remain just like they are today.[9]

I interviewed and followed the campaigns of 11 candidates for this research, 8 of whom were ethnic Gayo, and interviewed members of several other candidates' success teams. It was striking that *all* the

---

[9] "Siapa Wakil Gayo untuk DPRA …?" [Who Are the Gayo Representatives for the DPRA?], *Lintas Gayo*, 19 Oct. 2013. Available at: http://lintasgayo.co/2013/10/19/siapa-wakil-gayo-untuk-dpra.

Gayo candidates interviewed for this research agreed that playing the ethnic card was important to their campaign strategies. Sri Wahyuni, a district candidate for the Nasdem party, pointed out that it was precisely because "The Gayo ethnicity in Aceh's geopolitics is a minority, while the Acehnese ethnic group is the majority" that "if possible, all the people who get seats in electoral district IV should be indigenous Gayo".[10] Hendra Budian, a provincial Golkar candidate, agreed that mobilising ethnicity was necessary. The formation of the new electoral district was:

> a challenge for the Gayo community to choose Gayo sons and daughters; there is no reason not to vote for Gayo people, because now Bener Meriah and Central Aceh are in one electoral district, not like in 2009 when, because we were with Bireuen, there could be a reason for us to lose. This time there are no excuses.[11]

In practical terms, how did such views manifest themselves? In the campaign events I witnessed and campaign materials I collected, Gayo candidates used several techniques. First, some (such as Ismaniar, Muhlis and Yunis Shofiasti—all PAN candidates) explicitly used the *pilih singkite* slogan. A similar technique involved referring to non-Gayo candidates as "imported candidates", implying that they were standing in the uplands only for personal gain, rather than to build or develop the region for its own sake. The use of Gayo terms and other ethnic symbols was a second technique for mobilising the Gayo vote. The three PAN candidates all used the Gayo language in their campaign leaflets, beginning them with the words *Ama, Ine, Sudere* (Mother, Father, Brother). Ismaniar was especially assiduous: at his campaign events, he distributed a DVD featuring himself singing various Gayo and Acehnese language songs, most prominently *Tawar Sendenge* (Cool Home), a local song that is a sort of unofficial Gayo anthem. He and many other candidates also habitually referred to their region as *Bumi Linge* (Land of Linge), referring to an old highlands kingdom. Third, as already alluded to, candidates promised that, if elected, they would work

---

[10] Interview, Sri Wahyuni, 18 Mar. 2014.
[11] Interview, Hendra Budian, 22 Mar. 2014.

to deliver development benefits back to their local area, depicting the Gayo lands as being in competition with the rest of Aceh for limited resources. As a leaflet distributed by one candidate, Yunis Shofiasti from PAN, put it:

> If the community can prove the meaning of self-respect in politics, God Willing, the Gayo will be able to compete and derive strength from the local and national political structure. It is our joint goal and aspiration to reorganise the Gayo lands for the better in the future. Gayo community representation in the Aceh parliament will be most beneficial for the social and economic life of the Gayo. The Gayo community hope that their representatives in the Aceh legislature will be able to influence government development policies for the benefit of the Gayo.

It should be stressed, therefore, that much of the identity politics in the election also fundamentally concerned the distribution of material resources: many Gayo candidates promoted the perception that their region had been neglected by the Acehnese-dominated legislature in Banda Aceh, and promised to redress this neglect.

We should note one important exception to the general pattern described so far: Partai Aceh candidates and campaign workers tended to deny that primordial politics, and the Gayo vs non-Gayo cleavage, were important in this election. Some of them even tried to pass off ethnic politics as attempted provocation being promoted by unnamed third parties. Joni Suryawan, for example, a provincial Partai Aceh candidate, explained that voters did not differentiate between Gayo and non-Gayo interests, and were only interested in candidates' visions for developing the region.[12] This position makes sense when we remember that Partai Aceh candidates were primarily appealing to ethnic Acehnese voters—who represented a minority locally, even if they were a majority in the province as a whole—and that their overall approach was informed by an Acehnese ethnonationalism that emphasises what unites Acehnese as a group rather than the various subregional identities that divide them.

---

[12] Interview, Joni Suryawan, 29 Mar. 2014.

In contrast, candidates from the national parties and those of Gayo ethnicity tended to stress the importance of the Gayo political awakening. In fact, most Gayo candidates tended to target only their fellow Gayo for votes, and construct success teams that also mostly consisted of co-ethnics. At the very least, they tended to avoid campaigning among the ethnic Acehnese who, in the words of a PAN candidate, "are very ideological and are certain to go to Partai Aceh, so it's very hard to get through to them".[13] On the other hand, there were some Gayo candidates who tried to attract support from other migrants, such as the Javanese.

THE POLITICS OF PATRONAGE

Yet there was much more than ethnicity to this election. Most candidates shared as a starting point a simple proposition: "We have to give something to the constituents", whether that something was money, goods or political contracts promising future benefits to a village or group. Analysts have identified patronage delivery as being central to electioneering in Aceh.[14] In part, it is central because of community expectations that politicians will deliver concrete benefits to them. This expectation, however, arises in a context where many community members feel their politicians offer little else. As one villager complained:

> Candidates only start to show up and start coming to the communities when an election approaches. Beforehand, we rarely see them visiting the people; they only need us when it gets close to voting day. After they get elected, they forget us again. So we clearly cannot trust them. As a result, we put a price on our votes, and the candidates have to pay that price.[15]

---

[13] Interview, Muhlis, 7 Apr. 2014.

[14] See Samuel Clark and Blair Palmer, "Peaceful Pilkada, Dubious Democracy: Aceh's Post-Conflict Elections and their Implications" (Indonesian Social Development Paper no. 11, World Bank, Jakarta, 2008); Blair Palmer, "Services Rendered: Peace, Patronage and Post-conflict Elections in Aceh", in *Problems of Democratization in Indonesia*, ed. Edward Aspinall and Marcus Mietzner (Singapore: ISEAS, 2010), pp. 206–306.

[15] Interview, villager, Bener Meriah, 25 Mar. 2014.

Candidates who refused to distribute money or goods risked alienating their constituents. The aforementioned Sri Wahyuni explained: "If you give nothing to the voters they'll marginalise you. This is what I experienced in Bener Meriah. People asked: 'What good is she as a candidate if she can't give us anything?'"[16]

Candidates viewed the open-list proportional representation system as the source of such transactional politics. According to Golkar candidate Hendra Budian:

> The electoral system we use now brings forth a transactional process, so it becomes a real struggle to get people to vote for you on the basis of ideas, rather than transactions. In electoral district IV, only a very small percentage of people vote on the basis of ideas compared to the much larger number who vote on a transactional basis. It's seventy to thirty—30 per cent vote for ideas and 70 per cent or more believe in transactions. Almost all the constituents hope for gifts of money or goods.[17]

Some candidates engaged relatively openly in certain forms of patronage politics. Electoral politics in Aceh often involves a form of bargaining between candidates and village leaders in which "candidates commonly attempted to highlight how they had assisted communities in the past, and engaged in further distribution of such 'assistance' as part of their campaign strategies".[18] One such candidate who tried to lock in village leaders' support in 2014 was Golkar's Hendra Budian who, as well as being the deputy secretary of Aceh's Golkar branch, was a former NGO human rights and judicial reform activist. His campaign slogans were "With the people, opposing corruption" and "From the farmers, by the farmers, for the farmers". Instead of direct gifts he offered formal "political contracts" to farming communities, promising them favoured treatment should he be elected (see Box 3.1 for an example). If a group of constituents requested money or goods prior to a meeting, he would avoid going to that meeting, and if such requests were made during a meeting, he would explain why he could not meet that request and would generally then not hold any follow-up meetings with the same group.

---

[16] Interview, 17 Apr. 2014.

[17] Interview, Hendra Budian, 22 Mar. 2014.

[18] Palmer, "Services Rendered", p. 298.

Box 3.1: Example of a "Political Contract" in Bener Meriah District

Contract
Before the Almighty
The Community of Tebok village
Central Aceh District

I Hendra Budian, aged 36 years, a legislative candidate for the DPRA from the Golkar Party, with all my heart state my commitment to always pay attention to, look after, listen to and struggle for the interests of the community with all the abilities that I possess.

I also commit myself to fighting for the agricultural sector by promoting the concept of the creative economy and by helping to create a Village Owned Enterprise (BUMD) in Tebok village, with the hope that such a BUMD would then act to support the people's economy in the village. I also promise to struggle to make available a budget of 100 million rupiah for the village in carrying out this program, if I receive a mandate from the people to become their representative in the Aceh People's Representative Council.

This letter is part of my commitment to the people of Tebok village in Pegasing subdistrict. I am willing to face a legal suit if I fail to fulfil this commitment.

I make this contract in full awareness and without being under pressure in the hope that this letter of commitment can be used in the future by the community of Tebok village for the purposes of carrying out my commitment.

Sincerely
Hendra Budian

Witness I   Witness II   Witness III

…….....…..   …….....…..   …….....…..

Hendra offered such "contracts"—which he signed on a *materai* (a paper stamp that is used to seal official documents in Indonesia)—to about 20 villages through Bener Meriah and Central Aceh, all containing the same promise about special funding for village economic activities, which he promised he would be able to secure through "political lobbying". He usually first contacted the village head, then read out the document and signed it at a village meeting attended by village officials and residents. He timed most meetings to take place in the week or two leading to voting day. The goal of providing such formal contracts was to try to reduce the mistrust that many community members felt about politicians and their promises. He also explained, "I chose this approach to avoid money politics and as a result of my background as an activist".[19]

Though Hendra Budian's approach was particularly formal, in fact many candidates used this pattern of providing—or promising—pork barrel projects. Members of the provincial legislature in Aceh had access to "aspiration funds", a form of constituency development fund (see Chapter 7 for Muhammad Mahsun's discussion of this phenomenon in South Sumatra) in order to pay for projects in their electorates, with allocations averaging Rp 5 billion annually per legislator. In the Gayo lands, it was primarily new candidates rather than incumbents who made promises of future aspiration fund projects, trading on the feeling that the uplands had been neglected by their Bireuen-focused representatives who had been directing their projects to the coast. Thus, one ethnically Gayo Gerindra candidate promised aspiration funds in every village he visited, according to one of his success team members: "We tell the constituents that if our candidate wins in the areas we visit, that we will bring aspiration funds to that area and use it to promote the welfare of the coffee farmers."[20]

Many candidates also made "donations" of "assistance" (club goods) that would benefit an entire community. For example, Fariz Reza Firmandez, an ethnic Acehnese candidate for Partai Keadilan dan Persatuan Indonesia (PKPI, Indonesian Justice and Unity Party) who was

---

[19] Interview, Hendra Budian, 5 Apr. 2014.
[20] Interview, 2 Apr. 2014.

also one of Aceh's wealthiest businessmen, received many requests from village heads and other community leaders for contributions. According to one of his campaign coordinators:

> The donations that Fariz give vary in size, but he doesn't give everybody everything they ask for. For instance if, when he visits the constituents, they ask him for 30 sacks of cement to build a *meunasah* (prayer hall), Fariz might give them only ten sacks, or he might give them exactly what they want.[21]

Ismaniar, a Gayo PAN incumbent, made good use of her position as the head of the Aceh branch of the Ikatan Tata Boga (Ikaboga, Cooking Class Association), handing out assistance in the form of cooking utensils, serving equipment and similar material to Pembinaan Kesejahteraan Keluarga (PKK, family welfare guidance groups, a ubiquitous form of women's association) groups in about 17 villages across the electoral district. She also donated farming equipment and bags of fertiliser to farmers' groups. In her meetings with constituents she always explained all she had done for the region, and how she would continue to lobby for more funds for community-development projects for local communities.

Gifts and payments to individuals were also commonplace. One common technique was to give small sums to individuals who attended meetings or other campaign events. Such payments, typically in the vicinity of Rp 20,000 to Rp 50,000 per person, could eat up most of a candidate's campaign budget. Participants at outdoor campaign events—even those held by parties such as Nasdem and Partai Aceh whose candidates strongly denied that they engaged in money politics—were also typically paid for attending. In fact, persons I met at such events often stated that they would not have come but for the payment.

In contrast, money politics in its crudest form—retail vote buying—was much more hidden. Most candidates denied that they practised it and asserted that it was *haram* (forbidden) for them and their parties. Some suggested that it would be shameful to be caught distributing cash to voters. As a result, patronage politics tended to be carried out carefully

---

[21] Interview, Irwanto, 6 Apr. 2014.

and clandestinely. However, even if retail vote buying was largely hidden, this does not mean it did not happen at all. Various candidates' success team members monitored their rivals' efforts, and were one source of information about the distribution of cash in villages—payments that were called by various names including "transport money", "polling booth fee" (*ongkos ke TPS*) and *uang lelah* ("tired money"—here, as elsewhere in Indonesia, candidates used the argument that they were compensating voters for the trouble of going to the polls when they paid them).

It was mostly, but by no means exclusively, incumbents from the national (rather than local) parties who made these payments. The amounts paid varied: for example, I received one report of a Gayo incumbent who paid voters sums of Rp 200,000, 150,000 or 60,000 each to vote, with those payments distributed via village heads (in this case my source was a village head who received this money, but had in fact already committed to a candidate from a rival party). Village heads regularly played the critical brokerage role in transferring payments from candidates to voters in this region. I also received several reports of an ethnic Acehnese candidate from a local party who paid residents in several parts of Central Aceh Rp 200,000 for their votes—but required that they surrender their government ID cards to him before the vote, with the implicit threat they would not receive them back if the village voted for rivals. Though it is hard to be certain about how widespread such individualised vote buying was in Aceh IV, it was not rare.

A VICTORY FOR GAYO ETHNIC POLITICS?

As might be expected given the readjustment of the electoral district's boundaries, the election in 2014 did deliver victories for more Gayo candidates than in 2009. While only one of the ten candidates elected to the provincial legislature in 2009 was Gayo, in 2014 the number shifted to five out of six. Also notable is the fact that the major ethnic minorities in the uplands—the Acehnese and Javanese—were poorly represented (the former only by one successful candidate; the latter not at all). The redrawing of the boundaries had created new under-represented minorities.

Moreover, there were other changes that were also significant. None of the candidates elected were from Bener Meriah, the less populous of the two *kabupaten* contained in the new electoral district. The domination of Bireuen in 2009 had been replaced by the domination of Central Aceh in 2014. The fact that three of the five victorious Gayo candidates lived in either Jakarta or Banda Aceh shows that this was in fact a victory for the upper echelons of the Gayo elite, rather than for Gayo candidates more generally.

A comparison of victorious and losing candidates within the individual parties further tempers the conclusion that this was a simple victory for ethnic politics. For example, of PAN candidates, it was Yunis Shofiasti and Muhlis who had most assiduously played the Gayo ethnic card. Yet they were defeated by Ismaniar, whose primary advantage was greater financial resources, and consequently, greater ability to deliver patronage. Likewise, within Golkar, Iberamsyah far outspent his party rivals and was further advantaged by the fact that he was the brother of the incumbent district head (*bupati*) of Central Aceh, Nasruddin—he was mentioned by virtually all my informants as the financially strongest candidate in the constituency. Strategising by other Golkar candidates—such as Hendra Budian's attempt to lock in community-level support by offering political contracts—could not counter this great advantage.

Meanwhile, the victory of Nasdem's Ramadhana Lubis—the only non-Gayo candidate to be elected—can be explained by an organisational advantage: he built an exceptionally large success team of about 1,000 persons from the various ethnic communities, each of whom he provided with a formal letter acknowledging their status, and thus providing them with some hope of a continued relationship of mutual advantage should he win.

CONCLUSION

The election in the central highlands of Aceh in 2014 provides a dramatic example of the political consequences of electoral boundaries, with a major redrawing of boundaries prompting a dramatic change in the tenor of electioneering and the nature of representation. An electoral district that was dominated by the ethnically Acehnese lowlands district of Bireuen became, in 2014, an exclusively highlands constituency with a Gayo majority. Long-standing grievances about the marginalisation of the Gayo were now not only voiced, but had a chance to sweep the electorate. A "Gayos should vote for Gayos" mood became influential, and Gayo candidates achieved great electoral success.

Yet ethnic mobilisation was not the only—or arguably even the dominant—strategy of electoral mobilisation. Money politics and patronage remained critical. Indeed, even the mobilisation of ethnic Gayo sentiment was framed by patronage politics, with it being assumed that Gayo legislators would work harder to deliver development projects and other patronage goods to the highlands and to co-ethnics. This was a critical subtext in much of the election campaigning. More importantly, in a context in which numerous Gayo candidates competed for the votes of the same ethnic group, in the end it was candidates' financial resources, and the reach of their clientelistic networks, that determined success. In short, ethnic mobilisation and patronage politics were far from being in conflict in this election: instead, they fed off one another.

chapter **4**

Medan, North Sumatra: Between Ethnic Politics and Money Politics

Ahmad Taufan Damanik

The people of North Sumatra have experienced their fair share of embarrassing political scandals. In January 2008, Abdillah, the mayor of the capital, Medan, was arrested by the Komisi Pemberantasan Korupsi (KPK, Corruption Eradication Commission), along with his deputy, Ramli Lubis, for their part in a corruption scandal centred on the purchase of fire engines. In October 2010, it was the turn of the province's governor, Syamsul Arifin, to be arrested by the KPK. An earthy and funny politician, Arifin ended up in jail for corruption during his earlier term as head of Langkat district. Then, in March 2014, the new mayor of Medan, Rahudman Harahap was sentenced by the Supreme Court to five years' jail for budget irregularities when he had been a bureaucrat in South Tapanuli district. A number of senior bureaucrats and directors of local state enterprises have also been jailed for corruption. Add the scandals that have ensnared legislators in the province, and no wonder North Sumatra (Medan in particular) has a reputation for corrupt politics.[1]

---

[1] Vedi R. Hadiz, "Power and Politics in North Sumatra: The Uncompleted *Reformasi*", in *Local Power and Politics in Indonesia: Democratisation and Decentralisation*, ed. Edward Aspinall and Greg Fealy (Singapore: ISEAS, 2003), pp. 119–31.

One source of this corruption in North Sumatra, as in other parts of the country, is campaign financing. Candidates who expend great sums on getting elected typically try to replenish their funds once they are in office. It is thus a particular concern that in 2014 the city of Medan witnessed levels of money politics that exceeded those in all previous elections, with candidates distributing unprecedented amounts of cash and goods to voters and brokers. In practice, however, one of the distinguishing features of money politics in North Sumatra is how it becomes entangled in the politics of identity. Identity politics often provide the mechanisms or networks for the distribution of patronage. Candidates often also invoke identity appeals to reinforce the effectiveness of their patronage delivery, seeking whatever will give them a winning edge.

This chapter explores the entanglement of identity and patronage politics in the 2014 legislative elections in Medan. After briefly sketching the city's ethnic and political background, the argument proceeds through three main sections. In the first, I outline the ethnic and/or religious targeting that was central to the campaign strategies of most candidates, with almost all first identifying a core base and then deciding which communities might supplement that base. In the next two sections, I explain the patterns of organisation that candidates relied upon to reach out to these groups, and the forms of patronage they distributed in order to mobilise them.

BACKGROUND: THE POLITICS OF MEDAN

North Sumatra is a richly multi-ethnic province. Its population of 12.9 million (here and later I use 2010 census figures) consists of dozens of ethnic groups, both indigenous to the province and migrants or their descendants. The indigenous groups include the various Batak subgroups, such as the Batak Toba (21 per cent), Batak Mandailing (9.5 per cent) and Batak Karo (5.6 per cent), as well as Malays (4.4 per cent) and people from Nias Island (7 per cent). Others are descendants of historical migrants, including those who came to work in plantations and trade during the colonial period, plus the usual mix of more recent migrants. The migrants include Javanese, the biggest single group in North Sumatra at 33 per cent of the population, Minangkabau (2.6 per cent), Chinese (2.6 per cent), and many others.

The city of Medan, the provincial capital, is Indonesia's fifth most populous city with a population of a little over two million, and is equally diverse. The Javanese are the largest group, at 33 per cent, followed by Batak Toba (17.4 per cent), Batak Mandailing (9.9 per cent), Chinese (9.5 per cent), Minangkabau (7.8 per cent) and then a plethora of smaller groups. As well as having an unusually large Chinese population, with many still maintaining fluency in their ancestral Chinese languages, notably Hokkien, Medan is one of the few places in Indonesia to have a large Indian population, of about 15,000. Despite this great diversity, Medan has generally harmonious interethnic relations, with relatively little mass interethnic violence (though there was anti-Chinese rioting in 1998 in the lead-up to the fall of Suharto). At the same time, ethnicity plays an important role in housing and settlement patterns, and it is an important basis for affiliation both in daily social interaction and political life.

Ethnic associations (*paguyuban*) have a long history in the city, catering to the cultural and social support needs of the various communities. Their numbers expanded rapidly after democratisation. In the past, for example, the ethnic Javanese had only the famous Pujakesuma (Putra Jawa Kelahiran Sumatera, Sons of Java Born in Sumatra), but now there are more than a dozen ethnic Javanese associations, many of which become involved in politics at election times. Other ethnic groups native to North Sumatra, such as the Minangkabau, Malays, Toba Batak, Mandailing, Karo, Simalungun, Nias and Pakpak have their own organisations, as do migrants from elsewhere such as the Madurese, Betawi, Sundanese and Acehnese. The major Chinese organisations are Paguyuban Sosial Marga Tionghoa Indonesia (PSMTI, Indonesian Social Association of Chinese Clans) and Perhimpunan Indonesia Tionghoa (INTI, Indonesian Chinese Association), both of which are nationwide organisations, as well as a local splinter group led by Iskandar, a businessman-politician affiliated to the Nasdem party, called Paguyuban Suku Tionghoa Indonesia (PASTI, Indonesian Association for the Chinese Ethnic Group). Such organisations are often used for electoral mobilisation, though their primary functions are social.

Despite the city's renowned pluralism, primordialism is sometimes a factor in its local politics. In the most recent mayoral election, for example, although most of the Muslim residents of the city knew that Rahudman Harahap had a questionable background, there was a very effective campaign to mobilise Muslim support behind him, given that his main rival was Sofyan Tan, an ethnic Chinese and Buddhist. The ethnic Chinese and (to a lesser extent) non-Muslims rallied behind Sofyan.[2] Something similar happened during the gubernatorial election of 2013 when Gatot Pujo Nugroho, a Muslim candidate with a PKS background, received high votes in most Muslim residential areas, and Effendi Simbolon, a Toba Batak Christian backed by the PDI-P, was supported in Christian neighbourhoods. The same pattern of religious voting was seen throughout the province, with Simbolon doing well on the west coast, in Nias Island and the mountains, where many Christians live, and Gatot sweeping the majority Muslim east coast.

Ethnic and religious affiliation is not the only factor that influences voting behaviour in Medan, or in the wider province, however. Voters also take account of factors such as the candidate's charisma or programmatic offerings. Medan is also known as being a centre of *premanisme* (gangsterism), and the various gangs also play a role in organising election campaigns and mobilising voters.[3] As in many parts of Indonesia, the role of the bureaucracy is also important, so that in the 2014 legislative elections it was obvious that a party would do particularly well in a district if one of its members was the district head and was thus able to mobilise the bureaucracy in its favour.[4]

---

[2] Edward Aspinall, Eve Warburton and Sebastian Dettman, "When Religion Trumps Ethnicity: Local Elections in Medan, Indonesia", *South East Asia Research* 19, 1 (2011): 27–58.

[3] Muriyanto Amin, "Kekuasaan dan Politik Lokal: Studi Tentang Peran Pemuda Pancasila dalam Mendukung Syamsul Arifin dan Gatot Pujo Nugroho sebagai Gubernur dan Wakil Gubernur Sumatera Utara Periode 2008–2013" [Power and Local Politics: A Study of the Role of Pancasila Youth's Support for Syamsul Arifin and Gatot Pujo Nugroho as Governor and Deputy Governor of North Sumatra, 2008–2013], PhD diss., Universitas Indonesia, Jakarta, 2013.

[4] On the role of party machines in North Sumatra's politics, see Ryan Tans, *Mobilizing Resources, Building Coalitions: Local Power in Indonesia* (East-West Center Policy Studies No. 64, Honolulu, 2012).

The leading party in Medan's city council has changed with each post-Suharto election: it was PDI-P in 1999, PKS in 2004, Partai Demokrat in 2009 and then back to PDI-P in 2014, though with a smaller margin of victory than in 1999. At the provincial level, there have been similar fluctuations: from PDI-P in 1999, to Golkar in 2004, Partai Demokrat in 2009 and back to Golkar in 2014, but with only a margin of one seat (18 in total) ahead of PDI-P (17 seats). Islamic parties feature in the province's politics, but the large Christian population (27 per cent Protestant, 4 per cent Catholic) ensures that pluralist-nationalist parties are the main players.

CANDIDATE STRATEGIES: SOCIOPOLITICAL MAPPING AND ETHNORELIGIOUS TARGETING

One of the first steps any candidate takes when planning an electoral strategy is to map the sociopolitical features of voters in their electoral district. Most serious candidates running for DPR seats in North Sumatra electoral district I, made up of Medan and the districts of Deli Serdang, Serdang Bedagai and Tebing Tinggi, built campaign structures that covered all four of these districts. But when deciding on where to focus their energies, they generally identified particular subdistricts or even villages whose populations had the "right" ethnic and/or religious composition.

Take, for example, Chinese candidates. In the New Order period, the Chinese were famously divorced from political life, but this gradually began to change in North Sumatra in the *reformasi* era, gathering pace in the 2009 election when there was a dramatic increase in Chinese representation in several local legislatures, with people like Sonny Firdaus (from PPIB, or Partai Perjuangan Indonesia Baru, New Indonesia Party of Struggle, a party that was not qualified to compete in 2014) and Brilian Moktar (PDI-P) in the provincial parliament, and Ahie (Partai Demokrat), Jan Lie, Lily MBA (PPIB) and Hasyim (PDI-P) in the Medan DPRD. Many of these candidates relied on growing political consciousness within the Chinese community, which was their main voter base. Sofyan Tan, the Chinese PDI-P candidate for the national parliament in 2014, who had been the party's Medan mayoral candidate in 2010 (a campaign that had itself been a major marker of growing Chinese political confidence), concluded frankly that "my main support base is in the Chinese community, and they are mostly found in Medan".[5] In his case, this turned out to be a successful strategy. Sofyan was elected to the DPR with a personal vote of 113,000, much larger than his nearest intra-party rival at 46,000, and with most of those votes coming from subdistricts with large Chinese populations, such as Medan Kota, Medan Area, East Medan, Medan Sunggal and Medan Petisah.

In the provincial and city DPRDs, Chinese candidates with backgrounds in the same community organisation as Sofyan, PSMTI, duplicated his success. They included Brilian Moktar in the provincial legislature, and Hasyim and Wong Chun Sen in the city DPRD. All four men received strong support in the same Chinese neighbourhoods of Medan, and all of them ran as PDI-P candidates, a party which, partly under the influence of Sofyan Tan's rising political star, had experienced an influx of new Chinese members in recent years. A Chinese Gerindra candidate for the provincial parliament, Sonny Firdaus, also successfully focused on Chinese voters, though in his case he had a background in a different Chinese organisation, INTI. But plenty of other Chinese candidates, such as Firdaus's associates from INTI, Jan Lie and Lily MBA (both Gerindra incumbents) and Edy Suwandy (who was standing with Partai Demokrat), as well as Iskandar, a Nasdem candidate and the founder of PASTI, failed to get elected when using the same strategy. Obviously, ethnic appeals are in themselves insufficient to ensure election when numerous candidates from the same group target a particular ethnic voter base.

In these cases, two factors were critical to a candidate's electability, given that patronage politics was generally not a strong factor within the relatively prosperous Chinese community. One was the individual candidate's personal reputation for integrity, achievements as a public figure, and social activism, often within a particular clan. A second factor was community or organisational endorsement. Halim Lo, the head of the Medan chapter of PSMTI explained:

---

[5] Interview, Sofyan Tan, 18 Mar. 2014.

Chinese candidates are increasing in number so we need to carry out internal selection, who is it that the community should support, and who they shouldn't support. Because if a candidate turns out to act improperly in the legislature then we, the entire Chinese community, will feel the effects.[6]

A similar statement was made by Darsen Song, a young community leader who worked to raise funds from wealthy members of the Chinese community for several approved candidates.[7] Darsen was a member of both PDI-P and PSMTI, and though he had official PSMTI endorsement for his fundraising efforts, it also happened that all the candidates he supported were from PDI-P.

Candidates from other ethnic groups tended to use a similar strategy: determine a voter base and only then look for additional votes. Tahan Manahan Panggabean, for example, was a Partai Demokrat Toba Christian incumbent in the provincial parliament. He focused his efforts on fellow Toba Bataks in his electoral district (no. II), which consisted of 11 subdistricts within Medan. He ran as part of a tandem arrangement with Ruhut Sitompul, a nationally famous Partai Demokrat legislator with the same ethnoreligious background, along with several similar candidates for the city parliament. He stressed, however:

To promote our campaign I don't just work among the Protestants. We also have good relations with all groups, including with Muslims. Just a few days ago we carried out a social service activity and planted trees in the yard of the Sunggal mosque.[8]

Conrad Parlindungan Nainggolan, a Catholic Toba Batak who was a Golkar incumbent in the city DPRD, likewise claimed to be "close to all groups, I'm also close to Muhammadiyah [the major modernist Muslim organisation in Indonesia]. I helped them several times with tens of millions of rupiah when building Muhammadiyah mosques … and I've also helped with Protestant churches."[9] Despite such outreach,

---

[6] Interview, Halim Lo, 27 Mar. 2014.
[7] Interview, Darsen Song, 27 Mar. 2014.
[8] Interview, Ruhut Sitompul, 15 Mar. 2014.
[9] Interview, Conrad Parlindungan Nainggolan, 1 Apr. 2014.

Nainggolan felt it necessary to initiate a new ethnic association, Pasada (Persatuan dan Pengembangan Adat dan Budaya Batak, Unity and Development of Batak Tradition and Culture) and tried to shore up his Batak voter base through this organisation.

In fact, this dual strategy—reliance on a base, supplemented by outreach to other groups—was often also visible in the banners, posters and other advertising material that candidates produced. Such material often included symbols (traditional dress, pictures of traditional buildings) or tag lines that stressed the candidate's primary ethnic identity, but then also added secondary identity affiliations such as their professional background and any ethnic ties they might have by marriage. Such purely symbolic concessions, however, had to be backed by the distribution of patronage to the target groups.

Unlike non-Muslim candidates, Muslims tended to first emphasise their religious identity, and only then their ethnic affiliation if needed. This resulted from the fact that Muslim voters were a clear majority, and that many of them emphasised their religious over their ethnic identity in daily life. Candidates like Hasrul Azwar, Ikrimah Hamidy (both PKS) and Amiruddin (Demokrat) emphasised their Islamic identity in their campaign material and grassroots campaigning, and hardly emphasised their ethnic backgrounds (as Mandailing and Malay-Minangkabau). Even so, there were some candidates, such as Surianto (a Javanese running with Gerindra in the Medan DPRD) who fused ethnic and religious appeals:

> My main supporters are the Javanese community who live in large numbers in Medan electoral district V. In addition, well, the Muslims are a majority. So I target activities like *pengajian* (Islamic study groups), mosque youth groups, as well as Javanese *paguyuban* (associations). Every now and then I also help Christian groups, just to try to disrupt the votes for my competitors who are Christians. After all, some of the Christian candidates try to get votes in the Muslim community.[10]

Various Karo Muslim candidates also reached out to Muslim voters by targeting the Karo community (both Muslims and Christians) in order to maximise their votes.

---

[10] Interview, Surianto, 31 Mar. 2014.

CLIENTELIST NETWORKS AND SUCCESS TEAMS

After determining their primary and secondary support bases in ethnic and/or religious terms, and deciding on which identity aspects to highlight in their campaigns, candidates would then select the right networks to reach out to those voters.

Typically, those networks reflected the campaign's focus on identity. For example, Hasrul Azwar, the PPP's deputy general chairperson and head of the DPR's Commission VIII, worked mostly through networks of Islamic groups, principally Al Jamiyatul Washliyah—the major traditionalist Islamic organisation in North Sumatra—and through the government bureaucracy, which he was able to access as a senior politician. Ruhut Sitompul, by contrast, largely worked through church networks, as did Nurdin Tampubolon and several other Christian candidates.

Sofyan Tan did the same thing. As well as relying upon PSMTI, he drew upon various social-activism networks which he had been supporting for decades, such as traders' cooperatives, as well as educational networks and alumni from the school he supported through his organisation, Yayasan Pendidikan Iskandar Muda (Iskandar Muda Education Foundation). As he explained: "I have been working for many years for social projects, cooperating with lots of other stakeholders. Voters should know a figure like me, compared to those who don't originate from or live permanently in this region."[11] His colleague, Brilian Moktar, added to this mix networks of youth organisations, sports clubs and medium-sized traders in Medan, as well as PSMTI and other Chinese associations.

Most incumbents also used bureaucratic networks to support their re-election efforts. In Medan, however, this was less effective than in rural districts. In rural districts, bureaucrats are often the dominant figures in local communities, so it is relatively easy for them to influence voters; Medan, by contrast, is much more open and voters are subject to multiple social and political influences. Bureaucrats in Medan, too, are much more varied in their political affiliations, so the bureaucracy cannot

---

[11] Interview, Sofyan Tan, 18 Mar. 2014.

be relied upon for monolithic mobilisation, as in some rural districts. This is reflected, for example, in losses in 2014 by strong incumbents known for having excellent access—and lobbying power—within the local government, including Amiruddin, the Partai Demokrat speaker of the Medan DPRD, Conrad Parlindungan Nainggolan (Golkar) and Jhony Allen Marbun of Partai Demokrat.

Almost all candidates said that they did not want to organise their campaigns by relying on their parties. They typically explained that, with open-list PR, the party machine would not focus on a single candidate, party cadres might be disloyal, and it was more expensive to use party members than to construct success teams involving outsiders. Of course, candidates who were themselves party leaders—or close to those leaders—were generally able to make use of the party machinery, but they almost always also built non-party success teams. These success teams were then managed either by the candidate him/herself, a family member or another trusted associate.

Often, there would be some degree of overlap between the teams working for candidates running at different levels but who considered themselves to be part of the same faction or grouping. For example, Sofyan Tan's success team overlapped considerably with those formed by fellow ethnic Chinese candidates Brilian Moktar, Hasyim and Wong Chun Sen. They were not competing against each other because while Sofyan was running for a national DPR seat, Brilian was competing for the provincial DPRD and the other two for the city DPRD, but in different electoral districts. All four were not only running for PDI-P but were also leaders of PSMTI. Often these cooperative arrangements (tandems) were based on ethnic and/or religious affinity—not least because this would mean that the candidates involved were targeting similar voters. In some cases, however, tandems could cross identity lines, and even involve candidates from competing parties. For example, Conrad Parlindungan Nainggolan, the Golkar party Toba Batak discussed above, cooperated closely with his good friend, Ibrahim Sakty Batubara, a Mandailing Muslim and senior PAN politician who was running for a seat in the DPD.

Most success teams were informal and flexible. Some candidates, however, created formal organisations. Amiruddin (Partai Demokrat), for example, created an organisation called "Rumah Cerdas" (Smart House) headed by his son, Destanul Aulia. Amiruddin had established this organisation two years prior to the election, with salaried staff and a social work programme of providing skills training for youths, English lessons for students, religious instruction for poor residents and micro-enterprises for women. Destanul explained that the concept was based on NGO-style community development, though they also aimed for the organisation to be the main support body for Amiruddin's re-election.[12]

Every success team, no matter how large, will always include core members, usually a few people who are particularly trusted by the candidate. Sofyan Tan, for example, as well as having many volunteers responsible for grassroots campaigning, cooperated closely with a few people who worked as political analysts, media liaison officers, programme managers and members of a special "lobby team" whose job was to build links with Chinese community leaders and businesspeople. Some of those who worked for him (and for Brilian Moktar) did so because of their links through social activism. Likewise, some of the PKS candidates, such as Ikrimah Hamidy, attracted much voluntary support as a result of their grassroots Islamist activism—Ikrimah was a former leader of the Islamist student group, Kesatuan Aksi Mahasiswa Muslim Indonesia (KAMMI, Indonesian Muslim Students Action Front) in Medan and had a history of involvement in various forms of activism. Such candidates also tended to get strong grassroots support: Sofyan Tan was backed by market stallholders whom he had a history of defending, and Ikrimah gained support from the blind, having in the past fought for budgetary allocations for social services for them. It is hard to judge how important such support was, but it is important to note that grassroots activism also fed into electoral campaigning, and not all electoral dynamics were dominated by patronage politics.

On the other hand, it should be emphasised that most participants in success teams received direct or indirect material benefits for their participation. Some members were repaying favours they had received in the past: in Ikrimah's team, for example, were numerous "honorary" (casual) teachers at *madrasah* (Islamic schools) who had benefitted from his efforts to have their salaries raised. Other individuals

---

[12] Interview, Destanul Aulia, 20 Mar. 2014.

gained reputational or networking benefits: for example, Darsen Song, mentioned above as a fundraiser for Chinese candidates, was able to build his own links as a businessperson among wealthy Chinese entrepreneurs and party figures through his lobbying work. Yet others were paid in cash: members of Surianto's team received regular payments of "pocket money", members of Ikrimah's team also received a monthly incentive payment, and the same happened in many other teams.

PATTERNS OF PATRONAGE

We can divide patronage into two basic categories: first, patronage which is distributed long before the election; second, that which is distributed in the immediate lead-up to it.

Incumbents could usually rely largely on the first category, because they had typically been cultivating their base areas long before the election was held. Some first-time candidates, however, also had records of patronage distribution they could build upon. One such candidate was Sofyan Tan who, as explained above, had a long history of social activism and charitable works via various NGOs and his own educational foundation. This activity had long ago earned him a reputation as a leader in provincial education and social reform, winning him various awards even before he went into politics with the PDI-P and stood as mayor in 2010. Indeed, social activism became the basis of his political career and it was difficult to distinguish between his social and political activities.

In the months leading to the election, Sofyan Tan remained active, giving out free medical treatment, scholarships and economic assistance to poor families. Sofyan also admitted that during this period he frequently gave donations to community groups that sought funds from him, and of course he always paid for food and drink at all his campaign meetings in poor neighbourhoods. However, unlike many candidates, he said he refused to pay "transport money" to attendees, or to engage in vote buying. It should also be noted that his meetings with members of the Chinese community were always different from the pattern just described: usually in these cases the group who invited him would pay for the event and, if they found him impressive, at the end of the meeting attendees often collected funds for his campaign. In addition to such community donations, Sofyan also received many contributions from Chinese entrepreneurs, though he claimed he was always selective in doing so and would only take donations from "clean" businesspeople, not from "black conglomerates".[13]

Sofyan, Brilian Moktar and Hasyim were also assisted by PSMTI colleagues who raised money both for their campaigns and for social assistance for poor communities. Darsen, one of the key players in these fundraising efforts, explained that Brilian in particular was "increasingly poor" after he became a politician, because he neglected his private business and gave much of his money to needy citizens.[14] Brilian had a history of individualised constituency service, especially in helping people who needed support dealing with the authorities: supporting workers protesting at the DPRD, defending Chinese people who had trouble with the police or gangsters, and so on.

There were also candidates like Surianto, the ethnically Javanese Gerindra candidate in the Medan DPRD mentioned above, who built his base through provision of social assistance, but without any particular political consciousness or clear plan. He was a wealthy businessman and had in the past distributed a lot of financial aid to the poor, mosques, religious groups, women's cooperatives, Javanese cultural groups and the like. He described the ability to help others as a blessing from God: "I believe that we should pass on to others each *rejeki* we receive from Allah" (*rejeki* is a blessing or material benefit from God).[15] For example, one of his gifts had been of land for a graveyard in the Marelan subdistrict (a supporter explained: "He doesn't only help the living, he also helps the dead").[16] After Surianto decided to run for the DPRD, these previous good works could be turned into political capital, and both Surianto and his success team revisited recipients to remind them of Surianto's generosity. Many of his team members were themselves members of religious organisations Surianto had helped in

---

[13] Interview, Sofyan Tan, 15 Mar. 2014.

[14] Interview, Darsen Song, 27 Mar. 2014.

[15] Interview, Surianto, 8 Mar. 2014.

[16] Confidential interview, 8 Mar. 2014.

the past. At the same time, Surianto also spent a great deal on his campaign, distributing foodstuffs, giving money to the poor, paying for neighbourhood infrastructure, sponsoring social, sports and religious events, and so on. Two weeks prior to the election he had already spent Rp 1.2 billion, with still plenty of expenses to go in the form of paying for over 800 polling booth witnesses, operation costs for his team to go house to house, payments to his team members, and distribution of cash and goods to poor voters. In fact, he tended to give more to non-Javanese and non-Muslim voters, being less confident in their support.[17] Surianto's efforts, and his past record of generosity, paid off, and he was elected to a seat in the Medan city council, with the second-highest personal vote among Gerindra candidates.

Amiruddin, the Medan DPRD speaker, through his Rumah Cerdas, had been running various social programmes for *becak* (motorcycle rickshaw) drivers, women and teenagers for two years, mostly in the form of skills training and grants for micro-enterprises. He had also provided considerable assistance to his constituents through various pork barrel schemes involving social assistance grants and infrastructure. He felt confident of victory, having not only done all these things but even published a book about his achievements, and relying mostly on his home village for votes. Yet he lost, and suspected one of his rivals from within his own party (Partai Demokrat) of having defeated him by way of vote buying and bribery of electoral officials.[18] Many other candidates who lost—Conrad Parlindungan Nainggolan was another—explained their defeat by pointing to these factors.

Another interesting example was Ratna Sitepu, a Hanura candidate for the Medan DPRD. The daughter of Bangkit Sitepu—a famous former leader of Pemuda Pancasila (Pancasila Youth, Indonesia's largest and best-known *preman* organisation) who had himself served multiple terms in the city council—ran a campaign based on the slogan "Let's Wear the Hijab" (*Mari berhijab*). A Karo Muslim, she spent the campaign period targeting women's Islamic study groups promoting the use of the Islamic headscarf, teaching women how to put it on correctly, and, of

---

[17] Interview, Surianto, 31 Mar. 2014.
[18] Interview, Amiruddin, 28 May 2014.

course, distributing free scarves in great quantities. At these meetings she also handed out foodstuffs and equipment that the groups would find useful for their activities. Ratna described her campaigning as a religious duty: "I teach people how to wear the *hijab*, and hand them out, not just because of the election. I'll keep doing it after the election, too. This is part of my *dakwah* [proselytisation] duties."[19] Ratna Sitepu narrowly defeated her nearest Hanura rival, Budiman Panjaitan, by 3,893 to 3,642 votes, but said that she did not do so by distributing cash to voters (unlike her father who was caught on camera by journalists doing just that). Budiman Panjaitan did, however, allege that she had won by manipulating the counting process, but his case at the election supervisory committee failed.

In fact, there are many indications that vote trading was very widespread in Medan, as was elsewhere in North Sumatra. Candidates reported frequently being approached by brokers claiming to be close to election officials who offered to "sell" them a set number of votes during the count, usually at prices varying between Rp 25,000 and Rp 100,000 per vote. For example, one Hanura candidate recounted being offered thousands of extra votes at a price of Rp 1 billion. After the elections, there were numerous complaints of irregularities in the counting process, with recounts being required in several subdistricts. The fact that the Dewan Kehormatan Penyelenggara Pemilu (DKPP, Honour Council of Election Administrators) stood down several members of the regional election commission in North Sumatra points to how widespread these irregularities were.

CONCLUSION

The 2014 election in Medan was a highly individualised affair. Candidates had the responsibility for designing, running and funding their own campaigns. Rather than relying on their parties—or taking direction from them—they mostly decided upon their target constituencies themselves and then designed campaign teams that would provide them with access

---

[19] This quotation is taken from Ratna Sitepu's Facebook page after her victory.

to these communities. Patronage was also critical, though it came in many forms—not just distribution of individual gifts and cash, but also long-term programmes of social assistance that candidates had in some cases been providing for years. As a result, it tended to be only the wealthiest candidates—those who had significant personal assets at their disposal, or who could take loans or donations from relatives or sponsors—who had a strong chance of victory. Only a few candidates entered the political competition with clear ideas about the development policy or government programmes they wanted to promote, and even these candidates were forced to adapt to the increasingly pragmatic logic that governs grassroots politics in Indonesia.

Map of Bangka Belitung and South Sumatra

chapter **5**

Bangka Belitung: Patronage and Identity Politics in a Plural Society

Ibrahim

The province of Bangka Belitung, a group of islands to the east of Sumatra, hosts a heterogeneous and dynamic society. A long history of commerce with, and maritime connections to, other parts of Indonesia and Southeast Asia has produced a community that prides itself on its openness and ethnic pluralism. Since the beginning of the reform period, after a brief flurry of mobilisation that led to the formation of the province two years after the fall of Suharto, the province has been largely politically stable. Ethnic pluralism, for example, has not given rise to violence, and though there has been intra-elite rivalry (much of it focused on the political economy of tin mining), it has rarely led to significant social tension.

In the 2014 legislative elections, programmatic politics featured little in the campaigning of candidates running for seats in the national, provincial and district parliaments in Bangka Belitung. Instead, as in many parts of Indonesia, candidates concentrated on building personal success teams and winning voters over with patronage. This chapter examines these patterns of political mobilisation by focusing on three aspects of electoral dynamics. After a brief background section, the chapter analyses, first, the varieties of patronage politics that candidates engaged in. This section notes that, although most candidates denied involvement in money politics, in fact patronage was central to most of their strategies, and they demonstrated great creativity in devising new forms of gifts and means of delivery. Second, the chapter investigates the campaign structures used by candidates, noting a basic division between casual and unstructured methods used by poorly resourced candidates and more elaborate and effective structures built by wealthier candidates. Third, the chapter examines patterns of identity-based networking by the candidates. Here, we face something of a puzzle: though Bangka Belitung society is remarkably open and ethnically tolerant, candidates often relied on narrow identity appeals and networks when reaching out to voters.

BACKGROUND: LOCAL POLITICS IN A MULTI-ETHNIC SOCIETY

Bangka Belitung was established as a province relatively recently, when it was split from South Sumatra in 2000.[1] Consisting of an archipelago of some 256 islands to the east of southern Sumatra, the province is dominated by the two large islands which give it its name. About 70 per cent of the population live in the four districts and one urban municipality that make up Bangka island; most of the remainder reside in the two districts of Belitung.

Easily accessible by sea from Sumatra, Jakarta, Malaysia and elsewhere in island Southeast Asia, these islands have long been centres of maritime commerce. Bangka and Belitung have also been among Southeast Asia's major centres of tin mining since the 18th century. This long commercial history has produced waves of migration and trade in the islands. As a result, local society is not only highly heterogeneous but also relatively open and dynamic. The population of 1.3 million is about 82 per cent Muslim, and about 50 per cent Malay, including various local Malay subgroups with distinctive *adat* (customs) and dialects, but with very fluid boundaries, assimilating freely with more recent Malay

---

[1] Minako Sakai, "Resisting the Mainland: The Formation of the Province of the Bangka-Belitung (Babel)", in *Autonomy and Disintegration in Indonesia*, ed. Damien Kingsbury and Harry Aveling (London: RoutledgeCurzon, 2003), pp. 189–200.

migrants from other parts of Sumatra.[2] The Chinese are the second-largest group, and constitute, according to the 2010 census, 8 per cent of the population. However, many local experts believe the true figure is higher, with many persons of Chinese descent—especially in villages—describing themselves as Malays to census enumerators, meaning the real number might be 20–25 per cent, making Bangka Belitung a province with one of the largest populations of Chinese Indonesians. The Chinese population have a strongly *peranakan* or indigenised culture, which has developed since the beginnings of Chinese settlement in the 16th century.[3] The remainder of the population are migrants from other parts of Indonesia, drawn by tin mining and other industries: Javanese, Bugis, Butonese, Bataks and virtually all of Indonesia's significant ethnic groups can be found in the islands. Interethnic relations in daily life tend to be fluid and relaxed, with much interaction and intermixing; however, each significant ethnic group also has its own ethnic association (*paguyuban*) for organising community activities.

Despite the province being known for its tin mining, this industry only employs a minority of the workforce, with large numbers employed in sectors such as rubber, pepper and palm oil production, and fisheries. Though mining issues, such as conflicts between national and regional regulations or the role of illegal mining, tend to be prominent in direct elections of local government leaders (who have significant powers over licensing), they are much less prominent in the legislative elections.

---

[2] Ibrahim et al., "Pakaian Adat, Rumah Adat, dan Upacara Adat Melayu di Provinsi Kepulauan Bangka Belitung" [Traditional Dress, Traditional Houses and Malay Traditional Ceremonies in Bangka Belitung Province], A report of joint research project with Disbudpar Bangka Belitung Province, 2013, unpublished; Ibrahim, "Bisnis, Kekuasaan, dan Identitas: Studi terhadap Politik Identitas Etnis Tionghoa di Bangka Belitung Pasca Orde Baru" [Business, Power and Identity: A Study of the Post-New Order Identity Politics of the Chinese in Bangka Belitung], PhD diss., Gadjah Mada University, Yogyakarta, 2014.

[3] Anthony Reid, "Chinese on the Mining Frontier in Southeast Asia", in *Chinese Circulations, Capital, Commodities, and Networks in Southeast Asia*, ed. Eric Tagliacozzo and Wen-Chin Chang (Durham, NC: Duke University Press, 2011), p. 23; Mary F. Somers Heidhues, "Company Island: A Note on the History of Belitung", *Indonesia* 51 (1991): 2.

Politically, the islands are broadly representative of national trends. Due to its small population, the province elects only three members of the national DPR. In both 2009 and 2014 these three came from each of the largest nationalist parties: PDI-P, Golkar and Partai Demokrat, respectively. Other medium-sized parties such as Gerindra, PKS, PPP and PKB are all represented in Bangka Belitung's provincial and district parliaments. One distinctive feature of the province's political scene has been the relative strength of the small Islamist party, Partai Bulan Bintang (PBB, Crescent Star Party) which had eight seats in the provincial parliament in 2004, three in 2009 (almost as many as the big three of PDI-P, Golkar and Partai Demokrat), but fell to just 1 out of 45 in 2014. PBB's local strength did not reflect particularly strong Islamist politics, but the influence of its former leader, Yusril Ihza Mahendra, a Belitung native who held several national ministerial posts between 1999 and 2007. As his political star faded (his last senior national post was as Minister of the State Secretariat, which ended in 2007), so too did the local fortunes of PBB.[4]

FROM POT PLANTS TO WATER REFILLS: MODIFICATIONS OF MONEY POLITICS

My research on the 2014 elections in Bangka Belitung incorporated candidates for district, provincial and national legislatures. Almost every candidate and success team member I interviewed claimed that they did not engage in "money politics". Most of them condemned money

---

[4] Along with Yusril, a prominent local politician who has made a mark on national politics is Basuki Tjahaja Purnama, commonly known as Ahok, who had been elected (as the running mate of Joko Widodo, Jokowi) as deputy governor of Jakarta in 2012, then governor in November 2014. Ahok, who is Chinese, was formerly the *bupati* of East Belitung, the runner up in the 2007 Bangka Belitung gubernatorial race, and a Golkar national legislator. However, his impact on the legislative race in Bangka Belitung was limited. Unlike Yusril, a founder and consistent supporter of PBB, Ahok's career has been marked by shifts between parties.

politics as reprehensible and unhealthy. In this regard, they followed national political discourse which tends to interpret money politics literally, as the direct exchange of cash for votes, and as both illegal and immoral. But this did not mean that they rejected patronage politics, understood broadly. In this respect, Kohar (not his real name—I am using pseudonyms for most informants in this chapter), a PBB candidate in the East Belitung DPRD, was typical:

> As for money politics, I'm opposed. I won't use it because our people are smart already. They will take the money, but they won't necessarily vote for us. I prefer holding meetings where I can explain my ideas and the programme I will carry out. I have already held about 27 such meetings in almost all the villages in my electoral district. The attendance varies, from about 20 to 70 people. I give them assistance in accordance with their needs—for instance, sporting equipment for youths, shirts or headscarves—but not money. I've even sponsored a special festival in a fishing village.[5]

Darwan, a PPP candidate in the Pangkal Pinang city DPRD, had a similar attitude. Not only was he spending a lot on his success team, he also distributed unusual gifts to women voters: seedlings of *pucuk merah* (a red-leaved decorative plant) and palms. He believed that these were not only unique but also well-targeted gifts, because many women householders were fond of using such plants in their front yards. Another candidate, an incumbent in South Bangka, also distributed seedlings—but this time rubber trees intended for productive use. Neither candidate regarded such gift-giving as money politics.

Almost all candidates, no matter how vehemently they condemned money politics, distributed goods in this way. There was even a local term for such goods: *alat kontak* (contact tool), the gift being a tool to forge a connection between the giver and recipient. Some of the goods candidates distributed were standardised: many, for example, handed out headscarves, women's prayer robes (*mukena*), *sarung* and batik shirts—standard gifts when approaching religious groups or when trying to build an image as a caring person. It also helped that such goods can easily be bought in bulk in Java and shipped cheaply to the province,

---

[5] Confidential interview, 8 Apr. 2014.

and that they are useful to practically all recipients. Some candidates also distributed staple foods, typically rice, to voters. The typical method here was for the candidate or his/her success team to strike a deal with the RT (subneighbourhood) head and then distribute an agreed amount (for instance, 5 kg of rice per household) in the neighbourhood immediately before the election.

Some candidates avoided these gifts, however, thinking they were too commonplace. Thus, like Darwan above, some devoted much thought to making their gifts distinctive and memorable. In Pangkal Pinang, for example, one PPP candidate, Hera, cooperated with a drinking water depot to provide free refills of the 20-litre water tanks people use in dispensers in their homes. When his customers came in to ask for the refills, the depot manager would provide them the water for free, tell them Hera was paying for it, and ask them to vote for him. The manager kept a tally and regularly billed Hera, who was pleased with the arrangement as being an original idea, though he admitted there was no way of ensuring that those who got the water actually voted for him. He was also concerned that quite a few customers were taking advantage of the arrangement to ask for Aqua brand refills, which were four times more expensive than the standard water tanks.[6]

Some candidates paid for major events involving community service on a much larger scale. Rudianto Tjen, a PDI-P DPR candidate, for example, brought in teams of qualified doctors to provide free health checks and treatment in many kampung; he then paid for half-page advertorials in local newspapers to report on these events (such advertorials alone cost between Rp 5 and 7 million). The goal was to build a "brand" as a man of action who was concerned for the poor. Sam, a PKS candidate for the South Bangka DPRD, paid for mass circumcisions, using the opportunity to promote his candidacy and his party to the assembled masses. Det, the incumbent speaker of one of Bangka's DPRDs, did the same, also sponsoring free concerts by local bands.

It was also relatively common for candidates, especially strong ones, to invest their funds in club goods: donations to fund community

---

[6] Interview, 19 Mar. 2014.

infrastructure or construction projects. Bud, a Bangka district DPRD candidate, explained how he spent Rp 5 million on a small jetty for fishers in one community; Anto, a West Bangka district PBB candidate, was negotiating with a youth group in his constituency on how much it would cost for him to create a football field in their village—he estimated it would be about Rp 5 million.[7] Meanwhile, Cik, an RT head and campaign worker supporting three Golkar candidates, boasted of how he had succeeded in bringing in three packets of assistance for his neighbourhood from these candidates: two were for fixing the drains; one was for widening an intersection. In return, Cik organised a meeting for these candidates and personally encouraged residents to vote for them.[8]

Another common technique was to invite community members to attend a meeting, and then provide them with generous "transport money" as the meeting ended. A multi-level marketing agent dealing in high-quality clothing related how one candidate—with the help of a relative who occupied a senior position in the marketing network—pulled together a large meeting of about 300 persons. After talking about running for the election, the candidate gave Rp 100,000 to each participant, which they used to join up as members of the multi-level clothing network, each acquiring a fine shirt as a result.

Despite candidates' protestations, cash payments were in fact critical to much of the 2014 campaigning. Numerous terms were used to camouflage such payments to supporters, and sometimes, to ordinary voters—*uang makan* (food money), *uang transport* (transport money), *uang pulsa* (mobile telephone voucher money), *uang lelah* (money to compensate someone for performing a task—"tired money"), *uang saksi* (witness money) and the like. The timing and structure of payments to success team members varied widely: some members were paid regularly throughout the campaign, some only once near voting day, some were paid according to how much work they did, some were paid during the campaign, but then given a bonus if their candidate won, and so on.

---

[7] Confidential interview, 28 Apr. 2014.
[8] Confidential interview, 15 Mar. 2014.

And many candidates did engage in conventional vote buying. It is difficult to ascertain how widespread this phenomenon was, though it was clearly more widespread among district-level candidates than among provincial or national ones. For example, Darwan, the PPP candidate in Pangkal Pinang mentioned above, admitted that he needed to make cash payments of Rp 50,000 each to voters. I was present when he negotiated with provincial and national candidates from the same party about cost-sharing for this purpose, with these candidates pooling their vote-buying money and hoping that doing so would increase their individual votes.[9] Such financial deals between candidates were not unusual. Some parties also organised deals whereby victorious candidates would compensate losing candidates from the same party and constituency whose personal votes had helped them win (thus in the Bangka DPRD, the PPP, according to one candidate, set the price at Rp 40,000 per vote, to be paid within two years of the victorious candidate taking office).

Overall, we are left with an impression of the candidates' innovative and creative adaptations of patronage politics to local circumstances. Candidates used a wide variety of social networks and community activities—from religious meetings through to medical consultations and community development projects—to make themselves materially useful to constituents.

MOBILISING FOR VICTORY: UNSTRUCTURED AND STRUCTURED SUCCESS TEAMS

In Bangka Belitung, as was elsewhere in Indonesia, most candidates formed individual success teams to run their campaigns and to connect them to voters. But these teams varied widely in their levels of organisation. There were two basic patterns. In the first, candidates relied on rather casual methods and generally unstructured teams, drawing in only a few people from their personal and family networks. Almost every candidate was able to rally at least a handful of associates

---

[9] Field observations, 21 Mar. 2014.

to accompany them to campaign meetings without payment. Some such people would support a candidate because of personal friendship; others might have an organisational connection of some sort. Candidates of this type tended to be inexperienced first-timers. Lacking the resources to build large teams, they instead often professed confidence in their individual campaigning skills and ability to personally "say hello" (as some put it) to as many voters as possible. A few candidates with limited resources tried to marshal them for purposes they thought would be effective: a Hanura candidate in East Belitung spent his money on hiring a "Sales Promotion Girl" (SPG, a widely used Indonesian term for young, generally attractive and fashionably dressed women employed to promote products) to accompany him on his house-to-house visits.[10]

Such candidates, lacking the financial resources to build teams that stretched beyond their immediate personal networks, also tended to share another characteristic: their political support tended to be concentrated in only one geographic and/or social setting, which they usually described as their *basis* (base). Thus, Tri, a PAN candidate in the Bangka district DPRD, explained that his success team was truly solid only in a few RT around his home. Sri, a Golkar candidate in Pangkal Pinang, admitted she was strong only in her own subdistrict, and that she lacked network connections to campaign elsewhere.

One problem for such candidates was that there were almost always rival candidates competing for the same base, so that friendship networks could rarely deliver victory. Their lack of money also meant that they tended to be unable to pay for polling booth witnesses to ensure their votes were not stolen. Add this to their inability to expand beyond their narrow base, and it should not surprise us that such candidates were rarely victorious.

The second pattern, favoured by better-funded and more experienced candidates (especially incumbents), involved the formation of more structured success teams. The key here was the creation of hierarchical structures which tried to ensure that team members were present in at least the most important regions in the electoral district:

---

[10] Confidential interview, 8 Apr. 2014.

> I have a success team that consists of 20 people at the electoral
> district level. I recruited them way back, when I was beginning the
> nomination process. Then I have also formed success team branches,
> each consisting of four people, in each village. These are the ones who
> have the job of carrying out socialisation and countering negative
> issues about me. As for the costs, I cover them. We know if you want
> to win, you've got to spend money on winning.[11]

This candidate, who was standing for PBB for a seat in the East
Belitung DPRD, claimed that his team remained "solid" until voting
day, with no members defecting to other candidates.

It was generally expensive to run a well-structured success team.
Langit, the head of a Gerindra DPR candidate's success team, explained
that he had built a team consisting of three layers: Alpha Team consisted
of the strategic and conceptual planners, most of whom came from
Jakarta, like their candidate; Bravo Team consisted of locals who
concentrated on networking; and Gamma Team's job was monitoring
what the other two teams were doing. The total cost of running these
teams was about Rp 50 million per month, with expenditure lasting
for several months.

Though there was a big gap between the better-organised and
funded candidates and those who lacked the capacity to build strong
success teams, most candidates shared one thing in common: they
concentrated their efforts on their personal campaigns, rather than
on party efforts. In fact, as a result of the open-list PR system, most
candidates saw their strongest competitors as being rivals from within
their own parties. Most viewed competition with candidates from other
parties as much less significant, because they believed that each party
more or less had its own constituency and it could be predicted how
many seats it would win in a particular electoral district. What was less
predictable was which individual candidate would win. This situation
could lead to candidates from different parties—both at different levels
and sometimes even competing in the same constituency—supporting
each other's campaigns. Thus, in the Mentok-Simpang Teritip electoral
district in West Bangka, three candidates, representing PBB, PDI-P and

---

[11] Interview, Kohar, 8 Apr. 2014.

PKB respectively, often got together to exchange experiences and urge each other on in their contests against—as they saw it—their respective intra-party rivals.

IDENTITY POLITICS IN A PLURAL CONTEXT

As noted above, one characteristic of Bangka Belitung society is its ethnic pluralism, tolerance and egalitarianism, a product of its maritime character and of centuries of trade, migration and other interaction with the outside world. Amongst the province's Malays, the boundaries separating the various subgroups are fluid, and there is significant assimilation between Malay and other migrants. The Chinese are also highly assimilated, typical of the *peranakan* cultures of island Southeast Asia. The Chinese-language phrase, *tong ngin fan ngin tjing jong* (which roughly means the Chinese and the natives are equal) is a widely known and accepted term for depicting interethnic relations in the province. Accordingly, ethnic violence in the province is relatively rare: for example, there was no anti-Chinese rioting during the transition to democracy of 1998, and relations are harmonious in daily life.

Despite this background, it was striking that many candidates made identity politics central to their strategies. Religion and ethnicity, in particular, were often seen as convenient tools of mobilisation. Tri, for example, was a PAN candidate in the Bangka DPRD who openly described making ethnic sentiment central to his campaign. Of Javanese descent, he also lived in an urban precinct—called Kampung Jawa— whose population had previously voted for non-Javanese candidates from elsewhere. He drew almost all the local RT heads into his success team. The team coordinator explained that the Javanese residents were now ready to vote for one of their own:

> In every election we have always supported others, who get elected but then make no meaningful contribution back to us. Now there is a son of this place, born here, and part of our ethnic group, and we think he is smart, so we are going to support him. We don't need money, we need him to be elected and then he'll be able to do a lot for us. We have been regularly building support for him, and now we are sure that the masses in Kampung Jawa will be solidly in favour of

him. With more than 2,000 voters we are convinced we'll be able to ensure he becomes a council member.[12]

In the final event, Tri was not elected, missing out by a mere 50 votes. Anto, a PBB candidate for the West Bangka DPRD, explained that he was mostly relying on fellow members of the Jering-Malay subethnicity, learning from his experiences as a DPD candidate in 2009, when he discovered that it was mostly co-ethnics who voted for him (he ultimately failed to be elected in 2014, too).[13] Rah, a success team member of a PKB candidate running for the provincial DPRD, explained that he was mostly targeting regions with significant populations of Bugis, given his candidate's ethnicity. Amongst other methods, he sponsored friendly football matches among local Bugis youth groups.[14] Overall, almost all candidates used identity appeals in order to first try to ensure that their vote would be solid "internally", that is, within their own ethnic group. Even so, this was usually done in a quiet manner, by using informal campaigning techniques and within social contexts and spaces that were identified with the ethnic group in question—such as the *paguyuban* or ethnic associations.

There were also some distinctive ethnic voting patterns. For example, it has been apparent over several election cycles that members of the ethnic Chinese community tend to support the PDI-P. As mentioned, the PBB vote has been concentrated in Belitung because of Yusril Ihza Mahendra's role. Bugis voters, meanwhile, tend to be attracted to Golkar, in part because many prominent national leaders of the party, such as Jusuf Kalla and Nurdin Halid, are from that group.

Of course, candidates did not rely only on ethnic networks; they also used those based on other identity categories, such as religion. Many candidates, especially those from the Islamic parties, used Muslim organisations and networks. Hera, a PPP provincial candidate who was a teacher at a Quranic school for children, for example, had easy access to *majelis taklim* (religious study groups) and similar networks, and frequently appeared at religious events such as the

---

[12] Confidential interview, 4 Apr. 2014.
[13] Confidential interview, 18 Apr. 2014.
[14] Confidential interview, 20 Mar. 2014.

Quranic recitations carried out to pray for the deceased, known as *tahlilan* or *yasinan*, typically distributing religiously tinged "contact tools" such as headscarves, prayer robes or prayer mats. Pasca, a Demokrat candidate, targeted the Christian vote, emphasising church symbols in her newspaper advertisements and other campaign activities.

Perhaps the most ubiquitous social identity drawn upon by candidates, however, was place of origin and domicile. Almost all candidates stressed their local roots when interacting with constituents. Emphasising that they came from the same locale as voters was not only a way for candidates to encourage voters to identify with them but also raised the issue of where candidates would direct patronage should they be elected. Sam, a PKS candidate for the South Bangka DPRD, always told voters in his village to vote for him because if he won they would then be able to access government decision-making and so ensure that they obtained their fair share of projects and other benefits. As he put it: "Vote for people from your own kampung, why cross over to some other village? If you choose a candidate from the same kampung, it will be much easier to present your aspirations directly."[15] Many voters—such as those in Kampung Jawa mentioned above—felt, rightly or wrongly, that their particular community was neglected by the government. Electing a local was seen as a way to remedy such neglect.

What this reliance on identity appeals points to is partly that candidates were keen to use whatever social networks they could access in order to build connections with voters and invoke emotional bonds with them. Thus, as well as ethnic, religious and regional ties, candidates who had access to women's organisations would use them (as one female Golkar candidate put it: "In every meeting, I appeal to the women for them to vote for a woman") whereas those who worked in a particular social organisation would likewise make use of that network.

Overall, the prominence of identity networks and appeals in the election was thus a reflection of the clientelistic nature of politics in Bangka Belitung. It did not point to wider salience of ethnic and other identity cleavages in political and social life. To be sure, there was

---

[15] Confidential interview, 16 Mar. 2014.

something anomalous about the utilisation of identity networks in the province, given the pride that most locals take in their community's openness and heterogeneity. And perhaps, too, the reliance on identity points to the underdeveloped nature of democracy here, given that identity politics is often a sign of the underdevelopment of more programmatic appeals.[16] Yet what occurred in Bangka Belitung was at most a "soft" form of ethnic mobilisation in which "contestants for political office mobilize ethnic symbols in order to garner support but do not claim to be pursuing dominance or primacy for their own group at the expense of others".[17] In short, though identity politics was common, it was not necessarily *conflictual*. It also rarely involved substantive discussion of policy or programmatic issues, and was indeed a means for candidates who lacked the competence to engage with such issues to avoid doing so.

CONCLUSION

Bangka Belitung is not only a socially heterogeneous province; it is also one without a history of bitter political cleavages or contestation. In this context, legislative candidates felt they had to offer more than just party affiliation or a party programme to voters. As we have seen in this chapter, they often did so by providing patronage—in highly varied forms—to voters, and by building personal success teams to connect them with their constituents. It is in this context that the prominence of identity politics witnessed in the 2014 legislative election starts to make sense. At one level, there was something artificial about the proliferation of ethnic and other forms of identity politics, given Bangka Belitung's famous openness and interethnic tolerance.

---

[16] Purwo Santoso, "Merajut Kohesi Nasional: Etno Nasionalisme dan Otonomi Daerah dalam Proses Demokratisasi" [Knitting National Cohesion: Ethnonationalism and Regional Autonomy under Democratisation], *Jurnal Ilmu Sosial dan Ilmu Politik* 4, 3 (2001): 265–88.

[17] Edward Aspinall, "Democratization and Ethnic Politics in Indonesia: Nine Theses", *Journal of East Asian Studies* 11, 2 (2011): 292.

However, when we remember the context of patronage and personalised politics in which such identity mobilisation occurred, the logic of the phenomenon becomes clear. It is not simply that candidates needed to stress their personal connections with voters, with a common identity bond being a simple way to do this. It is also that they needed methods to convince voters that, if elected, they would take special care of their interests. Candidates who highlighted regional, ethnic, religious or other identity ties were typically making the promise— explicitly or implicitly—that they would keep certain voters in mind when delivering future benefits. In Bangka Belitung, patronage and identity politics thus go hand in hand.

chapter **6**

Musi Banyuasin, South Sumatra: Nine Steps to Victory

Alamsyah

"The winner of the 2014 election in electoral district III of Musi Banyuasin was Haji Sen." So said Wasjud, an unsuccessful PKS (Prosperous Justice Party) candidate when I interviewed him three days after the vote. A *haji*, of course, is somebody who has performed the pilgrimage to Mecca. In South Sumatra province, as in other parts of Indonesia, the title is also a signifier of wealth, because it is only well-resourced people who can afford the pilgrimage. "Sen", meanwhile, means money in the Sekayu language of Musi Banyuasin, a local Malay dialect. Haji Sen was Wasjud's term for a candidate with lots of money.

In this chapter I explore Wasjud's deceptively simple proposition, focusing on competition between candidates for the DPRD in Musi Banyuasin's electoral district III. Most of the chapter is structured around the steps that each candidate who wants to get elected must take. I identify nine such steps, starting with securing a party nomination right through to preparing for the eventuality of a court challenge. By exploring these steps I underline how the differing financial resources available to candidates were critical to determining what strategies they could use, though we shall see that incumbency was also an important factor. Finally, I show that although vote buying was not always the determinant of electoral success, it was nevertheless a last resort for many candidates in the campaign's last days.

BACKGROUND: A RESOURCE-RICH DISTRICT

Musi Banyuasin is a mostly rural district located to the north of South Sumatra's capital, Palembang. With a population of about 580,000, it is also one of Indonesia's most resource-rich districts, with significant production of oil, natural gas and coal. Electoral district III, which incorporates the three subdistricts of Bayung Lencir, Tungkal Jaya and Lalan, constitutes just under 50 per cent of Musi Banyuasin's land area, and has about 27 per cent of its population, about 157,000 people. Most economic activity in the electoral district is concentrated in the two subdistricts of Bayung Lencir and Tungkal Jaya, where a majority of the villages were established as part of the government's transmigration programme in the 1980s. There are also former transmigration settlements in Lalan, though somewhat fewer because this is a mostly swampy and riverine area that became accessible by road only in 2014 after the construction of a major bridge. Not surprisingly given this history, the electoral district is ethnically dominated by migrants, notably Javanese, Sundanese and Balinese. There are a few villages inhabited by local Musi people (such as Peninggalan, Mangsang, Bayat and Simpang Tungkal), but they are far outnumbered by transmigrants and their descendants.

The largest source of employment in the three subdistricts is the plantation sector, notably oil palm and rubber. Natural gas, oil and coal exploration and production (centred in Bayung Lencir and Tungkal Jaya subdistricts) have also produced some trickle-down benefits for local people, mostly in the form of outsourced employment in such functions as security, catering, office management, operation of heavy machinery, transport services and the hospitality industry. The entry of major oil palm companies, meanwhile, has generated not only economic opportunities but also many bitter conflicts over land, with locals often fiercely resisting land grabs by companies[1] with some candidates trying

---

[1] Elizabeth F. Collins, *Indonesia Betrayed: How Development Fails* (Honolulu: University of Hawai'i Press, 2007); Benny N. Joewono, "Perebutan Ruang Hidup di Lahan Sawit" [Struggle for Living Space in Oil Palm Areas], *Kompas*, 17 June 2011, available at http://regional.kompas.com/read/2011/07/17/18415991/Perebutan.Ruang.Hidup.di.Lahan.Sawit; "Konflik Lahan Bahaya terpendam di Muba" [Dangerous Land Conflict Hidden in Muba], *Palembang Today*, 1 Feb.

to capitalise on this—Edi Hariyanto, a Gerindra incumbent, for example, made his past advocacy for farmers against the plantations central to his campaign strategy.

Twelve seats were allocated to Musi Banyuasin electoral district III. It was not an easy task, however, for candidates to compete in this constituency. Roads are poor, and some villages can only be reached by river. A total of 120 candidates competed, including 9 of the 12 incumbents (who were particularly advantaged not only by their superior political experience but also by access to government aspiration funds, see Chapter 7 on Palembang by Muhammad Mahsun. Most candidates agreed that competition in 2014 was much more challenging than in 2009, in large part because the atmosphere of "money politics" had thickened noticeably, with many voters now openly asking them: *wani piro?* (Javanese: roughly, "How much are you brave enough to give?").

Despite, or perhaps because of, these challenges, the election produced remarkably similar results to 2009. Of the 12 members representing the electoral district in 2009, 6 were re-elected in 2012. Though some of the individuals changed, there were only minor adjustments in party representation (Golkar lost a place to PAN and a minor party, ineligible to run in 2014, was replaced by Nasdem). The open-list PR system is also starting to erode the significance of positions on the party list, with 8 of the 12 new legislators elected from third and fourth positions on their party lists (Table 6.1). It is also worth noting, however, that 23 per cent of voters in this electoral district still opted to vote for a party rather than an individual candidate.

CAMPAIGN STRATEGIES: NINE STEPS TO VICTORY

Every candidate in this constituency had a distinctive take on what they needed to do in order to win. But they all had to deal with the same basic institutional arrangements and face the same electors.

2012, available at http://palday.wordpress.com/2012/02/01/konflik-lahan-bahaya-terpendam-di-muba/.

Table 6.1
Musi Banyuasin III, Elected Representatives, 2009 and 2014

	2009		2014			
No.	Name	Party	Name	Party	Position on ticket	Status
1	Jaini	Golkar	Jaini	Golkar	1	Incumbent
2	Sugondo	Golkar	Sugondo	Golkar	2	Incumbent
3	Sri Retno Sari	Golkar	Ismawati	PDI-P	2	Incumbent
4	Ismawati	PDI-P	H. Ismail	PDI-P	4	Non-Incumbent
5	Desi Ulfa Anggraini	PDI-P	Ujang M. Amin	PAN	1	Non-Incumbent
6	Azwar Uncu	PAN	Riamon Iskandar	PAN	4	Non-Incumbent
7	Suparman Sy Bahri	PAN	Erni Eliyanti	PAN	3	Non-Incumbent
8	Edi Hariyanto	Gerindra	Edi Hariyanto	Gerindra	1	Incumbent
9	Iin Febrianto	Demokrat	Iin Febrianto	Demokrat	1	Incumbent
10	Iwan Aldes	PKS	Iwan Aldes	PKS	2	Incumbent
11	Parlindungan Harahap	PKB	Parlindungan Harahap	PKB	1	Incumbent
12	Novaili	PPRN	Kawairus Effendi	Nasdem	4	Non-Incumbent

Source: KPU Musi Banyuasin (2014).

Most of them thus proceeded through the same steps in the campaign process. These steps begin with registration as a candidate and end with possible legal action. Looking at these steps provides us with a useful framework for analysing variety among candidates, and helps explain the high incumbency return rate in this electoral district. As we shall see, probably the most important factor determining candidates' strategic choices was their access to financial resources, though incumbency also had an independent influence.

Step One: Securing Nomination

Each political party has its own internal mechanisms for recruiting candidates. My findings in Musi Banyuasin III suggest that candidates are increasingly unconcerned with what position they occupy on the party list (which was of course critical in earlier elections under the closed-list system). The practice of purchasing a high position on the list from party functionaries, which used to be commonplace, was in 2014 virtually unheard of because most candidates no longer believe that one's position can guarantee victory. Even so, most incumbents attained high positions (first or second) on their party lists because they were typically also party functionaries at the district level. Non-incumbents tended to be placed lower on the list, except in parties without a member holding a legislative seat.

How people came to be candidates varied greatly. Wasjud explained that PKS approached him to stand partly because he was seen as a potential vote-getter, given his status as a retired bureaucrat from the district education bureau who was also a *putra daerah* (local son), and partly because he had long been involved in PKS *dakwah* (proselytisation) activities and felt close to the party.[2] Most parties reserved a number of places for non-party community leaders as "vote getters" who could boost the party's total in this way. Ronny Fonardus Sengkeh, a PDI-P candidate, by contrast, saw his candidacy as the culmination of a long-held ambition and as a just reward for his service as a subdistrict-level party functionary: "Why would you be a party official if you didn't also get nominated as a legislative candidate?", he asked.[3] Riamon Iskandar, an ambitious would-be politician, stood with PAN for family reasons. His mother, he recalled, had warned him against standing for Golkar, his natural choice: "It's enough. Your father was a candidate for Golkar three times, and three times he got enough votes to be elected, but they never let him be sworn in."[4] Though some candidates felt strongly about their party identity, several indicated they would have been comfortable standing with any party.

---

[2] Interview, Wasjud, 16 Mar. 2014.
[3] Interview, Ronny Fonardus Sengkeh, 11 Apr. 2014.
[4] Interview, Riamon Iskandar, 14 Mar. 2014.

Step Two: Mapping a Victory Strategy

From my interviews, it was clear that all candidates considered one thing above all when designing their strategy: potential vote banks. Each candidate had a sense of how many votes he or she could potentially win. Their estimates were heavily influenced by their own social, economic, cultural and political backgrounds, especially with regard to two matters: the social networks they could access, and their sense of their own personal reputation and identity. These two factors were the cognitive foundations of candidates' clientelistic politics. With regard to social networks, almost all candidates said they would draw on their family, friendships, professional relationships, and on the areas where their party had done well in 2009. Their own identity concerned not only matters such as ethnicity and religion—and hence what networks they could access—but also whether they were incumbents or first-time candidates. Take, for example, the following extracts from interviews, from a PKS, PAN and Nasdem candidate respectively:

> I feel optimistic about being elected because I have worked for a long time in the Technical Unit of the Bureau of Education of Musi Banyuasin district. I have visited virtually every single school in electoral district III. If any teacher says they don't know me, that person would have to be someone who's only just started working in this region. The teachers and their families are my basic capital.[5]

> I was born and grew up here [Bayung Lencir]. My family were amongst the very first to settle here. My father was the longest-serving village head here. So it's no surprise that when he nominated himself as a Golkar candidate, he was always elected—though he was never able to take his seat because of internal intrigues within Golkar.[6]

> I am a native of Sekayu but I'm not from this area [electoral district III]. Although I don't have a lot of relatives here, I understand the character of the area and the people because I've had continual contact with them since I served as a PDI-P official at the district level.[7]

---

[5] Interview, Wasjud, PKS candidate, 16 Mar. 2014.
[6] Interview, Riamon Iskandar, PAN candidate, 14 Mar. 2014.
[7] Interview, Hairad Sudarso, Nasdem candidate and head of the Musi Banyuasin branch of the party; he was formerly a local PDI-P leader.

Virtually all candidates relied on kin and friends as a chief source of support. Incumbents had an added advantage: they could add social groups they had been supporting—and cultivating—from their positions in the legislature. Iin Febrianto, a Partai Demokrat incumbent, was typical in this approach, though he was a little unusual in that he had established an organisation, which he called FAS DA'I (Forum Amal Sosial Dunia Akhirat, Social Work Forum for This World and the Afterlife), to help him provide social services to constituents. This work gave him confidence:

> I am optimistic about the 2014 election because I've done a lot for the community in this area via FAS DA'I. So I ask the people to draw their own conclusion: which candidate has not yet done anything, and who has already done something concrete for them?[8]

Most incumbents had similarly confident attitudes. Of course, their confidence was based on a patronage logic: they had been directing government programmes—for instance, free ambulances or physical infrastructure projects paid for with their aspiration funds—to favoured areas, and they expected the residents to reciprocate with votes.

When candidates talked about their family ties they did not just refer to their immediate kin but to much larger networks, tied to them through shared descent, relations by marriage, emotional relationships and place of domicile or origin. With kinship relationships, people typically looked back several generations, thinking not only of immediate siblings and first cousins, but also second, third and fourth cousins, and including the same family networks of their spouses. But candidates also tried to evoke the language of family connections when talking about looser connections. For instance, I witnessed one candidate, Riamon Iskandar, addressing a meeting in the house of a resident of a village in Bayung Lencir:

> My late father lived here for quite a long time. Although he came here to *bekintang* [earn an income for the family], he always told us, his children, that you all, ladies and gentlemen, are part of our family. Because all we have today, it all started with this village. And

---

[8] Interview, Iin Febrianto, 22 Mar. 2014.

because you, ladies and gentlemen, are part of our family, thus I felt emboldened to come here.[9]

As for bonds based on domicile, people are influenced by Islamic teachings, with various *hadith* (sayings or deeds of the Prophet) encouraging people to cherish their neighbours and view them as akin to family. Little wonder, then, that candidates typically placed their family genealogy at the centre of their campaigning efforts, because it was often "family" ties, understood broadly, which were their first point of entry for communicating with voters.

Candidates also generally had clear targets for the number of individual votes they needed. They started by looking at the 2009 election results and working out the total quota of votes (Bilangan Pembagi Pemilih, BPP)—both party votes and votes for individual candidates—a party had needed to secure a seat that year; in Musi Banyuasin II this figure had been 6,000. Most incumbent candidates set themselves targets that were equivalent to or even slightly higher than this figure, with their confidence founded on the constituency work they had been doing over the preceding five years. Non-incumbents rarely felt so sure, and generally set a target of about 50 per cent of the total party quota, which most thought would be enough to make them the first-placed candidate in their party list and so get them elected.

It should be stressed, however, that no candidate met these targets. Most fell short by 50 per cent, or even more. No candidate managed to reach the BPP, which ended up being about 7,100 in 2014. The incumbents who were re-elected won personal votes that ranged from 1,400 to a little more than 3,500. All candidates I interviewed after the election identified money politics by rivals as the reason that they had fallen short. Indeed, the vote-buying strategies candidates discussed tended to fall into one of two categories: targeting the base areas of rivals, or defending one's own base from such attacks.

Step Three: Forming a Team

By definition, success teams (*tim sukses*) or victory teams (*tim pemenangan*) are groups of person recruited by candidates to help

---

[9] Field notes, 22 Mar. 2014.

them promote their candidacy and mobilise voters. The general pattern is for these teams to be structured along the lines of the territorial administration: a team coordinator, subdistrict coordinators (*korcam*, *koordinator kecamatan*), village coordinators (*kordes*, *koordinator desa*) and then witnesses at polling booths. In 2014 for the district elections in Musi Banyuasin, it was typically the candidate who acted as team coordinator, directing the team members below, making the key decisions and managing the finances. The functions of the *korcam* and *kordes* varied widely. They had no set roles apart from: (i) carrying out the candidate's instructions; (ii) helping in the candidate's promotional activities; and, (iii) connecting the candidate with voters.

In fact, not all candidates used this pattern. Iin Febrianto (Demokrat), for example, used the general pattern, but also integrated into his team FAS DA'I's charity network. He also formed an additional "Team of Volunteers Purely for the People" (Tim Relawan Ikhlas untuk Rakyat). Riamon Iskandar (PAN), Wasjud (PKS), and Abdul Wahab (PKS) followed the general pattern, but filled their structure with non-party cadres. In the case of Riamon this was because he was relatively new to PAN and though he was personally close to several subdistrict party heads, he was not confident about relying on the party machine because longer-term party cadres were using it. Wasjud and Abdul Wahab, meanwhile, recruited non-party teams because they both felt they had social networks at the village level that required special attention. Because the PKS candidates split the territory up between their candidates, to avoid duplication of effort, Wasjud and Abdul Wahab had much smaller teams than Riamon who had coordinators in all the villages and *kelurahan* (urban precincts) in Bayung Lencir and in part of Tungkal Jaya. Hairad Sudarso (Nasdem) built a team that included coordinators in just a few "spots" who were then charged with coordinating one or more villages. He did not use many party officials, because many of them were themselves candidates. A few candidates ruefully admitted they could not establish a team at all, because they lacked the funds. Even so, such people usually had a few friends or family members who helped them out.

People recruited into these teams can be divided into two categories: party officials (either at the subdistrict or village/precinct level), and non-party people. The non-party recruits were typically drawn in through the sorts of social networks and bonds of mutual trust referred to above. Candidates rarely recruited team members they did not already know well. Incumbent candidates tended to be advantaged, because they could reactivate networks they had formed at the preceding election or cultivated while sitting in the legislature (including by distributing aspiration fund projects). Non-incumbents often struggled to draw in significant numbers beyond their immediate networks.

It was at this stage that the Haji Sens among the candidates started to be advantaged, with money playing a key role. Most candidates paid subdistrict and village team members, whether party cadres or not, "transportation fees" to cover their costs. The amounts varied, depending on the kind of vehicle the team member was using (car or motorcycle) and the distances travelled. Only one candidate I interviewed (Hairad Sudarso of Nasdem) paid a flat-rate incentive (Rp 500,000 per person) to his village coordinators, though only to those in Lalan subdistrict where he lacked close friends and family.[10] Candidates paid additional sums (for example, to cover mobile telephone credit, food and drinks) to their subdistrict and village coordinators when they carried out particular tasks, like sticking up posters.

Step Four: *Sosialisasi*

Once the team was formed, the next step was *sosialisasi*, which basically means "promotion". The core task was getting the candidate's name, face, party affiliation and number on the ballot known by target voters (using sample ballot papers to show them how to locate the candidate was especially important as voting day neared). The timing differed somewhat: incumbents tended to hold their fire and reserve their most intense campaigning for the two months leading to the poll; first-timers often started four months or even longer beforehand—sometimes exhausting their funds and energy prematurely. The forms of *sosialisasi* varied widely, starting with meetings with groups of voters, public campaign rallies (*kampanye terbuka*), sporting events, Islamic study gatherings (*pengajian*), and door-to-door campaigning. Money

---

[10] Interview, Hairad Sudarso, 16 Mar. 2014.

was again a key determinant, especially seeing that most voters would request, or at least expect, something—whether goods or services— from the candidates.

During the few weeks leading to voting day, the most common forms of patronage politics were distribution of club goods and individual gifts, and vote buying (which occurred on average three days before the poll). Pork barrel projects and constituency services had typically been delivered over preceding years. In Musi Banyuasin, the terms *buah tangan* and *tanda mata*—two phrases whose closest English equivalents are "souvenir" and "keepsake"—were widely used to describe gifts provided by candidates. These could be club goods distributed to or via groups (volleyball or football equipment, or prayer books, for example) or individual gifts (such as headscarves or foodstuffs).

There was a distinction here between the approaches of incumbents and non-incumbents. Incumbents tended to minimise distribution of gifts in areas they had already cultivated through aspiration funds and constituency service. Instead, they targeted populations who had not received such benefits. It was wealthier non-incumbents who invested most heavily in such "souvenirs". Note, too, that candidates often provided such gifts in response to requests from their constituents during *sosialisasi*. Thus, when I accompanied Riamon Iskandar on the campaign trail, I witnessed him fielding many such requests the moment he opened the question-and-answer session during constituency meetings. At one meeting, some of those present asked for repairs to their village road, while others asked for volleyball equipment. Riamon immediately told them that he would meet their requests, but that the shirts he had brought would have to do in the meantime and he would attend to the road and sports equipment within the week. In deciding whether to grant such requests, candidates would consider their financial means (some lacked the capacity to respond to any requests), the reasonableness of the requests, and the vote potential in the area concerned. Some candidates felt that such gifts were not appropriate in elections at all, and always refused to give them, but no such candidate that I identified was elected. Other candidates always tried to give whatever was requested.

In campaigning, candidates used two basic approaches: territorial and functional. Territorial campaigning involved targeting particular villages or urban precincts where they felt they had potential votes because of personal history, family or friendship networks, past party performance and so on. Functional campaigning involved targeting social groups through events that brought together members of a particular network from a wider geographic area, such as a sports tournament or religious gathering involving people from several villages.

According to Ronny Fonardus Sengkeh (PDI-P), public expectations of gifts were attributable to the two previous direct elections of district heads (*bupati*) that had been held in Musi Banyuasin. In these elections, candidates had competed to seduce voters by generously providing goods and services. The fact that Musi Banyuasin is particularly resource rich, and that the winning *bupati* would have access to huge government revenues, generated strong incentives for candidates to outbid one another. Voters transferred their expectations of largesse from this setting to the legislative election, without understanding that they were now electing people who merely play a control, budgeting and monitoring role—the formal role of the legislatures with regard to the local government—without being directly in charge of the district budget or directing expenditures.[11]

Other candidates, however, blamed incumbents in the legislature. There was even a local Malay-language *pantun* (rhyming verse) to express the idea: *cempedak bawa bilik, ado kendak baru nak balik* which implied that candidates only came to visit the villages every five years when they were seeking votes. Outside election campaigns, many DPRD members rarely visited their constituents, who for their part had come to see their elected representatives as merely supplementary sources of income to be exploited from time to time. Hence the frequent requests and demands made of candidates. As one non-incumbent PKS candidate put it: "In the morning, they tap their rubber trees; in the afternoon, they tap the candidates."[12]

---

[11] Interview, Ronny Fonardus Sengkeh, 11 Apr. 2014.
[12] Interview, Abdul Wahab, 12 Apr. 2014.

Step Five: Recruiting and Training Witnesses

Witnesses are persons whose job is to represent the candidate and his/her party in monitoring vote counting and tabulation at the polling booth, and then as votes pass up through the layers of village, subdistrict and district election bodies. These people are trained on the technicalities of observation, and it is particularly impressed upon them to get copies of the C1 and D1 forms that record the results at the polling booth and village respectively. Having reliable witnesses is critical to preventing manipulation of the count—either by rival parties in collaboration with electoral officials they have bribed or by candidates from within the same party who seek to boost their personal vote at the expense of intra-party rivals.

The law states that witnesses are appointed by the party. The bigger parties in Musi Banyuasin, notably Gerindra, Demokrat, PKS, PDI-P and PAN, prioritised the appointment of village-level party officials as witnesses. Only if they lacked enough party members in a particular location did they recruit ordinary citizens. Gerindra, Demokrat and PDI-P entrusted recruitment to their subdistrict branches and village sub-branches. PKS, PAN and Nasdem entrusted it to candidates, after divvying up the electoral district between them.

The parties differed somewhat in how these individuals were paid. Nasdem witnesses were fully funded by the party's central board (Nasdem is headed by the wealthy businessman, Surya Paloh). PKS witnesses were paid by the district party branch. But Gerindra, Demokrat, PAN and PDI-P handed responsibility to their candidates. The result was that wealthy candidates got direct access to full documentation of the count from polling booths and villages, whereas poor candidates only learned the results from friends, relatives or other supporters who sent their observations by text message (SMS).

Candidates also usually paid for the training of these witnesses, which could be costly once transport fees for participants, food and drink and trainer fees were taken into account. Incumbents could afford this, but Riamon Iskandar (PAN) was the only non-incumbent I met who could pull together the money to pay for this expense.

In addition to the party-sanctioned witnesses, candidates also often paid people to act as unofficial witnesses who remained outside the polling booths. Though their status was not recognised by the polling booth committee, they typically carried letters from the candidate attesting to their status and were paid transport fees of Rp 50,000 to Rp 100,000 each. On voting day, there were three to ten such persons at each polling booth. In fact, appointment of such unofficial witnesses was often just a subtle mode of vote buying.

Step Six: Using the Quiet Period

During the three days immediately before the poll (6, 7 and 8 April 2014) contestants were officially prohibited from engaging in campaign activities. In fact, these three days were the peak of patronage politics, during which other forms of gift-giving made way for vote buying. As Ikhsanudin, a PKS subdistrict official, put it: "The quiet period is the time when the candidates drop their bombs on the voters."[13] Unlike in some parts of the country, all candidates and team members in this electoral district denied that they themselves engaged in the practice. However, all blamed their failure to reach expected vote targets on vote buying by competitors during the quiet period. Through field research and triangulation I ascertained that in fact some candidates I had interviewed, both incumbents and non-incumbents, did indeed buy votes in certain locales. In Musi Banyuasin III, the typical rates paid to voters were Rp 100,000 to Rp 200,000 for a single vote at the district level, a relatively high rate that presumably reflects the natural resource revenues generated in the district.

The modes of distribution are straightforward. First, the candidates call in their teams for last-minute planning, and it is typically team members who propose distributing cash, saying they are being pressured by voters in the villages, or that they have learned that rival teams have begun handing out money, or plan to do so soon. Second, the candidate asks for these team members to provide voter lists "by name by address" (English is used for this term) that they have been collecting, and who are in fact often already conditioned to expect payments. Third, the candidates provide money to the team members, partly or fully matching

---

[13] Interview, Ikhsanudin, 12 Apr. 2014.

their demands. Fourth, the team members then pack the cash in plain white envelopes, usually along with the name card of the candidate, though in a few cases cash was distributed without using envelopes. Finally, team members go door to door in areas where they hold lists, distributing envelopes in accordance with the number of voters in each household and the entries in their lists.

Step Seven: Monitoring the Results

On polling day, voting stops at 1 p.m. and booth officials open ballot boxes and begin manually counting ballots within half an hour. Candidates and their teams are immediately active, monitoring this counting to see if they will be elected and endeavouring to prevent fraud directed against them. The party witnesses mentioned above would play the key role at this point, ensuring that the initial count produced valid data and communicating them to candidates. Counting at booths and formal recording of results was very time-consuming in some places; many booths were not finished till 9 p.m. and some concluded only close to the dawn prayers the following morning (4 a.m.). The causes were varied: technical errors by polling booth officials in filling out forms, disputes between them and party witnesses, excessive breaks and so on. The result was that most witnesses were able to pass their copies of the C1 forms to village coordinators only on the next day, 10 April. Generally on that same day, the forms were then collected by subdistrict coordinators and passed to the candidates. C1 forms from a few remote villages reached candidates only on 11 or 12 April. Parties generally compiled these documents at a single point, often the home of a particular candidate. This procedure advantaged candidates who were party functionaries, but it also added to their workload. Only a few candidates had the capacity to collect C1 forms in this way and thus ascertain whether they had been elected in advance of the official announcement of results (two weeks after the vote). Only one (Iin Febrianto, a Demokrat incumbent) had a very reliable method that included a complex formula for calculating the estimated party vote and, hence, the personal vote he needed. Other candidates, especially those who lacked party leadership positions or the funds for their own witnesses, found it difficult to keep track of results and were vulnerable to manipulation of the count by officials bribed by rivals (though I should stress I did not find evidence of such manipulation in this constituency).

Step Eight: Monitoring Vote Tabulation as it Moves Through the System

Well-organised and well-funded candidates do not stop monitoring the count at the polling booth level, but instead ensure that their team members and party witnesses continue monitoring tabulation at the village and then subdistrict level. These witnesses need transport money, money for consumables, and honoraria. From the Panitia Pemungutan Suara (PPS, village-level voting committee), witnesses get hold of the D1 form (which includes a recapitulation of all the polling booth results in the village). It can take three days for these forms to make it to the Panitia Pemilihan Kecamatan (PPK, subdistrict election committee), and the PPK officials then work night and day totalling the various village results, an arduous task given the large number of individual candidates. In 2014, in contrast to 2009 when a large paper form was used, the PPK in Musi Banyuasin used Microsoft Excel spreadsheets for this process, making it more accessible for party witnesses. The more a candidate could ensure that his or her personal team members were acting as party witnesses at these levels, the more he or she could be confident of not losing votes as they were transferred from the booth, to the village, to the subdistrict and then, eventually to the Komisi Pemilihan Umum Daerah (KPUD, Regional General Elections Commission) in the district capital. Conversely, candidates lacking direct access to the count were vulnerable to having some of their personal votes stripped away by other candidates.

Step Nine: Getting Ready for a Legal Challenge

In Musi Banyuasin III in 2014, no conflicts over the results made it to the Constitutional Court. A total of 767 such cases from around the country did end up in the Court, however, including many from other parts of South Sumatra. Because it is the political parties that have legal standing at the Court to bring misconduct cases in the legislative elections, many of the bitterest conflicts between candidates within a single party could not be resolved in this way. Though I cannot comment directly on candidates' experiences at this stage, the more experienced candidates set aside funds for this eventuality, knowing that, if their result was challenged in the Constitutional Court, they would have to contribute to the costs of taking witnesses to Jakarta and legal fees.

CONCLUSION

These nine stages encapsulate the general pattern followed by candidates. Each stage, at least from number three onwards, had cost implications and included elements of material exchange between the candidate and supporters—whether those supporters were voters or campaign organisers. The critical stages for victory in Musi Banyuasin III in 2014 were numbers three through six—forming a team, *sosialisasi*, recruiting witnesses, and using the quiet period to buy votes. Without a team, it was impossible to reach out to enough voters. Without *sosialisasi*, voters would not know who the candidate was, let alone want to vote for him or her. Without witnesses, it was hard to monitor and safeguard the results. But most crucially of all, without conducting vote buying in the quiet period, candidates would run the risk that all their work in wooing voters would disappear without a trace. As Wasjud (a non-incumbent PKS candidate) put it: "Spraying voters with money is more effective then spraying them spiritually, with speeches, political oratory or dialogic communication."[14]

Financial strength was thus critical in determining which candidates won. In this context, Wasjud's labelling of "Haji Sen" as the winner of the 2014 election in Musi Banyuasin III seems accurate. Each of the non-incumbents elected in this constituency was a wealthy businessperson, whether in the plantation sector, entertainment or trade. Riamon Iskandar (PAN) was active in multiple sectors, owning a sawmill, an entertainment business (hiring out a stage and equipment for musical shows, weddings and the like), rental accommodation and large oil palm and rubber holdings. Erni Eliyanti (PAN) was the wife of a village

---

[14] Interview, Wasjud, 12 Apr. 2014.

head, and also owned an entertainment hire business and rubber and oil palm plantations. Haji Ismail (PDI-P) held a forestry licence and was a well-known local construction contractor, while his father-in-law owned a gold shop in Kota Sekayu. Kawairus Effendi (Nasdem) was best known as an NGO activist, but was also a contractor with a record of working on district government projects. Incumbents, meanwhile, were advantaged by access to aspiration funds and other government monies, but most of them, too, were wealthy prior to entering politics. The implication, as Ronny Fonardus Sengkeh (an unsuccessful PDI-P candidate) explained, was that not a single candidate elected in this constituency was one of the common people.[15] In Musi Banyuasin in 2014, elections were a rich person's game.

---

[15] Interview, Ronny Fonardus Sengkeh, 11 Apr. 2014.

chapter 7

Palembang, South Sumatra: Aspiration Funds and Pork Barrel Politics

Muhammad Mahsun

Since 2010 the government of South Sumatra province has provided an allocation of "aspiration funds" (*dana aspirasi*) for each member of the DPRD (provincial parliament). This programme funds development projects aimed at improving the welfare of legislators' constituents in their respective electoral districts. The idea is that constituents can propose (hence the use of the term "aspiration") to their representative a project that has not been covered by the government's normal development planning procedures. With the legislator's endorsement, the project can then receive government funding. In 2013 and 2014, the annual aspiration fund allocation for each member of the provincial parliament was Rp 5 billion, a fantastic amount when compared to the initial rate of Rp 250 million in 2010.

These large allocations in 2013 and 2014 allowed candidates who were incumbent members of the provincial DPRD to use their aspiration funds to mobilise electoral support in the 2014 election. These funds were a useful tool for this purpose, given the context of Indonesia's open-list PR electoral system, in which each individual candidate has to try to win a personal vote large enough to defeat intra-party rivals. Candidates thus came up with many creative means to increase their personal votes, most of which meant demonstrating their personal value to their constituents.

My research was conducted in provincial electoral constituencies I and II, which together covered the provincial capital, Palembang. Here, most incumbents facing re-election not only distributed patronage goods but also politicised the aspiration funds they had at their disposal. In effect, they distributed aspiration fund projects to community groups as a form of club good or pork barrel. They also used their access to these funds to build clientelistic networks to help their re-election efforts, using "success team" members as brokers who helped them distribute aspiration fund projects to target groups in the community, who were in turn expected to reciprocate with their votes.

In exploring this topic, I have two basic goals. First, I set out to explain how incumbents used their aspiration funds to build clientelistic relationships with voters and success teams, and so mobilise votes. Second, I explore the effects of these aspiration funds on the electoral success rate of incumbents, and on the nature of electoral democracy in Palembang.

BACKGROUND: THE CITY OF PALEMBANG

The city of Palembang, the capital of South Sumatra province, consists of 16 subdistricts (*kecamatan*) and 107 precincts (*kelurahan*), and in 2011 had a population of 1.7 million.[1] Rapid growth of the city's population in recent years resulted in it being split, prior to the 2014 election, into two electoral districts: South Sumatra I, on the southern part of the city, and South Sumatra II in the north, each consisting of eight subdistricts. However, this splitting of electoral districts did not increase the total number of seats being contested in the city: in the 2009 election the electoral district had contained 14 seats; the 2 districts combined had only 13 seats in 2014 (6 in district I and 7 in district II). Candidates felt that this change tightened the competition in 2014.

The challenge was especially great for first-time candidates, who had to face 13 incumbents who decided to recontest their seats. It

---

[1] Badan Pusat Statistik Palembang, *Palembang dalam Angka 2012* [Palembang in Figures 2012] (Palembang: BPS Palembang, 2013).

was widely understood that these incumbents were advantaged by their possession of significant social, political and economic capital, in part because of their ability to distribute Rp 5 billion worth of aspiration fund projects in the lead-up to the election.

The potential for these funds to have a significant electoral impact was great, given Palembang's social composition. The city has many poor residents, especially those living on the urban fringes, and along the banks of the Musi river which runs through it. Many factory workers, itinerant traders, livestock farmers and fish farmers live in these areas. Their low socioeconomic status means that many voters have a pragmatic attitude toward elections, judging candidates on their ability to deliver cash or other forms of patronage. In the lead-up to the 2014 elections, this tendency was deepened by elections of local government heads—notably, the Palembang mayoral election of April 2013 and the South Sumatra gubernatorial election of June 2013—both of which involved extensive money politics.

The city has a relatively complex ethnic and religious structure, with considerable segregation in residential and employment patterns. Palembang has significant populations of local South Sumatran groups, as well as of Javanese, Sundanese, Minangkabau, Bugis, Malay, Chinese and Arabs. Though Muslims are a large majority, there are also Protestant, Catholic, Hindu, Buddhist and Confucian minorities.[2] Some candidates adapt to this complexity by invoking ethnic and religious ties in their voter mobilisation efforts; often candidates make significant material donations to associations representing the various communities.

Voting patterns in the city have tended to favour Indonesia's major nationalist parties, notably PDI-P, Golkar and Partai Demokrat, rather than Islamic parties. In the Palembang city DPRD between 2009 and 2014, the largest party was Partai Demokrat with 11 out of 50 seats, followed by Golkar and PDI-P with 7 each, and 4 Islamic parties with only 12 seats between them, as well as a number of smaller parties.

---

[2] M. Ridhah Taqwa, "Pola Segregasi Ekologis: Kelompok Etnis-Suku vs Kelas Sosial di Kota Palembang" [Ecological Segregation: Ethnic Group vs Social Class in Palembang City], 2014, available at: http://sosiologi.fisip.unsri.ac.id/userfiles/Segergasi%20Ekologis%20Komunitas%20Kota%20Plbg.pdf.

In 2014 party representation flattened out: PDI-P led with 8 seats, followed by Partai Demokrat with 7, Golkar with 6 and then 8 parties with the remaining 29 seats between them. There were similar trends at the provincial level, the focus of this chapter. In 2014, in the 75-seat provincial parliament, PDI-P was the major party with 13 seats, and it also led the contest in South Sumatra I (one seat with 55,420 votes) and II (2 seats with 78,610 votes). Overall, the shift between 2009 and 2014 in the provincial race was in PDI-P's favour: in 2009, Partai Demokrat won the most votes and two seats in the city provincial contest, followed by Golkar and then PDI-P also each with two seats; in 2014, PDI-P won three seats in both new city constituencies; Gerindra, Partai Demokrat and Golkar each won two seats.

ASPIRATION FUNDS: MANIPULATION AND VOTER MOBILISATION

As explained above, aspiration funds are provincial government budget items that are allocated to each DPRD member with the purpose of allowing each legislator to provide project assistance to improve welfare in his or her electoral district. The DPRD members are supposed to identify potential projects to address community needs as part of the working visits they make to communities in their constituencies during periods of parliamentary recess, which happen three times a year. They then recommend the projects to the relevant government agencies, which release the money to the target beneficiaries. Payments usually take the form of social assistance grants, made directly to recipient community groups, or are issued by the relevant provincial government bureau, Satuan Kerja Perangkat Daerah (SKPD, Regional Apparatus Work Unit) and the Badan Keuangan dan Anggaran Daerah (BKAD, Regional Finance and Budget Agency).[3]

This pattern of government spending is not unique to South Sumatra, or even to Indonesia. Several countries, including the Philippines and several countries in Europe have programmes that resemble aspiration

---

[3] Interviews, Irmaidi, 21 Mar. 2014; Sakim, 20 and 21 Mar. 2014.

funds, with legislators able to influence, and sometimes exercise complete discretion over, allocation of projects to their home constituencies.[4] Such programmes are typically known as constituency development funds, constituency development grants, or, more simply, pork barrel programmes.[5] In many countries, including the Philippines, legislators use such pork barrel spending as a patronage resource when building clientelistic relations with constituents, and even as a form of collective vote buying at election times.[6]

In Indonesia, aspiration funds vary greatly in magnitude from region to region. In South Sumatra, they were first allocated to individual legislators in 2010 under governor Alex Noerdin, at a rate of Rp 250 million per legislator per annum. They have increased at a rate much faster than the growth of the provincial budget, to Rp 500 million per legislator in 2011 and then Rp 2.5 billion in 2012, doubling again to Rp 5 billion in 2013, and stabilising at that rate in 2014.[7] Given their magnitude, these funds have the potential to generate significant development benefits. The problem is that, in allocating such projects, legislators rarely take into account where social investment might yield the greatest improvements, but instead focus on where they might gain the greatest political benefits.[8]

In the lead-up to the 2014 election, many sitting members of the provincial DPRD manipulated the allocation of aspiration funds to try

[4] Azyumardi Azra, "Dana Aspirasi: Anomali Politik" [Aspiration Funds: A Political Anomaly], *Kompas*, 17 June 2010; Takeshi Kawanaka, "Who Eats the Most? Qualitative Analysis of Pork Barrel Distribution in the Philippines" (Institute of Developing Economies (IDE) Discussion Paper 26, IDE-JETRO, Tokyo, 2007).

[5] Kohei Noda, "Politicization of Philippine Budget System: Institutional and Economic Analysis on 'Pork Barrel'" (Policy Research Institute Discussion Paper 11A–04, Ministry of Finance, Tokyo, 2011); Edward Aspinall, "Money Politics", *Inside Indonesia* 116, Apr.–June 2014, available at: http://www.insideindonesia.org/weekly-articles/money-politics-2; Edward Aspinall, "Money Politics: Patronage and Clientelism in Southeast Asia", in *Handbook of Southeast Asian Democratization*, ed. William Case (London: Routledge, 2015), pp. 299–313.

[6] Kawanaka, "Who Eats the Most?".

[7] Interview, Anita Noeringhati, Golkar legislator, 28 Mar. 2014.

[8] Interview, Sakim, 20 Mar. 2014.

to build clientelistic connections with constituents and gain votes. The absence of any mechanism requiring executive government officials and legislators to come together to jointly discuss aspiration fund project proposals submitted by community members made it easy for legislators to prioritise only projects which they thought would be politically advantageous. One indication of this was the way in which sitting legislators responded when the old electoral district covering the city of Palembang was split in two before the 2014 election. Quite a number of incumbents postponed the release of their 2013 aspiration fund projects to the period very close to the election campaign period in early 2014, and also ensured they would be allocated only to neighbourhoods that would be part of their new electoral constituency. As one Golkar candidate explained:

> Incumbents, well, obviously they use their recess funds, their aspiration funds. You don't have to do a special survey to ascertain this, everywhere people are shouting about it, community members are discussing it … Right now they are using their 2013 aspiration funds, they haven't started with their 2014 funds yet … looking at it, they deliberately release the funds in the campaign period as bullets for the 2014 election … For example, let's say I used to represent the Palembang electoral district, but then in 2014 it was split and I was nominated to stand in electoral district II, well, I'd automatically make sure my aspiration funds were focused on that electoral district. And this is what's happening now. Because they are now working to get sympathy from their people, and votes in their electoral district, if they keep working on [aspiration funds in parts of their old district, where they are not standing for re-election], well, they would think of that as a waste, as pointless. Like Ms. N [he named a sitting legislator]. She's really splurging in electoral district I now. But she's doing nothing at all in electoral district II.[9]

A similar view was expressed by a PDI-P incumbent candidate:

> These [aspirations funds] are now only for eight subdistricts [constituting his new electoral district], but last year I distributed my 5 billion of funds throughout the whole city of Palembang. But

---

[9] Confidential interview, 3 Apr. 2014.

because we are now approaching the election, well, of course we are all focusing now only on our own electoral districts.[10]

These statements illustrate how incumbents viewed these aspiration funds, derived as they were from public funds, primarily as a patronage resource to be used to mobilise electoral support. If the primary consideration was development need, then legislators might have been expected to approve project proposals from all 16 subdistricts in the city (they were, after all, elected as representatives of all these subdistricts in 2009). Instead, almost all focused their projects in 2014 exclusively only on the eight subdistricts where they were standing for re-election in the forthcoming election.

The politicisation of aspiration funds in the period leading up to the election took two forms. The first was distributing funds to community groups with some sort of social connection (such as ethnicity or religion) to the candidate. Such distribution typically took the form of club goods. This could range from business development assistance to *bakso* (meatball soup) sellers' cooperatives and donations of crockery and kitchen utensils to PKK (family welfare guidance) groups, to donations of *rebana* (tambourines) and other musical instruments to Islamic prayer groups or funds to assist the construction or renovation of houses of worship. To illustrate, one PDI-P candidate used his aspiration funds for donations to assist the educational activities of the Keluarga Mahasiswa Budis Palembang (Palembang Buddhist University Students' Family), the provision of an ambulance to Persekutuan Gereja Tionghoa Indonesia (Indonesian Alliance of Chinese Churches) and the purchase of a set of gamelan instruments and *wayang kulit* (shadow puppet) equipment to the Paguyuban Seni Anggodo Laras, a Javanese traditional arts group.[11]

The second form of assistance involved geographic targeting. In this case, incumbents directed aspiration fund projects toward areas they considered to be personal vote bases. Usually such targeting happened at the *kelurahan* (urban precinct) level or at the lower-level RW (neighbourhood) and RT (subneighbourhood) levels and took

---

[10] Confidential interview, 21 Mar. 2014.
[11] Documents from, and interview with, Sakim, 21 Mar. 2014.

the form of allocations for small-scale infrastructure projects, such as the construction or repair of roads, irrigation canals, bridges, street lighting, community halls or other social facilities, as well as funding for community social enterprises known as KUBE (Kelompok Usaha Bersama, Joint Business Ventures) in aquaculture, animal husbandry and the like. Drawing on the comparative literature on patronage politics, we can think of such geographically targeted spending as a form of pork barrel politics.[12]

Candidates distributed assistance packages that varied in value from Rp 25 million to Rp 250 million per group, depending on the needs of the group putting forward the project proposal. Despite the varying size of the grants, the goal was the same, namely to attain political support and, ultimately, votes from the recipient group. Most incumbent candidates I interviewed were open about this being their goal. Even so, not all candidates were convinced of the reliability of this method, and some doubted that project beneficiaries would repay them with votes. They believed that voters in Palembang were becoming increasingly "pragmatic" and "transactional". Even residents who benefitted from aspiration fund projects often asked candidates or members of their success teams for goods or money in exchange for votes. One Golkar incumbent complained:

> As for whether they [aspiration fund projects] are beneficial, I would say they can be, but not always. Our society has changed. I say it's changed because now sometimes you can go to people who ask you for aspiration funds, but they will still adopt a "take and give" [he used the English phrase] attitude when it comes to voting. So there's been a shift since 2008 [*sic*]. At that time, when I went down to

---

[12] Frederic C. Schaffer, "Why Study Vote Buying?", in *Elections for Sale: The Causes and Consequences of Vote Buying*, ed. Frederic C. Schaffer (Boulder, CO: Lynne Reinner; Quezon City: Ateneo de Manila University Press, 2007), pp. 1–16; Susan Stokes, "Pork, by Any Other Name ... Building a Conceptual Scheme of Distributive Politics", paper presented at the American Political Science Association Annual Meeting, Toronto, 3–6 Sept. 2009, p. 10, available at: http://ssrn.com/abstract=1449057; Kevin Milligan and Michael Smart, "Regional Grants as Pork Barrel Politics", CESifo Working Paper 1453, CESifo Group, Munich, 2005.

the community, though I wasn't anybody yet, people would help me
without expecting anything. Now, though I have already given them
what they wanted [aspiration funds], why is it that they still ask for
stuff from me?[13]

Such attitudes on the part of candidates, and not only incumbents,
led them to adopt transactional methods in dealing with voters, providing
them with gifts of goods or cash aimed at securing their votes. Very
few candidates, including incumbents, responded by emphasising
broad programmes or even providing written "political contracts" to
communities. Incumbents should have been able to point to their past
records of delivering aspiration fund projects, and promise more in the
future. However, my field observations suggest that very few incumbents
relied exclusively on this path. Instead, in addition to politicising the
delivery of aspiration fund projects in ways described above, they
tended to mobilise voters using methods similar to those used by other
candidates, namely by the politics of patronage and reciprocity.

Patronage distribution in various forms was the essential ingredient
of most candidates' campaign strategies in Palembang. The most common
form was the distribution of goods (for example, basic foodstuffs,
headscarves, sports uniforms, *rebana* or other musical instruments,
prayer robes, hats, prayer mats, T-shirts, cups, rubbish bins, balls,
calendars, key rings, and pens), provision of free social services (most
commonly, medical services and ambulances) and vote buying, where
cash was distributed in exchange for individual votes (the amounts varied
from Rp 30,000 to Rp 100,000 for candidates for the provincial DPRD
and Rp 50,000 to Rp 150,000 for candidates in the city DPRD). Rich
candidates even funded private club goods and pork barrel spending, by
paying for small-scale road, irrigation or mosque repairs in communities.
In fact, some first-time candidates paid for such items precisely in order
to show communities that, should they be elected, they would return
to the community and provide future concrete benefits. One PDI-P
candidate explained it like this, when describing a meeting he held in
one community:

<hr>

[13] Confidential interview, 28 Mar. 2014.

They asked for 100 electricity poles, but how much would that cost? I said I didn't have the money. So I told them that if I helped them with all that now, lots of them would just forget me. So instead I just gave them four poles to show I was serious about wanting their votes here, and I told them that if I was elected then they could send a new proposal to me, and that would be my homework. They agreed.[14]

Thus, as in other contexts, candidates distributed patronage in order to tie voters to them. They typically targeted low income voters, because the poor tend to sell their votes more cheaply.[15] Cash and other gifts are less effective in winning over middle-class voters. It is not surprising, therefore, that aspiration fund projects tended to concentrate in areas inhabited by the urban poor.

Though patronage distribution did respond to community needs—and even to explicit demands from voters and community leaders—mobilising votes by disbursing patronage, in my view, tends to trap candidates in long cycles of transactional politics, which continue once they are elected as members of parliament. Transactional campaign methods are costly, so elected legislators typically engage in transactional politics of other sorts—corrupt deals with bureaucrats or business actors—in order to recoup their initial outlays. By opening the political process to predatory interests, this cycle is a serious impediment to democratic deepening in Indonesia.[16]

---

[14] Confidential interview, 26 Mar. 2014.

[15] Mulyadi Sumarto, *Perlindungan Sosial dan Klientelisme: Makna Politik Bantuan Sosial dalam Pemilihan Umum* [Social Protection and Clientelism: The Meaning and Politics of Social Assistance during General Elections] (Yogyakarta: Gadjah Mada University Press, 2014), p. 37; Susan C. Stokes, "Is Vote Buying Undemocratic?", in Schaffer, *Elections for Sale*, p. 82.

[16] See Vedi R. Hadiz, *Dinamika Kekuasaan: Ekonomi Politik Indonesia Pasca Orde Baru* [The Dynamics of Power: The Post-New Order Indonesian Political Economy] (Jakarta: LP3ES, 2005); Muhammad Mahsun, "Local Predatory Elite?: Potret Relasi Politisi-Pengusaha dengan Penguasa" [A Local Predatory Elite?: A Portrait of Relations between Politician-Entrepreneurs and Power-holders] (MA thesis, Gadjah Mada University, Yogyakarta, 2013); Henk Schulte Nordholt and Gerry van Klinken, eds., *Renegotiating Boundaries: Local Politics in Post-Suharto Indonesia* (Leiden: KITLV Press, 2007).

CLIENTELIST NETWORKS AND MODES OF DISTRIBUTION

Aspiration funds in South Sumatra in general, and Palembang in particular, are generally distributed in one of two ways. The first mechanism is for the funds to be directed to a relevant government agency (SKPD) to work on the project concerned. Typically, a community member or group will put forward a project proposal (often drafted with the help of an *asisten dewan*, legislator's assistant); the proposal then attains the approval of a legislator, and is passed on to the BKAD, and/or the relevant government unit by one of his or her personal assistants. The relevant unit then carries out the designated project. With this method, all of the work is done by the government agency; the target community is not involved directly in its execution and may indeed know little about the project. This mode of delivery is usually used for local infrastructure, as a pork barrel project.

The second mechanism takes place when the BKAD directly transfers the funds to the bank account of a beneficiary community group. In this case, typically the group will be a KUBE with at least 15 members. Such a group can submit a project proposal to a legislator, who then issues a recommendation letter endorsing it, and sends it, via a personal assistant, to the BKAD. When this method is used the grant will typically be for club goods: it will pay for some sort of activity by the group concerned, typically for an income-generating activity, or it could also be for a pork barrel project such as road or irrigation repairs.

The two mechanisms have different consequences. The first form of delivery, where the government agency handles the project, is vulnerable to corruption; the second form is particularly suited to electoral manipulation. Corruption in aspiration fund projects occurs when the government agency concerned subcontracts the work to a company owned by the legislator or, more commonly, a relative or friend. Typically, corrupt SKPD staff also levy informal fees on the contractor and divide up the proceeds with the legislator who sent the project their way. This form of rent seeking, involving collaboration between politicians and bureaucrats, is common in Indonesian public life.[17]

---

[17] Hadiz, *Dinamika Kekuasaan*; Vedi R. Hadiz, *Localising Power in Post-Authoritarian Indonesia: A Southeast Asia Perspective* (Stanford, CA: Stanford University Press, 2010); Muhammad Mahsun, "'Local Predatory Elite'".

The second form, where aspiration funds are transferred directly to community groups, is particularly common in the lead-up to an election. This was certainly the case in both of the Palembang provincial electoral districts in 2014, where this form was particularly widespread. Brokers and success team members played crucial roles in this variety of aspiration fund manipulation, by bringing project proposals to the incumbent, helping community groups with the paperwork, and then ensuring that the funds were transferred to them. For a minority of legislators, notably those from PDI-P, success team members were primarily party cadres. For most other legislators, their key success team members were non-party community leaders who were—or who hoped to be—project beneficiaries themselves, either as heads of KUBE, RT, RW or social organisations. In other words, incumbents (the patrons) build their vote brokerage networks using individuals (clients) who are expected to repay their patrons' generosity in distributing aspiration fund projects to them by helping their re-election efforts. A Gerindra incumbent in the provincial legislature explained it like this, when asked whether local people living in the vicinity of one of "his" aspiration fund projects would know that he brought it to their location:

> Oh yeah, definitely. They have to know it was me who got it for them. Usually the local community leaders will tell them that this is all thanks to my struggle for them. And they generally know me anyway … the ones I know the best, I make them members of my success team. I don't have success team coordinators everywhere, just in places where I have a potential vote … and that usually means places where I have helped them [with aspiration fund projects] … and where they have emotional ties with me.[18]

In a few cases, incumbents helped non-incumbent candidates from the same party by allowing them to distribute part of their aspiration fund allocations. Incumbents in the provincial DPRD did not, of course, help candidates who were competing against them in the same electoral district, but rather candidates competing for seats in the city legislature, or who were competing for a provincial seat in a different electoral district. A first-time PDI-P candidate explained:

---

[18] Confidential interview, 22 Mar. 2014.

I have been distributing aspiration funds. I have been helped to do this by friends who already sit in the council, they have aspiration funds of Rp 5 billion per head each year … So those friends have been helping me. The funds don't come from me, it's they who have the Rp 5 billion worth of aspiration funds, so I said to them, "Come on, please help me out here". Well, they did, they helped me and I was able to forward funds to my own electoral district. That's been a big help for me because I don't have money of my own. I've been giving out Rp 25 million per group, each group has to have at least 20 members … The hope is that if there's 20 people in 1 group, well each of them will have a family, let's say each has just 3 children, well that's already 60 votes.[19]

It is thus obvious not only that candidates targeted voters with their aspiration funds, but also that they used these funds to construct their campaign teams. In fact, the promise of access to such funds often drew community leaders into success teams.

Candidates typically did not distribute aspiration funds evenly throughout their entire electoral district. Most believed that certain areas constituted their "base" and they tended to target these areas for projects. Usually, such areas were concentrated in just four or five of the eight subdistricts in the electoral district. Candidates usually identified such areas on the basis of past election outcomes, focusing on neighbourhoods where they had received a strong personal vote in 2009, or where their party had done well. Sometimes, they also looked to the ethnic composition of the area, focusing on neighbourhoods inhabited by co-ethnics. Candidates tended to cultivate these populations, and their community leaders, with aspiration funds in the hope of building up long-term relations and loyalties.

IMPLICATIONS FOR CANDIDATE SUCCESS AND ELECTORAL DEMOCRACY

In an open-list PR system such as Indonesia's, where each candidate competes for a personal vote, programmes like aspiration funds—where sitting legislators provide direct material benefits to their constituents—

---

[19] Confidential interview, 18 Mar. 2014.

are expected to provide considerable advantages to incumbents. This view was certainly common in South Sumatra, where most incumbents in the provincial parliament disbursed their Rp 5 billion with the explicit goal of building loyal base areas of voters and creating clientelistic ties with community leaders who could mobilise votes.

Nevertheless, in the 2014 election only 6 out of 13 provincial incumbents standing for re-election in Palembang city were re-elected. They were Anita Noeringhati (Golkar) and Kartak SAS (PKB), both in electoral district I and, in district II, Fahlevi Maizano (PDI-P), Budiarto Marsul (Gerindra), Yansuri (Golkar) and Imam Mansyur (PKS). This result was stronger than the wider outcome throughout South Sumatra, where 50 of the 75 seats in the provincial parliament were won by first-time candidates.

What accounts for this outcome? There was no obvious pattern in terms of parties, with losing incumbents in Palembang coming from a range of major parties, both nationalist and Islamic. A general anti-incumbency mood borne of disillusionment with official politics was a likely influence. Another plausible explanation is that the losing incumbents were simply less adept at managing their aspiration funds and turning them to their political advantage. Many of the losers were candidates who had failed to capitalise on their aspiration fund projects by recruiting beneficiaries as success team members, making the neighbourhoods they had helped vulnerable to "attacks" by first-time candidates distributing cash payments to voters. The incumbents who secured re-election tended to be those who had from the start realised how they could turn these projects to their political advantage and used them to build longer-lasting clientelistic networks. At the same time, the six incumbents who managed to be re-elected in Palembang were also well known for distributing religiously symbolic patronage goods (such as *peci* hats, *sarung*, headscarves and so on) to mobilise voters. It is more difficult to be definitive about their engagement in retail vote buying; there were some indications that at least some incumbents did participate in this practice. Even so, it is important to stress that most of the incumbents interviewed for this research stated that aspiration funds made it easier for them to approach voters, and to become known at the community level. They mostly also agreed that the funds significantly reduced the cost of their election campaigns, suggesting that—in a climate in which voters expect tangible benefits from candidates—at least some incumbents used aspiration funds to substitute for funds they otherwise would have had to raise privately. Presumably without aspiration funds, the incumbency return rate would have been even lower.

Costly election campaigns are of course not only confined to South Sumatra, but are characteristic of elections throughout Indonesia. It is therefore not surprising that legislatures all over the country have adopted aspiration fund programmes. Two examples of provinces which have introduced their own schemes—in fact they were the earliest— are Aceh and East Java. In both provinces, legislators use these funds in very similar ways to their South Sumatran counterparts, building clientelistic relationships with local-level brokers and mobilising voter support in base areas.

In Aceh, sums allocated per provincial legislator between 2009 and 2014 were also Rp 5 billion, with some reports suggesting the amount increased to Rp 10 billion in 2015.[20] If in South Sumatra many legislators delayed the release of aspiration funds until the campaign period for the 2014 election, in Aceh such funds were mostly distributed six or seven months before the election. In East Java, there is an equivalent scheme, funded from the provincial budget using social assistance, grant and recess funds (see Chapter 16 by Rubaidi). Unlike in Aceh and South Sumatra, in East Java allocations vary according to a legislator's position: commission chairs receive more than ordinary parliamentarians, and the speaker and deputy speaker receive the most. Allocations for legislators between 2009 and 2014 thus ranged from Rp 3 billion to Rp 7 billion each. The management of these funds in East Java is also now more tightly controlled than in South Sumatra, with proposals having to be approved not only by the legislator, but also by bureaucrats in the relevant agency, and with recipients and legislators also required to fulfil rigid reporting requirements explaining their use of the funds. These accountability mechanisms were introduced in 2009 after the first period during which aspiration funds had been used in the province

[20] "Dana Aspirasi DPRA Bertambah" [DPRA Aspiration Funds Increased], *Serambi Indonesia*, 17 Jan. 2015, available at: http://aceh.tribunnews.com/2015/01/17/dana-aspirasi-dpra-bertambah.

(2004–09) resulted in several spectacular corruption prosecutions of parliamentarians and brokers.[21]

CONCLUSION

This study of South Sumatra, and the brief comparison with Aceh and East Java, suggests that politicians in Indonesia allocate aspiration funds in ways that diverge considerably from the developmental and welfare goals they are supposed to fulfil—as often happens with constituency development funds in other countries. Politicians typically use aspiration funds as a source of patronage with which they can build clientelistic relationships with community leaders and voters, and thus reap electoral benefits. When we add the corruption that often occurs in these programmes, it is no surprise that aspiration funds have attracted adverse commentary from civil society groups and academics.

In fact, it is not my intention in this article to argue for the elimination of aspiration fund programmes. The goal of providing a mechanism to connect legislators to their constituents, and to allow them to identify areas of need that have been missed by other government programmes, is not in itself negative. Proper targeting and accountability mechanisms—such as a requirement that legislators confer formally with relevant government agencies in identifying recipients and that field surveys are conducted to ensure programmes go to those who need them most—would help to reduce their vulnerability to electoral manipulation.

Moreover, as we have seen, it is far from certain that aspiration funds always confer the electoral benefits that incumbents hope for. During the course of my research in Palembang, almost all informants agreed that aspiration funds helped make incumbent candidates virtually unbeatable. Many were surprised when fewer than 50 per cent of them were re-elected. In the context of the patronage-oriented contestation that occurred in 2014, aspiration funds were just one resource that candidates drew upon, and did not always trump other forms of electoral mobilisation.

---

[21] Private communication, East Java researcher, 6 June 2014.

Map of Banten, Jakarta and Bekasi

chapter **8**

Banten: Islamic Parties, Networks and Patronage

Gandung Ismanto and Idris Thaha

A little over a week before the April 2014 election, a man was part of a motorcycle convoy driving through Tangerang on the outskirts of Jakarta. Like other people in the convoy, he was supporting a candidate from PKB, one of the Islamic parties. When asked what he wanted from this candidate, the man gave a straightforward answer:

> Just concrete stuff, brother. After this, well there's no guarantee is there, it's not even certain he'll remember his promises. Moreover, according to us, [taking payments and gifts] is no problem. It's not a sin. It's got nothing to do with sin. We get stuff from the various *ustad* in our place too, they told us there's no problem with that. It's just something we get as a way of saying thanks for helping the candidate.[1]

Like other participants in the rally that day, this man went away with a payment: Rp 30,000 for those who came by themselves by motorcycle, Rp 50,000 if they brought a passenger. A few days earlier at a nearby location, several candidates from another Islamic party, PPP, had come together to hold an open-air rally. Though some of the messages touched on religious issues, the speeches were directed

---

[1] Confidential interview, 30 Mar. 2014.

mostly at people who had come as part of the particular candidates' entourages. Some candidates had brought 100 people, some fewer than that. Speakers stressed that 2014 was an opportunity for the party's "big family" to make big gains. The coordinator of each candidate's contingent of supporters paid each person in their entourage with sums averaging Rp 50,000 each as "petrol money" to compensate them for their trouble and expense. When each candidate was introduced to the crowd, their respective contingents competed at cheering the loudest. There were *dangdut* music performances by women in tight clothing. Everybody got free snacks and drinks, and there were "door prizes" for a lucky few who answered questions about the candidates correctly. It was a festive occasion, not much different in style or content from campaign rallies organised in support of nationalist parties in the same area.[2]

These vignettes raise questions about the relationship between Islamic parties and patronage politics in contemporary Indonesia. Not surprisingly, much of the literature on Indonesian Islamic politics has focused on ideological factors, especially the over-arching issue of how Islamic parties and groups see the relationship between Islam and the state, as well as the various nuanced differences between them.[3] But what happens when Islamic parties and networks are used for patronage delivery? Does the mixing of patronage politics with Islamic networks and identities undercut Islamic messaging or reinforce it? How does it contribute to the alleged convergence between Islamic and nationalist politics?[4]

This chapter explores these questions by examining Islamic parties and informal institutions in Banten electoral district III, a mixed constituency that includes a large part of the peri-urban fringe to the west of Jakarta, major industrial zones, as well as coastal and agricultural

---

[2] The authors thank Argoposo Cahyo Nugroho for his field notes of this campaign event.

[3] For example, Anies Rasyid Baswedan, "Political Islam in Indonesia: Present and Future Trajectory", *Asian Survey* 44, 5 (2004): 669–90; Sunny Tanuwidjaja, "Political Islam and Islamic Parties in Indonesia: Critically Assessing the Evidence of Islam's Political Decline", *Contemporary Southeast Asia* 32, 1 (2010): 29–49.

[4] Tanuwidjaja, "Political Islam and Islamic Parties".

villages. After providing a brief introduction to this setting, our analysis takes us in two directions. First, through a focus on campaigning by candidates from Islamic parties running for seats in the national DPR in the constituency, we examine the patronage politics these candidates utilised, and ask what was distinctive about it. Second, to explore the role of grassroots Islamic institutions, we present a localised case study that zeroes in on candidates running for seats in one electoral district for the South Tangerang DPRD. Specifically, we focus on how these candidates engaged with one widespread and popular form of institution used for religious study and devotion: *majelis taklim*. Our analysis pinpoints one source of convergence between Islamic and nationalist parties, with candidates from Islamic parties using patronage strategies that resembled those used by nationalist competitors, and with candidates from both types of party targeting grassroots Islamic institutions.

BACKGROUND: POLITICS IN A PERI-URBAN ZONE

The province of Banten, formed in 2000 out of West Java province, and located at the western tip of Java, is a region with a particularly strong Islamic identity. This can partly be traced to the Banten sultanate, a major centre of trade and Islamic learning, which reached its high point in the 17th century.[5] It also relates to contemporary social formation, whereby the *ulama* have particularly strong influence in village society.[6] Despite this background, however, Banten is also a major site of industrial and urban modernisation, and as a result contains diverse social settings, ranging from agricultural villages through to industrial regions such as the city of Cilegon (home of Krakatau Steel and other heavy industries) and Tangerang on the western fringe of Jakarta, one of Indonesia's major sites of light, export-oriented manufacturing. Our research site

---

[5] Claude Guillot, *Banten: Sejarah dan Peradaban Abad X–XVII* [Banten: History and Culture from the 10th to the 17th Centuries] (Jakarta: Kepustakaan Populer Gramedia, 2008).

[6] Syarif Hidayat, "'Shadow State'? Business and Politics in the Province of Banten", in *Renegotiating Boundaries: Local Politics in Post-Suharto Indonesia*, ed. Henk Schulte Nordholt and Gerry van Klinken (Leiden: KITLV Press, 2007), pp. 203–24.

was the Banten III national electoral district, consisting of the district (*kabupaten*) of Tangerang and the municipalities (*kota*) of Tangerang and South Tangerang, an area that is part of the sprawling peri-urban fringe that surrounds the major world city of Jakarta.

Banten III is highly diverse. Its coastal, western and southern edges include rural villages with relatively traditional economic patterns. Much of the western part of the constituency has been swallowed by Jakarta's urban sprawl, with major industrial estates, shopping areas and middle- and working-class housing estates. This urban concentration accounts for why this electoral district contains a large part of Banten's population, with 6.4 million people or about 57 per cent of the total.[7] The rural parts of the electoral district are mixed ethnically: in the northern coastal fringe there are many Javanese speakers, but farming communities in the south include Sundanese and a few Betawi. The urban-industrial zones are areas of high migration and are ethnically plural.

Our research focused on two levels of electoral competition: one of us (Gandung Ismanto) focused on Islamic party candidates competing for seats in the national parliament (DPR), with the research therefore ranging across the entire electoral district; the other (Idris Thaha) conducted a local case study exploring just one electoral district for the South Tangerang DPRD—electoral district VI, covering Pamulang, the district capital. Pamulang is a feeder suburb for Jakarta. Though it has thriving trade, services and industry, it has also been marked by uncontrolled residential growth over past decades and includes many middle-class housing complexes whose residents commute daily to Jakarta.

Politically, the region does not stand out dramatically from national trends. In the 2014 DPR election, seats in Banten III were won by nine parties: one seat each for Partai Demokrat, Golkar, Gerindra, Hanura, PKS, PPP, PAN and PKB and two for PDI-P. This represented a slight adjustment on 2009, when Partai Demokrat had gained three seats and PKS two. The balance of seats across the Islamic–nationalist party divide showed a slight shift in favour of Islamic parties between the two

---

[7] Badan Pusat Statistik, Provinsi Banten, *Banten dalam Angka 2012* [Banten in Figures] (Banten: BPS, 2012).

elections: in 2014, four of ten seats went to Islamic parties (PKS, PPP, PAN and PKB); in 2009 only three seats had gone to Islamic parties (two to PKS and one to PPP). In Pamulang's electoral district VI, there was a similar proportion: in 2014 the nationalist parties Golkar, PDI-P and Gerindra each won two seats, while six parties (PKB, PKS, Partai Demokrat, PAN, PPP and Hanura) won one each, making a total of 12 seats, four won by Islamic parties. Broadly speaking, these results were in line with the national results, with the Islamic parties gaining 31.4 per cent of the national vote in 2014, up slightly from 29 per cent in 2009.

It is of course important to bear in mind that such results for Islamic parties are only a minor expression of religiosity in Banten: around 96 per cent of the population of the province are Muslims, and, as in most of Indonesia, a dense web of Islamic organisations and networks are present in rural and urban communities. The rural and coastal fishing villages in Banten III constituency are strongholds of traditionalist Islam, and the institutions normally associated with this socioreligious stream—such as *pesantren* (Islamic boarding schools) and Nahdlatul Ulama (NU)—are strong here. In the small towns and peri-urban sprawl, modernist organisations such as Muhammadiyah and Persis (Persatuan Islam) are strong, but so too, as we shall see, are a range of informal, highly localised Islamic prayer groups. Mathlaul Anwar, a Banten modernist organisation also has a presence, though it is concentrated more in other parts of Banten, notably Lebak and Pandeglang. This dense web of Islamic networks provides an important base of recruitment into formal politics, with many aspiring politicians attaining their first introduction to associational life through such organisations. It also provides an organisational resource candidates can use when reaching down to voters.

ISLAMIC PARTIES

The Islamic parties that contested the 2014 election can be divided into two broad groups: those that are linked culturally to major Islamic organisations with deep roots in Indonesian society (thus, PKB is associated with the traditionalist NU; PAN is close to its modernist equivalent, Muhammadiyah); and those that go one step further and declare in their party statutes that Islam is their "foundation" (*asas*) (PKS, PPP and PBB), and which might therefore be considered to be not just Islamic, but Islamist. It is a standard part of political discourse in Indonesia for representatives of the Islamic parties to claim that their goal is to represent the interests of the Islamic community in government. The Islamist parties claim to want to Islamise state policy. As one PPP DPR candidate explained:

> The Islamic *ummat* has to make progress, the Islamic *ummat* in Indonesia has to rise up, it has to change. That's why we have to win, why we have to seize power so we can control the policies of this beloved republic and make them accord with the wishes of the Islamic *ummat*.[8]

In contrast, the goals of PAN and PKB are more ideologically modest, but also more sectional, insofar as they aim to further the interests of their parent organisations and communities. As K.H. Ma'ruf Amin, a national PKB spokesperson, explained at a rally in Tangerang, PKB was simply the "vehicle of the community of Nahdlatul Ulama".[9]

But what effect does such rhetoric about advancing the interests of the Islamic community have on the nature of campaigning by Islamic party candidates? Does it make their campaigning distinctive? One of the key conclusions from our observations of electioneering in 2014 in Banten III was that there were no fundamental differences in the campaigning modes used by candidates from Islamic parties and those from nationalist parties, at least in respect to their reliance on patronage. Islamic party candidates, just like other candidates, relied overwhelmingly on providing "concrete stuff" to their constituents. Candidates from both types of party were equally cognisant of the voters' mood of pragmatism, and tried hard to meet their expectations of material rewards.

This is not to say that there was nothing at all distinctive about the campaign styles of Islamic party candidates, many of whom still relied

---

[8] Confidential interview, 30 Mar. 2014.
[9] Field observations, 5 Apr. 2014.

strongly on their parties' religious networks, and concentrated their patronage efforts through those networks. In other words, there often *were* distinctively "Islamic" networks for, and recipients of, patronage. For example, the PAN candidates we observed relied disproportionately on Muhammadiyah's various organisational affiliates—student organisations, schools, clinics and the like—in their campaigns. A PAN candidate we interviewed spent most of his campaign funds on various forms of "social assistance"—such as medical expenses of constituents, foodstuffs for voters, mosque and *musholla* renovations and donations for *ustad*, *ulama* and teachers. He distributed this material in a centrally planned and organised manner, through his success team. Though he used his Muhammadiyah connections in building this team and distributing the benefits, however, the recipients were not only from Muhammadiyah circles.[10]

Likewise, PKB candidates still relied largely on NU networks. In fact, one of the PKB candidates we interviewed stressed that one of her main motivations for standing for the party was to gain leverage over government programmes and budget allocations which she could then direct toward her constituents. She cited a saying of the Prophet, *Khairunnass anfa'uhum linnass* ("the best of people are those who give the greatest benefit to their fellows"). As an activist in Fatayat, NU's younger women's organisation, she had seen that significant funds were available to DPR members for community development activities that could benefit groups like Fatayat and others in the NU network, and she wanted to access them:

> I wanted to get into politics because, for one thing, I've been doing a lot for the people up to now. For example, through Fatayat I have cooperated [on programmes] with several ministries. We are only able to pressure them, to try to get them to link up [with our work] through that kind of cooperation. But it's not possible if you care about your organisation, just to entrust that to someone else and hope that they will do their best to get it into the budget. If we are on the inside, we can do it ourselves.[11]

---

[10] Confidential interview, 7 Apr. 2014.
[11] Confidential interview, 11 Apr. 2014.

Accordingly, party candidates sometimes presented themselves primarily as candidates who would care for their traditional constituencies, especially by directing future government programmes and pork barrel spending toward them.

The campaigning style of PKS was not far different, despite this party's reputation as a cadre-based and ideological party with Muslim Brotherhood roots. One significant difference was visible at open-air PKS rallies, which tended to be attended by party cadres and sympathisers, rather than the casual attendees and rent-a-crowds present at other parties' events. PKS events also did not feature singing, let alone scantily-clad entertainers, unlike some events sponsored by other Islamic parties. Otherwise, for their face-to-face campaigning, PKS candidates intensively made use of *majelis taklim* and *kelompok pengajian* (synonymous terms for Islamic-study groups) and door-to-door visits, and on these occasions distributed club goods and other gifts in ways that were identical to the practices of other parties.

It should be noted, however, that many Islamic party candidates "beautified" their patronage practices with religious doctrine. Thus, one PPP candidate, who talked about his party being the "only party that is blessed by Allah", took great trouble to direct some of his resources toward poor children, framing these gifts as religious charity, but really targeting the votes of their parents and relatives. Likewise, the PKB candidate mentioned above described her patronage politics as a manifestation of her religious duty to care for others. At the same time, these candidates were sometimes hard-nosed about what they were doing. As one experienced and successful PPP DPR candidate—the same man quoted above who stated that the goal of his party was to represent the *ummat*—explained a few days before the election:

> [Now] people don't care what party you're from, what your ideology is, what you do, whether you're corrupt, whether you are going to really try to stay true to the mandate they give you. They look at how big the concrete contribution is that you can give to the community. There's been a very sharp shift. Now voters are much more bold [about requesting gifts], and much more open about it. It's much worse than in 2009. It's out in the open now.[12]

---

[12] Confidential interview, 30 Mar. 2014.

Candidates built campaign structures that allowed them to respond to this mood. Every Islamic party candidate we encountered relied at least partly on religious networks—preachers, Islamic organisations, schools, and so on—in order to mobilise voters. But the best-funded and organised also built territorially organised success teams characteristic of campaigning throughout much of Indonesia, seeking to recruit and mobilise neighbourhood-level brokers who were often quite unconnected to the world of Islamic associational life. These brokers were instead often RW or RT (neighbourhood or subneighbourhood) heads, or informal community leaders of various sorts. This PPP candidate's success team, for example, contained approximately 3,000 persons, including 250 village coordinators. The main PKB and PAN candidates we interviewed had similarly large success teams. This structure was designed to identify grassroots voters' preferences for patronage and to deliver it to them, with team members acting as mediators between the candidate and voters, compiling lists of persons prepared to vote for the candidate, communicating voters' aspirations and requests to the candidate, and distributing on his or her behalf various benefits—whether in the form of individual payments or club goods. And in Banten III as in other parts of the country, this campaign style is very costly. Though most DPR candidates refused to give precise figures, it appears serious candidates spent between Rp 2 billion and Rp 5 billion.

Grassroots Campaigning on the Urban Fringe

If one force driving convergence between Islamic and nationalist parties was that Islamic party candidates were building territorially organised campaign structures that had little to do with Islamic politics, another was that many Islamic organisations and networks were increasingly targeted by candidates from nationalist parties. We illustrate this proposition by focusing on a particular form of informal, community-based religious institution, known as *majelis taklim* (*majelis ta'lim*) in the urban centre of Pamulang. Most candidates in Pamulang, including all ten candidates who were the focus of this research, promoted their campaigns at least partly through *majelis taklim*. Several of them made these bodies their main campaign focus; some candidates themselves had personal reputations as *ustad* or *ustadzah* (male or female preachers) who led such bodies and saw this background as their main political asset. Critically, not all of these candidates ran with Islamic parties.

Majelis taklim are a profusely abundant form of religious organisation in contemporary Indonesia. There are over 200 *majelis taklim* in Pamulang alone.[13] *Majelis taklim* are a form of informal religious educational institution which are open, flexible and voluntary in nature. They carry out their activities at any time and any place: morning, noon or night; in mosques or *musholla*, offices, schools, private homes and other locations. People from all ages, ethnic groups and educational and professional backgrounds, take part in *majelis taklim*; they are generally for women only, some are for men, but very few are mixed gender. Historically, this form of organisation began to grow rapidly in Indonesia in the mid-1980s, as one sign of a wider Islamic revival then occurring. They gained government support through a coordinating body, the Badan Kontak Majelis Taklim (BKMT), which was headed by Tutty Alawiyah, the daughter of a famous Betawi *ulama*, K.H. Abdullah Syafi'i (Tutty Alawiyah later became Minister for Women's Affairs in Suharto's final cabinet and under President Habibie).[14] The use of the term *majelis taklim* is unique to Indonesia, though it is derived from Arabic: *majelis*, meaning a place to sit, and *taklim* meaning teaching.[15] In other parts of the Muslim world similar organisations exist, but they are known by different names, such as *ḥalaqah*, *zâwiyah*, and *majelis al-'ilm*.[16]

---

[13] Eka Rahayu, *Bentuk Komunikasi Badan Kontak Majelis Taklim (BKMT) Kecamatan Pamulang dalam Mengkoordinir Majelis Taklim* [Forms of Communication in BKMT Pamulang District for Coordinating the Majelis Taklim] (Jakarta: Universitas Islam Negeri Jakarta, 2006), p. 35.

[14] Murodi, "Tutty Alawiyah: Pengembang Masyarakat Lewat Majlis Taklim" [Tutty Alawiyah: Developing the Community Through *Majelis Taklim*], in *Ulama Perempuan Indonesia* [Female Islamic Scholars of Indonesia], ed. Jajat Burhanuddin (Jakarta: Gramedia and PPIM IAIN Jakarta, 2002), pp. 205–15.

[15] Hasan Alwi, *Kamus Besar Bahasa Indonesia* [Dictionary of Indonesian] (Jakarta: Departemen Pendidikan Nasional Balai Pustaka, 2001), pp. 699, 1124; Ahmad Sunarto, *Kamus al-Fikr* [Dictionary of Fikih] (Surabaya: Halimjay, 2002), pp. 95, 470.

[16] Azyumardi Azra, *Paradigma Baru Pendidikan Nasional: Rekonstruksi dan Demokratisasi* [New National Education Paradigm: Reconstruction and Democracy] (Jakarta: Kompas, 2002), p. 236.

The basic aim of each *majelis taklim* is to improve the Islamic knowledge and piety of participants. Members will recite Quranic verses together and listen to religious advice from a preacher. Typically several members of a group will take turns to preach, though groups often invite outside preachers, especially for major religious holidays. *Majelis taklim* are also a forum for building close interpersonal connections among people living in the same neighbourhood. Occasionally, group members come together to help one another in case of a death in the family or other problem, but their primary function is religious learning. They are typically informally organised, and are usually led simply by an *ustad* or *ustadzah*. They are usually formed at the level of a single RT, so their members are usually neighbours; indeed, often each RT has a *majelis taklim* of its own. Mostly, though not exclusively, they are associated with the traditionalist variant of Indonesian Islam.

Because they are such a vigorous part of community life, and because so many individuals are organised through them, *majelis taklim* are an entry point for candidates seeking to promote themselves to constituents. In Pamulang, many candidates made visiting *majelis taklim* central to their campaign strategies. In fact, among the ten such candidates we studied, three had reputations as preachers in local *majelis taklim*. One example was Maesaroh, a 50-year-old woman, who had an established network of ten local *majelis taklim*, mostly based in and around the *kelurahan* (urban precinct) of Pondok Cabe Ilir. Educated in Islamic institutions from elementary to tertiary level, she regularly preached in these ten *majelis taklim*, whose total congregation was around 500, all women. As the election neared, Maesaroh often slipped into her sermons that she was running for Partai Nasdem in the district and asked the congregration to pray for her success, as explained by Hajjah Limah, a friend she had made through her *majelis taklim* activities and who was a major supporter.[17]

Maesaroh was not financially well resourced. But she did not complain much about how this limited her ability to campaign, believing that her religious network, the respect in which she was held within it, and her piety, meant she had a chance. As she put it:

---

[17] Interview, Hajjah Limah, 1 Apr. 2014.

I don't have a success team. I'm just doing it myself. I have the support of the mothers from the congregations of the various *majelis taklim*, who have volunteered to help campaign for me and promote me in the community hereabouts. I've long been building up a network among the women of the *majelis taklim*. There are at least one or two women in each *majelis taklim* who help promote my candidacy. I am struggling with strength from the heart, and with prayers. I am with Allah.[18]

Ibu Roayah, another of Maesaroh's *majelis taklim* friends and supporters, was not so confident: "Though she has many students in her *majelis taklim*, I don't know if they will want to vote for Bu Maesaroh. I hope all of them will, but it's up to them."[19] In fact, Ibu Roayah was putting her finger on a key weakness not only for Maesaroh but for many candidates with *majelis taklim* backgrounds. Many candidates who run for election, especially at the district level, do so because they feel confident in the strength of their social networks, as they do when they lead a *majelis taklim*. However, in a patronage-oriented electoral landscape, social networks are not the only key to success; material resources are also critical. Many candidates with *majelis taklim* backgrounds foundered as a result of this factor: their networks were strong, but their resources were weak.

Another preacher-candidate was Landi Effendi. A graduate of the Interpretation and Hadith programme at the nearby Syarif Hidayatullah State Islamic University, he also headed a *majelis taklim* of his own, which he named Majelis Dzikir (literally, a forum dedicated to chanting the name of God) and which was also active in promoting alternative medicine. He was also frequently asked to lead *pengajian* (Quranic study sessions) in other *majelis taklim* and *tahlilan* (ritual prayers for the deceased) when there was a death in his neighbourhood. His main constituency was poorer residents. Indeed, one of Landi's major claims of success was that through his *Majelis Dzikir* he had taught around 2,000 locals to be able to recite the Quran. A major aim was to expand his programme for wiping out "Quranic illiteracy" in the city,

[18] Interview, Maesaroh, 19 Mar. 2014.
[19] Interview, Ibu Roayah, 1 Apr. 2014.

especially by targeting older and poorer residents.[20] Interestingly, Landi was running through PDI-P, a nationalist party long identified primarily as the party of heterodox *abangan* Muslims and non-Muslims.[21] However, over the decade, as part of the wider convergence between Islamic and nationalist parties, PDI-P had reached out to devout Muslims, including by establishing a Muslim organisation affiliated to the party, the Baitul Muslimin Indonesia, which Landi directed at the city level.

Like Maesaroh, Landi had limited resources. His campaign events were modest, and he travelled to them by motorcycle. He jokingly referred to himself as a member of ICMI (Ikatan Caleg Miskin)—the Association of Poor Candidates—playing on the name of the well-known Ikatan Cendekiawan Islam se-Indonesia (All-Indonesia Association of Islamic Intellectuals). He explained, "We are just making do, our only capital is *li-Llâhi Taʾâla* [Sincerely for the sake of Allah] and prayers. Whatever I have is a product of my 'busking' in *pengajian*", by which he meant he funded his campaign by way of the appearance fees he received for his preaching.[22] He was confident, however, that his reputation in *majelis taklim* would carry him to victory and, although he gave donations to the *majelis taklim* he visited, they were rather modest, and funded by a DPR candidate with whom he was cooperating.

Two other PDI-P candidates—neither of whom were incumbents— were Dwi Untari and M. Rusli. They also targeted voters through *majelis taklim*. Rusli who had worked as contract staff in the local Department of Transportation, and was originally from Bangka Island, paid particular attention to the *majelis taklim* in the neighbourhood around his residence, and was on the board of one group that operated out of the *musholla* he had built in front of his house. Like Maesaroh, he saw his involvement in these groups as a way to build emotional links with neighbours, and so win their votes: "Without being close to them, how can the community know what kind of person I am? I try to never

---

[20] Interview, Landi Effendi, 11 Mar. 2014.

[21] Marcus Mietzner, "Ideology, Money and Dynastic Leadership: The Indonesian Democratic Party of Struggle, 1998–2012", *South East Asia Research* 20, 4 (2012): 511–31.

[22] Interview, Landi Effendi, 11 Mar. 2014.

let go of the bonds of *silaturahmi* [Islamic fellowship]."[23] One of Rusli's friends and assistants insisted that Rusli had been assiduously working his way through the various Islamic networks in the neighbourhood, and he was confident as a result:

> We have visited virtually all the *majelis taklim* and religious leaders. I have also given directions to my residents about what we should do in this election. That means: first, don't abstain. Second, vote for a Muslim candidate. Third, vote for a candidate who is close to us, whom we know.[24]

This local focus was central to Rusli's strategy, and the *majelis taklim* were just one—albeit the most important—method of reaching out to his neighbours. He also tried to provide them with concrete proof of what he could do for them, securing funds from a party colleague who was a sitting DPRD member to pay for road repairs in the housing estate where he lived.[25]

Dwi Untari, meanwhile, was a particularly poorly resourced candidate (she could not even afford any publicity material of her own, but had to rely on whatever was supplied by a DPR candidate with whom she was in a "tandem" arrangement). Her main campaign method was to visit women's religious study groups, especially in the *kelurahan* of Kedaung. Some of these groups were run by her husband's relatives (Dwi herself was a migrant and did not have many relatives in the area). She distributed free *jilbab* (headscarves), making sure they were red, the colour of her party.

Another female candidate was Agnes Harnasih, an incumbent with Partai Demokrat, a party whose credo is "national religious" and pioneered the fusing of Islamic and nationalist appeals. Agnes, originally from West Sumatra, also focused her campaign on all-female *majelis taklim*, visiting them and bringing with her "souvenirs" in the form of *jilbab* and "mementoes in the form of money".[26] At the end of her meetings, during which she would introduce herself and explain her

---

[23] Interview, M. Rusli, 13 Mar. 2014.

[24] Interview, Benzuarefi, 8 Apr. 2014.

[25] Interview, M. Rusli, 13 Mar. 2014.

[26] Interview, Agnes Harnasih, 11 Mar. 2014.

candidacy, she usually gave an envelope containing cash—typically Rp 300,000 or Rp 500,000—to the head of the group, as a symbol of her support for the community. But it did not stop there. According to the coordinator of her success team, Agnes also ran workshops for these *majelis taklim* on the role of women in the family. She took groups on bus tours. She even had a success team member whose special job was to organise and coordinate her contacts with *majelis taklim* in each *kelurahan* in her electoral district, to organise a schedule of meetings with them and to take along snacks and drinks. Agnes viewed these organisations primarily as a vehicle for *silaturahmi* and had no particular religious expertise herself.[27] The coordinator of her success team, Freddy Herianto, explained that she primarily used these meetings to explain her achievements as a council member, explaining that the goal was to "sell ... her experience, her friendliness and her simplicity. I package all of that in terms of programmes," by which he meant that he linked her personal characteristics to the education and welfare programmes she claimed credit for.[28]

Nur Kholiq, by contrast, was an incumbent DPRD member representing PKB, which as explained above is rooted in the traditionalist Islamic community. From Jombang in East Java, part of the NU heartland, Nur Kholiq regularly provided religious instruction at ten *majelis taklim* where he would teach, among other topics, *fikih* (Islamic jurisprudence) and *tauhid* (unity of God). He made use of one of the *kitab kuning*, the "yellow books" that have been used for religious study since time immemorial by traditionalist Muslims in the archipelago, the *Syafinah al-Najaah*, a classic text of the Syafii school of Sunni Islam. He was very well known in the Pondok Cabe Ilir *kelurahan* for his religious knowledge, his preaching, and for leading *tahlilan*, and would often be invited to officiate at religious events in the community. Unlike some of the candidates mentioned above, however, Nur Kholiq was relatively well-resourced, and also provided generous material aid to *majelis taklim*. In the words of a supporter:

[27] Ibid.
[28] Interview, Freddy Herianto, 28 Mar. 2014.

If the mothers in the congregation of a *majelis taklim* need a sound system or other aid, Nur Kholiq will always provide it. Nur Kholiq also will occasionally give money to *majelis taklim*. [But] that's in response to requests from the community or the head of the *majelis taklim*.[29]

Here we have one other electoral function of *majelis taklim*: as a site for disbursing patronage, and for representing that patronage as a form of religiously sanctioned charity. In Nur Kholiq's case, his giving to *majelis taklim* was just part of a broader approach; according to an associate, he was also known for helping out with people's health or educational needs, paying for hospitalisation or school fees when necessary with his own money, and for arranging government help to repair neighbourhood roads.[30]

These sketches provide a clue as to the intensity of interaction between candidates and grassroots religious institutions—in this case, *majelis taklim*—during elections. *Majelis taklim* provide one mechanism for contacting grassroots voters and, because of the atmosphere of community engagement and piety they foster, many individuals with *majelis taklim* connections seem particularly tempted to stand for elected office. However, social networks only go so far: *not one* of the ten candidates we focused on during this research in Pamulang who made *majelis taklim* an important part of their strategies was elected. The reason seems to be that they lacked other resources. While these candidates were concentrating on cultivating their *majelis taklim* networks, wealthier and better-organised candidates were building neighbourhood-level success teams and delivering club goods and individual gifts to their constituents. We might even go so far as to suggest that *majelis taklim* gave poorly resourced candidates unwarranted confidence: in the end, their network resources could not counteract the financial resources of more cashed-up candidates.[31]

---

[29] Confidential interview, 4 Apr. 2014.

[30] Interview, Suyuti HM, 4 Apr. 2014.

[31] This observation has also been made of district executive government elections: see Edward Aspinall and Muhammad Uhaib As'ad, "The Patronage Patchwork: Village Brokerage Networks and the Power of the State in an Indonesian Election", *Bijdragen tot de Taal-, Land- en Volkenkunde* 171, 2–3 (2015): 165–95.

CONCLUSION

The preceding discussion adds to the literature exploring contemporary Islamic politics in Indonesia and, especially, the convergence between Islamic and nationalist parties. Our analysis of electoral dynamics in Banten's constituency III shows, on the one hand, that Islamic party candidates are relying on patronage-focused strategies that do not fundamentally differ from those of nationalist competitors. On the other hand, the account also shows that grassroots religious institutions such as *majelis taklim* are just as open to candidates from nationalist parties as they are to Islamic party candidates. In short, both patronage delivery and network resources are driving convergence at the grassroots.

Of course, where patronage politics are conducted through the vehicle of Islamic social organisations and activities, arguably Islamic party candidates are advantaged by their longer track records and greater claims of legitimate authority in such spheres. Yet, in an electoral climate characterised by increasingly fierce inter-candidate competition, and by increasingly transactional calculations by voters, such resources only go so far. Candidates who are well resourced in terms of their Islamic credentials and networks often lack the material resources needed to organise large teams of brokers and provide gifts to community groups and voters. Religious morality does not inoculate Islamic party candidates from patronage politics, in part precisely because it often fails to provide a compelling alternative means to mobilise the voters.

chapter 9

Tangerang, Banten: Women Candidates in the Shadow of Men

Argoposo Cahyo Nugroho

One Friday not long after the April 2014 legislative election, I received a text message (SMS) from Riri, a woman who had been a DPRD candidate in the district (*kabupaten*) of Tangerang, Banten province:

> The votes of people in Tangerang were bought cheaply, at just Rp 10,000 each. Even a chicken costs more. Of all of them, it was only those who were for Bu Riri who were pure. It was only people who voted for Bu Riri who had good sense, healthy minds and noble hearts.

This message appeared on the screen of my handphone as a sort of summary of the story that Riri (I am using pseudonyms for all informants in this chapter) had already told me about various violations committed by other candidates. She blamed her loss on vote buying conducted by rivals.

For more than a month in the lead-up to these elections, I spent time living in Tangerang district, with a special research focus on efforts made by women candidates. Though not all the candidates I interviewed or observed were women, I wanted to know whether we would get a different perspective on the politics of patronage and clientelism if we focused on the experiences of women contestants. In particular, I followed three women who were running for the local district council. Each of them believed they had a good chance, but none was elected.

Though my conclusions cannot be taken to be representative of all women, these three candidates did have one thing in common: in each case they were encouraged to enter politics by a husband who had himself tried but failed to get nominated. Their husbands played important roles in directing and planning their campaigns. But these women had varying levels of access to material resources, and different campaign strategies and modes of patronage politics. Riri was the only one who did not distribute large quantities of material goods to voters; instead, she tried to help voters by providing advice and assistance on accessing government services. The other two provided both collective and individual gifts in ways that were broadly in line with male candidates' practices. Overall, my findings suggest that women's participation in electoral politics is still marked by the gender inequalities that characterise Indonesian society, pointing to broader lessons about female participation in public life.

BACKGROUND: POLITICS IN AN INDUSTRIAL ZONE

Tangerang has for more than two decades been one of the densest sites of industrial activity in Indonesia. My research was conducted in electoral district I of Tangerang district, an area that comprises six subdistricts: Tigaraksa, Solear, Jambe, Cisoka, Balaraja and Jayanti. Tigaraksa is the district capital and the location of its chief public buildings. Along with Balaraja, it is also the site of dense industrial activity, including the Millennium Industrial Estate and the 300,000 ha Balaraja Industrial Park. New industrial parks, meanwhile, are planned for Solear. Much of the electoral district, therefore, is covered by dense factory zones, as well as even more dense working-class housing estates. According to the local Bureau of Statistics, 45 per cent of the working population are employed in industry. The crumbling roads are packed with heavy trucks bearing manufactured products and construction materials. The factories, and the service industries that have sprung up around them, are also an employment drawcard for people from all over the archipelago, giving rise to a mixed, largely migrant population.

Nine seats were available in this electoral district, with each party running the maximum allowable nine candidates. With a 30 per cent minimum quota of female candidates, each party nominated exactly the same number of women: the required minimum of three. There were six incumbents standing for re-election, only one of whom was a woman, Suherni, a Hanura candidate who was re-elected. In the district DPRD as a whole between 2009 and 2014, only 5 of the 50 members were female.

The three candidates I focus on in this article are Ani, from Partai Demokrat, Riri of the Islamist PBB (Partai Bulan Bintang, Crescent Star Party) and Nida of Gerindra. All were standing for election for the first time. They also had one other thing in common: their husbands also acted as heads of their success teams. In fact, in each case, it was their husbands who first joined the party and wanted to stand as a legislative candidate, but—according to the men concerned, at least—they failed to achieve this goal because of the 30 per cent quota on female candidates (as required by Article 55 of Law No. 8 of 2012).[1] Set aside by their parties in favour of women (as they saw it), these three men decided to put forward their wives to replace them (though in Ani's case, she had independent political experience and was herself close to leading party figures, as we shall see). These men continued to participate politically by leading their wives' success teams and designing their campaign strategies.

During one relaxed discussion at the couple's house, Arto, Riri's husband, explained that it had been the party that had suggested to him that he should push his wife forward. The PBB wanted to meet its quota of women candidates:

> I can still play a political role through my wife, and PBB can still make progress in the election. Because of that, I decided to become the head of my wife's success team, brother. I will be the one who guards my wife from temptations if she is elected as a council member.[2]

Arto lacked sufficient political capital to shoulder his own way onto the candidate list. He was not an incumbent, he did not occupy a position in the party structure, and he lacked the financial resources to

---

[1] Law No. 8 of 2012 on General Elections of Members of the People's Representative Council, Regional Representative Council, and Regional People's Representative Councils.

[2] Interview, Arto, 14 Mar. 2014.

win mass support. Onal, Nida's husband, had a similar story. Like many Gerindra members, he had been a PDI-P cadre. Even after changing parties, however, he hit a dead end when he tried to gain nomination as a legislative candidate. So he, too, put his wife forward in replacement. In the case of Ani, the Partai Demokrat candidate, though her husband initially wanted to stand, she was also close to a local party leader, Wahidin Halim, who favoured her.

We are reminded here of T.O. Ihromi's description of a woman being akin to her husband's property.[3] Certainly, it seems these candidates were put forward as stand-ins for their husbands, perhaps even as their "puppets". The 30 per cent quota for women candidates has been subjected to debate on such grounds. Though some commentators have supported it, others have argued that it is not strong enough.[4] Another view is that in conditions under which women do not experience equality in the household this quota is unlikely to promote substantive female leadership. Shelly Adelina and Ani Soetjipto, for example, argue that quotas

> have the potential to be essentialist, only chasing a quantity or amount and marginalising quality and gender perspectives .... [A] focus on women based on the principle of representation of women can lead to essentialism, given that the category of "women" is far from homogeneous.[5]

Syarif Hidayat has explained a similar situation, also in Banten, in his piece on the "shadow state" in that province.[6] In this case, however, the power was of a father in relation to his daughter: in 2001 Ratu

---

[3] T.O. Ihromi, *Sosiologi Keluarga* [The Sociology of Families] (Jakarta: Yayasan Obor Indonesia, 2008), p. 445.

[4] Sharon Bessell, "Increasing the Proportion of Women in the National Parliament: Opportunities, Barriers and Challenges", in *Problems of Democratisation in Indonesia: Elections, Institution and Society*, ed. Edward Aspinall and Marcus Mietzner (Singapore: ISEAS, 2010), pp. 219–42.

[5] Shelly Adelina and Ani Soetjipto, "Kepentingan Politik Perempuan dalam Partai: Strategi Gender" [The Importance of Women's Politics in Parties: A Gender Strategy], in "Perempuan Politisi", special issue, *Jurnal Perempuan* 81, 19, 2 (2014): 53.

[6] Syarif Hidayat, "'Shadow State'? Business and Politics in the Province of Banten", in *Renegotiating Boundaries: Local Politics in Post-Suharto Indonesia*, ed. Henk Schulte Nordholt and Gerry van Klinken (Leiden: KITLV Press, 2007), pp. 203–24.

Atut Chosiyah was put forward as deputy governor of the province as a pawn of her father, Chasan Sochib, a powerful *jawara* (man famed for his fighting skills) and businessman. Atut became deputy governor to advance the economic interests of the family; Chasan wished to be free of the ties of formal office, allowing him to gain greater power by manipulating his daughter's authority. When she was in power, accordingly, numerous Banten government projects were handed to the family. Even if she later developed significant independent political authority, in Hidayat's analysis, when Atut gained office she lacked elite political experience, and gained the post primarily as a product of her father's power and planning.

Of course, it should be stressed that not all women candidates fit this pattern—there are plenty of women politicians in Indonesia with independent careers who exercise strong political leadership. Even so, in the electoral district which was my focus I had the experience of encountering several additional female candidates whose experiences were similar to those described above; indeed, several even refused my requests for interviews, saying that they were on the candidate lists just to help their party fill the 30 per cent quota, and had no particular desire to stand for election. One—who did not want to be interviewed because her campaign was left entirely to her father—in fact ended up being elected.

MOBILISATION STRATEGIES

What then of the strategies that these three candidates used? What networks did they draw upon, and how central was patronage distribution to their efforts?

One strategy that many candidates use in Indonesian elections is the mobilisation of religious or ethnic ties. Nida, the Gerindra candidate, used her minority status as a Christian Batak (an ethnic group from North Sumatra) to try to get out the vote. Her husband, Onal, the "brains" behind this campaign, argued that *marga* (clan) and church networks could take her to victory. Accordingly, since July 2013 the couple had been assiduously using their relations with a Protestant pastor and members of his congregation to promote Nida's candidacy, holding campaign events immediately after church services had finished. The couple also used the *arisan* groups of the various Batak *marga* in the district (*arisan* are a form of social group in which people get together to practice communal saving: every participant makes a contribution and takes a turn at getting the total sum donated at one meeting). The couple took advantage of their belonging to two separate *marga*:

> My *arisan*, the *arisan* of my husband, the *arisan* of my mother, my mother-in-law—there are lots of them. The members of any one *arisan* group will be married to someone from a different *marga*, so they will also bring in other families. That's just from one family. If you have 40 families, the numbers will be huge.[7]

As well as going through this *arisan* network, Onal also directed Nidal to reach out to migrants from their home region—Medan and North Sumatra. According to Onal, many such people worked in the car and motorcycle workshops in the district; he claimed that every workshop owner in the district was a Batak. Accordingly, they launched a programme of social assistance in which they provided tools to workshop labourers in order, so they said, to support employment in the sector. Nida and Onal felt confident that there was a sufficiently large group of voters with Batak and Church connections, though they did not explain the basis of these calculations.

Nida, like many other candidates, also provided other forms of "assistance". For example, she provided donations to help renovate several *musholla* and churches, though she insisted these donations were not large. She believed that her Christian identity, and the fact that she was relying on church networks, should not prevent her from trying to reach out to non-Christian voters. She gave the donations, she said, as a "spontaneous" part of her effort to build good relations with Muslim community leaders in several neighbourhoods in Tigaraksa subdistrict.[8]

One thing that assisted Nida's campaign efforts was that she and her husband were relatively wealthy. Nida works in the finance section of a Yemen-based textile company that operates in Tangerang, while

---

[7] Interview, Nida, 2 Apr. 2014.

[8] Ibid.

her husband is a contractor with experience in both city and province-level projects, and has occasionally worked for foreign companies. Thus her campaign was relatively well financed, allowing her to give fairly generous donations to religious groups and workshops, amounting to a total of roughly Rp 300 million.

Though her religious and party background was very different, Riri also had a similar campaign strategy, in that its most important component was the attempt—under the direction of her husband—to reach out to religious leaders who it was hoped would influence their followers to vote for her. Riri viewed *kyai*, *ustad* and *ulama* as her entry points to the communities that stood behind these Islamic leaders, though she did not feel the need to strike specific deals with any of them.

Unlike Nida, Riri's campaign was modestly financed. Her husband, Arto, worked as a staff member in a construction consultancy firm—thus, though he worked in the same industry as Onal, Nida's husband, he did so at a lower level and with a lower income (Onal owned his own company). Riri was a full-time housewife; previously she had worked as an administrator for an automobile showroom, but had given that up when she married. This meant that they had much less money to spend on her campaign, only about Rp 100 million.

However, Riri made her housewife status important to her campaign strategy, because she was able to use her connections with similar women, via *posyandu* (integrated health posts, the lowest level in Indonesia's healthcare system, and primarily focused on maternal and infant health) and a volleyball competition in her housing estate. By involving herself in these activities she was able to get to know the women in her neighbourhood and then use those relationships for her campaign. The *posyandu* activities involved health services for infants and other family health programmes, while volleyball involved competitions between RT in the same housing complex, or between different complexes, and were often held on the volleyball court near her house. In particular, Riri tried to use her knowledge of how to access health services, gained through involvement in the *posyandu* programme, to substitute the funds that many candidates used to cultivate connections with constituents. She targeted communities in the Adiyasa housing estate, in Solear subdistrict, as well as Tigaraksa and Cisoka subdistricts. According to Riri, the residents of this area were poor, and they lacked good information about health:

> I once visited a neighbourhood in Cileles, Tigaraksa for a *sosialisasi* and *silaturahmi* [promotion and fellowship meeting]; there was a woman there whose two-year-old child only weighed 3 kg, because it had hydrocephalus. I asked her why she hadn't taken it to hospital and she said she couldn't afford it, she didn't have the fee. I felt terrible, brother, I almost cried. I explained to her that care at the hospital was now free, that she just needed to get her documents from the RW/RT and the *kelurahan* [precinct]. There are funds available through your health card, through community health insurance [*jamkesmas*] or regional health insurance [*jamkesda*] programmes. So I told her to take her child to hospital straight away, and leave chasing up the administrative side to me. So I started just with her KTP [identity card] and got her a SKTM [Surat Keterangan Tidak Mampu, Statement of Disadvantage] from the subdistrict, then the community health centre and then Tangerang hospital. Praise be to God, it all went smoothly. In the end I cried, I was moved, oh God, I can be of some benefit to others. I can help, though only with my energy and my thoughts.[9]

Another thing Riri did was to promise to establish a savings and loans cooperative for the community of motorcycle taxi (*ojek*) and city transport (*angkot*) drivers in Solear, and those based around the Tigaraksa bus station. On one occasion I attended a meeting between her and members of this community in the yard of her house, facing the volleyball court. About 25 drivers were present, all men. Riri opened the meeting and started introducing the concept. At this time, I was interviewing her husband, Arto, as her success team head. When our interview finished, Arto joined the meeting and took over the discussion from Riri, explaining the technical side of the operation of the cooperative they proposed, how they wanted the drivers themselves to run it, and so on. Their basic proposal was that Riri would be able to access aspiration funds as a DPRD member, if elected, and direct some of those funds to the cooperative. Arto told those in attendance

---

[9] Interview, Riri, 12 Mar. 2014.

that he himself would remind his wife to fulfil her obligations to them should she actually be elected:

> I myself will *menjewer* [pull the ear] of Bu Riri if she forgets her promise when she sits as a member of the council. I myself will be the one to remind Bu Riri that she needs to fulfil her mandate.[10]

Arto also presented Riri to the drivers as being different from other candidates, who he said used money to buy the masses. Riri presented herself instead as a person who used her own energies and brains to help her constituents. At the same time, I could see for myself how much control Arto himself exercised over every major decision and action that Riri took.

The situation was somewhat different with Ani, the Partai Demokrat candidate, who had independent political experience before becoming a candidate. She was a teacher in a junior high school, and also a part-time lecturer in a private university in Balaraja, another subdistrict of Tangerang. Though this was her first time as a candidate, she was not new to politics, having worked on a success team for Wahidin Halim, a Banten gubernatorial candidate, in 2011. It was Wahidin who first encouraged Ani to run, though she of course also got the agreement of her husband, Imam, to do so. Both husband and wife were, like Wahidin, Partai Demokrat members and it was Imam who first tried to secure nomination as a candidate. When he failed, he passed on the task to his wife (both husband and wife agreed on this version of events). Wahidin viewed Ani as having greater potential, precisely because the party was seeking to meet the 30 per cent quota on women candidates.

Ani had also been active in social affairs, especially education. For example, she told me that before becoming a candidate she had helped found an early childhood education centre in one village in Solear subdistrict. She was now able to use her base in that institution to get votes in the village and its surrounding, where many people appreciated her contribution. But she also promised several concrete development

---

[10] Field notes, 14 Mar. 2014.

programmes for the area, which she said she would fund from the district budget, including aspiration funds, if elected. One was a clean water programme: the state water company was not yet servicing the area and people were instead drawing poor-quality water from wells. Ani also wanted to introduce training programmes for high school drop-outs, improve roads and increase community security by funding more neighbourhood guard posts.[11]

However, Ani did not limit her campaigning to promises of this sort; with her team, led by her husband, she also gave out three packages of instant noodles to each household she visited during house-to-house campaigning. She had been doing this for a long time, from August 2013 right until election day in April 2014. Riri, the PBB candidate often criticised an unnamed Demokrat candidate for handing out instant noodles in Solear; it seems she was targeting Ani.

In fact, these candidates used patronage politics that was quite similar to that of male candidates. Plenty of male candidates gave donations to places of worship or paid for small-scale kampung infrastructure like Nida, engaged in constituency service like Riri, or gave out small gifts of foodstuffs like Ani. What made these candidates distinct was how household dynamics interacted with their campaigns: none of the many male candidates I observed had success teams headed by their wives, and certainly none of them had replaced their wives when the latter had been unable to fulfil their own ambitions to stand. As far as I could tell, at most they positioned their wives as campaign supporters, and some did not even go this far.

In the end, as already noted, none of these three women was elected. Only two women succeeded in electoral district I: a Hanura candidate, and a PDI-P candidate. In all of Tangerang district, only 7 women were elected to the district parliament, an increase of 2, but given that there were 50 seats, this was only 14 per cent of those available, falling far short of the 30 per cent quota of women candidates.

---

[11] Interview, Ani, 17 Mar. 2014.

CONCLUSION

Much has been written about the patriarchal nature of Indonesian politics and how traditional views of women belonging in the private sphere of family life and the household continue to constrain women's public agency, including in politics.[12] The introduction of a 30 per cent quota for the nomination of women to legislative bodies has generally been seen as one tool to challenge male domination of political life, though many commentators see the requirement as not going far enough. Quotas have proved in some countries to be an important first means to break down gender stereotypes which see the public sphere and democratic politics as a male space.[13]

Other authors have highlighted weaknesses in the quota requirement itself, and pointed to other impediments women candidates face (such as unsupportive party hierarchies and lack of access to financial resources) as additional reasons for why women remain poorly represented in Indonesian legislative bodies.[14] My analysis complements such views by providing a micro-analysis of how some women become candidates and organise their campaigns. The three case studies suggest one important issue is that, for some women candidates, the husband still exercises a dominant role in determining campaign strategies and even in deciding whether the wife should enter politics at all. It is hardly surprising that the nomination of women candidates through the quota system in such circumstances will not always produce female engagement in ways that challenge traditional gender roles or allow women to act autonomously. To some extent, ironically, these women's political engagement was an extension of their husbands' frustrated political ambitions.

The construction of women as merely objects rather than subjects of the political process was far more blatant, however, in the campaigns run by male candidates that I witnessed. Women performers frequently

---

[12] See, for example, Julia Suryakusuma, *Agama, Seks, dan Kekuasaan* [Religion, Sex, and Power] (Depok: Komunitas Bambu, 2012).

[13] United Nations Development Program (UNDP) Indonesia, *Partisipasi Perempuan dalam Politik dan Pemerintahan* [Women's Participation in Politics and Government] (Jakarta: UNDP, 2010).

[14] Bessell, "Increasing the Proportion of Women".

provided the entertainment at election rallies, for example, singing *dangdut* songs and swaying sensually in front of mostly male crowds. In one PPP function, the male candidate allowed male participants to come up onto the stage and *menyawer* these performers—dance suggestively with them and offer them money. Another type of gender bias was visible at a PDI-P event where the candidate exclusively directed his patronage politics—"door prizes" consisting of kitchen utensils and other household items—to the women who were present, as if suggesting that women voters only respond to material incentives, especially those that evoke the household domain.

So it was important that these three women engaged in the political process as candidates, even if the context and framework of their campaigns were largely determined by men. We can also see that there were significant differences between them. Of the three, Riri was most constrained, being both politically and economically dependent on her husband. Nida was relatively independent economically, and though new to politics, developed considerable confidence in her ability to reach out to voters. Ani was the most autonomous of all, having political skills derived from her professional background and previous campaigning experiences. All three candidates used, in part, networks of women that were open to them not only because of their husbands, but also because of their own connections. And all of them gained new confidence and experience from their campaigns. Even Riri found a sense of empowerment in her new-found ability to help poor women access health services. Moreover, we should remember to view these three women *not* as representatives of all women candidates in Indonesia; clearly, many women candidates exercise greater political agency and enjoy greater political success.

There is one more sobering conclusion to be derived from these accounts, however, and that concerns money politics. These three stories do not suggest that women engage in patronage politics in ways that differ substantially from male candidates. The main determinant of the type and extent of material distribution they organised was instead household wealth and the networks they could access. As the quotation which started this essay made clear, Riri was the one candidate who did not engage much in material distribution, but she was also the poorest. If lack of access to material resources is a key impediment to female success in a political system fuelled by money, it is perhaps not surprising that women candidates trying to break into the system will use patronage politics like their male rivals. If many women who become candidates do so because they are spouses of men who lack the resources to become candidates themselves, it is equally unsurprising that women candidates will often lack the resources to fare well in patronage-based competition.

chapter 10

Central and South Jakarta: Social Welfare and Constituency Service in the Metropolis

Sita W. Dewi, S.L. Harjanto and Olivia D. Purba

This chapter focuses on electoral district II in Indonesia's capital city, Jakarta. The legislative election in this constituency, made up of the districts of South and Central Jakarta, is distinctive for several reasons. First, Jakarta II contains some of Indonesia's wealthiest voters. Jakarta is behind only oil-rich East Kalimantan province in gross regional product per capita, but it is far ahead of other provinces in prosperity measures such as the Human Development Index. Of course, not all of Jakarta's voters are middle class or wealthy, but there are more such voters here than in other parts of Indonesia. Second, there are some peculiar characteristics of election administration in the capital and this electoral district in particular. Unlike other regions, there are no elections at the district (*kabupaten*) or municipality (*kota*) level in Jakarta: residents vote only for representatives in the provincial and national parliaments. Jakarta II also happens to be the electoral district where votes cast by all expatriate voters are counted: any Indonesian overseas votes not for a candidate in that person's home town or village, but for one in this electoral district. Thus, candidates running in Jakarta II had the option of appealing not only to Jakarta residents, but also to expatriate Indonesians. Third, residents of Jakarta in 2014 were casting their votes in the shadow of a major nationwide political phenomenon that was rooted in their home city: the rise to prominence of Joko Widodo. Jokowi, as he is popularly known, was elected as Jakarta governor in September 2012, grabbed national attention at that time, rose meteorically to the top of opinion polls as the country's preferred next president in 2013, and was announced as the PDI-P's presidential candidate just before the legislative campaign began in 2014. Many people wondered how a "Jokowi effect" would shape voting patterns in Jakarta, and some PDI-P candidates tried hard to take advantage of the governor's popularity.

Despite these factors, we find that in many ways electoral dynamics in Jakarta II resembled those in other parts of the country. Most candidates targeted poorer voters and used patronage to attract their support. To be sure, we found relatively little of the one-on-one retail vote buying that occurs elsewhere in Indonesia. But there was much delivery of club goods—small-scale projects for communities, often with the neighbourhood and subneighbourhood (RW and RT) heads acting as brokers. As elsewhere, candidates mostly built personal campaign machines rather than relying on party structures to do their campaigning, and many used religious, ethnic and other networks to reach voters. There were, however, many candidates who combined these approaches with more programmatic appeals, media strategies and appeals to middle-class voters. Above all, electioneering in Jakarta was characterised by what might be called *clientelist social welfare*: many voters wanted access to health, education and other services; many candidates strove to deliver such services in ways that would generate personal political debts.

BACKGROUND: NEW POLITICS IN THE NATIONAL CAPITAL?

Jakarta electoral district II contains many of Indonesia's major public buildings and urban landmarks, from the presidential palace, the major financial and commercial centre of Jalan Thamrin-Sudirman to the national parliament building, as well as a plethora of hotels, shopping malls and skyscrapers. It also houses some of the wealthiest residential neighbourhoods in the country, including leafy and long-established elite suburbs like Menteng and Kebayoran Baru, as well as a growing number of multistorey apartment buildings for middle-class professionals.

Yet Jakarta is also a city of great contrasts. Jakarta's population is 9.6 million, according to the 2010 census, but the city proper—Daerah Khusus Ibukota, the Capital City Special Region—blurs into a much greater urban metropolis, including the industrial zones of Bekasi in the east and Tangerang to the west. Each working day the city's population swells by about 3 million, as commuters travel from distant suburbs to their workplaces, and then leave again at night. Though the sprawling urban slums of past decades are now much reduced, there are still many crowded urban kampung where families live in dense and unsanitary conditions. In 2014, only 3.9 per cent of the population of the capital lived below the poverty line, the lowest proportion of any province.[1] However, according to the governor, some 40 per cent of Jakartans were vulnerable to falling into poverty should they be affected by a major life crisis or in the event of an economic downturn.[2]

Jakarta has massive challenges in terms of urban planning and development: the city suffers from overcrowding, land conflicts, flooding, poor-quality water and other facilities, and appalling traffic congestion. Public discontent with the poor quality of life was part of the background of Jokowi's election as governor in 2012.[3] A populist politician known for his trademark ability to connect with ordinary people, especially the poor, Jokowi also promised to wage war on corruption in the city administration, improve the quality of government services, and deal with major urban challenges such as flooding and traffic congestion. He also strongly emphasised improved education and health, and introduced a free healthcare system that was very popular and which generated a spike in health services utilisation.

---

[1] According to Badan Pusat Statistik, 2014, available at: http://www.bps.go.id.

[2] Sita W. Dewi, "RI Tycoons Lend City a Hand", *Jakarta Post*, 27 Feb. 2013, available at: http://www.thejakartapost.com/news/2013/02/27/ri-tycoons-lend-city-a-hand. html.

[3] Abdul Hamid, "Jokowi's Populism in the 2012 Jakarta Gubernatorial Election", *Journal of Current Southeast Asian Affairs* 33, 1 (2014): 85–109.

In other ways, however, politics in Jakarta have not deviated far from standard post-*reformasi* patterns. Other post-Suharto governors in the capital, Sutiyoso (1997–2007) and Fauzi Bowo (2007–12), were both old-style patronage politicians with roots deep in Suharto-era politics. Neither have previous legislative elections in Jakarta produced extraordinary results (though many candidates for DPR seats here are prominent national politicians, celebrities and other public figures). Voting in Jakarta tends to follow national trends. For example, in 2009 and 2014 the seven DPR seats elected from Jakarta II went five to two to nationalist over Islamic parties (in 2009 three seats went to Partai Demokrat, in 2014 PDI-P took two; other parties gained only a seat each). In the provincial legislature, Partai Demokrat also dominated in 2009, with 32 of the 94 seats; in 2014, as we shall see, a "Jokowi effect" put PDI-P in first place.

CANDIDATE STRATEGIES AND PATRONAGE POLITICS

How then, did legislative candidates in Jakarta go about campaigning in 2014? With few exceptions, most candidates said that they targeted voters from lower socioeconomic strata— "middle to lower" (*menengah ke bawah*) is the standard Indonesian term. This was largely because these voters constituted a majority. But it was also because they were easier to access. It was relatively simple, as we shall see, for candidates to find brokers who could arrange meetings for them with residents in the dense urban kampung where poor voters live cheek by jowl. It was more difficult to access wealthier residents in their apartment buildings, gated communities or locked private residences. Wealthier residents typically have much less to do with their neighbours, and lack influential community leaders who can act as vote brokers. Moreover, candidates tend to assume that wealthier and better-educated voters in places like Menteng would have already made up their minds about who they were voting for, so it would be a waste to approach them personally.

In reaching out to poor voters, there were four preliminary steps that candidates took. First, candidates mapped out areas to target where they thought their potential vote was high. Sometimes they did so on the basis of previous election returns. Eriko Sotarduga, a PDI-P DPR incumbent, employed a professional consultancy firm to map areas where he had received the highest number of votes in 2009, identifying 51 *kelurahan* (urban precincts) which he then made a special focus. Some PDI-P candidates identified areas where Jokowi had done particularly well in 2012, and made these their focus. Candidates also targeted areas where they had personal or network connections, or where they had a history of providing patronage and constituency service.

Second, candidates established "success teams" whose job was to reach out to voters in these target areas. Most teams adopted the basic structure of territorial organisation found throughout Indonesia. The largest team we found was that of PDI-P provincial candidate Prasetio Edi Marsudi, who claimed to have 9,000 "volunteers" (*relawan*) in his team, spread across 9 subdistricts (Prasetio was elected and became speaker of the DPRD). More typical was the team of Taufiqurrahman Rusdi (a Partai Demokrat incumbent in the DPRD) who claimed to have about 300 people involved, spread across 8 subdistricts, and organised into a pyramid of managers, subdistrict coordinators, *kelurahan* coordinators and RW (neighbourhood) coordinators. Depending on the candidate's resources, some of the people occupying apex positions in these structures were paid honoraria, but typically these were modest, in the vicinity of Rp 400,000 to 2.5 million, though at different rates (thus the Rp 400,000 payment was for distributing flyers, the higher payment was a monthly salary). In addition, candidates also worked through whatever social networks they had access to in order to mobilise support. Wibi Andrino, from Nasdem, partly relied on a network of cyclists he was part of; Firman Abadi (more commonly known as Dibo Piss), a PAN candidate, was known for his association with the famous rock band, Slank, and he drew on the network of "Slankers", as the fans of the group are known. More typically, candidates used ethnic or religious networks: thus Ruddin Akbar Lubis, a DPRD incumbent representing Golkar, claimed to have a network through the Islamic organisation Al Jamiyatul Washliyah, an Islamic organisation through which he could secure 6,000 votes.

Third, candidates then mobilised their teams to boost their name recognition by distributing paraphernalia: posters, banners, stickers and suchlike through areas identified as targets. As a result, even the narrow alleyways that wind through Jakarta's most crowded housing areas were festooned with banners and posters. Some candidates, aware of the saturation advertising on the roadsides, tried to cut through the noise by using more inventive methods. One PDI-P candidate paid street cleaners and coffee sellers Rp 500,000 to wear his T-shirts. A PKS candidate gave out bottles of chilli sauce with his picture on them; as he put it: "Chilli sauce is a basic component of the menu for all Jakartans. So if they eat, they will remember me."[4]

Fourth, these success teams organised various forms of *blusukan*—a term for meet-the-people campaigning popularised by Jokowi. Most candidates believed that direct personal contact with voters was critical for success. Jokowi used the term *blusukan* for meetings in public spaces such as marketplaces; candidates used it to describe face-to-face meetings of all sorts. The typical method was small meetings facilitated by RW or RT leaders, but a huge variety of contact points were possible: visiting religious gatherings organised by *majelis taklim* or *kelompok pengajian* (Islamic study groups) and Pembinaan Kesejahteraan Keluarga (PKK, Family Welfare Guidance) or *arisan* (communal savings) group meetings involving the women of a particular locale were common. The basic goal was to ensure that as many voters as possible felt they had some personal connection with the candidate and could have easy access should they need anything in the future. Some candidates thus took extraordinary efforts to make themselves accessible: Firman Abadi in his visits to kampung distributed material that listed not only his telephone numbers, but also his contact details via five forms of social media: BlackBerry Messenger (BBM), Twitter, Facebook, Yahoo Messenger and WhatsApp. The goal was to convince constituents that they could contact him whenever, and through whatever medium, they wanted to.

Beyond those basic steps, perhaps the most striking thing about election campaigning in the capital was that so many candidates— at least, the truly competitive ones—emphasised delivery of what in many settings would be considered part of normal government service: provision of healthcare or ambulances, repairs of roads, help with accessing government agencies, and so on. The basic thinking motivating

---

[4] Confidential interview, 7 Mar. 2014.

this strategy was simple. In Jakarta, as throughout the country, most candidates believed that voters were not interested in vague programmes or general promises about what the government could deliver to the country, or city, as a whole. Instead, they believed, "What the people need, what they hope for, is concrete things."[5] Or, put a little more crudely: "The people only think about their stomachs".[6]

In providing such concrete benefits, most candidates avoided giving direct cash payments to voters. To be sure, many handed out small gifts and keepsakes when they met constituents. But most patronage came in the form of club goods (donations conferring some collective benefit to a community) or constituency service. Most candidates thus insisted that they avoided "money politics" even as they relied on patronage as their main strategy. For example, a PDI-P DPRD candidate, Prasetio Edi Marsudi, differentiated between "political costs" and "money politics", with the latter consisting of cash payments to supporters, which he eschewed. Donations of assistance that would benefit communities, however, fell into the "political cost" category:

> [Fixing] damaged roads, public lavatories or bathing facilities, [supplying] street lighting, or carpets in a *musholla*—that's all fine. Those are part of my political costs. But giving money to them? I don't do that. Money feeds pragmatic politics. What I do makes me closer to them.[7]

Some of the stronger candidates had sophisticated machinery to provide constituents with such benefits. One of the most elaborate was that of Ruddin Akbar Lubis, a Golkar DPRD incumbent. Shortly after being elected in 2009 he established a non-profit organisation known as the "Rudal Family" through which he provides social assistance to poor residents, with the goal of maintaining connections with his campaign team and constituents. In particular, he opened health clinics in three neighbourhoods where he got a high vote in 2009: Utan Panjang, Menteng and Pegangsaan (the latter two clinics are called Rudal Medika). They are open every weekday, offering free treatment

---

[5] Interview, Latifa Al-Ansori, Nasdem DPR candidate, 11 Mar. 2014.
[6] Interview, PAN candidate success team member, 29 Mar. 2014.
[7] Interview, Prasetio Edi Marsudi, 4 Mar. 2014.

to the poor but charging wealthier patients, and funded, Rudal said, by his own contributions with help from relatives and friends. During the campaign in 2014 he handed out coupons offering free check-ups to an additional 3,000 voters for each clinic, explaining that this was an effective electioneering technique: "If we give people coupons for free medicine, they are really happy."[8] His Rudal Family staff collected data on the recipients, with the implicit understanding that they would repay their free treatment with votes.

Eriko Sotarduga, a PDI-P DPR incumbent, by contrast, emphasised fogging—spraying insecticide throughout a kampung in order to kill the mosquitoes that spread the dengue fever that is endemic in Jakarta. This method was popular with candidates. Eriko explained that he favoured fogging not only because it was relatively cheap, but also because it was an effective way to meet constituents and demonstrate his usefulness to them: while the fogging was going on, people had to leave their houses for three hours, during which time Erico would have the opportunity to personally greet about 1,000 people. Eriko also ran a programme during the campaign period which he called "Kampung Eriko" in six *kelurahan* (precincts), through which he offered various benefits: free motorcycle servicing, free haircuts and free medical consultations. Eriko claimed that people were likely to remember such services, and that though constituents often teasingly asked him for money he was never tempted to engage in individual vote buying, both because this was disallowed and because, "even if you give it to them, it's far from certain that they'll vote for you".[9] He funded the activities, he claimed, from the corporate social responsibility budget of his motorcycle spare-part shops; in fact, Eriko is a rich man, and also owns oil palm plantations in Riau and Kalimantan, gas stations and automobile workshops.

Other examples included Bambang Marsono, a Hanura DPR candidate, who handed out hundreds of thousands of brochures offering a 75 per cent discount in student fees at an Economics High School in Rawamangun which he owned.[10] Yora Lovita Haloho, a Gerindra DPR

[8] Interview, Ruddin Akbar Lubis, 4 Apr. 2014.
[9] Interview, Eriko Sotarduga, 29 Mar. 2014.
[10] Interview, Bambang Marsono, 13 Mar. 2014.

candidate, through her "Yora Centre" got her success team to compile lists of voters who pledged to support her. She promised constituents that should any registered voter die she would provide payments of Rp 500,000 to assist with the funeral costs, and made more than 20 such payments.[11] Like many candidates, she also provided a free ambulance service, with ambulances on standby at her Center and ready to be used whenever any of her field coordinators called in to say a community member was in need. Firman Abadi (Dibo Piss), the PAN candidate mentioned above, also ran a free ambulance service, and funded Quran lessons for orphans and children.

CONSTITUENCY SERVICE

As well as funding benefits directly, many candidates also emphasised their ability to deliver what in many settings is known as constituency service: helping residents in their dealings with government agencies, especially those providing education, health or other programmes. In other words, candidates—especially incumbents—positioned themselves as intermediaries between their constituents and the government's own social welfare machinery.

DPRD candidates from parties close to the city government offered citizens help in accessing the government's new social programmes. For example, Wa Ode Herlina was a PDI-P candidate trying (unsuccessfully) for the third time to get into the DPRD. She had been a member of Jokowi's campaign team and had formed an NGO, Sahabat Jakarta (Friends of Jakarta), at the time of the 2012 gubernatorial election, through which she helped poor residents who were experiencing difficulties, especially in relation to health, education, land disputes or getting on the population register and accessing ID cards. A lot of what she offered was help in accessing the government bureaucracy, even, if necessary, by arranging meetings with the governor or his deputy: "The image in the community is that if I get involved, your problem gets solved", she said.[12] Likewise, Michael Victor Sianipar,

---

[11] Interview, Yora Lovita Haloho, 12 Apr. 2014.
[12] Interview, Wa Ode Herlina, 18 Mar. 2014.

a Gerindra candidate who was part of the deputy governor's personal staff, helped citizens to get birth certificates for their children, and in his campaign meetings explained to residents how they could get the "Healthy Jakarta Cards" and the "Smart Jakarta Cards" in order to access Jokowi's signature programmes. He also explained that the Jakarta budget in 2013 made available aspiration funds totalling around Rp 2.5 trillion, which DPRD members could access for neighbourhood development programmes. (The total amount of these funds is set every year during negotiations between the DPRD and the provincial government, and was particularly high in 2014, allegedly due to the election.)

In fact, it was not only candidates linked to the city government who could provide such services. For example, Kastorius Sinaga, a Partai Demokrat DPR candidate, provided not only services which he personally funded—including fogging—but also assistance for residents who wanted to obtain birth certificates, who needed financial help when a family member died, or who wanted scholarships for their children—all provided through various Jakarta government programmes. Much of his focus was thus on assisting people to get documentation or financial aid to which they were entitled from government agencies: Sinaga provided expert staff who could tell people about their entitlements, assist them to fill in forms and even accompany them to relevant offices.

Of course, such assistance was provided with the expectation that the recipients would reciprocate with their votes. Typically, success team members would keep a list of the persons who had been helped by a candidate, either in the lead-up to the election or earlier. They would then contact them close to the election and remind them of this help. Agus, a success team member for a Partai Demokrat candidate explained, "Usually, they understand straight away, [saying:] 'Oh, of course my whole family and I will vote [for the candidate].'"[13] Other candidates tried to reduce some of the uncertainty by locking in blocs of votes at the community level by drawing up "political contracts" under which they promised to provide benefits to residents of a community, in return for votes. Taufiqurrahman Rusdi, a DPRD incumbent from Partai Demokrat, for example, had spent much of his

---

[13] Interview, Agus, 2 Apr. 2014.

time in office providing various social programmes to constituents, with the expectation they would reciprocate at election time. During the campaign period proper, he visited many communities where his team members prepared "political contracts" which were signed on behalf of the residents whose names were compiled on voter lists in particular neighbourhoods. The contracts included eight items that he promised residents, including help in getting land certificates for their residences (a major issue in a city which in past generations was settled largely by way of squatting), assistance in getting birth certificates—without charge—for their children, and three-monthly visits to check on how his promises were being realised.

Critically, access to urban neighbourhoods for many candidates was mediated by neighbourhood-level brokers. Very often, these were the RW and RT heads—the elected heads of local neighbourhood government units responsible for basic community government functions such as household registration and documentation and basic community services. As Taufiqurrahman Rusdi put it, "The RT head, the RW head, they are usually guiding lights, respected figures in their own areas. If you can bring on board the RT/RW head, then you have a good chance of getting votes there."[14] Candidates viewed these figures as a bridge between themselves and residents, and as the key to unlocking access to grassroots voters. Accordingly, most worked hard to draw such persons into their success teams, or at least to get them to facilitate neighbourhood meetings, typically involving 20 to 100 voters at a time. Sometimes, candidates offered special benefits to bring them on board: for example, Kastorius Sinaga provided free cataract operations for RT/RW heads who needed them.

In many cases it was the RT/RW heads who took the initiative in contacting candidates, with the goal of seeing what benefits they could get for their community, while perhaps also making some money on the side. Often they did so by way of local "communication forums" of the RT/RW heads in a particular locality. For example, the subdistrict coordinator of a Gerindra DPRD candidate, Maeky Robiko, recalled receiving a written proposal for a campaign event to introduce his

---

[14] Interview, Taufiqurrahman Rusdi, 2 Apr. 2014.

candidate to residents of the *kelurahan* of Mangga Dua Selatan. The proposal came from a local "Coordination Forum" of the RT and RW and requested a budget of Rp 6 million for the event, covering food, drinks and "transport money" for participants. He managed to knock the price down to Rp 2.5 million.[15]

Of course, RT/RW heads were not the only conduit for accessing urban neighbourhoods. Many candidates also worked through community-based organisations, such as PKK groups or neighbourhood youth groups (*karang taruna*). Islamic party candidates sometimes substituted, or at least supplemented, networking through neighbourhood government structures with networking through religious institutions. They also adjusted their patronage distribution accordingly: rather than (or in addition to) contributing to neighbourhood improvement schemes, they provided donations to *majelis taklim* or *kelompok pengajian* (Islamic study groups), mosques, Islamic associations, *pesantren* and other religious bodies. They gave either cash or goods (such as loudspeakers, carpets and water pumps) that would be useful to such institutions. In such cases, substituting for the role of the RT/RW heads as the key vote brokers were *majelis taklim* heads, members of Mosque Welfare Councils (Dewan Kemakmuran Masjid, DKM), and *ustad* or *ustadzah* (male or female preachers). One DPR candidate from PKS, for example, mentioned that he regularly gave donations of Rp 500,000 to *majelis taklim* he visited during the campaign.[16] A Jakarta DPRD incumbent from the same party gave Rp 1 million in donations to *majelis taklim* and also helped direct government grants (*dana hibah*) to religious organisations in his constituency.

Reaching out to community members through religious networks was thus not far different from using neighbourhood government or other associations. Religious networks were simply another way of accessing voters, and what politicians offered members of these groups was similar to what they offered other voters: access to government patronage and personalised assistance. Thus, at a meeting with a Quranic study group in Cilandak, South Jakarta, Abdul Wahid Maktub, a PKB

---

[15] Interview, Maeky Robiko, 16 Mar. 2014.
[16] Confidential interview, 7 Mar. 2014.

candidate and former ambassador to Qatar, promised: "If you ladies vote for me, then you will have a friend as a member of parliament. If that's the case, then everything will be easy if you experience a problem. I will help you."[17]

Finally, it should be emphasised that the social welfare approach to political campaigning described above did not just deliver votes. It also helped create personalised political networks. Candidates created success teams partly by drawing in beneficiaries of their social welfare assistance or other largesse. Out of many possible examples, let us mention Aca, a success team member of a Demokrat incumbent in the DPRD. Aca was campaigning for this candidate in his neighbourhood in Galur, Central Jakarta, where he was an RT official. Aca had been helped some years back, when the candidate paid the fees when one of Aca's children had to be hospitalised. After the candidate won in 2009, Aca started working for the NGO the candidate had established to run his social programmes. Another example is Ruhiyat, a member of the success team of a Golkar candidate. Ruhiyat lived in Pegangsaan, Central Jakarta, and had first developed a relationship with the candidate when he joined his success team in 2009. After the candidate won in 2009, he became a manager of one of the clinics he had established to serve his constituents and received a scholarship from the candidate to support his further studies. Within almost every strong candidate's success team, we found such relationships: relationships rooted in the exchange of material assistance—sometimes, assistance at critical moments in the recipient's life cycle—for political support. Classic clientelistic relationships lay at the heart of the city's politics.

ALTERNATIVES TO PATRONAGE

Yet patronage politics was not all there was to the election in Jakarta II. We also found candidates—even if they were a minority—who also emphasised programmatic appeals. For example, Bondan Winarno, a well-known journalist and presenter of television cooking shows

---

[17] Field observations, 31 Mar. 2014.

who was running for Gerindra in the DPR, promoted an "*Indonesia Bergizi*" (Nutrition for Indonesia) programme, highlighting the need for better nutrition and introducing healthy Indonesian food to voters. The PAN candidate Yoga Dirga Cahya promoted a "*kampanye putih*" (white campaign), which he conceived as a social movement of young professionals to restore public faith in political life by rejecting money politics and "black campaigns". Special cases were candidates for the provincial parliament who were associated with Governor Joko Widodo (PDI-P) and Basuki Tjahaja Purnama (Gerindra) and who tried to ride on the coattails of their popular programmes. Thus, it was common for PDI-P and Gerindra DPRD candidates to stress the success of the city's new "pro-people" programmes, especially in health and education, and to promise that these programmes would continue if their parties won handsomely in the election. PDI-P candidates often featured photographs of Jokowi in their publicity material. And there was a real "Jokowi effect" in the results of the election in Jakarta, with PDI-P attaining over 25 per cent of seats in the Jakarta DPRD, up from 20 per cent in 2009.

Although, as noted above, most candidates focused on mobilising lower-class voters, some did target the middle classes. Those who did so generally felt they possessed some sort of reputational advantage among such voters. The best example was the aforementioned Bondan Winarno, who made maximum use of his high media profile and reputation as a celebrity chef, visiting diners at "culinary precincts" famous for their roadside eating stalls to hand out leaflets and discuss his platform. He also paid an SMS-blasting firm to send out mass messages to 200,000 mobile telephone numbers with material on matters culinary as well as his candidacy, and adjusting the message to the recipient (thus, young women learned about fruits or vegetables that make one's skin beautiful, housewives received favourite family recipes). Damayanti "Ine" Hakim, a PAN DPR candidate and well-known socialite, and owner of a famous PR company, also targeted upper and middle-class voters, focusing on elite *arisan* and similar networks.

Another feature that distinguished Jakarta candidates from others is that on average they expended more energy and resources on traditional and social media strategies. Many of them saw media campaigns as the main way to reach wealthier voters, even as they focused patronage delivery in poor neighbourhoods. Some candidates employed special consultants to manage their social media campaigns (social media has very high penetration in Jakarta; it is, for example, the biggest Twitter city in the world). Others expended significant funds on advertising in traditional print and electronic media.

Finally, the fact that the votes of Indonesian expatriates were counted in Jakarta II opened up an entirely new constituency. We were not able to observe at first hand how candidates organised their campaigns overseas. But we did come into contact with several candidates who focused to varying degrees on expatriate voters. For example, Yoga Dirga Cahya was a young PAN candidate for the DPR who was a long-time resident of Singapore, where he had pursued university studies. He was recruited to the party specifically with the goal of mobilising the expatriate vote, and he ran a campaign that heavily focused on gaining support from Indonesian domestic workers, especially in Singapore and Hong Kong. He had a large campaign team in these countries, about 300 people in total. He also relied strongly on social media, and on promoting both individual advocacy for, and policy reform on, migrant workers.[18]

A Hanura candidate, Sayyid Tohir Bin Yahya, as well as forming success teams in South and Central Jakarta, did the same in Malaysia, a country with approximately one million Indonesian voters, or about half of the expatriate total. Tohir aimed to get about 300,000 votes from Indonesian construction sector and plantation workers there. He sent four *kyai* from Madura and East Java to Malaysia in order to mobilise voters from their home regions.[19] In the end, he complained, the electoral committee in Malaysia did not provide sufficient "drop boxes" (mobile polling booths) in his supporters' workplaces and he fell far short of his target, getting less than 20,000 votes in Malaysia.

We heard from some candidates that vote buying was common among Indonesian migrant workers in some overseas settings, notably Malaysia. We were, however, unable to verify how widespread the practice was or how it was organised, though one candidate talked about foremen at oil palm plantations acting as brokers.

---

[18] Interview, Yoga Dirga Cahya, 25 Mar. 2014.
[19] Interview, Sayyid Tohir Bin Yahya, 2 Apr. 2014.

CONCLUSION

The Jakarta electorate is generally more prosperous, better-educated and more media-savvy than voters elsewhere in Indonesia. However, although there were candidates who focused on wealthier voters and did not emphasise patronage, in general those candidates were unsuccessful. Bondan Winarno, the media personality who tried to get elected on the back of the Jakarta middle class's fascination with good eating, failed by a solid margin. So too did Yoga Dirga Cahya, the young Singapore-based PAN candidate who tried to mobilise overseas voters and middle-class Jakartans through his "white campaign". The socialite, Damayanti "Ine" Hakim, also from PAN, was likewise unsuccessful.

Candidates who succeeded were those who focused on poor neighbourhoods and built strategies around patronage delivery. In this regard, the capital proved similar to most parts of Indonesia. Yet this conclusion, too, requires qualification. First, programmatic and media campaigning were not irrelevant, even if they were rarely decisive: most successful candidates combined patronage with these other strategies. Second, the fact that the Jokowi effect was important in the capital shows that some voters were interested in programmatic delivery, given that Jokowi's reputation was so closely linked to his trademark health and education policies. A third, and perhaps most important, qualification is that the patronage politics practised in Jakarta tended to represent a rather distinctive mix. As we have seen, there were relatively few individual cash payments as found elsewhere in Indonesia. In Jakarta, most patronage politics was of what might be called a social welfare type. It often involved provision of services such as healthcare to individual voters and collective assistance with local development goals to communities, mixed with a great deal of constituency service in the form of personalised assistance to voters who wanted to access government programmes.

Clientelist politics typically flourishes in the absence of state provision of welfare protection for society's more vulnerable citizens: when citizens cannot get the social protection they need from the state, they turn to the individual politicians who can provide it. This is certainly part of the context for the patronage politics we saw in Jakarta. But Jakarta's experience was shaped by the growing importance of government social welfare schemes. The rise of local politicians such as Jokowi has shown that many Indonesian voters—at least in direct elections of local government leaders, or *pilkada*—are interested in education, healthcare and other programmes; there has been a proliferation of local healthcare schemes like Jokowi's "Healthy Jakarta" programme as a result of such local elections.[20] In this context, it is striking that, in their interactions with candidates in the more fragmented context of open-list PR elections, voters in Jakarta seemed to support candidates who provided welfare services and not simply cash or goods. Many politicians also connected voters with state agencies to help them access programmes they were legally entitled to. It seems we see in Jakarta a hybridised form of politics, caught somewhere between programmatic delivery of social welfare and the pattern of clientelistic relationships between voters and politicians we are familiar with from other parts of Indonesia.

---

[20] Edward Aspinall, "Health Care and Democratization in Indonesia", *Democratization* 21, 5 (2014): 803–23.

chapter **11**

Bekasi, West Java: From Patronage to Interest Group Politics?

Amalinda Savirani

Is it truly the case that electoral politics in Indonesia is simply a matter of money politics, patronage and transactional deals? This chapter seeks to test the patronage perspective on Indonesian politics by providing a case study of the electoral politics of the metalworkers' movement.[1] In 2014, this movement tried to break into formal politics by having some of its cadres nominated as legislative candidates in the district (*kabupaten*) of Bekasi, east of Jakarta. These cadres took the bold step of standing as candidates, though they did not have much money. They called this experiment *"buruh go politics"* (workers go into politics). Through this effort they tried to resist money politics by organising and mobilising movement cadres as the backbone of their campaign. These volunteers were unpaid.

Other writers have looked at previous attempts, in 2004 and 2009, by Indonesian workers to enter the electoral arena.[2] These studies

---

[1] The author thanks Iqbal Basyari who assisted in carrying out data collection in the field, but takes full responsibility for the contents of this article. She also thanks Michele Ford for her comments.
[2] Teri Caraway and Michele Ford, "Labor and Politics under Oligarchy", in *Beyond Oligarchy: Wealth, Power, and Contemporary Indonesian Politics*, ed. Michele Ford

focused on electoral experiments in the industrial areas of Tangerang and Bekasi, but these were attempts that were not fully backed by the relevant unions (SPN in Tangerang and FSPMI in Bekasi) and which were carried out without strong mapping of union membership in the relevant constituencies. In Bekasi in 2009, worker candidates ran with small parties, and many union members did not even know they were competing. As a result, these early efforts were disappointing.

The study presented here focuses on the 2014 election and contextualises the workers' campaign in terms of the centrality of patronage in Indonesian electoral politics.[3] In doing so, it also touches on two other topics: linkages between social movements located in civil society and parties located in political society; and the character of the contemporary Indonesian workers' movement, and specifically whether it is shifting from focusing on issues of concern only to workers toward broader programmatic politics.

BACKGROUND: A WORKERS' TERRITORY WITH WORKER CADRES

The district of Bekasi, located about 30 km east of central Jakarta, has a population of about 2.8 million, of whom about 70 per cent are of working age. About 450,000 work in the formal sector. There were just over 2 million voters in the district, with 568 candidates competing for 50 seats in the district's DPRD.

Bekasi is one of Indonesia's main industrial zones. Official statistics list 864 manufacturing plants in the district, producing, among other

and Thomas Pepinsky (Ithaca, NY: Southeast Asia Program, Cornell University, 2014), pp. 139–56; Michele Ford, Teri Caraway and T. Nugroho, "Translating Membership into Power at the Ballot Box? Trade Union Candidates and Worker Voting Patterns in Indonesia's National Election", *Democratization* 22, 7 (2015): 1296–1316, doi: 10.1080/13510347.2014.930130.

[3] For another account of this worker campaign, see Kirsty Hoban, "Workers Go Politics!", *Inside Indonesia* 116, Apr.–Jun 2014, available at: http://www.inside. indonesia.org/current-edition/workers-go-politics.

things, electronic components and automotive spare parts, with many of them located in seven large industrial parks: Jababeka, MM2100, Delta Mas, Lippo Cikarang, Hyundai EJIP and Bekasi Fajar.[4]

Bekasi is an area of contrasts. In the industrial parks, roads are smooth and wide, but outside them the roads are often poor, both narrow and potholed. During the rainy season, congestion is severe. Housing is divided between crowded residential zones housing workers and management-level estates, with a stark difference between the two. Lippo Cikarang, for example, is a famous and expensive middle-class estate, with house prices starting at Rp 400 million; in comparison, houses designed for labourers in the Mega Regency estate have a starting price of Rp 100 million.

Despite being a major site of industry, politics in the district are in many ways typical of those found in other peri-urban zones of Indonesia. The current *bupati* (Neneng Hasanah Yasin) and her deputy (Rohim Mintareja) were nominated by a coalition of Golkar, Demokrat and PAN. The DPRD contains a typical mixture of large and small, nationalist and Islamic parties (see Table 11.1).

CANDIDATE-REPRESENTATIVES OF THE UNION

The Indonesian Federation of Metalworkers Unions (Federasi Serikat Pekerja Metal Indonesia, FSPMI) has a strong presence in Bekasi. This union, which was formed amidst the post-Suharto liberalisation of union organisation in 1999, had 82,000 registered members in 324 factories across the country in 2014. It is known as one of the most militant unions in Indonesia, pioneering new forms of industrial action and responsible for some of the most dramatic mass mobilisations and strikes of the last decade.[5] In 2014, it encouraged its cadres to enter parliament, and to do so with institutional support, not merely as individuals.

---

[4] Badan Pusat Statistik Kabupaten Bekasi, *Bekasi dalam Angka 2012* [Bekasi in Figures 2012] (Bekasi: BPS, 2013).

[5] Edward Aspinall, "Popular Agency and Interests in Indonesia's Democratic Transition and Consolidation", *Indonesia* 96 (2013): 101–21.

Table 11.1

Bekasi District DPRD, Party Representation,

2009 and 2014

Party	Seats, 2009	Seats, 2014
Golkar	9	10
Demokrat	9	5
PKS	8	5
PDI-P	7	8
PAN	4	5
PPP	4	3
PKB	3	1
PBB	2	1
Hanura	2	2
Gerindra	1	7
Nasdem	0	3
PKP	2	0
Total	50	50

Source: KPUD Kabupaten Bekasi.

A process of strategic rethinking underpinned this decision. Union leaders have increasingly recognised that workers' interests are not confined to wages and workplace conditions, but also encompass citizen welfare issues, such as education and healthcare. They also recognise that, in order to achieve those broader goals, they will need to go beyond their existing strategies of union organisation and mobilisation. The union also learned from the 2009 elections, when several union members tried to get into parliament but did so as individuals without institutional support, and failed.[6] With formal support from the union in 2014, they believed the union would be able to instruct its members to vote for endorsed candidates, boosting their chances.

Getting into local parliaments was just one of the FSPMI's strategies to advance the workers' agenda of improved welfare. By placing its cadres by stages in legislative bodies, first in district parliaments, and later in provincial and national legislatures, the union believed that workers

---

[6] Ford et al., "Translating Membership into Power".

would gradually get access to decision-making in the policy arena. As well as going into parliament, FSPMI has involved itself in other instances of electoral politics, such as by supporting the candidacy of Rieke Diah Pitaloka (a PDI-P national legislator with a reputation for sympathy for workers' demands) in the West Java gubernatorial election in 2013. For workers, this campaign was an important training opportunity on how to organise their base for electoral purposes.

The fact that it was the union rather than individuals who were nominating the candidates, plus its large membership base in Bekasi, made the FSPMI's attempt to get its members into parliament in 2014 different from previous election campaigns involving union candidates. There is, of course, no social democratic or union-based party in Indonesia (some were attempted after 1998, but did not succeed in attracting significant electoral support), and no provision for independent candidates in legislative elections, so the union had no choice but to approach mainstream parties if it wanted its members to run. For its candidates who lacked prior party connections, the union did all the negotiating with the parties to ensure nomination (see below), and these people stood, not merely as individuals, but under formal instruction from the union. For candidates who had pre-existing party links, the union let them settle their candidacies individually, intervening only if problems arose.

In 2014, FSPMI nominated nine of its members as legislative candidates in the greater Bekasi region, including district, provincial and national races, though my discussion here focuses on district-level candidates. Two stood for the Bekasi city (*kota*) DPRD, five for the *kabupaten* and one each for the provincial and national parliaments. The five candidates running in the *kabupaten* were Nurdin Muhidin (electoral district I), Suparno (district II), Aji (district III), Susanto (district V) and Nyumarno (district VI). In Bekasi city, they were Hendi Suhendi (district II) and Masrul Zambak (district V), while the provincial and national candidates were Rustan and Iswan Abdullah respectively, both running in West Java electoral district VII.

In selecting its candidates, FSPMI tried to follow several principles, chief of which was to choose union cadres with deep organisational experience. All the candidates selected had either held (or were still holding) union leadership positions (for example, as head of the education division, or of the advocacy unit) at the district level, or had been or were still heads of its workplace units, the union's lowest level of organisation. All had good knowledge of labour issues, and had been, or were still, members of the Dewan Pengupahan (Wage Council), the government's tripartite body for fixing wages. Branch chairpersons were not allowed to stand because they were expected to take charge of organising the campaign.

The union also tried to ensure that its candidates were distributed through the six electoral districts that made up the *kabupaten* of Bekasi, and that candidates fully represented the six member unions of the federation (in the end, the candidates represented only four, namely, Serikat Pekerja Elektronik dan Elektrik [SPEE, Electronics and Electricity Workers' Union], Serikat Pekerja Aneka Industri [SPAI, Miscellaneous Industry Workers' Union], Serikat Pekerja Automotif, Mesin dan Komponen [SPAMK, Automotive, Machine and Components Union], and Serikat Pekerja Logam [SPL, Metalworkers' Union]. Initially, too, the plan was that candidates would be chosen from below.

The final agreed principle was "anti-money politics": candidates would not attempt to buy votes, either from individual voters or collectively by providing club goods. It was also agreed that the union would not pay the parties which agreed to nominate its cadres.[7] In the end, five parties were chosen as the vehicles for the union candidates: PDI-P (Nyumarno and Rustan), PAN (Nurdin Muhidin and Aji Narwi), PKPI (Suparno, Susanto and Masrul Zambak), PPP (Hendi Suhendi) and PKS (Iswan Abdullah). The choice of using multiple parties was deliberate, a strategy union activists called "zigzag politics", described below.

Some of these principles were adapted in practice. For example, the idea of selecting the candidates from the bottom up by way of a general election involving all union members was cancelled, both because time ran short and because leaders decided it would be better to focus on mobilising for the legislative election rather than for an internal one. In the end, top-down selection of candidates by the FSPMI branch took place, though the grassroots experience of candidates was still important in deciding who would run. The goal of full representation

---

[7] Interviews, Obon Tabroni, chair of Bekasi branch of FSPMI, 7 Apr. 2014; Sukamto, head of SPEE, 12 Apr. 2014.

was also not achieved, because two unions, Serikat Pekerja Dok dan Galangan Kapal (SPDG, Dock Workers and Shipbuilders Union), and Serikat Pekerja Dirgantara (SPD, Aerospace Workers Union) did not contribute candidates.

THE UNION AGAINST MONEY POLITICS

The union played the key role in nominating these worker candidates, determining who would stand, where they would stand, and through which party. The union also took responsibility for providing the logistical support and educating the volunteer team (*tim relawan*) whose job it was to mobilise voters (the union deliberately avoided using the phrase "success team" because of its money politics connotations). In short, FSPMI took care of four matters: administration of the campaign, logistics, the team and training. As noted above, it did these things within a framework of rejecting money politics, by which it meant rejecting distribution of cash or goods to parties, voters or other actors.

Even so, any political campaign entails costs. FSPMI covered most of these, paying for banners, stickers and other campaign materials. Its total expenditure on all of its nine candidates' campaigns through 2014 was Rp 200 million, a sum that is of course much smaller than that spent by many individual candidates even at the district level. As we shall see, however, many candidates also raised additional campaign funds through their Pimpinan Unit Kerja (PUK, Workplace Leadership Units) or via personal networks.

The rejection of money politics started early, at the point at which the union was seeking party vehicles for its candidates. At that time, union leaders approached leaders of various party branches in Bekasi, offering their cadres as candidates. They also said that they would not pay for these nominations (a common practice with Indonesian parties, especially when enrolling candidates who are not party cadres). But FSPMI had a strong bargaining chip: its large membership base in Bekasi. Its leaders offered the parties an attractive deal: trouble-free access to this mass base, promising that the party machine would not have to do anything to get out the union vote, which the union itself would mobilise.

Not all parties accepted this bargain. Though parties which accepted the deal could expect to boost their total party vote, the risk was that the union candidates would attain higher personal votes than other candidates nominated by these parties, beating them to legislative seats. Some party leaders were fearful of such competition and therefore rejected the deals. Others asked for money. Hendi Suhendi, a FSPMI candidate in Bekasi city, for example, was initially going to run with PAN, but the party branch asked for a payment. To be consistent with the pledge against money politics, Hendi shifted to PPP. Another worker candidate, Suparno, was initially going to stand with PDI-P in electoral district II but, because a local party leader who was also a DPRD incumbent saw him as a threat to his own re-election prospects, Suparno was rejected by the party branch. Suparno tried to shift to PAN, but because time was running short this proved impossible and he eventually ran with PKPI, a small party with limited electoral appeal.[8] In contrast, two of the unionists who ran with PDI-P, Nyumarno and Rustan, had long been active in that party, and had actively supported PDI-P member Rieke Diah Pitaloka's gubernatorial campaign in 2013.

This multi-party strategy was labelled by the worker activists as "zigzag politics", by which they meant they were not supporting any particular party at the district, provincial and national levels. Instead, they campaigned simultaneously for the various individual union candidates—which, of course, was quite possible with open-list PR—who were in most cases running for different parties. For example, in electoral district I in the *kabupaten* of Bekasi, the union supported Nurdin Muhidin, who was running with PAN, as its district candidate, Rustan (PDI-P) as its provincial candidate and Iswan Abdullah (PKS) as its DPR candidate. In electoral district III the same thing happened: here it was Aji Narwi (PAN) who was the district candidate, alongside the same higher-level PDI-P and PKS candidates. Collectively, the union labelled all its candidates a "*paket hebat*" (great packet) and they displayed banners and handed out brochures with all their photographs and party affiliations so that workers would be able to identify them.

---

[8] Interview, Suparno, 31 Mar. 2014.

No other social organisation in Bekasi engaged in this sort of "zigzag politics".

This approach had certain implications, however. In particular, the parties disliked it and protested to the FSPMI. They did not like their candidates' supporters simultaneously promoting candidates from rival parties. The union ignored such protests. Its candidates participated in party campaign events alongside other candidates from the same party, but rejected all offers or instructions to enter into "tandem" arrangements with non-union candidates at the national or provincial level, focusing on the union campaign instead. Another problem, however, was coordination between the three levels; volunteers working on the district-level campaigns in particular complained that the province and national teams made few concrete contributions and mostly depended on their district colleagues' grassroots work.

Each candidate had his own volunteer team, none of whom were paid. Team members worked only for the worker-candidate in the electoral constituency to which they were assigned. This resulted, however, in an uneven distribution of effort. Electoral district I, for instance, was the base of much industrial activism, being where many members of Garda Metal, a militant wing of FSPMI, lived. The campaign was so active and well-organised here that it gave rise to complaints from activists in other electoral districts that they were being neglected. Nyumarno, the candidate in electoral district VI, complained about favouritism in FSPMI in his online communications with fellow activists.

The zigzag strategy shows how loosely connected the union and its candidates were to the parties that were their vehicles. By openly encouraging workers to vote for candidates from different parties at different levels they were calling on them to place their identities as workers—and their loyalty to the union and unionism—above party affiliation. At the same time, the strategy was also a response to what they knew about how parties functioned. Union activists knew that union candidates would be placed low on party lists and that the parties nominating them would expend little or no effort or expense to support them—that would all be reserved for local party bosses running as candidates. If the union did not organise to get their members elected, nobody would.

CAMPAIGNING AMONG WORKERS

In order to get out the vote, and to resist the rampant vote buying that was occurring in Bekasi, the union used two separate strategies: factory-based mobilisation targeting workers, and a territorial strategy targeting general voters. Though the first strategy was more successful, both were attempts to resist patronage politics.

Campaigning among workers started with the lowest-level union organisations, the PUK (Pimpinan Unit Kerja, workplace leadership unit) in the factories. Most of the FSPMI candidates had strong roots at this level because they had themselves been PUK heads for at least two periods, or six years, except for Nyumarno (electoral district VI) who was not part of a PUK. The others, however, were well known in their own factories, because as PUK leaders they had been involved in handling industrial issues such as wage and bonus negotiations and advocacy on behalf of workers in disputes with management. The PUK are at the coalface of workers' efforts to defend and extend their rights and improve workplace conditions. The candidates' track record of leadership in these bodies typically created considerable loyalty from their fellow workers. Aji Narwi (electoral district III), for example, twice appointed as a PUK head, was famous even beyond his own factory for his fierce defence of workers' interests. He spent much time commuting between Bekasi and Bandung, where the court dealing with industrial issues is located. The first time we met, during a training session on voter mobilisation, he had just arrived from Bandung where he had been taking charge of one case. Suparno (district II) was the PUK chair in the PT Aisin Indonesia factory, a plant which employs 1,500 people. The core of his *tim relawan* consisted of four fellow PUK members at that factory. Nurdın Muhıddın (dıstrıct I) was famous as a unıon actıvıst who had done a great deal for workers in the electronics sector.

Nyumarno (district VI) was not a PUK leader, but was well known among militants and workers for other reasons. He was one of several worker activists who had played a leading role in the campaign to push the DPR to pass a new social security law in 2012, and had then set up a team to monitor the new system's implementation in Bekasi. He was not a PUK leader because the company where he had worked, PT Kymco Lippo Motor Indonesia, had gone bankrupt and closed down in

2010, leading to the dismissal of its workforce. Along with FSPMI colleagues, Nyumarno had played a leading role advocating on behalf of the sacked workers to ensure that they received severance pay. They took the company—the first manufacturer of automatic motorcycles in Indonesia—to court, winning the case, with the judges ordering the company to pay wages and other allowances that had not been paid between June 2009 and April 2010, at a total cost of Rp 7 billion.

Campaigning through the PUK took several forms, including distribution of brochures and other campaign materials, as well as mass campaign meetings in factories. The PUK were also used to mobilise financial support. Suparno, for example, got members of his PUK to donate whatever they could afford to help cover the costs of campaign materials. The candidates who either lacked a PUK (Nyumarno) or who had poor relations with their PUK (like Hendi Suhendi whose PUK was in the PT Showa factory) were at a considerable disadvantage.

The relationship between these union candidates and the worker-voters who supported them did not involve exchange of material goods for political support, so it cannot be classified as clientelistic. Instead, it involved embryonic interest group politics, with candidates chosen and supported because they had promoted the broad interests of workers. Their brochures and other material made much of the candidates' records of defending workers' rights. At public meetings and in small-scale interactions with workers, campaign volunteers tried hard to reawaken workers' memories of the past services these activists had performed. They also strove to remind workers of other achievements by these candidates, the union and the workers' movement more generally—such as successful worker participation in the district's Wage Council and resulting wage rises, or their campaign for the new social security system. When it targeted workers, the campaign single-mindedly focused on promoting working-class politics.

CAMPAIGNING AMONG NON-WORKERS

An election is, of course, all about getting as many votes as possible. These worker candidates thus needed to reach out to non-workers, whose numbers were much greater than FSPMI members in Bekasi.

Moreover, voting occurs in places of residence, not in workplaces. Even if campaigning was going well in a particular factory located in an electoral district where that factory's PUK head was standing, many of that factory's employees might reside, and thus vote, in a different district.

Campaigners divided general voters, who could be reached only through a territorial rather than a factory-based strategy, into those who lived in housing estates and those in villages. The former tended to be migrants to the area, and were generally factory workers themselves, while the latter were natives of Bekasi and were generally farmers. Labour candidates focused on migrant areas. They considered the kampung where locals lived as tough going, believing that not only were these hard core money politics areas where voters expected payments but also that many local residents disliked migrants like them, and were much influenced in their voting preferences by instructions from local community leaders.

In several electoral districts with predominantly non-factory worker populations, the campaigners established *tim relawan* based on territorial administrative divisions—housing estate, neighbourhood (RW) and subneighbourhood (RT). These teams consisted of workers who lived in the electoral district, plus local members of the nominating party. This was a standard way to organise a campaign team, with many candidates around Indonesia using exactly this pattern. In Bekasi, the formal neighbourhood (RW and RT) leaders often played the critical role in mobilising voters, acting as gatekeepers for candidates who sought to access their communities. They often acted as brokers, facilitating efforts by candidates to engage in collective vote buying by providing public facilities or services such as ambulances.[9]

Outside the factories, the logic of electoral politics is transactional. "*Cendol* money" (*cendol* is a popular sweet coconut-based iced drink) is the popular local term for the cash payments voters receive for supporting a candidate. Many voters would ask candidates for "*cendol* money" quite openly. FSPMI candidates responded to such requests by emphasising the role they had played in promoting policy changes

---

[9] Interview, Supriadi, 13 May 2014.

that benefitted the general public, especially the social security law. This method, however, was not very successful. FSPMI candidates who ran in non-working class areas, notably electoral districts II, III and IV, were all defeated.

Aji Narwi, for example, was the candidate in the largely urban electoral district III, whom I accompanied on the campaign trail. One day he visited a housing estate in the South Tambun area, going from door to door, introducing himself to residents and asking for support. Many of those he visited, especially the women, appeared very pleased, saying that they had never been visited by a candidate before. But many of them also asked for T-shirts or "*cendol* money". Aji told them that he did not want to distribute cash, but was committed to defending the interests of the general public, and joked that he was a poor candidate. In his campaign speeches, he strongly emphasised the embryonic national social security system, saying that if elected he would push the district parliament to issue a regulation to ensure its proper implementation locally. However, with no "*cendol* money" to give out to voters, Aji's efforts counted for little: he gained only about 2,300 votes, far short of what he needed.

In contrast, Suparno, who was running in electoral district II, a similar area, tried to fulfil at least some requests from residents and community leaders. In particular, he paid for fogging (pesticide spraying)—a common activity during dengue fever season—in some kampung.[10] He also approached community leaders and leaders of kampung youth groups (*karang taruna*), either providing them with modest payments or buying them things they could use collectively, such as sports equipment. His campaign thus resembled that of many mainstream candidates. FSPMI leaders were critical of this approach; one of them told me, "It's a shame Suparno spent money like this and it's not in accordance with the union's campaign principles."

Another case was Susanto, who was running through PKPI in electoral district V. He was a worker in PT Gunung Steel and spent relatively lavishly on his campaign. His campaign structure and strategy were almost identical to those of mainstream candidates. He built a

---

[10] Interview, Suparno, 31 Mar. 2014.

pyramidal success team, with *korcam* (subdistrict coordinators), *kordes* (village coordinators) and *korlap* (field coordinators). One of his team members reinvigorated part of the old success team that had been built by Taufik Hidayat, an independent who had stood as a *bupati* candidate in Bekasi in 2012. He also tried to recruit influential local community leaders such as *dukun* (shaman) and *ulama* (religious scholars) to his team. To generate personal loyalty, he distributed "pocket money" (*uang saku*) to his team members. He also had an entertainment budget to pay for karaoke sessions, meals and similar activities.

Suparno was the FSPMI candidate who spent most on his campaign, with an expenditure of about Rp 200 million which he raised personally. Much of this was money he raised by selling off land he had bought with savings, and by getting help from his parents back in their home village, who also sold land (many workers in Bekasi have assets in their home villages, typically in the form of land or small informal businesses). His willingness to risk his personal assets in this way was unusual among the worker candidates of Bekasi, but not especially unusual in Indonesian electoral politics writ large. Many candidates have inflated ideas of their own electability and are willing to risk their meagre fortunes on, or go into deep debt for, the chance to be elected as a legislator. Suparno had been planning to stand for election before the union decided on its "go politics" campaign. Though an FSPMI member, he was not particularly active; when FSPMI cadres learned that he was planning to stand they integrated him into their team. Suparno's campaign was thus rather individually focused and he tended to ignore the union's instructions, especially when it came to campaign expenditure. Even so, the money he spent on his campaign did not produce a successful outcome.

Throughout Bekasi, in the few days leading to the vote on 9 April, demands for "*cendol* money" became ever more intense. Everybody knew that envelopes containing cash payments and name cards of candidates were being distributed everywhere. Also in circulation were many "political contracts" in which candidates promised to provide water supplies, sports facilities, rubbish collection or similar facilities for residents of a particular community, typically facilitated by a village, RT or RW head. In this climate, the FSPMI campaigners erected banners with the message "Movement against money politics" (*Gerakan anti*

Table 11.2
Bekasi District, Votes for FSPMI Candidates, 2014

Name	Party	Electoral district	Personal vote	Elected?
Nurdin Muhidin	PAN	I	10,891	Yes
Nyumarno	PDI-P	VI	6,092	Yes
Suparno	PKPI	II	5,600	No
Aji	PAN	III	2,200	No
Susanto	PKPI	V	2,700	No
Total			27, 483	

Source: FSPMI team.

politik uang) at many key points, especially in the housing estates where their candidates lived.

In the end, such techniques had limited impact, and the FSPMI campaign largely failed to successfully reach out to voters beyond the ranks of organised workers. When campaigners could access voters on the factory floor or through union networks, and target them with sectoral appeals, they were generally successful. Out in the general electorate, where most voters were not factory workers, the logic of money politics was all-pervasive, and proved difficult to defeat with programmatic appeals. Even the two candidates who tried to adapt to this prevailing logic found they lacked the material resources to compete against more cashed-up candidates.

SAFEGUARDING THE VOTE

Patronage politics does not stop when votes are cast. Another arena of patronage is the vote counting and tabulation process, when officials at the polling booth level, or higher up as the votes are collated, manipulate the count to benefit certain candidates in return for payments. The FSPMI candidates tried to stop this happening by relying on their volunteers. These volunteers were unpaid. Indeed, they generally covered even their own transport costs when travelling around the constituency—something that is highly unusual in Indonesian election campaigns. The candidates only paid for their volunteers' drinks and, sometimes, food.

The candidates' homes came to resemble cafes, with coffee sachets ready for the volunteers to stir into glasses of hot water. At night-time meetings, the candidates typically provided cheap snacks or meals, but sometimes everybody chipped in to cover the costs.

On voting day, these same volunteers then became the polling booth witnesses. The Trade Union Rights Centre (TURC), an NGO with a history of training labour activists, provided special training on how to observe proceedings and identify irregularities (staff from Universitas Gadjah Mada also participated in the training). FSPMI provided enough witnesses for each polling booth in the district, and issued each of them with an official duty letter. Because they were not officially endorsed by the parties, however, these witnesses could not enter the polling booth interior (though these were as a rule open air so they could still observe the proceedings), nor could they ask for the C1 forms that recorded the polling booth results and which can provide strong evidence of fraud when tabulation is manipulated higher up. The official witnesses were provided by the parties and, as a rule, paid small fees by them.

I had the opportunity to attend one of the training sessions two nights before the vote, which was carried out in an abandoned factory that had once belonged to PT Kepsonic Indonesia, in South Cikarang. About 100 workers attended, some of whom had just returned from work and were still wearing their factory uniforms; others were about to go on the night shift. The training was clear, but the allocation of polling booths to volunteers was rather chaotic. Even so, on election day monitoring activities went well. The presence of so many volunteers helped pressure polling booth committees not to engage in fraud. I was at one polling booth at the Bumi Cikarang Makmur (BCM) housing complex, together with four FSPMI cadres. One of the committee members told me that he had been involved in vote counting three times, and had never seen so many volunteers monitoring the booth. Not all the booths were covered, however. In electoral district I, for instance, no more than 2 per cent of the 589 booths were covered. The most important phase was the counting of votes at the village level, which FSPMI cadres attended in shifts, staying at the village offices while tabulation took place.

CONCLUSION

The 2014 union election campaign marked a significant advance on previous union electoral efforts. The "workers go politics" experiment began in 2009 in various working-class areas around Indonesia, notably Bekasi, Tangerang and Batam. The 2014 experiment involved much fuller support from the union, something that was not forthcoming in 2009 in Bekasi.[11] Another difference from 2009 was that in 2014 workers decided to focus their political efforts at the lowest-level political unit, namely the districts. In 2009 in Batam, by contrast, the main target was the national parliament, and the challenges of getting elected were thus much greater.[12] The local strategy pursued in 2014 allowed workers to target their mobilisation efforts more narrowly, and it did produce some victories.

In the end, two of the worker candidates were elected (see Table 11.2). Their personal votes were not especially high, but they were high enough to defeat other candidates on their party slates. This itself caused some friction with these parties: Nurdin Muhidin, for example, was accused by other PAN candidates of profiting from their personal votes and they asked him to pay them financial compensation to cover the costs of their campaigning. The union forbade him to accede to this request.

Despite these successes, we must note some important qualifications. The two constituencies where FSPMI candidates won had particular characteristics. Nurdin Muhidin was advantaged by running in an electoral district (I) in the heart of Bekasi's industrial district where many workers lived. Most of his voters were mobilised through factory-level campaigning. Nyumarno competed in a constituency (VI) that was also heavily populated by workers and which was also a strong base for PDI-P, the party he was standing for. FSPMI candidates found it hard to break out beyond their industrial base into the general community; candidates running in non-labour constituencies faced great difficulties in competing with the transactional politics which ruled there.

---

[11] Ford et al., "Translating Membership into Power".

[12] Michele Ford, "Learning by Doing: Trade Unions and Electoral Politics in Batam, 2004–2009", *South East Asia Research* 22, 3 (2014): 341–57.

There were limits, too, to the union-focused campaign. The total of 27,483 votes for the FSPMI candidates was only a third of the total FSPMI membership of 82,457 in the *kabupaten* of Bekasi. Of course, not all of these union members lived in the district and were eligible to vote there, but many of those who did would have had spouses or other close relatives who might have been expected to also support the union candidates. Clearly, not all FSPMI members or supporters voted for the union candidates, so even the vote of this most militant of Indonesian unions was far from being consolidated.

Overall, then, how are we to understand this political experiment? As well as marking a further milestone in organised labour's steady efforts to expand its political influence in Indonesia, we can see it as a modest example of broader attempts to challenge the patronage-based and clientelistic nature of Indonesian politics with more interest-based and programmatic appeals. The FSPMI candidates stressed workers' rights and interests in appealing to a worker vote, and they tried to campaign on broader issues of welfare and social security when appealing to the general community. The former strategy obviously worked best, with the campaign offering salutary lessons about how difficult it is to challenge the transactional logic that governs the wider electoral arena. Even so, in the victory of the two candidates we can still see positive lessons about how voluntarism, organisation and militancy can reap rewards for programmatic politics even in unpropitious circumstances.

Map of West Java

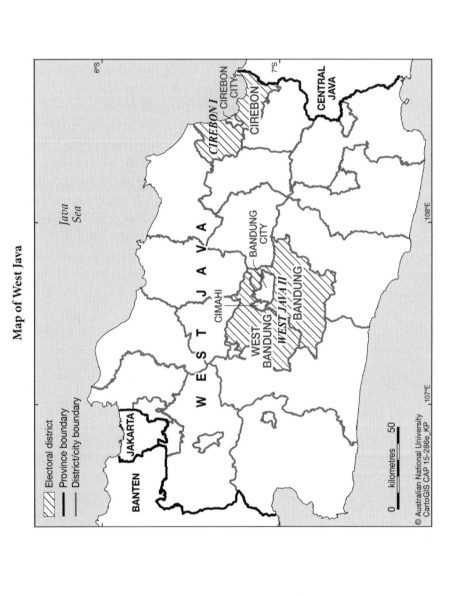

chapter 12

Bandung, West Java: *Silaturahmi,* Personalist Networks and Patronage Politics

Caroline Paskarina

This chapter provides an account of election campaigning in West Java's electoral district II, a national and provincial constituency that wraps around Bandung, Indonesia's third largest city. The focus of analysis is what virtually all the candidates I met here explained as being their core strategy: *silaturahmi*. This term most simply refers to the practice of candidates visiting communities in order to hear directly their aspirations and desires. But it also implies the forging of close personal bonds between social actors. All candidates believed this strategy was more effective than alternatives such as handing out free T-shirts or putting up banners and billboards. *Silaturahmi* has positive connotations, because it is associated with religious and social traditions. Accordingly, many voters saw face-to-face meetings as a positive way of building connections with their candidates and representatives. Generally, we can view the candidates' decision to adopt this approach as a product of the interaction between formal and informal institutions, where the formal institutions are the rules governing electoral competition and the informal institutions are norms, conventions and traditions governing social interaction.[1]

The formal institutional setting that counts, of course, is Indonesia's open-list proportional representation (PR) system, which has pushed Indonesian legislative elections toward personal competition between individual candidates, rather than programmatic competition between parties. Individual candidates prepare their own funds and campaign teams, and many voters look to what these candidates will deliver to them personally. In this context, the emergence of *silaturahmi* as a dominant mode of campaigning in 2014 was not a natural product of local culture or social structure, but rather arose from the interaction of that setting with formal electoral institutions. With formal political structures weakening—at least, many people see parties in particular as becoming weak or irrelevant—candidates turned to informal community-level institutions.

The *silaturahmi* approach in this context serves two purposes. First, it is a convenient means to present candidates to constituents in populist clothing and to furnish them with personal connections with voters. Second, it also allows candidates to build clientelistic networks down to the community level, and to strengthen those networks by injecting into them strong elements of cultural tradition and emotional bonding. As we shall see, many candidates do not simply select already influential local actors to populate their campaign networks; they often help to elevate the social status and leadership reputation of their clients by providing them with access to government funds and projects. As a result, personalist links connecting legislators and the grassroots shadow the formal institutions of both the parties and the state. After an introduction to the electoral district and the concept of *silaturahmi* campaigning, we explore how this approach connects to the distribution of patronage,

---

[1] Douglass C. North, *Institutions, Institutional Change and Economic Performance* (Cambridge: Cambridge University Press, 1990); Hans-Joachim Lauth, "The Impact of Informal Institutions on Democratic Performance: Theoretical Reflections and Empirical Findings", paper presented at the American Political Science Association Annual Meeting, 1–4 Sept. 2005, available at: http://www.allacademic.com// meta/p_mla_apa_research_citation/0/4/2/5/7/pages42574/p42574-1.php.

and to candidates' networking activities. We conclude by investigating how the approach worked in practice by focusing on two successful candidates: one who was running for a seat in the DPR, the other in the provincial DPRD.

BACKGROUND: WEST JAVA AND GRASSROOTS CAMPAIGNING

West Java is Indonesia's most populous province, with almost 33 million registered voters in the 2014 election. West Java II electoral district covers the districts (*kabupaten*) of Bandung and West Bandung, which surround the provincial capital of Bandung. Most of these two districts consist of rural areas and villages, but several regions, such as the subdistricts of Lembang (West Bandung), Cileunyi and Soreang (Bandung) are part of Bandung's peri-urban periphery. Both districts, like much of rural West Java, also have substandard infrastructure and poor transportation access. By making it harder for ordinary citizens to access formal institutions for quick solutions to their everyday problems, these conditions help nurture clientelistic politics. Thus, community leaders often act as mediators between citizens and government elites. Accordingly, ordinary people are often more inclined to invest politically in building personal relations with leaders who can provide them with direct benefits, than in hoping for systemic change.

In West Java, mainstream moderate nationalists have generally dominated electoral politics. Throughout the New Order years the province was a bastion of Golkar; PDI-P was placed first in 1999, followed by Golkar in 2004 and Partai Demokrat in 2009, with PDI-P regaining the top position in 2014. In West Java II, the map is similar: in 2009 the first-placed party was Partai Demokrat, followed by PDI-P and Golkar, and then various Islamic and nationalist parties; in 2014 the big three were PDI-P, Golkar and Gerindra at the national level, though at the provincial level it was PDI-P, followed by Golkar, PKS, Partai Demokrat, and then Gerindra. In fact, these results track national trends fairly closely, with many politicians viewing electoral district II as containing many swing voters easily influenced by dominant political trends.

Even so, as in other parts of the country, the introduction of open-list PR has generated intense competition among individual candidates, including those from the same party. In 2014, this system gave rise to a particular style of campaigning, involving direct visits by candidates to their constituents. Three keywords were widely used to sum up this approach and underline candidates' desires to forge direct, personal links with constituents: *blusukan, kukurusukan* and *silaturahmi*. The first, *blusukan*, is widely associated with the meet-the-people style of campaigning used by former Jakarta governor, now President, Joko Widodo (Jokowi). It derives from the Javanese word *keblusuk* which means to be lost. *Blusukan* is used to refer to someone who deliberately loses themselves to learn or find something—and hence was used to describe Jokowi's style of informal meetings where he grilled government workers or ordinary residents about government services, economic conditions, difficulties faced in daily life and similar matters.[2] *Kukurusukan* (Sundanese; from *kurusuk*, to walk or travel) means to walk through a place in search of something.[3] In contrast with these two terms, both of which imply a search for information, *silaturahmi* is from Arabic and means to join together two things that are separated or broken. Though the origins of these words differ, in the contemporary political context they all describe the same activity: a visit by a leader to a community in order to find out people's views and aspirations. In West Java II, virtually all candidates—whether incumbents or first-timers, and from whatever party—engaged in this strategy.

CANDIDATE STRATEGIES AND THE ROLE OF PATRONAGE

All the candidates (nine provincial DPRD candidates and one DPR candidate) interviewed for this research stated that the main approach

---

[2] W. Samirin, "Blusukan", *Kompas Online*, 12 Jan. 2013, available at: http://nasional.kompas.com/read/2013/01/12/11232457/Blusukan.

[3] R. Danadibrata, *Kamus Basa Sunda* [Dictionary of Sundanese] (Bandung: P.T. Kiblat Buku Utama, 1984).

they used to win votes was *silaturahmi*: visiting residents in their own communities. The basic concept of *silaturahmi*—face-to-face meetings when two or more parties seek to maintain or deepen their social relations—is part of local cultural practice and it is also, significantly, backed by Islamic teachings. For Muslims, engaging in *silaturahmi* is a religiously meritorious practice that brings blessings both in the present and the afterlife. There is a *hadith* (saying of the Prophet) that suggests that those who practice *silaturahmi* will be blessed by a longer life and greater prosperity.[4] This religious background helps legitimate the practice as a campaign method, and also means that the term *silaturahmi* is more commonly used in politics than the Sundanese alternative *kukurusukan* (which can have negative connotations because it is close to *tikusruk*, which means to stumble over something). The word *silaturahmi* is also close to *silaturahim*, which means to renew family or kinship connections, and therefore evokes a sense of close and warm emotional bonds between participants. *Silaturahmi* is thus a culturally powerful word, both religiously sanctioned and suggestive of close affective ties.

So how did candidates adapt the concept of *silaturahmi* for campaign purposes? The basic format of *silaturahmi*-style campaigning was small-scale meetings between candidates and community members, typically involving between 20 and 100 people, and often held at the house of a supporter within a particular village, or in a public place such as a mosque or village hall. Many candidates, however, engaged in *silaturahmi* by meeting with citizens in the context of some sort of organised social activity: a *pengajian* (Islamic study session), a community walk, provision of free medical treatment or even a sports tournament. Such events were intended to introduce the candidate to the community and at the same time create an image of him or her as a person who was one of the people, or *merakyat*.

In such social activities, patronage distribution occurred through sponsorship of the event itself. In practical terms, this typically meant the

---

[4] Anna Mariana and Milah Nurmilah, *Inilah Pesan Penting di Balik Berkah dan Manfaat Silaturahmi* [This Is the Important Message Behind the Blessing and Benefit of Friendship] (Jakarta: Ruang Kata, 2013).

candidate would provide cash to the campaign workers who organised it, covering at least "transport money" for the organisers and consumption costs for attendees. Candidates did not view such payments as being part of illicit money politics, because no cash would be distributed directly to voters.

At the same time, candidates liked such events because they could typically draw in large numbers at one time. First-time candidates in particular believed that such meetings were a more effective way of introducing themselves to voters than erecting campaign banners and billboards, which all too often would disappear or get damaged. Newcomer candidates thus tended to hold such events in one locality, and then shift elsewhere. After moving on, the candidate would leave the job of follow-up promotional activity to their local success team members. Such people would have the job of carrying out *silaturahmi* in the sense of cultivating ongoing personal relations with local community leaders, such as village heads (people who are considered a key to electoral success, because they have personal followings of their own and are able to predict where the votes will go in their village).[5] The local team members would then judge whether the candidate needed to personally revisit the community to reconnect with local leaders. In most cases, however, *silaturahmi* simply meant a one-off visit.

But there were also candidates for whom *silaturahmi* meant ongoing personal efforts to build relations with constituents, especially to strengthen existing ties with them. This was especially the case for incumbent legislators who had been routinely visiting communities in their electoral district for years. Maman Abdurahman, a PAN candidate for the provincial DPRD, explained the importance of personal connections as follows:

> Don't ever tell other people to maintain relations with the village heads on your behalf … it's the candidate who has the interest in doing this. … The people will feel closer to the candidate if they know him directly. Sometimes there are things they can only tell the candidate directly. It's like when we want to ask something in confidence from one of our parents and we don't want our brothers or sisters to

---

[5] Interview, Cecep Somantri, Gerindra campaign worker, 13 Apr. 2014.

know about it, because we're embarrassed. So we have to have good emotional connections with them.[6]

Such long-term trust building can occur through informal meetings, such as meals, or fishing trips, or even through regularly exchanging greetings via text messages (SMS).

However, the key weapon incumbents had in their arsenal for building such relations was access to the local government budget, especially through aspiration funds. Both provincial and district legislators could use these aspiration funds to pay for projects proposed by residents of their electoral district. Typically, legislators used these project funds to generate good relations with village RW and RT heads and other senior community leaders, who would in turn help them build a base among lower-level leaders, such as PKK (Family Welfare Guidance) cadres, village youth (*karang taruna*) and village security guards. The key incentive was the provision of funds for community development projects, such as renovations to the village office, or road repairs, which would help both the legislator and the recipient local elites build reputations as effective leaders. A campaign worker for one provincial candidate explained:

> Nowadays, it is no longer relevant to promote ideology, what people need is concrete service. Because of that my priority is to point to the concrete results of my past work. When my team does *silaturahmi*, people tell them about the concrete conditions of the area, and then the team explain what budget allocations and programmes are available for that area. They then suggest that the village should prepare a proposal to the province and that Pak Maman will take care of it as a member of the parliament. Members of parliament each have aspiration funds they can use to pay for such proposals. If the funds are released, they go straight to the village; they don't go at all to Pak Maman's account or those of his team.[7]

With this sort of arrangement, it is not simply that the funds tie the recipient village elite as client to the legislator as patron. The success of the local leader in gaining access to funds from the legislator and then

---

[6] Interview, Maman Abdurahman, 13 Mar. 2014.
[7] Interview, Wahyu, 5 Apr. 2014.

successfully executing the project also helps that local leader build his (or her) prestige and influence in the relevant community. This enhanced local prestige is often what counts most for the local actor, and what makes him or her especially grateful to the legislator. These local elites then support the legislator's re-election efforts in repayment; some will also use their enhanced prestige to nominate themselves for legislative office at the district level. In my research, I came across district legislative candidates who were campaigning in support of provincial incumbents with whom they had very close personal relations, and to whom they felt grateful for having helped build them up as locally-respected *tokoh* (figures). In short, this pattern of pork barrel politics does not simply help promote the legislator; it also helps create new local elites who are linked to that legislator through a clientelistic relationship.

MOBILISATIONAL STRUCTURES

In organising their campaigns, candidates used both formal party structures as well as informal teams of brokers (here mostly known as *relawan*, volunteers) to reach out to voters. Brokers were generally recruited on the basis of personal connections. Most candidates viewed their *relawan* as more effective, and relied on them much more than on their parties. When candidates wanted to use the party, they had to do so in cooperation with other candidates. Yet joint campaigning went against the logic of the open-list system, with its emphasis on personal competition. Accordingly, most candidates used party structures only to organise public campaign rallies, events which nobody thought were important. In organising face-to-face meetings with constituents, they used their *relawan*, and they funded these teams entirely with their personal funds. Although some candidates used party cadres in their *relawan* teams, they mostly did so by picking out individuals with whom they had strong personal relations, rather than using the party organisation per se. In short, personalism was the name of the game.

   Relawan were recruited from target communities, so they knew the local geographic, cultural and political terrain. They were crucial for candidates using *silaturahmi* strategies for a number of reasons. For example, they could identify villages which had not been visited or cultivated by rival candidates. They could be used to maintain the loyalty of voters in areas where a candidate believed he or she had strong support. Most candidates knew it was not enough to simply visit an area once or twice, strike up a good relationship with locals there, make a donation, and then assume that its votes could be counted on. Instead, they typically ensured that some *relawan* would continue to monitor and reinforce their work there. Cecep, a *relawan* for a Gerindra candidate explained:

> Usually there are several layers of *relawan* who visit an electoral district. The first layer has the job of carrying out *sosialisasi* [promotional] activities along with the candidate. The second layer then reinforces the motivations of the people in that area to vote for the candidate. Then, usually two days after the candidate's visit, these *relawan* will visit again to meet once more with the community leaders and strengthen their informal ties with them. A week before the poll, there will be a shadow team which will check the location. This team won't state they are working for the candidate, but just survey where the votes are going. If they are not going to the candidate, then the second layer will need to visit again to work on the location.[8]

Some, however, stressed the candidate's personal role in *silaturahmi* and explained the role of *relawan* as primarily arranging visits. Wahyu, a *relawan* for a PAN provincial candidate explained:

> Pak Maman [the candidate] goes down to the community via the village heads, so he is a figure who is very much in touch with the community [*memasyarakat*]. Pak Maman has been building his network with the village heads, because they are the ones who best understand conditions in their regions. If he visits one area, then the team does the follow-up work there. But he will visit the area two or three more times in order to create an emotional connection with the voters there.[9]

Another common pattern was for candidates from the same party to cooperate in a single "packet" so that three candidates standing respectively for the DPR, provincial DPRD and district DPRD would

---

[8] Interview, 13 Apr. 2014.
[9] Interview, Wahyu, 13 Apr. 2014.

cooperate in their campaign activities, with the latter two effectively also working as *relawan* for the most senior DPR candidate. Candidates could save money this way, sharing costs for campaign material and events. This cooperative approach was often also used by candidates at different levels who were related: for example Yadi Srimulyadi a PDI-P DPR candidate and local grandee, cooperated with his daughter, Nia Purnakania (a provincial DPRD candidate); Jacub Anwar Lewi (a provincial DPRD candidate from Nasdem) cooperated with his wife, Cucu Popon (running in the West Bandung DPRD), and Rachel Maryam (Gerindra, DPR) cooperated with her younger brother, Tobias Ginanjar (provincial DPRD). Again, personal connections were key.

The growing strength of such informal networks in electoral competition shows that informal institutions are not only complementing but also starting to substitute for formal structures, especially political parties, in election campaigns.[10] This is where the *relawan* come in. The use of this term is itself interesting, suggesting as it does supporters' voluntary commitment to the candidate, and therefore an emotional connection between both sides. In reality, of course, candidates often paid for the volunteers' activities, though many *relawan* were also motivated by the access that candidates could provide to government programmes. Indeed, it was often incumbents who were most able to rely on the loyalty and commitment of supporters, precisely because they had been providing such access for long periods.

BUILDING SUCCESS BY CULTIVATING NETWORKS: A STORY OF TWO CANDIDATES

In order to illustrate some of the preceding points, let us now look more closely at two successful candidates in West Java II: Maman Abdurahman of PAN, and Yadi Srimulyadi of PDI-P. Maman Abdurahman, already a two-term member of the provincial DPRD, was one of the only about 25 per cent of incumbents re-elected to the provincial parliament. Yadi

---

[10] Gretchen Helmke and Steven Levitsky, eds., *Informal Institutions and Democracy: Lessons from Latin America* (Baltimore, MD: Johns Hopkins University Press, 2006).

Srimulyadi had a history in both district and provincial legislatures, but had most recently served as deputy *bupati* of Bandung district (2005–10), and in 2014 he ran successfully for the DPR. Both of these candidates designed campaigns based on the *silaturahmi* approach, aiming to promote images of themselves as populist figures who were close to the people.

A first feature of both campaigns was that they relied significantly on their respective parties. This would seem to contradict what many candidates say, namely that personal teams trump party structures. However, when viewed closely it quickly becomes apparent that both Maman and Yadi used their parties in rather unstructured, uninstitutionalised ways. They recruited individual party members and sympathisers to their personal teams (especially Yadi, who was particularly dominant in the local party structure). They also worked with selected district candidates from their parties to cooperate in organising their campaign networking and events. By acting in these ways, they bypassed official party organs, such as the Badan Pemenangan Pemilu (Bapilu, Election Victory Body). In short, the parties acted as loose frameworks through which they constructed their own personal networks, rather than as machines that acted of their own volition.

Second, both candidates relied heavily on their past access to government funds, which they had used to build personal networks with people who became their *relawan*. Proving that they had records of using their formal positions to help communities was critical. Maman explained:

> During my ten years as a member of the provincial DPRD representing West Java II, I have continued to maintain ties of *silaturahmi* with the communities who have entrusted me with the mandate of being their representative in the council. It is my obligation to struggle for the aspirations of these communities, especially those from my own electoral district, both via *dana hibah* [grant money] or social assistance funds, including in the form of [provincial] assistance to the district. This is how I prove to the people that as their representative I am capable of struggling to meet their needs and fulfil their aspirations.[11]

---

[11] Interview, Maman Abdurahman, 13 Mar. 2014.

Yadi, a first-time candidate for the national DPR, had previously served not only as deputy *bupati* in Bandung but also as speaker of the district's DPRD (1999–2004) and briefly as a member of the provincial parliament (2004–05). In these capacities, he too had been an important policymaker with significant influence over government expenditure. He admitted this was an important source of his ability to build strong networks, not only among politicians and community leaders whom he had assisted in the past, but also with local businesspeople whom he had previously helped with licences.[12] In short, a history of successful patronage delivery—in the form of distribution of economic opportunities to local elites—was critical to both candidates' image building, and their networks.

A third shared feature was reliance on brokerage, by which the candidates themselves had helped to improve the social positions—and therefore the brokerage capacity—of the local leaders they relied upon to do their campaigning at the community level. Both Maman and Yadi's *relawan* tended to be people who had local social influence. But this social influence often partly depended on—or had been boosted by—the candidates themselves, who had provided these people with aspiration funds or other projects. Access to aspiration fund projects is provided by way of a formal proposal system, in which local leaders submit project requests to the DPRD, or to a particular legislator who represents the constituency. The legislator then takes action through the budgeting process to ensure that the project is allocated funds and that these funds are actually released. Accordingly, successful acquisition of a project boosts the reputation and status, not only of the sponsoring legislator, but also of the local leader making the request.

At one level, this suggests that formal government mechanisms are not working well, with successful execution of a project in a particular locale being seen as evidence, not of effective government performance, but of brokerage skills on the part of community leaders. One's reputation as a community leader (*ketokohan*) is thus closely tied to one's access to the political elite at a higher level. By helping create local leaders in this way, Maman and Yadi could in turn rely on loyal and hardworking

---

[12] Interview, Yadi Srimulyadi, 19 Apr. 2014.

teams to help their election efforts: these people were tied to them, not simply by one-off material exchange, but by debts of gratitude that went to the heart of their community identities and social positions. In turn, these *relawan*—some of whom were themselves standing as district DPRD candidates in 2014—acted as patrons for community leaders at a lower level, for instance, RW or RT heads, or youth leaders. As a result, both candidates were connected by brokerage chains right down to the neighbourhood level.

A fourth feature of both candidates' campaigning style was an emphasis on their personal qualities rather than their parties, programmes or even promises of future development projects. This was not simply a product of the general weakness of parties and programmatic politics that might be expected under an open-list electoral system, though this was important. More specifically, it was a product of the structure of Indonesian legislatures, where a legislator's ability to access particular government projects depends greatly on the commission on which he or she sits. Several candidates emphasised that, because they did not know which commission they would be placed on, they did not yet know what type of projects they would be able to access (would it be village roads or assistance for women's empowerment activities, for instance?). As a result, it was best to avoid making concrete promises about what they could bring to the community. It was better to simply promote themselves and get to know their constituents. Both Yadi and Maman also had this approach; they both believed that making promises of particular projects was not only ineffective but might haunt them in future years. Instead, like other incumbents, they promoted their track record in delivering past projects.

CONCLUSION

There is nothing in itself wrong with *silaturahmi* becoming a dominant mode of electioneering. That candidates devoted time and resources to visiting constituents can be seen as a positive product of the open-list system, and as a starting point for two-way communication between citizens and their political representatives. But when we view the practice in a broader light, it becomes less positive. The importance of direct meetings and other kinds of face-to-face interactions between candidates and voters is a sign of the weakening of party structures, despite the fact that parties are a fundamental institution of every electoral democracy. Moreover, this campaign style, as we have seen, was structured, not only by cultural traditions of *silaturahmi* that stress warm personal relations and affective ties, but also by the construction of tiered clientelistic networks that are kept alive by project funds and other patronage goods. The incumbent candidates who succeeded in being re-elected typically made large long-term investments of public funds to help them secure this goal. Moreover, a legislator's success in directing chunks of the public budget to constituents not only helped determine his or her chances of being re-elected. The legislator could also use that success to build up local leaders who owed their reputations and status to the legislator concerned, and would want to repay that debt by helping his or her re-election efforts. A personal, informal network is thus created that is outside the state, yet dependent on state funding to maintain itself.

chapter **13**

Cirebon, West Java: Where Materialism Defeats Personalism

Marzuki Wahid*

Rohana, a Gerindra candidate for the district (*kabupaten*) parliament in Cirebon, and Mutiwati, a Nasdem candidate for the same body, were both in for a nasty shock on election day, 9 April 2014. Not only did they fail to get elected, but they were also defeated by huge margins in their own villages, including in polling booths close to their homes. To make matters worse, they lost in these places to candidates who came from outside their villages, even outside their subdistricts. And many of their neighbours were relatives. Both candidates were born, grew up, lived and worked in these villages. In the weeks leading to the poll they had campaigned there too, dropping in on their neighbours one by one, going house to house, encouraging people to vote for them. In the end, these efforts had counted for little.

---

* I dedicate this chapter to the memory of my beloved late wife, Liya Aliyah al-Himmah. I was conducting the research, and writing up the findings, while she was struggling with breast cancer and finally passed away on 21 July 2014. May God always be with her in the afterlife.

Both Rohana and Mutiwati, and their success team members, blamed these embarrassing defeats on vote-buying efforts conducted by rivals on the day and evening before the vote. Just after the counting was finished, Faturrahman, a member of Rohana's success team, explained that the winner in their village was a Golkar candidate from a neighbouring village whose team, a day earlier, had given out Rp 50,000 notes to residents.[1]

Nuruzzaman, a Gerindra candidate for the national parliament, also felt there was something odd about this election in Cirebon. Of the nine candidates who won the largest personal vote in the national race, only two of them lived in Cirebon or Indramayu— the two regions that constituted the electoral district. Some of them had only started introducing themselves to the community at the beginning of the formal campaign period, or when the candidate lists were announced, a few months before. Some barely did any grassroots campaigning at all. Yet these people defeated candidates who lived in the region and had intensely carried out *blusukan* (Javanese; meet-the-people style campaigning). Nuruzzaman himself received many reports of "dawn attacks" carried out by some of the winners, especially on voting day itself, and put their victories down to this factor.[2] Nuruzzaman was only placed third among the Gerindra candidates, though he was a Cirebon native, grew up, lived and worked in Cirebon, had a long career as a social activist there, had links to a strong network of local *pesantren*, and had for four years been the head of the Cirebon branch of Ansor, Nahdlatul Ulama's youth organisation.

The analysis of the Cirebon election here confirms these candidates' suspicions. Despite analyses of clientelistic politics that stress the importance of personalistic connections between patrons and clients, in Cirebon strategies emphasising personal ties with voters were ineffective when not backed by material distribution. In other words, materialistic patronage defeated personalistic connections.

---

[1] Interview, Faturrahman, 9 Apr. 2014.

[2] Interview, Nuruzzaman, 5 June 2014.

In my field research, I found that almost all candidates from all parties used goods, money and services to build connections with voters and gain their support. Various sayings and terms circulated widely, pointing to the importance of material exchange, including: NPWP, *Nomer pira, wani pira* (roughly: What number on the ballot are you and how much are you brave enough to give?), with the standard response, "*Ana duit, ya dipilih*" (If you've got money, we'll vote for you); and *uang es* ("ice money"), a popular local term for small amounts of money, such as Rp 5,000 that could be used for minor purchases, and a commonly used euphemism for vote buying. Certainly, candidates themselves widely believed that voters paid little attention to their honesty, integrity, social activism or other qualities. Instead, in the words of one candidate, "The people just judge you on the basis of what you bring, not on what vision, mission or programme you offer."[3] Consequently, the 2014 poll was a very costly election for candidates and their financial backers.

BACKGROUND: A HETEROGENEOUS SETTING

This research was conducted for 45 days leading to and immediately after the April election in the district (*kabupaten*) of Cirebon. Cirebon has a distinctive subculture in Indonesia, located between Central Java to the east and the Pasundan heartland of West Java to the west. Cirebon people do not like to be considered either ethnically Javanese or Sundanese (the major ethnic group of West Java). Sandwiched between these two great ethnic groups, they form a hybrid community, mixing elements of both, and have their own distinctive language.

The focus of the research was electoral district I in Cirebon district. This area, consisting of six subdistricts to the west and north of the town (*kota*) of Cirebon was chosen for several reasons. First, it is socioeconomically heterogeneous, mixing urban, peri-urban and rural features. Some subdistricts, notably Kedawung and Tengah Tani are on the outskirts of Cirebon town, and most of their inhabitants work

---

[3] Interview, Ali Murtadlo, PKB DPR candidate, 1 Apr. 2014.

in petty trade, home industry, services and as factory workers. Other subdistricts, notably Panguragan and Suranenggala, are rural, with the population working as farmers and collectors and traders of second-hand goods and recycled materials. Gunung Jati and part of Suranenggala subdistrict are located on the coast and people here are fishers or processors of marine products. Though there are pockets of comfortable middle-class housing in the electoral district, and even a few genuinely wealthy people, most of the population are lower-middle-class or poor.

A second consideration was that, although most of the population here are traditionalist Muslims affiliated to NU, many are better described as *abangan* who engage in syncretic religious practices in accordance with Cirebon-Javanese traditions. The area covered by the electoral district includes many historic pilgrimage sites that are important for both *santri* (pious Muslims) and *abangan*, and varied religious festivals are celebrated enthusiastically here, including pilgrimages to holy tombs, *muludan* (Prophet Muhammad's birthday), *muharraman* (Islamic new year), *nadran* (a festival where offerings are made to the sea), and *sedekah bumi* (an equivalent festival of offerings to the earth). Despite this mixing of *abangan* and *santri*, in other ways the electoral district is not particularly heterogeneous: there are few significant ethnic minorities, and there are no churches or temples to compete with the many mosques and *tajug* (*musholla*, Muslim prayer halls).

Politically, some parts of the electoral district are thought of as being "red" areas: in other words, both *abangan* and PDI-P base areas. Some of these same villages are also known as being rather lawless *daerah preman* (gangster regions) and for their histories of inter-village violence. And though in religious terms NU is the largest group, since the New Order years the PDI-P and its predecessor, the PDI, have generally been the leading party here. This changed, however, in 2014 when PKB won the highest vote for the first time. Part of the reason was that NU, notably the organisation's national chairperson, Said Aqil Siradj, supported PKB more openly than in previous elections, and also because several prominent local NU leaders, such as the chair of the Cirebon district branch, KH Ali Murtadlo, became PKB candidates. PDI-P also faced significant competition from several candidates from the new Partai Nasdem.

Table 13.1
Election Results, Cirebon I, 2009 and 2014

Party	Total votes		Highest individual vote		Candidate who was elected	
	2009	**2014**	**2009**	**2014**	**2009**	**2014**
PDI-P	42,350	24,409	10,533	5.414	H. Tasiya Soemadi Al Gotas	Carila Rohandi
			5,301		Sawita	
Demokrat	25,825	15,656	5,222	3,925	Ach. Darsono	Tarseni
PKS	15,419	12,024	1,952	2,055	M. Arief Rahman	Nova Fikrotushofiyah
Golkar	13,844	22,204	2,154	7,447	Efendi Darmadji	H. Khanafi
Hanura	8,581	13,322	2,810	4,709	Supirman	Supirman
PKB	7,547	29,774	2,014	5,880	H. Abdullah Masrur	Pandi
Gerindra	7,421	19,500	2,512	3,925	Ibnu Hamdun	Mulus Trisla Ageng
Nasdem	–	13,483	–	2,542	–	H. Tarmidi

CANDIDATE STRATEGIES

Candidates used highly varied strategies in this electoral district. They were chasing fairly modest vote targets; two candidates scraped in with a little over 2,000 personal votes (Table 13.1). It should be noted, however, that not all candidates were especially committed, and some did not work hard to chase even such modest targets. Candidates who were resigned to not being elected tended to be either women who were on the list so that their party could reach the quota of 30 per cent female candidates or they were "vote-getter" candidates—prominent persons or leaders of social organisations added to the list to boost the party total, but not to win enough personal votes to secure a seat.

Most candidates did not favour public rallies or street convoys—
methods that used to be associated with Indonesian elections. Such
methods did not help candidates increase their personal vote tallies.
When candidates participated in such events, it was usually in response
to requests from party officials, and with the goal of maintaining the
party's public reputation. Some candidates who were not party officials
or long-standing cadres did not even bother to participate in such public
campaigning, and parties could do nothing to punish them. Everybody
knew that candidates were primarily concerned with boosting their
personal vote.

For ease of analysis, it helps to group candidate strategies into
two categories: personalistic politics and material exchange. Though
there was much overlap, this division captures two different paradigms
used by candidates. On the one hand, some candidates claimed that,
basically, residents vote for candidates whom they know, especially those
with whom they have close personal relations. The closer a candidate's
connections with the community, according to this paradigm, the greater
his or her chance of being elected. Many people thought this approach
was rooted in local culture, and that, in Cirebon, personal connections
count more than anything else.

On the other hand, some candidates believed that voters were above
all materially oriented, and that they voted for candidates who offered
them the greatest personal benefit, specifically material benefits in the
shape of cash, goods or services. In this paradigm, people's life choices
are guided by their economic needs. Many candidates believed that this
was how voters in Cirebon behaved. They did not always approve of
this approach, but sometimes viewed it as an unavoidable fact of life.

Let us succinctly run through some of the main strategies employed
by candidates, grouping them according to the two paradigms.

Personalistic Strategies

Socialisation. The most popular personalistic strategy is known by the
Indonesian word *sosialisasi*. Basically this term refers to promoting
something to the community, and it is often used to refer to campaigns
to promote an idea or a government programme. In the electoral
context, it means promoting one's candidacy by publicising one's name,

picture, candidate number and party symbol by way of billboards, posters, banners, calendars, pamphlets, name cards, sample ballot papers, T-shirts, shirts and stickers. Some candidates also distributed key rings, glass bowls, and cigarette packs bearing their images, as well as other promotional material. Almost every serious candidate engaged in *sosialisasi*, and usually plenty of it.

How and where candidates placed their stickers, pamphlets and billboards varied, however. Some put them up only in officially designated places, which usually meant on a few of the main roads and strategic public places. This could be expensive, however, and it restricted visibility. Thus, few candidates paid attention to the General Elections Commission rule which restricted them to placing only one banner in each zone determined by the KPU and local government.[4] Most put their material wherever they could: the roadside, bamboo poles, stuck on trees, the walls of houses or other buildings, bridges, public transport vehicles, private cars, motorcycles, boats—basically whatever had a surface and was visible from passing traffic.

Through the course of my research, I only met with one candidate who did not use this approach. Mutiwati, the aforementioned Nasdem candidate, who was still acting as the Head of Government Business (Kepala Urusan Pemerintahan) in the village of Sambeng in Gunung Jati subdistrict, only printed 200 name cards, without even her photograph. She explained that not only did she "not have any money" but that she preferred to rely on her "closeness to the residents" and her status as an important village official.[5]

---

[4] Article 4, *Peraturan Komisi Pemilihan Umum Nomor 15 Tahun 2013 Tentang Perubahaan Atas Peraturan Komisi Pemilihan Umum Nomor 01 Tahun 2013 Tentang Pedoman Pelaksanaan Kampanye Pemilihan Umum Anggota Dewan Perwakilan Rakyat, Dewan Perwakilan Daerah dan Dewan Perwakilan Rakyat Daerah* [General Elections Commission Regulation No. 15 of 2013 on Amendments to General Election Commission No. 1 of 2013 on Guidelines for the Implementation of Campaigns for the General Elections of Members of the People's Representative Council, Regional Representative Council and Regional People's Representative Councils].

[5] Interview, Mutiwati, 18 Mar. 2014.

Meeting residents. Another popular strategy among candidates was known as (using the English phrase) "door-to-door" or *silaturahmi* (bonds of fellowship or brotherhood). All candidates used this strategy, except for some of the provincial DPRD and national DPR candidates who were not from the area. Non-native candidates would tend to meet with residents collectively, either at events which were arranged by their success teams or by turning up at regular community events, such as women's Quran recitation gathering or meetings of the RW and RT (neighbourhood and subneighbourhood) or PKK (Family Welfare Guidance) group.

Door-to-door visits were generally carried out by the candidates themselves (remembering that they were not targeting a huge number of votes), though sometimes this job was also delegated to success team members. This approach required plenty of time and patience. Even so, candidates did not try to visit all the voters in the electoral district. Mostly they prioritised those whom they thought would be most likely to support them, or visited influential community elders and other key persons. Typically, they used these visits not only to promote their candidacy but also to map out their community-level support.

Candidates used various methods during such visits (I had the chance to accompany several candidates on their rounds). Usually, they would arrive at a house, introduce themselves, ask for the household's *doa dan dukungan* ("prayers and support"—a standard phrase), and leave without giving any money or gift. But some would bring a *bingkisan*—a small package containing basic foodstuffs valued at perhaps Rp 10,000 to Rp 15,000, in order to increase the personal connection.[6] Other candidates would slip the householders a small amount of cash, typically Rp 10,000, when saying their farewells.[7] As one of these candidates explained, these gifts were really about solidifying a social relationship, though the recipients perhaps viewed it differently:

> Our people are now quite pragmatic, aren't they? If I don't bring a *bingkisan*, and just give them a calendar or a name card, they'll say that other candidates have come and given out *bingkisan* and money.

---

[6] Interview, PKS candidate, 24 Mar. 2014.

[7] Interview, PKS candidate, 17 Mar. 2014

But when I do give them a *bingkisan* they say, "Why did you go to all that trouble to bring along a heavy package? Just giving me 5,000 rupiah would be quite enough" ... So, those packages are just for me to build my relations with the people.[8]

Some candidates paid these house calls alone, or with their spouse or a success team member. Some would come in groups of ten or so team members who would go from house to house. The frequency of the visits also varied. Some candidates would visit a resident's home just once, believing it was better to divide their time among many residents. Some visited each household twice: once in the campaign period and once just before voting day, with the view that they needed to remind the voters of the connection they had already established. Some visited just once, but followed up with brief text messages or telephone calls in order to reconnect.

Many candidates claimed making direct connections this way was effective in boosting their vote, because it touched the personal feelings and emotions of those they visited. Many candidates explained that people saw these visits as a sign that they valued them as individuals. Many could quote residents who had told them they were touched to be visited: "I've never been visited before by a DPR member, this is the first time any such person has spoken directly to me", recalled a PAN incumbent of one such encounter.[9]

Religious activities. Several candidates supplemented their normal campaign strategies with religious activities. For example, some candidates drew on "supernatural" methods. One candidate I interviewed did so by holding *istighatsah*, namely joint prayers involving the candidate, success team members and voters, using *dzikir* recitation and recounting the story of Syaikh Abdul Qadir al-Jilani, the great Sufi saint. The candidate I interviewed (in fact, several used the same strategy) was Pandi from PKB, and he held the prayers every Wednesday night during the campaign period, beginning immediately after the *isya* prayers and going on till late. He described it as a form of "spiritual strengthening" that, among other purposes, would prepare him for accepting the outcome of the election,

---

[8] Interview, PKS candidate, 17 Mar. 2014.
[9] Interview, Abdul Kholiq Ahmad, 15 Mar. 2014.

even if he lost, as God's will. Of course, it also had the practical benefit of improving his image in the eyes of his success team and voters, and in the end he recorded a strong vote and was elected.

Another candidate, Anis Khoirunnisa from PPP, invited groups of voters to participate in free trips or *ziarah*, pilgrimages, to a nearby famous and controversial Islamic boarding school: the Pesantren al-Zaytun in Indramayu. This *pesantren*, one of the wealthiest and best-appointed in Southeast Asia, has been controversial because of its connections with one wing of the banned Negara Islam Indonesia (Islamic State of Indonesia) movement and accusations that it was practising "deviant teachings". The candidate's success team members invited women, mostly elderly members of *pengajian* groups and *majelis taklim* (Islamic study groups) to visit the *pesantren*, providing them with free bus transport, food, drinks and souvenirs, and then inviting them listen to *mau'idhah hasanah* (literally, "good teaching", a kind of sermon) by the *pesantren*'s head, who also used the opportunity to endorse the candidate.

Technology. Only a few candidates used social media and other forms of electronic communication to reach out to voters. At most, this meant using Facebook, Twitter and text messaging, for example by providing on their Facebook page basic information about themselves, promoting positive media coverage they received, and the like. In the electoral district where I was conducting research, no candidates set up their own websites to explain their programmes to voters. A few used their success teams to collect thousands of mobile telephone numbers from voters while on house-to-house visits, or in meetings, and then used these lists to send text messages to them in the lead-up to the poll, urging them to vote for the candidate. Most candidates, however, believed that the penetration of electronic communication was low among poorer voters, and preferred face-to-face strategies.

Materialistic Strategies

Helping with practical needs. Many candidates made contributions of money or goods to voters, either because they viewed this as an effective strategy, or because they felt they could not refuse direct requests for such assistance. Such contributions could be for collective benefit, such as when a candidate helped pay for construction or renovations of a mosque or *musholla*, a road, an irrigation ditch or some other community infrastructure, or helped defray the cost of a traditional community event (such as a *muludan* or *tahlilan*). Or they could be to help individuals: paying for repairs to poor voters' homes, for instance, or distributing foodstuffs or basic goods. The most common gifts were snacks and drinks—and often "transport money"—for people who attended meetings with candidates. This practice was all but ubiquitous.

Without going into detail, the modes and types of distribution varied greatly. Some candidates distributed such gifts personally at public events precisely in order to attract attention. Some delegated the task to their team members in order to avoid being accused of (or even being charged for) engaging in money politics. One of the more ingenious methods I encountered involved a candidate who distributed clothing and basic foodstuffs by handing out coupons and an invitation to come to her house. At the house, the voter could then hand over the coupon, pay Rp 10,000 (which did not come near to covering the cost of the items) and then take away an item of clothing and a packet of foodstuffs that also contained the candidate's stickers and pamphlets.

Most candidates claimed they had little choice but to provide such gifts. As Bintang Irianto, a Nasdem candidate, put it with regard to payments of "transport money" to those who attended his meetings: "These are all requests from the community, it feels really hard to say no. And it's just to make up for the income from their employment they gave up [in order to meet me]."[10] Others claimed altruistic motivations, including Euis Suhartati, a provincial candidate from the same party:

> If I can afford to do it, I will fulfil such requests from the people, because I want to *shadaqah* [give something to the people in the name of God] and I want the people to *shadaqah* their votes to me.[11]

Providing services. As well as providing goods, some candidates provided services. These varied according to the candidate's skills and connections, and voters' requests. One candidate provided training in

---

[10] Interview, Bintang Irianto, 12 Mar. 2014.
[11] Interview, Euis Suhartati, 16 Mar. 2014.

small business skills—he had a master's degree in economics and was a businessman himself. Others organised teams which provided basic medical services or accompanied patients at hospitals—these candidates either had medical backgrounds themselves (for example, as midwives), or they hired doctors to provide the services. One candidate, with a NU background and a history of interfaith dialogue, offered his services helping a local Christian community to ensure that its church would not be closed down. Yet another candidate, who had a background in NGOs helping female victims of domestic violence, drug users and sex workers, continued with her social work and advocacy, turning this to her electoral benefit by mentioning her candidacy in events involving her clients.

Promising club goods. As in other parts of Indonesia, elected representatives in Cirebon have access to aspiration funds and other special funds that most feel that they can—or will—turn to electoral benefit. Accordingly, many candidates, at their meetings with voters, promised that they would ensure these funds would be used to benefit their constituents, that they would not syphon them off in corruption, and so on. Often, community members demanded written statements setting out these commitments, and candidates were happy to oblige. A few tried to make more specific and elaborate commitments to convince potential supporters of their sincerity. For instance, one provincial PKB candidate promised that, if elected, he would establish a foundation to distribute all aspiration funds and similar government grants within the constituency. He would cover the foundation's administrative costs himself, and would endeavour to attract as much government money as possible to it. He also promised that if he got 5,000 votes in a subdistrict he would donate a motorcycle to the subdistrict branch of the party (there were 76 subdistricts in his electoral district, so this was a potentially extravagant promise). A PKS candidate promised a subdistrict branch of Muslimat, the NU women's organisation, that he would donate Rp 200 million to build them an office if he got a high vote in that subdistrict (he did achieve a reasonable vote and made good on his promise).

The dawn attack. One strategy that was very popular with candidates in Cirebon—and awaited by many voters—was the so-called dawn attack. The term is widely used in Cirebon to apply to the direct distribution of cash, usually, but not always, enclosed in envelopes, to individual voters. The term's origins date back to the revolutionary struggle against the Dutch when Indonesian fighters often launched their raids in the early morning; it has since been adapted to politics because cash, too, is often distributed before voting starts on election day. In 2014 in Cirebon, however, the dawn attack often occurred in the days leading to the poll.

Almost all candidates from all parties used this strategy, either planning to do so from the start, or feeling they had no choice once they saw that others were preparing to use it. Those who distributed the cash were usually village success team members who knew local circumstances and recipients. Some candidates also gave their envelopes to village heads to distribute onward to voters. A few candidates handed out the cash themselves.

As elsewhere in Indonesia, the dawn attack strategy was full of uncertainty for participants. While some candidates distrusted their success team members, some of those distributing money also felt deceived. One RT head in Arjawinangun subdistrict, for example, complained:

> I was tricked. At first I was promised by [A], a relative of mine, to get votes at Rp 10,000 each for a provincial candidate from PKS. I got more than 200 votes for him at my polling booth. Afterwards, when I asked for the money from [A], he refused to give it to me. He said the candidate had given Rp 5 million to the village head.

He continued, "Every resident could receive three or four envelopes from different candidates. So this is not a matter of a vote for a party, but a vote for money."[12]

The sums of money distributed varied significantly, though Rp 5,000 and Rp 10,000 notes were most in circulation. The lowest sums were paid by DPR candidates (Rp 5,000 to 10,000) and provincial DPRD candidates (Rp 10,000 to 20,000) though these candidates were all running in the same electoral district (West Java X). It was at the lowest level (where candidates were chasing far fewer votes) that the variation was greatest

---

[12] Confidential interview, 11 Apr. 2014.

(Rp 10,000 to 50,000) and where candidates tended to pay higher sums per voter.

Some candidates supplemented these cash gifts with other gifts, such as headscarves, cakes, packets of instant noodles and other foodstuffs, and some even arranged breakfasts of porridge and rice cakes on voting day.

CONCLUSION

What is striking from this brief summary of the strategies used by candidates is how little programmatic politics featured, and how little candidates dealt with fundamental issues of importance to the welfare of the people and the future of the country or the district. Such issues barely rated a mention in candidates' speeches, printed propaganda or personal interactions with voters. This absence had a tremendous impact on the nature of the election and the sort of choices that voters could make. Though most candidates used a mixture of what I have described as personalistic and materialistic approaches, it tended to be those offering the bigger material rewards who won.

Observing voters in the lead-up to the 2014 election in Cirebon sometimes seemed like watching buyers in a supermarket or shopping mall. Each voter had a choice of 4 candidates from among 346 on offer (87 in the district DPRD, 117 in the provincial DPRD, 106 in the DPR and 36 in the DPD). As with a well-informed consumer in a shopping mall, voters who had access to information about the candidates, and who were reasonably prosperous, were well positioned to make their choices. But many voters were more akin to consumers who lacked the information, time, or means to choose carefully, and so bought whatever product seemed most attractive at first glance.

Accordingly, many voted for whoever they thought promised them personally the greatest material rewards. Not surprisingly, it was the wealthiest candidates who were advantaged. Ultimately, in my view, it is the open-list proportional representation system that must bear the responsibility for this outcome, with its emphasis on personal competition between candidates and the incentive this provides for them to downplay party, ideology and programme, and to win over voters with whatever gifts and electoral bribes they can. In this context, I would like to leave the last word to Abdul Kholiq Ahmad, a PAN candidate for the DPR in Cirebon. At the height of the campaign period, before even the flurry of vote buying on the final days, he was already describing this as "the most expensive, the most chaotic and the most ugly election I have known … [E]verything now is about the money".[13]

---

[13] Interview, Abdul Kholiq Ahmad, 15 Mar. 2014.

Map of Central and East Java

Electoral district
Province boundary
District/city boundary

kilometres

0   50

Java
Sea

EAST
JAVA

REMBANG

PATI

CENTRAL
JAVA III

BLORA

GROBOGAN

CENTRAL
JAVA

MOJOKERTO
CITY

MOJOKERTO

EAST JAVA VIII

JOMBANG

NGANJUK

MADIUN

MADIUN
CITY

6°30'S

7°30'S

111°E

112°E

© Australian National University
CartoGIS CAP 15-286K_KP

Pati, Central Java: Targets, Techniques and Meanings of Vote Buying

Noor Rohman

In the district of Pati in Central Java, most politicians describe voters as pragmatic, explaining that locals typically follow the Javanese language adage *"ora uwek ora obos"* (no money, no vote) during elections. Accordingly, a large majority of candidates in Pati engaged in vote buying during the 2014 legislative election. In so doing, they typically viewed the *voters* as the source of this practice, arguing that candidates were only responding to voters' desires for rewards. In fact, if we carefully analyse the source of this phenomenon, it is to be found in the behaviour of these elites themselves. Once elected, politicians in the district are rarely accountable to the voters who put them in place. To the extent that they benefit their constituents, they typically target only groups which have helped them get elected for aspiration funds, social assistance packages, or other forms of patronage. Popular disillusionment with official politics is one result. My argument in this chapter, therefore, is that the massive vote buying witnessed in Pati arose due to failure on the part of local elites to understand the factors that are making their citizens increasingly pragmatic, even apathetic, at election time.

To make this argument, and in order to understand the practice of vote buying, I address three questions. First, who were the targets of vote-buying efforts? Was it voters who were already considered to be core supporters of the candidate in question, or was it swing voters, or supporters of rivals? Second, what techniques were used to distribute cash and goods to voters, and what measures did candidates use to ensure that these gifts reached the intended recipients? Third, how were these cash gifts interpreted and understood by the recipients?

My findings suggest that the priority targets of candidates were voters they considered to be their "base" supporters, as recorded in voter lists compiled by success team members. However, the compilation of these lists was itself often highly problematic, with team members also often listing the names of people who were uncommitted, or even supported rival candidates. Distribution of cash or other gifts, meanwhile, occurred at the household level, and was carried out by team members located in the lowest-level neighbourhood (RW) or subneighbourhood (RT) unit. Some candidates distributed cash on a per voter basis, others per household. To ensure the effectiveness of these gifts, some candidates required photographic evidence of ballots, but most teams simply appealed to the recipients to vote for the candidate when they handed over the cash. Ensuring that recipients delivered their vote was very difficult, because many residents received payments from multiple candidates. The social meanings accorded to these cash gifts, meanwhile, varied, though many interpretations did not in fact oblige recipients to repay the "buyer" with a vote.

Before elaborating on these findings, we first need to explain the basic anatomy of the district of Pati, the strategies used by candidates, and the mobilisation structures they relied on.

BACKGROUND: JAVA'S AGRICULTURAL HEARTLAND

Pati is located on the northern coast of Central Java province. With a population of about 1.3 million, it has the maximum of 50 members in its district DPRD and, together with the neighbouring districts of Rembang, Blora and Grobogan constitutes the Central Java III electoral district for the national and provincial legislatures. Its economy is primarily agricultural, notably wet rice farming (with rice fields covering about 40 per cent of the district), though fisheries are also significant. It is a Muslim-majority region, and though there are significant followings of both the traditionalist NU and the modernist Muhammadiyah in the district, the majority of the population are identified with the syncretic *abangan* stream.[1]

Given this *abangan* composition, it is not surprising that Pati is known as a strong base area for PDI-P, which has been the winning party in the district in every post-Suharto election, though its vote has declined: in 1999 the party won 21 seats in the district legislature, 16 in 2004 and 12 in 2009.[2] The party's vote in the district's DPRD declined again from 141,547 votes (24.3 per cent) in 2009 to 117, 644 votes (16.9 per cent) in 2014, yielding only 8 seats. One factor causing the drop was a bitter internal conflict over the *bupati* election in 2011, which prompted several leading PDI-P politicians to jump ship to Hanura, whose share of the vote increased from 3.6 per cent in 2009 to 9.3 in 2014. The other big winner in 2014 was Gerindra, whose vote share of 16.2 per cent in 2014 was a major increase from 4.8 per cent in 2009. This increase was above all due to the fact that several sitting members of the DPRD from small parties which had not passed the verification process for party registration in 2014 joined Gerindra. The new Nasdem party also did relatively well in Pati, with 50,725 votes (7.3 per cent), in large part because of the support of former PKB politicians who, as supporters of former president Abdurrahman Wahid, had lost out in past internal conflicts within that party.

CANDIDATE STRATEGIES AND STRUCTURES

The strategies of candidates at all levels (the national DPR, and the provincial and district DPRDs) in Pati district were based on a combination of the distribution of goods, cash and economic opportunities (deriving from aspiration and social assistance funds) to voters and success team members.

---

[1] Clifford Geertz, *The Religion of Java* (New York: Free Press, 1960).

[2] "Sebagian Ketua PAC PDI-P Pati Diapelkan" [Several PDI-P Sub-branch Chairs Required to Parade], *Suara Merdeka*, 29 Apr. 2004, available at: http://www.suaramerdeka.com/harian/0404/29/mur3.htm.

The distribution of cash came in two forms: vote buying, which took place at the time of voting or a few days beforehand, and the disbursing of "transport money" to success teams, which could occur at any time during the campaign period. I encountered several candidates who explained from the start that they would engage in vote buying, though they mostly kept the amounts secret. Others denied they would engage in the practice, but in reality did so. I also encountered a few district candidates who were planning to distribute cash, but were unable to do so when they did not receive the hoped-for financial support from their party or DPR candidates they were paired with. Virtually every serious candidate engaged in the practice. This phenomenon is explored below. The typical amount of "transport money" given to success team members or polling booth witnesses was in the order of Rp 50,000 to 100,000 at each "consolidation" meeting with candidates, which happened at least once, but more often several times in the lead-up to the poll.

Cash gifts were just one part of a wider range of patronage politics engaged in by candidates. A few also distributed foodstuffs such as bags of rice to voters.[3] Another common form was donations for repairs or renovations of mosques or *musholla*, roads, school buildings or *pesantren*. The value of these donations was typically around Rp 5 to 10 million and most incumbents, as well as some other candidates, engaged in this form of giving. Others provided social services; in particular, two candidates were particularly well known for providing health services. One of these, Sumijah (a Gerindra candidate) provided her private vehicles for use as ambulances in her subdistrict (where she had received a strong vote in 2009). She also helped residents access the government's health insurance scheme and other government services.[4] In this case, as with many others, the goal was to build long-term clientelistic linkages with supporters.[5]

---

[3] Confidential interviews, 12 Mar. 2014, 15 Mar. 2014.

[4] Interview, Sumijah, 13 Mar. 2014.

[5] Herbert Kitschelt, "Linkages between Citizens and Politicians in Democratic Politics", *Comparative Political Studies* 33, 6–7 (2000): 845–6.

Candidates who were incumbents also typically facilitated the provision of financial assistance, using their access to government aspiration funds and social assistance programmes, to community groups such as farmers' groups (*kelompok tani, kelompok ternak*). The beneficiaries often joined success teams to help candidates with their re-election efforts. Almost all candidates promised future access to these programmes to community groups where they campaigned. In fact, some candidates saw making promises of future access to such programmes as an *alternative* to money politics, sometimes making semi-formal "political contracts" with groups they promised to assist.

Meanwhile, in order to run their campaigns, most candidates said they relied both on party structures and informal success teams. However, it was mostly national and provincial candidates who emphasised their parties; they tended to be more senior in party organisations, and also faced greater personal expenditure if they wanted to establish personal success teams through the entire Central Java III constituency. Most of the other candidates said that parties were unreliable, because rival candidates competed for the loyalty of every individual party cadre. Accordingly, most candidates relied on their personal teams. As in other parts of Indonesia, these usually consisted of a core team of the candidate's most trusted confidants, and then a structured pyramid of subdistrict and village coordinators with, at the base level, *korlap* (field coordinators, the term used for the lowest-level brokers in success teams) who worked in a particular RT or in the catchment area of a single polling booth.

THE DYNAMICS OF VOTE BUYING

Vote buying in this study is the giving of material rewards, both money and goods, to an individual or household with voting rights, on the day of the poll or several days beforehand. This practice was also distinguished by its outright illegality, something which should not be forgotten while reading the following description.

In the 2014 legislative election in Pati, most informants, including candidates, their team members and ordinary voters, agreed that there was a much greater volume of money circulating than in previous elections. This significant financial incentive probably increased voter participation in Pati: 74 per cent, up from 72 per cent in 2009. However, when voters come to the polling booths in response to cash gifts, I would argue they did so more as targets of political mobilisation, rather than as active participants in the political process. In this system, voters are positioned as supporters of elites, not as individuals with real freedom or sovereignty to determine and express their own preferences, and thus improve the quality of democracy.[6] The high voter participation rate in Pati can thus hardly be a source of pride.

Of course, not all candidates engaged in vote buying, but almost all did so. The amounts they distributed varied significantly, from Rp 10,000 per recipient through 15,000, 20,000, 25,000 and 30,000 up to 50,000 at the upper level. Candidates standing for election in the provincial and national parliaments gave out smaller sums (typically Rp 10,000 or 15,000) than district candidates. Some candidates supplemented their cash payments with gifts of food (typically rice). The individual value of all these gifts was perhaps not great, but if a voter received envelopes and gifts from five or more candidates, as was often the case, the accumulated value was significant in local terms. Not surprisingly, on voting day there was a visible jump in residents' buying power, with many local foodstalls selling out their stock early.

Targeting: Loyal Not Swing Voters

Most candidates in Pati believed that in their vote-buying efforts they needed to target voters who already supported or were sympathetic to them. They mostly identified these voters by using success team members who compiled lists of residents who were prepared to vote for the candidate. Most team members were instructed to each enlist about 20 to 30 persons, so as not to swell the lists beyond the candidate's capacity to pay. Typically, they enlisted people who had close relations with the broker: family members, neighbours, friends and so on. Even

---

[6] A.E. Priyono, Willy Purna Samadhi and Olle Törnquist, *Menjadikan Demokrasi Bermakna: Masalah dan Pilihan di Indonesia* [Developing a Meaningful Democracy: Issues and Options in Indonesia] (Jakarta: Demos, 2005), p. 77.

so, many district DPRD candidates ended up with large lists, upwards of 20,000 persons. In fact, these lists were often very unreliable: they contained not only the names of truly loyal supporters, but also many uncommitted voters and even persons committed to other candidates.

In identifying supporters, candidates often targeted members of groups or communities which the candidate had helped in the past through aspiration or social assistance funds. However, many candidates and success team members believed that the provision of such assistance was by itself insufficient to ensure that the recipients would reciprocate with their votes. They felt beneficiaries could be bought off by rival candidates. This was why their "loyalty" had to be ensured by vote buying. In fact, however, from the voters' standpoint, the problem was that aspiration and social assistance fund projects often involved significant corruption, so that they received few benefits from them; little wonder that "beneficiaries" were therefore often unsympathetic to the politicians who delivered these projects.

By focusing on voters whom they thought of as sympathetic, candidates believed that they were enhancing the likelihood that their vote-buying efforts would not go to waste. As one candidate explained:

> With regards to execution [this word, *eksekusi*, was often used by candidates to describe the distribution of envelopes on or near voting day], our priority is obviously the masses who we are sure of, rather than the floating masses [*massa mengambang*, a New Order era term that is today used to describe uncommitted voters]. I prefer to hand out transport money, or money to compensate them for the cost of buying petrol [to go to the polling booth] on voting day, to the masses who have already clearly been guided by the members of our team.[7]

Of course, there was a logic to this argument because, even though there were considerable risks even in handing out money to voters whose details had been entered on vote-buying lists, the risks were much greater in giving out money randomly to voters who might lack any sort of commitment to the candidate.

---

[7] Confidential interview, 12 Apr. 2014.

Another candidate confirmed the widespread belief among candidates that they needed above all to "secure" (*mengamankan*) the votes of loyal supporters:

> If in a particular village our team is strong and we want to go all out, we'll actually try to increase the number of team members there. In other words, we don't build our teams in any old place. For instance, in my own village we have 300 people in my team. It means that if we have a base area, we have to get as many team members as possible there, because we have to secure it. Some people might think it's best to cast their nets into the sea, but I'm not like that. I think it's better to cast my net into a fishpond where we know there are plenty of fish.[8]

The problem that arises from such descriptions, however, was that often the job of defining who was "loyal" or a "supporter" of the candidate was effectively outsourced to the brokers. If what candidates meant by the term "supporter"—and this often seemed to be the case—was simply individuals whose names were included on the lists compiled by their success teams, this was an exceptionally minimalist and unreliable definition. Success team members were often slapdash when entering the names of voters on these lists, and some entered names without even the knowledge of the individuals concerned. It was thus often far from certain that an individual on a vote-buying list was in fact committed to voting for the candidate in question.

Overlap in data collection by success team members was another problem. For example, in the village of Grogolan, around one polling booth where I conducted much of my research, numerous *korlap* working for different candidates included the same citizens on their lists. As a result, many voters received multiple payments. It was not uncommon for one person to receive six envelopes. Obviously, many so-called uncommitted voters, or supporters of rival candidates, were being mixed with "loyal supporters" in many lists.

In fact, it is worth noting that some candidates also believed it was important to target not only so-called loyalists but also swing voters. One PDI-P candidate for the district parliament explained:

---

[8] Confidential interview, 7 Apr. 2014.

I also carried out execution [of vote buying], and did so not only by using the voter list we had fixed. We also mapped areas that we thought we could attack. The floating mass after all don't really care about what party you are from, for them what's important is that the candidate gives them money.[9]

The problem here was that almost all candidates distributed money so it was unlikely that there would be any area where such an undirected "attack" would yield significant results, at least if the amounts of money being distributed were not large (and in this case the candidate was distributing envelopes containing only Rp 10,000, at the lower level of the scale of distribution in Pati). Indeed, one of this candidate's success team members explained that even his more directed vote-buying efforts were not very successful: though he had distributed cash to the 100 persons on his list, the candidate only got 20 votes at the relevant polling booth.[10] And in this case the 100 persons had been on the list from early in the campaign period, and were considered to be "loyal".

Vote buying thus typically involved a huge failure rate (candidates often used the English term, "margin error"). For example, one success team member related to me that the 107 envelopes he distributed around his polling booth produced only 62 votes for his candidate.[11] Another explained how in the village of Alasdowo, 1,700 envelopes were handed out, yielding only 350 votes. This success rate of 21 per cent was not particularly unusual. Several team members who worked for other candidates also pointed to success rates in the 20–25 per cent range. According to one success team member the candidate she supported spent a total of Rp 300 million on vote buying, distributed in about 15,000 envelopes each containing Rp 20,000, but won a little under 2,000 votes and failed to get elected.[12]

These high failure rates were partly products of the failings of the success teams. Many team members, especially the low-level *korlap*, adopted a casual attitude to their work and simply aimed to provide their candidates with lists, without ensuring that the persons on those

---

9   Confidential interview, 14 Apr. 2014.
10 Confidential interview, 11 Apr. 2014.
11 Ibid.
12 Confidential interview, 10 Apr. 2014.

lists were truly committed to supporting the candidate. Many of these team members were likely to be what Aspinall calls "opportunist brokers", whose goal was to misappropriate part of the money they were handling.[13] One candidate confirmed that many team members passed on only part of the money they were supposed to distribute, or even none at all:

> In the village of Kembang, according to a report I received, they were handing out only Rp 10,000 notes, though they received Rp 20,000 per person from the candidate. When my relative put it in the envelopes, nobody was supposed to get just 10,000. In Grogolan village, a former village head was entrusted to distribute Rp 5 million, but the candidate only got about 30 votes there.[14]

From such cases we can see that the success team played a critical role in determining which candidates were elected. As one candidate put it, the key to victory in the 2014 election in Pati was not the individual candidate, and certainly not the party, but rather the success team members who were in direct contact with the voters.[15]

Modes of Delivery: From House to House

Most success team members knew that distributing cash to voters was illegal. Most were unconcerned, however, as a result of the extremely lax enforcement of the election regulations. At the same time, most residents were highly permissive of vote buying, although some of them interpreted it negatively, as we shall see. Election officials, for their part, often hid behind the excuse that such practices were difficult to prove. In fact, vote buying took place so openly in Pati that it would have been easy to find evidence for prosecutions. Accordingly, if the officials from Panitia Pengawas Pemilu (Panwaslu, Elections Supervisory Committee) had acted more boldly, the circulation of cash might have been significantly reduced.

---

[13] Edward Aspinall, "When Brokers Betray: Clientelism, Social Networks, and Electoral Politics in Indonesia", *Critical Asian Studies* 46, 4 (2014): 545–70.
[14] Confidential interview, 10 Apr. 2014.
[15] Interview, Teguh Bandang W., 7 Apr. 2014.

Distribution was generally a straightforward process: *korlap* went from house to house, visiting the voters on their lists and handing out the money in envelopes. Here and there, voters themselves would take the initiative and visit the broker's home, asking for their money. When they handed over the money, most *korlap* provided a brief demonstration of how to vote for the candidate on the large and complex ballot paper, usually also handing out a sample ballot, or a card highlighting where the candidate was to be found on the ballot paper. Some, however, would just hand over the cash to the voter and verbally request support for the candidate, without explaining the technicalities of how to cast a vote accurately. As a result, many voters received money without being really sure who it was they were supposed to vote for.

Mostly, candidates distributed individual payments for each voter on their list in a household, though some only made a single payment for each household. The money was usually distributed inside blank envelopes. A few teams distributed cash without using envelopes. One candidate (a major political powerbroker in Pati) had his team distribute gifts of rice (2 kg per voter) about four days before polling day as a form of down payment (*panjer* in Javanese). After that, about a day before polling, he also distributed payments of Rp 20,000 to each of the voters on his lists.

Most candidates worried greatly that some of the money they were distributing would go missing, as it had to pass through several sets of hands (usually, those of a subdistrict coordinator, a village coordinator and then a *korlap*) before it reached the voter. Candidates used various strategies to try to overcome this problem. For example, at one polling booth where I conducted research, one candidate used mostly female success team members to distribute cash because, like many others, she believed that women were more trustworthy. Another candidate sent especially trusted deputies to accompany the *korlap* when they handed over the envelopes. He believed that this was an effective way to pre-empt embezzlement:

> To control the distribution, I indeed have a strategy but I can't explain it because later other candidates will copy it. All the candidates will be ripped off [*kebobolan*] but me, as someone who's been in the business

of politics for nine years, I'm convinced that the chances that anyone
will misuse my money are very small.[16]

In fact, many candidates used this or similar methods, with varying
effectiveness. A member of another candidate's team explained:

> He sent members of his family or people he really trusted to accompany
> [those handing out the cash] to ensure it really went to its intended
> targets. If you didn't do that, it could be dangerous. But I didn't want
> anyone to accompany me; I was really helping him out as a friend.[17]

Another candidate commented similarly:

> In controlling the distribution, well, yes, I did check, but just by doing
> sampling [by which he simply meant visiting target areas to check
> whether he was being mentioned by locals as one of the candidates
> distributing envelopes]. In a few places we could cover we did direct
> monitoring [while the cash was being handed out]. But of course I
> did most of my execution in my own area. As for the effectiveness of
> that execution, it's only about 25 per cent for all parties.[18]

This candidate was typical: most candidates paid special attention,
including in the distribution of cash and other gifts, to their base areas.
For district candidates, this meant their home villages or subdistricts.

If ensuring that the money reached the voters was problematic,
candidates had even greater difficulty in ensuring that voters who
received cash actually reciprocated with a vote. Asking for evidence
could cause affront given that the sums being distributed were relatively
small. One vote broker related how she tried to get voters to document
their votes by taking photographs using their handphones, but even she
did not end up pursuing this strategy seriously:

> In the end, if there was a voter who came to me and said he or she
> would really, truly vote for the candidate I supported, yeah, I gave them
> the money. Then [after voting day] some also came to me and showed
> me a photo of their vote, well I gave them Rp 50,000 straight away.[19]

---

[16] Confidential interview, 12 Apr. 2014.
[17] Ibid.
[18] Confidential interview, 11 Apr. 2014.
[19] Ibid.

Of course, photographic evidence in itself might not be a guarantee, given that digital technology allows photos of the relevant section of ballot papers to be copied and distributed widely among voters. In the end, everybody assumed it was very hard to provide evidence of exactly what a voter does in the polling booth. Most candidates simply handed out cash before the vote, and hoped for the best.

THE MEANING OF MONEY: FROM GIFTS TO PUNISHMENT

Studies of vote buying in other parts of the world indicate that cash payments from politicians can have multiple meanings for recipients. As Schaffer and Schedler explain, some voters can view these payments as a wage, a gift, reparations for past misdemeanours, a source of affront, a sign of virtue on the part of a candidate, a sign of vice, or a sign of strength.[20] Several of these constructions were found among the voters of Pati.

In particular, in the Pati context, it cannot be assumed that, just because a person received money from a candidate, that person's vote had been bought. This was especially the case given that there was so much overlap in the distribution of cash, with many individuals receiving payments from two or more candidates competing at the same level, confusing them as to whom they should support. Some households responded to this dilemma by dividing their votes among candidates who provided them with payments. Others believed that they should vote for the candidate who gave them money first, with the rationale that when something is being distributed, it is always the people who come first who get a share, not those who arrive late. Yet other voters determined their choice on the basis of their relations not with the candidate, but with the person who gave them the cash on

---

[20] Frederic C. Schaffer and Andreas Schedler, "What is Vote Buying?", in *Elections for Sale: The Causes and Consequences of Vote Buying*, ed. Frederic C. Schaffer (Boulder, CO: Lynne Reinner; Quezon City: Ateneo de Manila University Press, 2007), pp. 25–7.

his or her behalf, for example, voting for a candidate whose success team member was a relative.

However, some voters were undeniably influenced by the money they received, especially when one candidate gave a larger sum than others. Typically, if a household received multiple envelopes and one of them contained more cash than the others, they would direct at least one of the family's votes to that candidate. Likewise, if a candidate did not distribute money at all, voters were unlikely to take that candidate seriously and he or she would get few votes. Almost all candidates believed that both the giving of cash and the size of the gift had a determining effect on voter choices, with them mostly viewing voters as "pragmatic". Of course, there were also a few voters who said that money, including the size of the payment, was a critical factor influencing their preference. However, we must not forget that money was never an instrument that stood in isolation from other factors such as family ties, friendship and other connections to the candidate.

Moreover, many voters I spoke to interpreted the cash payments they received in ways which did *not* imply reciprocity. First, some felt that the money they received was *rejeki*—a blessing or material benefit received from God which they therefore should not reject. In addition, refusing the money would mean offending the success team members who were handing it out, who were usually neighbours. There was also a feeling that turning down the money could be considered arrogant or pretentious, especially if those doing so were from a poor family. Many voters accepted the payments on the basis of such considerations, rather than according to the logic of a transaction between buyer and seller, which is what many candidates assumed was happening. Precisely because many voters felt that they had not asked for the money, they viewed it as an unencumbered gift which imposed no burden or requirement on them.

Second, some religiously inclined voters viewed the money as being *syubhat*, meaning it was not clear whether it was sanctioned (*halal*) or forbidden (*haram*) according to Islamic law. Accordingly, although these voters accepted the money they did not use it to purchase food or drink that they would consume and which then would pass into their bodies. Instead, they used it for other purchases, such as petrol, telephone charges or cigarettes. One candidate who was trained in Islamic law argued, however, that it was permissible to accept such money so long as the recipient still voted according to his or her conscience.[21]

Third, some voters viewed the payments as in fact being their own money: the payments were derived from public funds that had been "taken" by candidates while in office, typically via corruption. Accordingly, voters had every right to receive the money without feeling bound to vote for whoever was giving it out (this attitude, of course, applied only to candidates who were incumbents). Fourth, some voters went even further and saw these payments as a way to punish politicians, by taking their money, but voting for someone else. This especially applied to candidates who were seen as having failed to deliver tangible benefits in the past or as being especially pragmatic in their dealings with residents—for instance, only interacting with them in the lead-up to an election.

Obviously, such attitudes were connected to wider disillusionment among voters with existing political institutions, which many see as being incapable of improving their welfare. They point to deep cynicism about politicians, who are often seen as being concerned only with pursuing their own self-interest and engaging in corruption. Overall, these problems add up to deep challenges when it comes to developing a sense of universal citizenship among voters.

Overall, given the range of attitudes summarised above, it is clearly no exaggeration to say that vote buying is a strategy that is full of uncertainty, and which often involves a significant gamble on the part of those practising it. A candidate who relies only on this approach, without developing supplementary strategies, such as building direct relations with voters or encouraging an esprit de corps in the success team, will very likely be disappointed. In the end, money is not the only tool that can be used to influence voter preferences, even in a place like Pati where vote buying is so widespread.

---

[21] Confidential interview, 19 Mar. 2014.

CONCLUSION

Vote buying was rampant in Pati in the 2014 legislative election. Yet my findings also suggest that it was a strategy that was not only very costly for those who engaged in it but also often ineffective. With a success rate that rarely exceeded 20–25 per cent and was sometimes even lower, many candidates distributed cash to 10,000 voters, at great personal cost, and yet only got 2,000 to 2,500 votes, a number that was usually not enough to be elected (the candidate with the lowest vote total to be elected in the Pati DPRD was Sri Lestari Wahyu Anggraeni, a Partai Demokrat candidate in electoral district V, who gained 2,587 votes). Obviously, vote buying was a very risky strategy. Moreover, though many candidates believed they were distributing cash to a loyal base, in fact this so-called base was often itself simply a construct of the lists that their success teams provided, teams that were themselves often not monitored closely. Many voters ended up on more than one list, and many success team members performed their tasks poorly, if at all.

But if it was so ineffective, why did so many candidates engage in vote buying? One answer suggested by this research is that candidates themselves failed to understand the roots of voters' pragmatism. Viewing voters as being ruled by transactional logic, candidates responded not by promoting a programmatic politics which could have eroded such perceptions but as traders, assuming they would be able to simply purchase the commodity—votes—they needed. As we have seen, many voters viewed the transaction very differently, and hence did not feel obliged to vote for the "buyer".

chapter 15

Blora, Central Java: Local Brokers and Vote Buying

Zusiana Elly Triantini

"Well, it's a people's festival, but this festival is only fun because the candidates are spreading cash around." This statement, made by a grassroots vote broker in Blora, Central Java expresses a view that was widely held in this district during the lead-up to the April 2014 election. In Blora, the buying and selling of votes is no longer a taboo. Community members often openly asked the question: *Wani piro?* (Javanese: How much are you brave enough to pay?) of their candidates. Well-funded candidates frequently answered with *piro-piro wani* ("as brave as you want").

Despite the festival atmosphere, however, and the obvious delight that many voters took in their ability to extract payments from candidates, not all was as it seemed. Some of the candidates who responded most generously to their constituents' requests did not end up being elected. Many voters took money or other gifts without intending to vote for the candidate. In such circumstances, what then determined electoral success? My findings in the field suggest that one critical factor was the methods candidates used to recruit success team members, and then the methods these teams used in the field to target voters and deliver cash and goods to them.

Candidates and others used many different terms to describe their networks, such as *tim sukses* or *tim survei*, and to describe the individuals that made up these teams, including *kader* (cadres) and *korlap* (field coordinators). The most commonly used term was *sabet* (Javanese: "to whip"), which has long been used in Blora to describe brokers who distribute envelopes containing cash to voters at election time. *Sabet* came from many different social backgrounds. Many were ordinary villagers, others were village government functionaries or RW and RT heads, and still others were spiritual actors (*dukun*, shaman) or leaders in social organisations.

These *sabet* played a critical role in vote buying by candidates, in particular by collecting lists of voters—a process known locally by the English-language phrase, "by name, by address". However, not all the names that ended up on these lists were of people who actually intended to vote for the candidate. Many *sabet* used rather slipshod methods in drawing up the lists, writing down people's names without knowing anything about their voting preferences, or without inquiring about who among them had been contacted by other teams. How well the *sabet* created these lists was critical to a candidate's success or failure.

The effectiveness and loyalty of brokers was thus central to election outcomes in Blora. Accordingly, brokerage networks are the focus of this chapter. The discussion proceeds as follows. First, after a brief introduction to Blora, three forms of patronage politics used by candidates are surveyed, along with the critical role played by *sabet* in each. Second, the process by which *sabet* drew up their vote-buying lists is analysed more closely. A third section explores the role of big-time gamblers (*botoh*) in distributing cash in some locations on voting day, in order to swing the results. A final discussion focuses on women candidates and asks whether there was anything distinctive about the methods and networks they used.

BACKGROUND: SOCIAL AND POLITICAL SETTING OF MONEY POLITICS

Blora, an inland district of Central Java, is one of the rice bowls of the province, with most of the population engaged in agriculture, notably growing corn in addition to rice. It is, however, rather mountainous, and just under 50 per cent of the district is given over to state forests producing teak. Another industry of note is oil, with many small-scale oil wells left over from the Dutch colonial era still in production and managed by local entrepreneurs.

Blora is, overall, an *abangan* part of Java, with many residents still holding strongly to animist beliefs and practising traditional rituals such as visits to sacred tombs on important occasions. *Dukun*—traditional healers and spirit mediums—are a prominent feature of local communities, and they also play a political role, whether as spiritual advisors to candidates or as vote brokers. Of course, as elsewhere in Java, the local community is by no means monolithic, and there are also many Nahdlatul Ulama (NU)-aligned traditionalist Muslims with several important *pesantren* in the district and a smattering of modernist Muslims and adherents of other religions in the town.

In party terms, Golkar and Partai Demokrat have dominated the local parliament for several electoral cycles. An underlying trend is that both the district parliament and its executive government are dominated by what might be called local oligarchs. In 2004, for example, two leading PDI-P members of the district DPRD were local entrepreneurs who had grown rich from sugar and teak, and were famous equally for their great wealth and their charitable works. A Golkar legislator was a local oil entrepreneur, with wells in Blora and Bojonegoro, and was famous for spreading money around the district (he was re-elected in both 2009 and 2014). In 2014, another local oil boss was elected, this time through the Nasdem party.

Another slice of the local political elite consists of PKB and PPP politicians who originate from prominent local *pesantren* families and who are active in wholesale trade and have strong networks with market traders. The Blora market—and more generally trade throughout the district—is itself dominated by traditionalist Muslims with *pesantren* links, who then become a formidable political base for these politicians.

Interestingly, though money politics—especially vote buying—is now massive in local elections, many local informants can date its arrival on Blora's political scene very precisely. Most blame two of these local entrepreneurs when they first stood for the district legislature in

2004. It was they, people say, who introduced large-scale individual vote buying in legislative elections (though the practice was previously already well known in village-head elections). By 2014 it had become firmly entrenched in electoral politics throughout Blora.

For this research, I focused on two electoral districts with contrasting social, cultural and economic features. Electoral district I includes the town of Blora itself, as well as the neighbouring subdistricts of Jiken, Jepon and Bogorejo; electoral district V consists of the subdistricts of Ngawen, Banjarejo and Tunjungan, 15–30 km from Blora town. District I is demographically mixed, with a large ethnic Chinese minority, as well as many civil servants, and religion factors little in local political alignments. District V, by contrast, is primarily agricultural and NU heartland territory. Though in many respects political competition in the two electoral districts was similar in 2014, the average size of cash payments to voters was different: between Rp 20,000 and 30,000 in district V, and 30,000 to 100,000 in district I.

PATTERNS OF PATRONAGE POLITICS: OPEN, SEMI-CLOSED AND CLOSED

It should be noted from the outset that all my respondents agreed that a key plank of political campaigning in Blora was giving cash, goods or services to voters. All described using some form of patronage politics in order to get elected. However, how open these strategies were—by which I mean the extent to which they were carried out in the public gaze—varied.

When candidates wanted to confer benefits on a whole community—by distributing club goods—they were generally open about doing so. In fact, they had to be. If they wanted to outbid offers coming in from other candidates, they had to know about them, and this usually required open discussion at meetings with voters. One PAN candidate explained how this happened:

> I would bargain [*tawar-menawar*] with residents about what assistance
> I needed to give them. For instance, some residents told me that they
> had already been helped by a Hanura candidate who had provided

them with the materials they needed to asphalt their road. I offered them the service of actually laying that asphalt down. In my opinion, that was a valuable offer for them.[1]

Provision of such club goods to communities usually occurred early on, during the formal campaign season or even a few months beforehand, rather than close to voting day. It was also a high-cost strategy. If a candidate wanted to make a mark on a community, he or she usually had to spend over Rp 1 million per "donation": gifts of livestock, such as cows or goats to constituents (a PKS candidate), agricultural equipment (a Golkar candidate), road construction (another Golkar candidate), provision of street lighting and repairs to drainage (a Demokrat candidate) and distribution of foodstuffs (a PAN candidate). One Golkar candidate, a former official in the local government's Education and Culture Bureau, sponsored an inter-village volleyball competition, buying uniforms for the teams, and paying a prize of Rp 600,000 for the winning village and Rp 300,000 for the runner-up.

Candidates who were incumbents were advantaged in this approach, because they could draw on aspiration funds they could access through the legislature to pay for such projects. Several candidates who were former local government bureaucrats could also call up officials in relevant government agencies to get them to supply whatever the community needed. But whether they were mobilising public or private funds, by necessity this form of patronage occurred out in the open: if candidates wanted to reap electoral benefit from their largesse, the recipient community had to know who was responsible for it.

The main form of semi-closed campaigning candidates engaged in was house-to-house visits. The typical approach here was that candidates would come to a household, usually on advice from their *sabet* about who in the village was likely to be most sympathetic. The *sabet* would invite along some neighbours and an informal meeting would be held. As well as explaining a little about his or her background, vision for the district, and how to locate his or her position on the ballot paper, the candidate would typically ask those present for their "prayers and blessing" (*doa*

---

[1] Confidential interview, 16 Mar. 2014.

dan restu)—and their support on voting day. Many candidates ended such visits by giving small gifts, which could be foodstuffs (such as rice, tea or sugar) or small amounts of money.

The main closed strategy was vote buying. Although almost all candidates in Blora engaged in this practice, they were aware of its illegality. All wanted to avoid being caught in the act by the election monitoring agency, and therefore they tried to hide their involvement to one degree or another. Of all the 19 candidates I interviewed, only 2 (both women candidates, one from PAN, one from Gerindra) said they were not going to distribute cash to voters. Neither of these candidates believed they would win, and were running mostly to support their parties and their "tandem" partners running for higher-level seats. Everyone else explained they were planning to distribute cash one or two days prior to the vote, ranging from Rp 15,000 to 50,000 per voter in rural areas and from Rp 50,000 to 100,000 in and around the town of Blora. They used various terms to describe the practice: "bomb" (*bom*), *kenpyuran* (dissemination) or "transport money" (using the conceit that voters had to cover the costs of getting themselves to the polling booth, though it was usually just an easy stroll).

Most candidates combined cash payments with other strategies. One candidate I followed was generous in providing club goods—funding numerous mosque and *musholla* repairs and buying uniforms for *hadroh* (a form of Islamic music) groups. He was a Partai Demokrat incumbent, who was close to the *bupati* (district head) and thus able to access government funds to pay for projects for his constituents—such as street lighting for one housing estate. Yet he still prepared Rp 500 million to "bomb" the villages on voting day (he did not distribute cash in the town, believing this approach was not effective there).[2] In contrast, a PKB candidate, who was much less well-resourced, turned down all requests to give money for road or mosque repairs, precisely because he was saving all his cash to distribute in the days leading to the vote. He tried to compensate by forming village youth groups into business cooperatives and promising them he would deliver aspiration fund projects to them should he be elected. But he believed that he

---

[2] Confidential interview, 17 Mar. 2014.

needed to save his resources for vote buying. The wealthy Demokrat candidate similarly believed that, although he had helped community groups very generously in his target villages, he still needed to give the voters cash, both because other candidates were doing the same and because he believed it was fair to recompense them for income they would lose by going to the polls.

Sometimes distribution of individual payments arose as a result of face-to-face bargaining between candidates or their brokers and community members. People often used the phrases *wani piro* and *piro-piro wani*, mentioned at the start of this chapter, as well as *ono duite coblos wonge* (I'll vote for whoever has money) when talking about such bargaining. More often, vote buying was an initiative of the candidates— something they had planned to do without having to be asked. In either case, in order to ensure that distribution was systematic and that money actually made its way to the individual voters, the success teams and *sabet* played a critical role. All candidates who practised vote buying used *sabet* to collect data on voters who were prepared to exchange their votes for cash. Team members typically did this simply by writing the voters' names and contact details on lists that were then compiled centrally by the candidate, though some candidates also insisted that their *sabet* also provide photocopies of these voters' ID cards. In one case (that of a PAN candidate who was running in a "tandem" pair with a DPR candidate), brokers handed out promotional stickers which included a peel-off label the voters could fill in.

The *sabet* thus played a critical role in organising vote buying, but in fact they were often central to the other forms of patronage politics as well. Village-level brokers typically facilitated the informal contacts and community meetings through which donations of club goods were negotiated, and they were also key in identifying the people candidates should visit on their campaign tours. In short, candidates relied almost completely on their brokers.

MOBILISING VOTERS "BY NAME, BY ADDRESS"

As noted above, most candidates used their *sabet* to list voters willing to vote for them, and used those same lists to deliver cash payments. These lists were typically called "by name, by address". This system typically involved the candidate assigning one or more *sabet* to a set geographical area: a village, a *dusun* (hamlet), an RW or RT, or a particular polling booth. All sorts of variations were possible: for example, some women *sabet* were charged exclusively with recruiting female voters. All types of people could be *sabet*: often they were people who had personal connections with the candidate (relatives, workmates, friends), but many *sabet* also put themselves forward for their positions on a team.

This system was absolutely necessary for any candidate who wanted to execute a vote-buying strategy. However, though the *sabet* were the crucial link in the chain, they were sometimes a weak link. Given that they were motivated at least partly by material rewards they had an incentive either to inflate their voter lists or fill them with names of voters whose voting intentions they did not know. The result was that *sabet* often provided very lengthy lists, sometimes even from voters outside their designated territories, to their success team coordinators. One success team coordinator (working for a Golkar candidate) explained that he did not take the lists supplied by his brokers at face value, but instead sifted them based on what he knew about the areas they came from:

> I don't just accept all the data that comes in. I still question the *kader* about their validity and I ask them to make sure they are all correct. I've been cutting out a lot of the data we've been getting because some don't seem rational. For example, one of them deposited 200 names, but from the base area of another candidate. So I asked him to start again and when it came back the data had gone down from 200 names to 74.[3]

There were in fact three separate patterns by which candidates collected their voter data "by name, by address". A first pattern involved tightly administered and monitored data collection. Many candidates running in the urban centre of electoral district I used this pattern. What this typically involved was that one or two people helped the candidate (as in the example of the Golkar candidate above) to

---

[3] Confidential interview, 18 Mar. 2014.

cross-check the data supplied by the *sabet*. They would seek other informants—often *sabet* from nearby neighbourhoods or villages—to cast their eyes over the list and check its credibility based on what they knew about the size of the community, the strength of rival candidates there and other local factors. If they had any doubts, they would call in the original *sabet* and get him or her to recheck the voters and their intentions.

Second were candidates who collected written lists, but with only loose administration and monitoring. These were mostly candidates who were not intimately familiar with the areas where their *sabet* were working, and perhaps also lacked close personal relationships with those *sabet* and the voters in these areas. These candidates also did not cross-check the data they received, typically because they lacked the personal networks for doing so. Many of these candidates spent great sums on vote buying, but received few votes in return. Many people on their lists ended up on the lists of other candidates.

Third were candidates who had the confidence to use less formal methods of collecting their data and targeting their vote-buying efforts. Such candidates required only rough written lists from their *sabet*, relying more on verbal communication with them, and trusting them to monitor political developments at the grassroots—particularly the vote-buying efforts of rival candidates—in the days and hours leading to the poll. In these cases, the *sabet* would use their close personal connections with the voters to monitor their voting intentions virtually to the last minute. In fact, in such cases the *sabet* usually had direct personal or cultural connections with the voters on their lists, for example, as members of the same football team or fishing club, or being alumni of the same *pesantren*. This method was often more effective than the more tightly administered lists, because it relied on more committed brokers and stronger identity-based networks: it was often PKB candidates, or other candidates working in the NU milieu and relying on *pesantren* networks who used this approach.

In short, a candidate's success was to a large degree determined by the quality of the work performed by his or her *sabet* at the grassroots. Strong connections between a *sabet* and voters would produce a strong vote. In contrast, as Aspinall has observed, some brokers were highly opportunistic, and saw their work for candidates purely as a profit-making enterprise, with little regard for the votes they delivered.[4] In Blora, I met several *sabet* who took such opportunism to an extreme by working for several candidates at the same time, providing them with the same voter lists. As one *sabet* who was working simultaneously for three candidates competing against each other explained:

> I am working for Bimo from Golkar, as well as Arjuna from Golkar and Krisna from PPP [not their real names]. I've gone to each of their houses and taken them the data that I've drawn up. On voting day I will invite each resident I've listed to come to my house and collect their envelopes.[5]

Such doubling and tripling up was fatal for many candidates because it meant that many of their payments went to waste. I witnessed one *sabet* distributing four envelopes from two different candidates to one voter (for the voter and his wife) and, when I later talked to the recipient, he told me he did not vote for either of those candidates, but rather for another candidate with whom he had long-standing clientelistic ties and who did not pay him anything.

The results were visible on polling day. One candidate from Golkar (the man I have called Bimo above) admitted to distributing 12,000 envelopes (one of his success team members told me it was 40,000) with amounts of cash that varied from place to place (depending on whether it was in the town or a village, and depending on what his rivals were distributing), but only received 6,200 votes. He failed to get the largest personal vote in electoral district I and, though he was elected, he was very disappointed with the result, having received a larger vote in 2009. In contrast, the PPP candidate Krisna got 2,200 votes though he only distributed 6,000 envelopes, and was elected. His organisation was much tighter and he distributed cash only to constituents whom he thought were truly loyal. Bimo used a much looser method of selecting his *sabet*, and rarely checked their data. His campaign was thus far more wasteful of resources. But it should be stressed there were far worse

---

[4] Edward Aspinall, "When Brokers Betray: Social Networks, and Electoral Politics in Indonesia", *Critical Asian Studies* 46, 4 (2014): 545–70.

[5] Confidential interview, 22 Mar. 2014.

stories: one Golkar candidate distributed 11,000 envelopes, received only around 1,800 votes, and failed to be elected.

BOTOH: THE INFLUENCE OF GAMBLING BOSSES

One phenomenon of interest in Blora's 2014 election was the role played by *botoh*, or local gamblers, in vote buying. There is a major subculture of gambling on electoral races in many parts of Java. In Blora, most of these *botoh* came from neighbouring Pati district, forming rival groups who often bet against each other in predicting the outcome of a particular election.

In 2014, in the cases I am aware of, the bets were substantial, at around Rp 50 million per race. Given such an investment, it could be worthwhile for those betting on a loss by a particular candidate to invest substantially in negative vote buying of their own, with potentially destructive results on the efforts of the target candidate. The *botoh* thus sometimes targeted the base areas of the candidate they were betting against, and distributed cash to voters with the instruction for them not to vote for that person. One day after the election I visited a Golkar candidate, whose success team member explained:

> This is the first time that the *botoh* have come into the legislative election; it has been quite normal for them to play a role in village head elections. They came from outside Blora; in our area they came from Pati. They handed out money, Rp 100,000 for each voter on voting day. What's important for them is just that they hurt the vote of candidates they bet against. They usually come in groups, with one group normally containing five to ten people.[6]

The individual payments the *botoh* distributed typically far exceeded the money being distributed by the candidates they targeted. In this particular case, the Golkar candidate had been distributing only Rp 20,000 to each voter, which she had done two days earlier. However, she had also paid for repairs to two *musholla* and was very confident

---

[6] Confidential interview, 10 Apr. 2014.

that she would sweep the village. This prediction was shattered on voting day when 60 per cent of her voters shifted to other candidates, as a result of this intervention by the *botoh*.

The *botoh* do not have larger political goals. Their goals are simply to win their bets. But they do research their interventions carefully. The *botoh* collected information about where the candidate's strengths were and which voters were being targeted by his or her vote-buying efforts by sending out agents to meet with residents in foodstalls, motorcycle taxi ranks and such places. Sometimes, they paid local residents to collect information about the target candidate's campaign. They often targeted just two or three base areas (typically, villages) of the candidate they sought to bring down, singling out younger voters (especially young men) whom they consider to be more amenable to payments. The goal is to wreck the vote of the target candidate in these locations, without giving any instructions to the voters as to where they should direct their votes. The *botoh*, however, have underworld connections and they play it rough, often following up their cash gifts with threats to the recipients that they will be punished if the candidate does not lose.

Experienced and skilful *sabet* will typically be able to detect operations by a *botoh* in their home village—indeed *sabet* themselves sometimes have connections of their own with *botoh* networks, and are used by them. But the inexperienced are often caught unawares.

WOMEN CANDIDATES AND CLIENTELIST POLITICS

Did gender matter to the patterns of clientelist politics and vote buying described above? In particular, was there anything distinctive about the campaigning and networking strategies employed by women candidates? In my research I made a special effort to interview and observe campaign activities of female candidates, meeting with 11 of them. In the Blora DPRD itself, in the 2009–14 period 12 of the 45 elected members were women, but this number fell to 8 out of 45 in 2014.

One starting point for our analysis here is the observation that men still played a critical role in most of these campaigns. If we liken the election to a film, the women candidates were often simply the actors, while the key role was often played by male "directors"—often, the candidate's husband who acted as chief advisor or success team head. Women candidates were rarely able to independently determine their own role and campaign themes.

There were exceptions, however. The only female candidate I considered to be truly independent who was elected in 2014 was an incumbent PKB candidate who was simultaneously a head of the Blora branch of Fatayat, the NU organisation for younger women. She was widely known for her knowledge and skills, including for her ability to recite the Quran and as a speaker at religious gatherings. She made great use of the Fatayat network as the backbone of her campaign. She also did not draw much upon funds provided by outside donors, instead using her access to government funds, especially aspiration funds, to cultivate her constituents. These mostly consisted of women—many of whom were brought together through Fatayat—and she had concentrated during her years in the DPRD on providing them with access to various economic empowerment projects, especially those targeting women through funding for small business cooperatives known as KUBE (Kelompok Usaha Bersama). Her success team was particularly large, consisting of 4,000 people, most of whom were Fatayat members and functionaries spread out through the subdistrict-level branches (*cabang*) and village-level sub-branches (*ranting*). She was very confident of this network's loyalty, as they were bound not only by ideological and gender ties but also by her clientelistic delivery of government programmes over preceding years. This PKB candidate was similar to most of the other women candidates I met, insofar as she mostly relied on women as her success team members and *sabet*.

Apart from a PDI-P candidate—another incumbent with a strong record of bringing aspiration fund projects to her constituency—most of the other women candidates I met, were running in order to help their parties meet the 30 per cent quota of female candidates. Many of them were standing because they had been encouraged to do so by family members, or their party. One PKB candidate was typical:

I joined the party because my husband, who is the party secretary, asked me to do so. Actually, I wasn't too keen, and I never ask the people to vote for me. I think that whichever candidate gets elected is a matter of choice for the voters, so I let them choose for themselves. Those who will choose me are those who know me. I don't have a success team and I only use social media to promote myself. And I am convinced I will get votes.[7]

Another woman candidate from the same party had similar views:

I joined because I enjoy being in an organisation and my father asked me to go to PKB. It's also a good medium for me to start learning about politics. My family and friends are helping me to promote my candidacy. I'm not convinced I will win, but my role is just to increase the vote for the party.[8]

Although I met other female candidates with similar attitudes, not all were like this. There were PDI-P, Golkar and PAN candidates, for example, who, although their funding primarily derived from their husbands, still worked hard to win their seats, including by engaging in door-to-door campaigning and vote buying. These women used success team structures that were similar to those used by male candidates, except that, as noted above, they tended to use women as their *sabet*, and recruit them through female networks such as *arisan* groups, Dasa Wisma (a neighbourhood-level women's group focused on healthcare) and the like.

Moreover, candidates widely believed that female *sabet* were more loyal than male brokers. Of the many female campaign workers I met while conducting this research, none was working for more than one candidate (outside of "tandem" arrangements), while several males I encountered were doing so. The PKB candidate with the Fatayat background mentioned above viewed her reliance on women supporters as a key to her success. In other ways, however, female *sabet* tended to work in similar ways to their male counterparts, except that they tended to target female voters.

---

[7] Confidential interview, 29 Mar. 2014.
[8] Ibid.

CONCLUSION

As with other locations surveyed in this book, the politics of patronage were central to electoral dynamics in Blora. In both electoral districts I focused on, most candidates distributed club goods and built clientelist networks that allowed them to reach down to voters at the grassroots. One distinctive feature of electioneering in Blora, however, was the prominence of vote buying. As noted above, almost all candidates distributed cash gifts to individual voters in the days before the poll.

A mixture of incumbents and first-time candidates were elected in the two electoral districts that were my focus. Though I did not follow all these candidates closely enough to be certain that they all used vote buying, all the successful candidates whose campaigns I did study engaged in the practice. Yet many candidates who invested heavily in vote buying did not succeed, and some of them even lost large sums of money. One woman Partai Demokrat candidate spent Rp 600 million but was not elected; a female Golkar candidate spent Rp 400 million and lost (this was the one whose victory was snatched by a *botoh*). Vote buying per se was thus not the determinant of success, because virtually every serious candidate did it. Nor, as far as I could see, was the amount of money that a candidate distributed the overriding factor in determining who got elected. On the other hand, vote buying was critical, to the extent that many voters viewed themselves as being bound by the money they received, so that candidates could hardly win without distributing some cash.

In most cases, the determinant of success was the strength and reliability of the candidate's brokerage network. Some candidates kept a tight rein on their *sabet*, and closely monitored their data collection; others had highly reliable *sabet* who were both loyal to their candidate and skilled at reading the shifting political moods in their communities. Other candidates, however, had rather lax approaches to recruiting and monitoring their brokers, and received vote-buying lists that were inflated and unrealistic. The extreme opportunism of some brokers, and their willingness to claim payments from multiple candidates for the same vote banks, points to the traps that lay in wait for unwary candidates. Though vote buying may sometimes seem like a surefire means of political success, the experience of Blora suggests that it is actually a highly risky and costly strategy.

chapter **16**

East Java: New Clientelism and the Fading of *Aliran* Politics

Rubaidi

Over the last decade-and-a-half of democratic politics, there has been a recurring debate about the extent to which the old system of *aliran* (streams) that once dominated Indonesian politics has broken down. According to the *aliran* view, first propounded by Clifford Geertz, politics in Indonesia, or at least in Java, was based on deeply rooted socioreligious communities, or streams.[1] An important division was between the *abangan* (syncretic or nominal Muslims) and the *santri* (devout Muslims), who were in turn divided into modernist and traditionalist streams. In the view of some scholars who compared the results of the 1955 election with those of the first subsequent democratic election, in 1999, the old pattern of *aliran* politics was largely unchanged.[2] Other observers, however, have argued that since 1999 the *aliran* pattern has begun to fade. Tanuwidjaja, for example, points to the long-term decline in votes for Islamic parties since 1955 as a sign

---

[1] Clifford Geertz, *The Religion of Java* (New York: Free Press, 1960).
[2] Olle Törnquist, "Dynamics of Indonesian Democratization", *Third World Quarterly* 21, 3 (2000): 413.

of the declining relevance of socioreligious identities in Indonesian electoral politics.[3]

In this chapter, by focusing on electoral district VIII in East Java—a constituency that incorporates four rural districts or *kabupaten* (Mojokerto, Jombang, Nganjuk and Madiun) and two urban municipalities or *kota* (Mojokerto and Madiun)—during the 2014 legislative election, I demonstrate that *aliran* politics are indeed facing serious challenge. Unlike other scholars, however, I point to Indonesia's changing electoral system, and the changing nature of its patronage politics, as causal factors. I present two major findings to support this argument. First, voting patterns are shifting as some voters replace *aliran* loyalties with more "rational" calculations in making their political choices. In the past, affiliation to *aliran* was based on what might be labelled an old culture of clientelism, whereby political and social relationships were based on unreserved obedience by a client to a patron within a single cultural community. The new culture of clientelism apparent in Java involves a strong element of calculation by clients regarding the material benefits they can gain from affiliating with a particular patron, and no longer necessitates blind identification with the party where a patron might be located. This shift is apparent during elections, when some voters are greatly influenced by the benefits they may gain through candidates' vote buying and other forms of patronage, rather than by fixed *aliran* or other loyalties.

Second, competition between individual candidates in Indonesia's open-list proportional representation (PR) system is increasingly crossing *aliran* lines. If in earlier elections rival parties competed primarily to mobilise separate *aliran* blocs, by 2014 it was apparent that many candidates were crossing freely between *aliran* in their chase for votes. This was made possible by candidates' reliance on their own clientelistic networks, including success teams, with which they mobilised a personal vote. In building these networks, candidates opportunistically made

---

[3] Sunny Tanuwidjaja, "Political Islam and Political Parties in Indonesia: Critically Assessing the Evidence of Islam's Political Decline", *Contemporary Southeast Asia* 32, 1 (2010): 29–49. See also Andreas Ufen, "From *Aliran* to Dealignment: Political Parties in Post-Suharto Indonesia", *South East Asia Research* 16, 1 (2008): 5–41.

use of whatever connections, relationships and institutions they could access, often without paying attention to the supposed *aliran* loyalties of voters or even to the *aliran* identities of the parties that nominated them. In other words, *santri* candidates were not just building links to fellow *santri* voters but also competing to win over *abangan* voters, and vice versa. Critically, this *aliran*-hopping was occurring, not just within newer catch-all parties, but also among candidates within parties (such as PKB and PDI-P) that were historically strongly associated with one or other *aliran*.

In making these arguments, I draw a distinction between "old clientelism" and "new clientelism". Old clientelism has been described in many anthropological and sociological writings on traditional agrarian societies and involved relations between patrons and clients that were relatively stable, long-lasting and marked by high levels of reciprocal loyalty. According to Putra's analysis of traditional society in South Sulawesi, for example, patron–client relationships were highly personalised in this part of Indonesia, such that harming a client was widely understood as being akin to harming the patron himself.[4] Following Jonathan Hopkin, "new clientelism" takes place in more modern societies marked by greater urbanisation and social mobility.[5] This context produces relations between patrons and clients that are "less hierarchical, more 'democratic'", with "less of a sense of deference and dependency on the part of the client".[6] Moreover, "as a result of this less hierarchical and personalized context, the new clientelism is more conducive to fluidity and change in electoral behaviour, opening up possibilities of greater competition and elite turnover".[7]

[4] Heddy Shri Ahimsa Putra, *Patron dan Klien di Sulawesi Selatan: Sebuah Kajian Fungsional-Struktural* [Patrons and Clients in South Sulawesi: A Structural-Functional Analysis] (Yogyakarta: Kepel Press, 2007), pp. 15–17.

[5] Jonathan Hopkin, "Conceptualizing Political Clientelism: Political Exchange and Democratic Theory", paper presented at the American Political Science Association Annual Meeting, Philadelphia, 31 Aug.–3 Sept. 2006, p. 3.

[6] Ibid.

[7] Ibid.

The shift from old to new clientelism captures much of the dynamic I observed during fieldwork in East Java in the lead-up to the 2014 legislative election. In Geertz's classic account of Javanese society, the division between the *aliran* were relatively clear, and ties between patrons and clients within them tended to be stable—especially in the traditionalist Islamic community where relations between politicians and their followers were simultaneously relations between *kyai* (religious scholars) and their *santri* (boarding school students). Now, open-list PR has downgraded the role of parties in electoral competition and increased that of individual candidates, leading to a more individualised and personalised pattern of electoral mobilisation. The number of would-be patrons competing for voters has multiplied. Candidates use varied clientelistic networks, patronage distribution and vote buying to attain support, increasingly transgressing *aliran* divisions. Voters, too, are becoming more cynical, as evidenced by the fact that there is often a large gap (typically, as high as 50 or 60 per cent) between the number of envelopes containing cash that candidates distribute and the votes they achieve at the ballot box.

BACKGROUND: *ALIRAN* POLITICS IN EAST JAVA VIII

With a total of 4.3 million registered voters, East Java electoral constituency VIII is divided into two cultural zones. In the east, and closer to the coast, are Mojokerto and Jombang—*santri* heartlands with a strong presence of Nahdlatul Ulama (NU) and many *pesantren*, including some of the most famous in the country, such as the Tebu Ireng *pesantren* founded by NU founder Hasyim Asy'ari. In the west, Nganjuk and Madiun are strongly *abangan* in character, and are part of the broad Mataraman Javanese heartland area of the interior of East Java (also incorporating Kediri, Ponorogo, Blitar and several other major centres).

Since 1999, a distinctive feature of electoral competition in East Java has been the continuing influence of *aliran* politics. As in other parts of the country, there is a complex multi-party system, but two leading parties in the province have in most post-Suharto elections been the two major *aliran*-oriented parties: PKB, which is linked to NU and broadly represents the traditionalist *santri* community, and PDI-P, which is based among *abangan* voters (and non-Muslims in other parts of the country). PKB attained the highest vote in East Java in 1999 and 2004, followed by PDI-P. In 2009, PKB was badly afflicted by internal conflict and then-President Yudhoyono's Partai Demokrat won in the province. In 2014, the leading party was PDI-P, followed by PKB. At the same time, a host of other parties, both Islamically-oriented and nationalist (or nationalist-religious, as the Partai Demokrat styles itself) compete for both *abangan* and *santri* voters.

PDI-P has consistently been the leading party in electoral district VIII since 1999. Broadly speaking, election results in the districts and municipalities that make up the constituency have followed the *aliran* map described above, though not always in a strictly linear fashion. Thus, Nganjuk has since 1999 consistently been a stronghold of the PDI-P, and Mojokerto has similarly been a bastion of PKB. In contrast, PDI-P has generally (except in 2004) been the leading party in Jombang, which, despite its strong *santri* image, in fact also has a large *abangan* population. In Madiun, PKB and PDI-P have tended to be balanced, and a PKB *bupati* (district head) was elected in the *kabupaten* in 2008.

PATTERNS OF POLITICAL MOBILISATION AND PATRONAGE DISTRIBUTION

My field research in constituency VIII focused exclusively on candidates competing for seats in the provincial legislature based in Surabaya. I interviewed and closely followed the campaign teams of ten candidates representing seven parties (two each from PDI-P, PKB and Gerindra, and one each from Partai Demokrat, Nasdem, PPP and Golkar). My research focused on candidates whom I believed were strongly placed to win seats (seven of the ten did), and who were distributed across Islamic and nationalist parties, and between individuals with *abangan* and *santri* backgrounds.

Before we discuss the networks these candidates used, which will take us directly to their *aliran* alignments, we need to provide background on the inducements they provided to voters. As in many parts of Indonesia, the campaigning in East Java VIII was strongly patronage-oriented. It came in two main forms: pork barrel politics and vote buying.

All candidates made promises of "programmes" during their campaigning. However, when candidates used the term "program", they were referring to small-scale economic development, health, education and infrastructure projects which they could personally deliver to their constituencies through the provincial parliament's Jaring Aspirasi Masyarakat (Jasmas) programme. The name literally means "net the community's aspirations", referring to the fact that legislators were supposed to visit their communities when the legislature was in recess, listen to community aspirations and report back on what they heard in order to determine priorities and allocate funds. Under this programme, a set amount (in 2014, Rp 5 billion) was allocated per legislator which could be used for various purposes, in accordance with the "aspirations" of community members. Legislators differed somewhat in how they expended these funds; some used most of their Jasmas allocations for agricultural programmes and farmers' groups, while others used it for mosque, *madrasah* (Islamic school) and road improvements (see Chapter 7 by Muhammad Mahsun for discussion of a similar aspiration fund programme in South Sumatra province).

While both incumbents and non-incumbents typically made promises about future projects they would deliver when they were campaigning, the former were advantaged because they typically had a record of past delivery they could point toward. Thus, one candidate I followed was a sitting legislator from the Golkar party. During his five years in the legislature, he told me, he had directed 60 per cent of his Jasmas funds to the district of Nganjuk, with the remainder spent through Jombang, Mojokerto and Madiun.[8] He deliberately focused these funds on assistance for farmers' groups (*kelompok tani*) and, when it came time for re-election, he was very confident that these beneficiaries would support him. Accordingly, he set aside a relatively modest amount (Rp 275 million) for vote buying, which he expended only in areas he had prepared with these programmes. This plan was unsuccessful,

---

[8] Confidential interview, 1 Apr. 2014.

however, and he was not re-elected, pointing, in this candidate's mind, to the growing importance of transactional politics.

Nevertheless, incumbent candidates generally believed Jasmas programmes were critical for their re-election efforts. Thus, one candidate (Renville Antonio, a senior Partai Demokrat figure) who was a sitting member of the DPRD explained how, once his party decided he would stand in East Java VIII in 2014 (in 2009 he was elected from electoral district VI), he immediately redirected his remaining *Jasmas* funds to the constituency where he would next face the voters.

In addition to promising pork barrel projects, or relying on their past delivery of such projects, candidates also delivered cash and other gifts to voters. This happened in two main ways. First, almost every candidate gave "transport money" to community members who came to the small-scale meetings their success teams organised for them, which were typically attended by 20 to 100 people. Second, vote buying in the form of the notorious dawn attack was widespread. My estimate is that about 95 per cent of incumbents and other serious candidates engaged in vote buying, with varying modus operandi. Vote buying typically happened on the day of, or the evening before, the vote, when success team members distributed cash door to door.

Members of our research team, including myself, had the opportunity to interview many candidates and success team members about this procedure, and to witness aspects of it. Data we collected in the field suggest that the typical sums distributed to voters ranged between Rp 20,000 and Rp 50,000, with amounts varying according to differing "market prices" in each district or municipality. The town of Mojokerto was widely known as having the highest price per voter, in part because its small population of about 22,000 meant that candidates here had to win a smaller vote total than elsewhere and could thus afford higher payments. According to one candidate there, with such intense competition among candidates, residents could expect to receive payments from multiple candidates and to get on average Rp 500,000 to Rp 700,000 from vote buying. Quite a number of provincial candidates avoided campaigning in Mojokerto town as a result. The "price" per vote was around Rp 50,000 in Madiun (both town and country), but in the rural districts of Mojokerto, Jombang and Nganjuk it ranged from Rp 20,000 to Rp 35,000. The costs were often shared through "tandem" arrangements between district, provincial and national candidates (thus the rupiah sums mentioned above were typically not for each vote, but per voter, with an expectation that the voter would repay with three votes, one at each level).

This reliance on money politics meant that serious candidates expended considerable sums on their re-election efforts. As one success team member (the husband of a PKB candidate) explained, "I have readied Rp 700 to Rp 900 million to anticipate these last days."[9] He added that he had also spent Rp 450 million on other campaign activities.

A Gerindra candidate, who was close to the governor and deputy governor of the province, was widely known to have spent the most on vote buying in the constituency, distributing not only cash but also two 10-ton trucks full of baked goods. One member of this candidate's success team told me, not long before the poll, that he was in charge of disbursing Rp 1.5 billion for vote buying in Nganjuk district alone, and that he knew the candidate had spent an additional Rp 1.3 billion for other campaign expenses in the same district. He did not know how much the candidate was spending in Jombang, Mojokerto and Madiun.[10] The candidate concerned was relying so heavily on vote buying because he believed that voters in this part of Java were no longer motivated by *aliran* loyalties as they had been in the first post-Suharto election in 1999. Angrily, he explained that community attitudes were now explained by a term that was widely circulating in the lead-up to the election:

> The people are extraordinary now! They're nuts! [They believe that] rather than dreaming of eating cake, you should eat cassava [a saying meaning, roughly, "A bird in the hand is worth two in the bush"]. Number one for them now is money, yeah money, that's obvious. It happens because of all those candidates who've just made promises [they don't keep].[11]

In fact, candidates who made distributing cash the central component of their strategy faced great uncertainties, and many badly miscalculated. The same Gerindra candidate distributed 109,000 envelopes containing

---

[9] Confidential interview, 18 Mar. 2014.
[10] Confidential interview, 2 Apr. 2014.
[11] Interview, Gerindra candidate, 25 Mar. 2014.

cash during his "dawn attack", but achieved a vote of only around 67,000 or about 60 per cent. A PKB candidate who, according to a campaign organiser, distributed cash to over 80,000 voters only attained a little over 40,000 votes, a success rate of 50 per cent, and only made it into the DPRD because she could rely on votes for other candidates and her party.[12] Success rates of this sort were common.

In this respect, it is important to note that, although most of the candidates we encountered used money politics, not all of them did so. Of course, some did not attempt vote buying simply because they lacked the money; such people were weak candidates who failed to get elected. But some successful candidates also refused to buy votes. For example, both PDI-P candidates elected to the provincial parliament from East Java VIII apparently did not engage in vote buying. Slamet Heru Nugroho, a local party leader who was not an incumbent, lacked the money to engage in this sort of politics, but he also said he opposed it in principle: "I wish to prove the power of *silaturahmin* [the bonds of fellowship] and of humanism." He explained that he spent a total of Rp 176 million for his campaign, most of it on the purchase of promotional material such as name cards and calendars, and to pay for snacks, drinks and cigarettes for the many informal meetings he held with residents.[13] Despite this relatively modest campaign style, Nugroho was placed first among PDI-P candidates in the constituency, defeating the incumbent.

The second PDI-P candidate who was elected without vote buying was Gatot Supriadi, the head of the Mojokerto town branch of the party, a businessman and former member of the town's parliament. He was often viewed negatively by members of the public in Mojokerto, because he was a prominent figure in its "grey" economy and in the world of the town's *preman* (petty gangsters), for example, providing security services at companies, cafes, karaoke bars and hotels, including places of ill repute. However, through such activities he had helped many otherwise marginal people secure employment, and he also had a record of helping the poor through various charitable works. He thus

---

[12] Confidential interview, 28 Apr. 2014.
[13] Interview, Slamet Heru Nugroho, 16 Mar. 2014.

had a reputation for generosity and social conscience which he used to build his popularity as a candidate. As with Nugroho, Gatot and his team stated they did not distribute money, and only paid for food and drink at campaign meetings.

Another unusual candidate was Halim Iskandar, a prominent PKB leader. As well as being the head of PKB in Jombang and having served twice in the Jombang DPRD, he was also the provincial legislature's deputy speaker. Though in the years leading to the 2014 election he had been responsible for distributing *jasmas* projects with a total value ranging from Rp 2.5 billion to Rp 4 billion annually, he said he made no use of these projects for campaign purposes: "I have never even gone and visited those who received *jasmas* assistance [from me]."[14] He also said that he did not distribute cash or other gifts to voters. Even so, he was re-elected with a handsome margin, and the highest individual vote in the electoral district. The reason for his success was largely his strong base in NU and PKB, including the fact that he was the son of the leading *kyai* of the Den Anyar *pesantren* in Tambak Beras, one of the three largest in Jombang.

Yet the situation is complex, and other examples suggest that money politics can indeed be the key to political success, even overriding *aliran* loyalties. For example, Gus Irfan (K.H. Muhammad Irfan), a PPP candidate, was one of the most respected *kyai* in the constituency. Most people predicted he would easily win a seat because he was the leader of Tambak Beras *pesantren* in Jombang, with tens of thousands of *santri* students or graduates, whose loyalty should have been enough to ensure his election. However, Gus Irfan was defeated by his own nephew, largely because he did not distribute cash to lock in the votes of his followers, many of whom deserted to other candidates. A similar example on the *abangan* side was Heddy Dediansyah, the head of Gerindra's East Java advisory board and a major construction contractor. He also did not resort to a dawn attack, instead distributing services and club goods—during his campaign, he provided ten vehicles that constantly travelled through the constituency providing free medical treatment and circumcisions. He too was not elected.

---

[14] Interview, Halim Iskandar, 4 Apr. 2014.

Thus, although the trends were not unidirectional, overall it is clear that financial calculations were increasingly remaking the connections between clients and patrons, voters and politicians *inside* the *aliran* in this part of East Java. Money politics can be used to reinforce *aliran* loyalties—if candidates are prepared to distribute cash or goods to back up their traditional sources of authority (such as those between a *kyai* and his followers), and many candidates do conduct their vote-buying efforts mostly within their own *aliran* community. Yet money politics can also undermine traditional *aliran* loyalties. When making their political choices, a growing number of voters look, not to the candidates' cultural capital, but to what can be attained from them—notably, cash. This tendency makes it increasingly possible for candidates to seek support beyond their own *aliran* bases, a point we turn to now.

NEW CLIENTELISM AND THE DECLINE OF *ALIRAN*

One implication of the intense competition between individual candidates generated by open-list PR—the *perang figur* (war of figures) as it is sometimes known in Indonesia—is that candidates draw upon increasingly diverse and fragmented networks to increase their chances of electoral success. The old *aliran* pattern described by Geertz has been characterised by Aspinall as a system of "pillared clientelism" in which most patron–client ties and patronage distribution occurred within relatively stable socioreligious communities, and the political and social organisations that underpinned them.[15] In contemporary conditions, though political candidates can still draw upon their traditional communities, they increasingly look beyond the old *aliran* identities to multiply their sources of political support.

Before elaborating, it is important to stress that this transition is still in progress. *Aliran* remain a prominent feature of political life in this region. Accordingly, most candidates can still be categorised as coming from, and mostly relying upon support from within, one of

---

[15] Edward Aspinall, "A Nation in Fragments: Patronage and Neoliberalism in Contemporary Indonesia", *Critical Asian Studies* 45, 1 (2013): 32.

the two mainstream *aliran—santri* and *abangan*. For example, *santri* candidates still mostly compete with other *santri* candidates for the vote of devout Muslims, and they do so by making use of the networks that undergird the community (or communities) of the pious. Thus there is an identifiable group of *santri* candidates with NU backgrounds who compete for the traditionalist vote, as well as candidates (notably from PAN and PKS) who compete for support from modernists. East Java VIII has more traditionalists, and candidates with NU orientations are found in numerous parties, not only Islamic parties like PKB and PPP but also nationalist parties such as Nasdem and Gerindra. In seeking support of traditionalist voters, such candidates typically rely above all upon the formal and informal networks that make up the large NU family. This includes formal organisations, such as Muslimat (older women), Ansor (male youth), Fatayat (younger women), IPPNU (female high school students), Pagarnusa (martial arts) and others, as well as informal institutions such as *tarekat* (Sufi orders), *pesantren* and their alumni networks, as well as cultural networks. Candidates make use of these networks informally, often by seeking the support of influential individuals within them. Kiai Hamam Ghozali, the head of Krempyang *pesantren* in Nganjuk, is an example. As well as being a charismatic religious scholar, he is also the chair of the executive branch of NU in Nganjuk. He positioned himself as a supporter of all candidates with NU backgrounds, and several of the candidates researched for this chapter, including Hadi Dediansyah (Gerindra), Lilia Agustina (PKB) and Makruf (Gerindra) claimed to have received his blessing.

In just the same way, there was also a set of identifiably *abangan* candidates who drew on distinctively *abangan* networks and institutions. There is no *abangan* equivalent to the network of religious institutions that underpin the *santri* community, but this community is traditionally identified with a range of other formal and informal institutions. These included the bureaucracy itself, including key actors such as subdistrict heads (*camat*) and village heads, professional organisations that touch on the direct interests of ordinary farmers and villagers, such as Himpunan Kerukunan Tani Indonesia (HKTI, Farmers Harmony Association of Indonesia), Lembaga Masyarakat Desa Hutan (LMDH, Forest Village Community Institution), Asosiasi Petani Tebu Rakyat Indonesia (APTR,

Sugar Growers People's Association), Kelompok Tani (Poktan, Farmers' Groups) and Koperasi Wanita (Kopwan, Women's Cooperatives), cultural or artistic organisations, martial arts groups and others. A large number of the candidates with an *abangan* orientation were particularly reliant on village heads and farmers' organisations for their campaigning. For example, Renville (Demokrat) was on the East Java board of HKTI and used his links there to build his electoral machine. He also had strong connections with the East Java governor and used them to mobilise support in the bureaucracy and, especially, among village officials; he claimed to dominate the village heads of Nganjuk district, who were organised in their own association.[16] Heru Nugroho (PDI-P), meanwhile, mobilised his *abangan* base, especially farmers in remote villages, by relying on the network of Kelompok Tani Andalan Nasional (KTAN), a farmers' network headed by Suyanto, the former PDI-P *bupati* of Jombang. Nugroho also worked through APTR, which was mostly concentrated in Madiun, and through HKTI.[17]

It was also, however, obvious that candidates were reaching across *aliran* lines to build their support networks. Many *santri* candidates, as well as trying to mobilise a *santri* base, were also trying to attract support—sometimes successfully—among *abangan* voters. In particular, there was not a candidate I encountered who did not claim to be using village heads and other village officials as part of his or her electoral machine. Thus, one Nasdem candidate, who was a prominent activist in NU circles, used his "tandem" connections with other Nasdem candidates to share the costs of vote buying in primarily *abangan* areas of Jombang and Mojokerto, relying on networks of village officials to do so.[18] One successful PKB candidate likewise targeted rural voters, both *abangan* and *santri*, especially by relying on village heads: "In Nganjuk I'm backed by around 50 village heads, in Madiun I have them working for me in 8 subdistricts, in Mojokerto in 5, no 6, subdistricts."[19] He complained that he did not want to seek support in the towns because "[t]hey are

---

[16] Interview, Renville, 16 Mar. 2014.
[17] Interview, Heru Nugroho, 16 Mar. 2014.
[18] Confidential interview, Nasdem candidate, 14 Mar. 2014.
[19] Confidential interview, 14 Mar. 2014.

all damaged ... It's all about money there". Even so, he won by using his rural networks to carry out vote buying.

The same was happening with *abangan* candidates. Some worked through village heads to penetrate *santri* areas, and several even very visibly relied on *santri* community leaders such as *kyai* based in *pesantren*, as well as village-level *kyai* (*kyai langgar*) and informal institutions such as *majelis taklim*. For example, Nugroho (PDI-P) who, as explained above, partly relied on *abangan* networks and voters, also mobilised networks of village *kyai* in some rural areas. Muchtar (Golkar) had likewise directed much of his *jasmas* funds to funding mosque, *musholla* and *madrasah* repairs, also with the goal of gaining support from *santri* voters.

Overall, and unlike the pattern that was visible in 2009, in 2014 vote buying and other forms of patronage politics were now no longer strictly confined within *aliran* communities. Candidates were making use of brokers—especially, village heads—who gave them access to vote banks from beyond their own communities.

CONCLUSION

Aliran have been a resilient feature of Indonesian politics. Many observers noted, in particular, their re-emergence in 1999 during the first democratic election after 1955. However, the continuation of Indonesia's democratisation process, and of social modernisation, has increasingly undermined the *aliran* pattern of convergence between socioreligious identities, political parties and voting patterns. In particular, the shift to an open-list PR system with its logic of intense competition between individual candidates, has gone hand-in-hand with the rise of a pattern of "new clientelism" in which stable patron–client relations are breaking down and being replaced with more fluid arrangements, where clients critically evaluate potential patrons and choose between them.

The preceding analysis of electoral dynamics in one constituency of East Java in 2014 thus shows that *aliran* politics are far from dead. Some candidates, especially those from parties such as PDI-P and PKB that are strongly identified with one of the major *aliran*, focused their voter mobilisation efforts on their own socioreligious community, and campaigned through social networks that were largely confined within it. The analysis also shows, however, that *aliran* politics are being undermined at its very heart by the proliferation of patronage politics. Within *aliran*, it is not only that many candidates with strong sources of cultural capital (for example, the social status that derives from being a respected *kyai*) still feel they need to engage in vote buying in order to "tie" (they often use this word: *mengikat*) their voters to them. It is also that candidates who rely on distribution of material benefits, in the form of pork barrel projects, club goods and vote buying, have many new possibilities to cross freely between *aliran* in their vote-getting efforts. Though patronage politics in many cases is constrained by *aliran* identities, in even more cases it is blurring the lines between the *aliran*. Even in the heartland of rural Java, patronage politics are trumping *aliran* loyalties.

chapter **17**

Madiun, East Java: Brokers in Territorial, Social Network and Vote-buying Strategies

Ahmad Zainul Hamdi

This chapter describes election campaigning in two electoral districts in the district (*kabupaten*) of Madiun in East Java. Electoral district I, incorporating the subdistricts of Jiwan, Sawahan and Madiun is known as a strongly *santri* (pious Muslim) area, whereas electoral district III, consisting of the subdistricts of Saradan and Mejayan, is an *abangan* (syncretist) and secular–nationalist area. Despite the differing sociocultural backgrounds, the strategies candidates used in the two electoral districts did not differ significantly. In particular, vote buying—the distribution of cash to individual voters in the days leading to the poll—was widespread in both areas.

Brokers were a key determinant of whether candidates' vote-buying efforts succeeded. Very few candidates used the party machine to try to get out the vote. Most put greater trust in their own success teams and, even if these involved party activists, their role in the teams did not differ from those of other members. Though candidates structured their teams in varied ways, the lowest stratum of members was always the key when it came to mobilising voter support. These base-level vote brokers are known in Madiun as *kader* (cadres), though the term does not necessarily connote membership in a party. The role of the *kader*

279

was vital to vote buying because it was from them that candidates received lists of voters to be targeted, and it was through them that they distributed cash.

In the final analysis, the success of any vote-buying effort greatly depended on the integrity and loyalty of these *kader*. Those who were not linked to the candidate by ideological, party or some other close tie tended to exploit the candidates for economic gain. When vote buying was entrusted to brokers of this sort, the effort could easily fail because the brokers would misappropriate much of the money. But when vote buying was carried out by brokers who were constrained by party loyalty or by loyalty to the candidate or to people close to the candidate, then the money was more likely to make its way to the hands of the voters.

In fact, vote buying tended to be combined with other forms of patronage politics, notably distribution of club goods and pork barrel projects. Club goods here mean donations or gifts that confer collective benefit to members of an association with significant community-level influence. This form of patronage reflects a social network approach to campaigning. Pork barrel projects, by contrast, implies a territorial strategy and geographic targeting, and occurred when candidates were trying to gain the support of voters in a particular locale—typically, a *dusun* (hamlet), RW (neighbourhood) or RT (subneighbourhood). In both of these approaches, too, brokers played a key role.

Candidates generally had to disguise their attempts to make use of formal social associations, which were mostly prohibited by internal regulations from participating in partisan politics. Thus, candidates tended to use associations by approaching their leaders or prominent figures within them and inviting them to join their success teams. The more open the involvement of a social association in a campaign, the more likely the candidate concerned would reward it with club goods. But if the candidate could only make use of the brokerage role of an association's leader without openly drawing the association itself into the campaign, then the economic and political benefits would likely be enjoyed only by the leader concerned. In contrast, territorial strategies relied on the brokerage roles of informal and formal leaders in the location concerned, with those formal leaders typically consisting of RT and RW heads, *dusun* heads and so on. This territorial strategy, and the associated pork barrel spending, was absolutely dependent on the involvement of these influential local actors. When a significant proportion of them in a particular locality rejected an approach by a candidate, it was likely that pork barrel spending would be aborted.

BACKGROUND: THE LOCAL POLITICS OF MADIUN

Madiun is one of the most important urban centres of the western part of East Java, having played an important administrative role since the early 19th century as the chief town of the residency incorporating Ngawi, Magetan, Ponorogo and Pacitan, as well as Madiun itself.[1] These five districts now form part of the westernmost edge of East Java; not far across the border in Central Java is the town of Solo, the old capital of the Mataram kingdom. This geographic proximity, and the fact that the region was part of Mataram, means that culturally the region is now generally seen as being closer to the Mataraman culture associated with the kingdom, rather than to the Arek culture of the capital of East Java, Surabaya, and its surrounds further to the east. The Mataraman culture is agrarian, marked by a strong sense of social distinctions and traditional *kejawen* beliefs, while the Arek culture is more egalitarian and open, with people using a much coarser version of the Javanese language than the more refined language used in Mataraman.

The city (*kota*) of Madiun is an administrative entity separate to the rural district (*kabupaten*) which is the focus of this study. The district's capital since 2010 (previously, Madiun town still played this role) is Caruban, a small town on the main road between Surabaya and Solo. The district itself, which consists of 15 subdistricts, 198 villages and 8 *kelurahan* (urban precincts) is a typical inland district, with a population of about 770,000. In 2013, 40 per cent of the working

---

[1] Wasno, *Misteri Bulan Suro: Studi tentang Konflik antara Perguruan Silat PSH Terate dengan PSH Tunas Muda Winongo di Madiun* [The Mystery of the Month of Suro: A Study of the Conflict between the SH Terate and SH Winongo Silat Schools in Madiun] (Malang: PPS Universitas Muhammadiyah Malang, 2004), p. 50.

population were employed in agriculture, forestry and fisheries.[2] Some 58 villages are located on the edge of, or inside, forest zones.[3] Education levels are relatively low, and 32 per cent of households are classified as poor.[4]

The population is 99 per cent Muslim, but residents feel that the south of the district tends to be pious, or *santri*, while the north is populated by *abangan*. This supposition is reflected in the figures: the two subdistricts with the largest number of mosques and *musholla*—Dagangan and Kebonsari—are both located in the south.[5] Overall, however, Madiun tends to be seen as an *abangan* heartland.[6] Whereas Islamic parties fare well on the northern coast of East Java, the east and Madura, areas such as Madiun, Bojonegoro and Kediri to the west have historically been dominated by secular-nationalist parties. In Indonesia's first democratic election in 1955, the communist party, PKI, placed first in the residency of Madiun. Like much of Indonesia, Madiun voted strongly for Golkar during the New Order years (1966–1998). In post-*reformasi* Indonesia, between 1999 and 2009 the first-placed party in the district was always PDI-P.

However, in recent years the political dynamics of the district have begun to change, with traditionalist *santri* beginning to attain new dominance. The turning point was the election, in 2008, of Muhtarom as *bupati* or district head. Muhtarom, who has a background in the traditionalist community himself, was nominated by PKB, the major NU-affiliated party. He was re-elected for a second term in 2013, defeating a candidate backed by PDI-P and Golkar. Then, in the 2014 legislative election, for the first time PKB was the first-placed party with 110,000 votes. PDI-P was pushed to second place and Golkar to third, with PKB

[2] Badan Pusat Statistik Kabupaten Madiun, *Kabupaten Madiun dalam Angka 2014* [Madiun District in Figures 2014] (Madiun: BPS, 2015), p. 92.

[3] Badan Pusat Statistik Kabupaten Madiun, *Kabupaten Madiun dalam Angka 2011* [Madiun District in Figures 2011] (Madiun: BPS, 2012), p. 8.

[4] Ibid., p. 140.

[5] Ibid., p. 160.

[6] For the *santri–abangan* distinction, see Clifford Geertz, *The Religion of Java* (New York: Free Press, 1960).

benefitting from holding the *bupati* position, but also from the demise of competitor parties that exclusively vied for the NU vote.

ORGANISING THE CAMPAIGN: TERRITORIAL AND SOCIAL NETWORK STRATEGIES

As in many parts of Indonesia, almost all candidates in Madiun said that they relied more on political machines they had built themselves—success teams—than on party structures. Yet none relied on a truly professional team. Instead, candidates built their teams by relying on family and friendship networks. In the inner circle, the candidate would place people she or he most trusted. Below them were the people charged with seeking votes. At the lowest level were the *kader* whose job it was to market the candidate to community members directly. No candidate had professional means of coordination or monitoring to organise these various layers.

Figure 17.1
Typical Success Team Structures in Madiun District

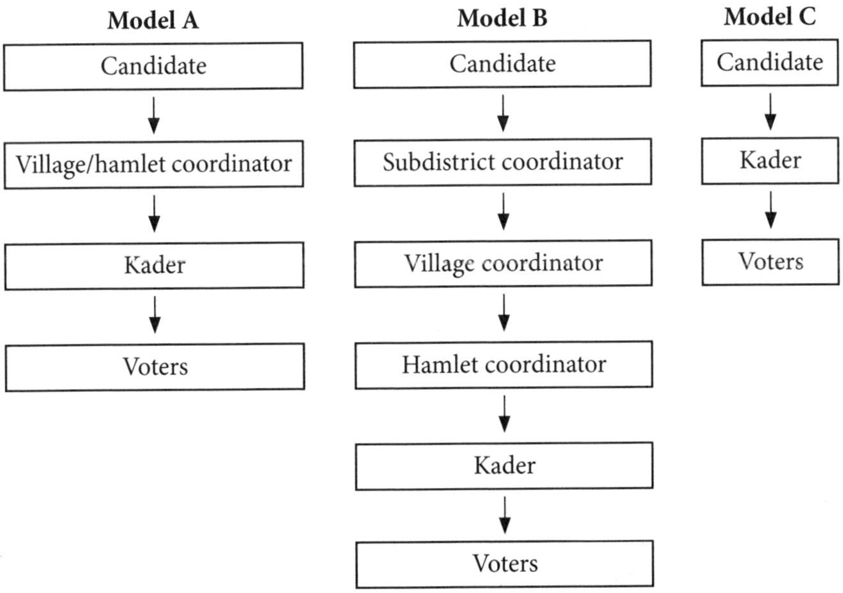

Model A

Candidate
↓
Village/hamlet coordinator
↓
Kader
↓
Voters

Model B

Candidate
↓
Subdistrict coordinator
↓
Village coordinator
↓
Hamlet coordinator
↓
Kader
↓
Voters

Model C

Candidate
↓
Kader
↓
Voters

Most team structures mirrored the territorial structure of government, with two main variations: model A, a simplified structure which did away with one or two intermediary layers between the candidate and voters, or model B, which was more complete (see Fig. 17.1). At the base level, however, there could be considerable variation: some candidates recruited just a handful of *kader* in each hamlet (*dusun*) whereas some would place them in each RT, with the consequence that there could be a large number in each hamlet. Some candidates allocated their *kader* to individual polling booths rather than to RT. Model C was a cut-down version, in which the candidate interacted directly with the brokers rather than using intermediary layers of coordinators. Candidates using this model tended to be motivated by a desire to save money, though in fact it made them vulnerable to deception because they often had to rely on brokers they lacked close relationships with but were forced to trust, given that they had no mechanism with which to control their brokers.

There was task differentiation within these structures. The higher an individual's position within the hierarchy, the more he or she had to do in terms of coordinating the work of those below them, monitoring them to make sure they were working hard and honestly, and ensuring that target locations were covered. Even so, the basic job of everybody in these structures was to chase votes. Every team member was expected to "secure" his or her own family's votes first, and then invite their friends, neighbours and then whoever else they could influence to support the candidate. At the base level, the *kader* were expected on average to bring on board only 5 to 15 votes each, though of course the more the better. We examine how they went about this task—in particular how they distributed cash to voters—in the next section.

These patterns, however, only deal with the territorial organisation of brokers. There was an additional pattern, too, which can be thought of as branching off from the candidate at the apex. This occurred when a candidate also recruited group coordinators (*koordinator kelompok*) charged with mobilising voters from a particular organisation or community group. Often such "recruitment" was highly informal, and the individuals concerned would not be officially enlisted as success team members. Typically, these individuals were prominent community, religious or associational leaders with influence over a particular network.

Their task was to seek votes from within that network, which might not be confined to one particular village or hamlet. Most candidates supplemented their territorial strategies with attempts to use whatever links they happened to have with social organisations in this way. Importantly, however, their attempts to reach out to such groups were rarely conducted openly or formally.

As an example of such social-network campaigning, consider one PPP candidate in electoral district I.[7] In his success team he personally played the role of coordinator. The team was in turn divided into two groups, each with a very different scope and focus. The first group consisted of PPP officials, and did the work of territorial organisation described above. The second group consisted of individuals who he hoped would garner votes within important social organisations. Specifically, they were:

- Leaders of two large and famous *pencak silat* (traditional martial arts) organisations in Madiun: SH (Setia Hati) Terate and SH Winongo. He chose carefully, drawing in a well-known SH Terate trainer in Sawahan subdistrict, and a senior leader of SH Winongo in Jiwan, knowing that SH Terate members who followed a particular master had the reputation of remaining very loyal to him, whereas SH Winongo members tended to respect seniority. Most importantly, these two organisations are exceptionally popular in Madiun, with very large followings of young men, as well as some women.
- Activists from Ansor, NU's (male) youth organisation, in both Sawahan and Jiwan subdistricts. As with the *pencak silat* groups, the candidate did not approach the organisation formally, but instead pulled in some influential leaders he knew.
- NU leaders, both individuals occupying formal leadership positions within its structure and influential *kyai*. The candidate explained it was impossible to use the formal structure of the organisation openly, but he knew it was quite practical to draw in its leaders.

---

[7] Confidential interview, 26 Mar. 2014.

- Leaders of Muslimat, NU's organisation for older women. In this regard he was assisted by his wife, who was the treasurer of a subdistrict branch of the organisation.
- Individuals from his personal friendship and family networks. Even though some of them lived outside the electoral district where he was competing, he still viewed them as a useful resource for influencing their own friends and families in the district.

None of these supporters openly used their organisation to support the candidate. This was the general pattern: no matter how much office-holders in a social association supported a candidate, they always avoided working openly through its formal structures. They always wanted to be able to deny accusations that they were abusing their association for political ends, and typically said that they supported the candidate only as an individual—though invariably they would use the network the organisation gave them access to for just that purpose. All this effectively meant, therefore, was that organisations' formal meetings were not used for political campaigning, and they did not issue public statements supporting any candidate.

In the Madiun context, the *silat* schools were especially critical to campaigning efforts. Both have large groups of members and fanatical supporters. Their enmeshment in political life dates back to the 1950s and 1960s, when SH Winongo was close to the PKI and SH Terate to its opponents; through the New Order years, SH Terate remained close to Golkar and the regime, while SH Winongo only began to experience a revival from the 1990s, when the PDI (the predecessor to today's PDI-P) was becoming re-energised as a site of opposition to the regime. SH Terate is still known for having very close relations with local politicians, and its officials admit its involvement in local political affairs. Even so, they typically take pains to ensure that this involvement does not contravene the formal proscription on political partisanship in the organisation's statutes. One SH Terate leader explained:

> The leadership of the organisation says members are free to vote for whoever they choose; there is no special instruction. Except, well, if there is a leader, if there is somebody who asks for help from the central leadership, you know. But then it won't be the general

chairperson who sends out the instruction, just certain people, so that nobody thinks the chairperson is siding with any particular party.[8]

Anwar Yadi, a prominent figure from SH Winongo, made a similar point:

Basically, SH Winongo is not allowed to locate itself under any particular political umbrella or be part of any stream. But when it so happens that there is a people's festival [that is, an election] then indeed there will be some party people who use SH people. But that's quite alright, because it's just the individuals. If you act in the name of the organisation and say that SH Winongo is following one of the parties, that's not allowed.[9]

This is the general pattern through which social organisations get involved in supporting a particular party or candidate, and it is a pattern which sometimes enables different people within the same organisation to back different candidates. Something similar happens, too, with informal organisations, such as *paguyuban* (a broad category of non-formal interest-based associations). One such organisation that was targeted by many candidates was Gapoktan (Gabungan Kelompok Tani, Alliance of Farmers' Groups), an organisation that brought together many of the small farmers' groups that are found at the village level and which are basically self-help groups, typically consisting of 20 to 30 persons, organised to share agricultural tasks, and often being the recipients of government assistance programmes. Candidates tried to approach informal groups like this also via their leaders, but treated those leaders merely as an entry point. Most candidates would then follow up such contacts with gifts of assistance packages such as seedlings and fertiliser, and making "transport money" payments to members at the meetings they held.

Finally, another variation in how candidates organised their networking might be thought of as a strategy of "territorial dominance". The outline of success team structures presented above makes clear that all candidates used a territorial approach in organising their campaigns.

---

[8] Interview, Sutoyo, 10 Apr. 2014.
[9] Interview, Anwar Yadi, 19 Apr. 2014.

In some cases, candidates took this logic further and tried to completely dominate a particular location, including by denying access to rival candidates and their teams. Many candidates viewed this strategy as particularly effective. They would only try this strategy in an area which they believed represented—or potentially represented—a personal "base".

For this strategy to work, the candidate would work closely with both informal community leaders and formal leaders (such as the village, RW and RT heads) in the location. If they reached a deal to "guarantee" the votes of that location for the candidate, the candidate would then try to "quarantine" it from rivals by targeting it with donations or assistance packages of some sort—typically funds for road repairs or other infrastructure, money for the mosque or *musholla*, or other club goods. The logic was that this assistance—and the endorsement of the community leaders—would win local residents over to the candidate, and that those local leaders would then be reluctant to open access to their community to rival candidates. This strategy would come unstuck, however, if any significant leaders in the community concerned opposed the deal, or had conflicting loyalties.

PATTERNS OF PATRONAGE POLITICS

In Madiun, virtually all candidates distributed patronage, whether as club goods, pork barrel spending or individual vote buying. Before we examine these one by one, we should make it clear that not all politics was patronage-based. For example, there also were candidates who talked programmatically—in other words, they promised they would work to ensure the local government allocated funds for programmes that would be distributed to entire categories of persons using criteria that were open and transparent, rather than contingent upon votes.[10] For example, one PKB incumbent made much of his past achievements in boosting

---

[10] Susan C. Stokes, "Pork, by Any Other Name ... Building a Conceptual Scheme of Distributive Politics", paper presented at the American Political Science Association Annual Meeting, Toronto, 3–6 Sept. 2009, p. 10, available at: http://ssrn.com/abstract=1449057.

funds available for religious bodies in the district, and for increasing district budgetary allocations for emergency infrastructure programmes in villages.[11] Candidates rarely, however, relied on programmatic politics exclusively, but combined it with patronage.

Club goods were distributed by candidates who approached social associations in pursuit of votes from their members. Some candidates were willing to go far in the pursuit of the big organisations. One PDI-P candidate, for example, explained that he had bought land for a *padepokan* (a training centre-cum-office) for a SH Terate branch in Madiun subdistrict, placing a deposit in 2004–05 and only paying it off in 2010.[12] A Gerindra candidate showed his commitment to a group of his supporters from the same organisation by promising that he would pay them Rp 1 million per month for two years if elected.[13]

Pork barrel projects were primarily used by incumbents, who could direct government-funded projects toward particular locations where they believed they had supporters. Nevertheless, I also came across several examples of candidates who privately funded such gifts, ranging from a Gerindra candidate who bought televisions for neighbourhood guard posts or a PDI-P candidate who paid for street lighting and lighting in a village cemetery to a PKB candidate who paid for *musholla* renovations.[14] Candidates who did not use this approach did so either because they could not afford it, or because they did not believe it provided value for money in terms of votes. This brings us back to the point made earlier about strategies of territorial domination: pork barrel spending could be effective if it occurred alongside cooperation from village authorities or other influential community figures. One success team member working for a Gerindra candidate in electoral district II recalled a case in his village:

> People in RT IX asked for 40 sacks of cement and 2 trucks full of sand. So I took [the candidate] there myself. But he asked them: "I

---

[11] Interview, 21 Mar. 2014.
[12] Interview, 26 Mar. 2014.
[13] Interview, 18 Mar. 2014.
[14] Interviews, 18 Mar. 2014; 26 Mar. 2014; 17 Apr. 2014.

want to give you that much but can you guarantee the votes from your
polling booth?" There were 275 votes in that booth. He only wanted
100, but the person who he was dealing with there wasn't confident
… so he still has not given any of those donations.[15]

In this case, the deal fell apart not simply because those making
the request could not provide the requested guarantee: they could not
do so, it turned out, because the RT head was working in the success
team of another candidate.

Almost all candidates engaged in vote buying. They were relatively
open about this to me as a researcher: almost all explained that they
would distribute payments to the people whose names their success
teams had collected. The local term for these payments was *sangu*, a
Javanese word meaning pocket money, or the food or other supplies
taken when going on a trip. Payments ranged from Rp 20,000 to
Rp 50,000 per voter, with no significant difference between the two
electoral districts. With virtually all candidates engaging in the practice,
there were no noticeable differences between candidates from Islamic and
nationalist parties, those from large and small parties, or incumbents
and first-timers. And though many people claimed that the key to
political success was a candidate's personal qualities and reputation, no
candidate I came across was so confident that he or she was willing to
stake their chances on their personal attributes alone: all tried to lock
in their prospect of victory by also distributing *sangu* to voters.

For example, one PPP candidate in electoral district I explained
that he was preparing *sangu* at a rate of Rp 10,000–20,000 for people
on the lists his *kader* had supplied (he ended up paying Rp 25,000 a
head). Those same *kader* had the job of distributing the cash. When
I interviewed him, he was hoping he would be able to enter into a
tandem arrangement with a provincial and central candidate so that
they could together increase the amounts distributed to each recipient
by Rp 10,000.[16] This did not happen, and I met one of his *kader* after
election day who confirmed that he had distributed envelopes containing

---

[15] Confidential interview, 18 Mar. 2014.
[16] Confidential interview, 26 Mar. 2014.

Rp 25,000, which the candidate raised himself. This was insufficient, and he was defeated by another PPP candidate who distributed Rp 50,000 to each voter. The *kader* attributed the loss to this gap.[17]

A first-time candidate from Gerindra in Madiun III also explained he was preparing *sangu* in the vicinity of Rp 20,000–30,000 per voter, with an additional Rp 10,000 that would be contributed by a provincial Gerindra candidate. This meant his *kader* would be distributing Rp 40,000 per envelope. "You can't get around that here," he said, "no way."[18] The only candidate I interviewed before the poll who said he would not engage in vote buying was a senior PKB candidate in Madiun I—but I later interviewed a *kyai* who acted as one of his brokers who said that he had distributed Rp 30,000 per head on this candidate's behalf.[19]

The brokers gained materially from participating in these networks of distribution. They usually received an envelope containing the standard payment, as well as additional fees when distributing *sangu*. Success team members also typically received payments ranging from Rp 30,000 to Rp 150,000 when attending team coordinating meetings. When they deposited voter lists with team coordinators, they also usually received Rp 25,000 to Rp 50,000. If the candidate was elected, he or she typically gathered all success team members and *kader* and gave them gifts, either goods, cash, or both.

Vote buying feels like an accepted part of local culture in Madiun. Its roots can be traced to village-head elections, where vote buying has been practised for many years. According to Anwar Soleh Azzarkoni, the head of the district General Election Commission, however, the practice also has cultural roots.[20] Candidates feel inadequate, or embarrassed, if they seek the support of voters without giving something in exchange. This attitude is an extension of local beliefs that it is impolite to visit someone's house, especially if you are seeking their help, without bringing a small gift. Accordingly, candidates who visit their constituents' homes but bring nothing will be labelled as *pelit*—stingy—and, once that label

[17] Confidential interview, 19 Apr. 2014.
[18] Confidential interview, 18 Mar. 2014.
[19] Confidential interview, 17 Apr. 2014.
[20] Interview, Anwar Soleh Azzarkoni, 20 Mar. 2014.

sticks, it is difficult to gain popular support. It is also accepted practice that when one *sowan*—makes a respectful visit—to a community leader's home, one should bring something.

Accordingly, none of my informants could name a significant local community leader or religious figure who refused to be involved in vote buying. On the contrary, many of them played brokerage roles. For example, one respected *kyai* in the Sawahan subdistrict explained that he personally coordinated the distribution of cash in his area for a PKB candidate. There was no indication at all that this *kyai* was particularly greedy. On the contrary, he did not try to seek government assistance to build his *pesantren*. That he was somewhat reluctant to discuss his role distributing *sangu* was simply because he knew it was illegal. He did not feel any guilt at what he had done because he felt he had not contravened any social norms or committed a sin.[21] I did, however, meet one PKB candidate who believed that it was wrong to give money to voters. However, he still did so after receiving advice from his *kyai* that it was only a minor sin that could be erased by way of reciting the *istighfar* prayer, seeking forgiveness from God. Accordingly, he felt he could carry out vote buying without experiencing a conflict with his conscience.[22]

This tradition can also be used to explain the embarrassment that success team members feel when their candidates are perceived as acting ungenerously, for instance by failing to distribute *sangu*. Take the story of Bejo (not his real name), a success team member from Saradan subdistrict, who was asked by a national DPR candidate to pull together a meeting of people from the area as potential village-level brokers. Bejo is not at all a person who is obsessed with making money. But when the candidate failed to provide money to the people he had invited, Bejo felt humiliated. He understood that the candidate did not want to engage in money politics (he was a rarity), but as a field operator he knew that nobody would want to come to such a meeting if they thought they were not going to receive a payment. Moreover, without providing money, his own credibility as a broker would decline, and he would be the target of mockery:

---

[21] Confidential interview, 17 Apr. 2014.
[22] Confidential interview, 7 Apr. 2014.

To vote for someone without getting any *sangu*, that's hard here, brother. Someone once sent me an SMS accusing me of running a *"partai tletong"* [cow dung party], when I brought together people from 15 villages to discuss them becoming *kader* … but then it turned out they only got food, there was no petrol money. So then people turned on me … I thought there would be envelopes with cash in the snack boxes—even if it was only Rp 10,000 or Rp 20,000 to cover people's petrol. People would salute that. But there was nothing. And just recently he [the candidate] rang me again: "How's it going brother? Are the kids ready?" [I replied:] "What do you mean ready? Ready to do what? These people don't have any trust in you now, sir."[23]

Just as "stingy" candidates could harm the reputation of their team members, so could "generous" candidates assist them. Local social norms view positively rich people who are charitable (*dermawan*), and so it can be a source of prestige to be associated with a candidate who is not only wealthy but also generous in providing donations to communities, social organisations and individual residents.

Of course, it should be stressed that vote buying in Madiun takes place in a context of considerable social inequality. As Nathan Allen explains, "low levels of economic development or sharp levels of economic inequality produce an environment conducive to personalized campaigns based on direct exchange relationships".[24] Candidates in Madiun explicitly targeted poorer voters for vote buying: a payment of Rp 25,000 or Rp 50,000 might not mean much to a middle-class voter, but it would be highly valued by somebody earning Rp 50,000 to Rp 75,000 for a hard day's labour. Many poorer voters I met explained how much they looked forward to receiving *sangu*. Even so, they were often quite cynical about candidates believing legislators did little that was valuable for them except at election times. They also knew that

---

[23] Confidential interview, 18 Mar. 2014.

[24] Nathan W. Allen, "Diversity, Patronage, and Parties: Parties and Party System Change in Indonesia", PhD diss., University of British Columbia, 2012, p. 147. See also Susan C. Stokes, Thad Dunning, Marcelo Nazareno and Valeria Brusco, *Brokers, Voters, and Clientelism: The Puzzle of Distributive Politics* (New York: Cambridge University Press, 2013), pp. 152–73.

candidates needed them for their votes, and believed that they thus had power not only to expect, but also to demand, cash.

Candidates in Madiun seemed trapped in a cycle of vote buying. They all realised that it was all but impossible to win elections without distributing money; even building an effective success team to reach down to voters needed large cash injections. Most candidates agreed that cash payments to voters and fees for success team members were their greatest campaign expenses. Yet few were confident that their vote-buying efforts alone were enough to secure victory. They all knew that their rivals were also preparing to distribute cash: this made it imperative for them to do the same, but it also made the outcome of their own efforts far from certain. Not surprisingly, all candidates believed this situation was unhealthy. They would all prefer, they said, elections without money politics, but none could take the risk of being the first to try. As soon as one candidate buys the vote, the rest follow.

On the other hand, no candidate believed that vote buying was the sole determinant of electoral success: nor could it be, when all candidates took part. With all candidates distributing money, other factors such as a candidate's personal reputation, party affiliation, the support of influential community leaders and links to social networks were often critical. Even so, if other candidates were distributing cash, who could be confident that they could be elected on the strength of such factors alone? This was the fear that gripped candidates, and made them participate in vote buying, no matter how excellent their qualities as a candidate. Vote buying was simply to neutralise the money power of one's rivals.

But there *was* one factor that could make vote buying fail: the brokers. Brokers played the key role in connecting candidates and voters.[25] It was they who knew conditions at the grassroots, including which voters had already made their political choices and who would be amenable to persuasion. This asymmetrical share in the control of knowledge between candidates and brokers provides the latter with

---

[25] Stokes et al., *Brokers, Voters, and Clientelism*; Edward Aspinall, "When Brokers Betray: Clientelism, Social Networks, and Electoral Politics in Indonesia", *Critical Asian Studies* 46, 4 (2014): 545–70.

opportunities to gain personal profit. Candidates had to rely on brokers and their superior grassroots knowledge and connections, but this meant brokers could expropriate part of the money or goods they were supposed to pass to voters.

Seen from the outside, the success team structure seems like a site of close collaboration between brokers and candidates. Viewed up close, this harmonious image falls to pieces. The collaboration is shot through with distrust and deceit. A Gerindra candidate in Madiun I put it bluntly: "Candidates have to get ready to be cheated."[26] A PDI-P candidate in the same electoral district expressed his lack of faith in his own success team: "There is no way those kids are just trying to help me honestly and without expecting any reward."[27]

A story of a broker in Saradan subdistrict illustrates the situation. Dwipa (not his real name) has been a youth leader in his village. Whenever an election happens—whether it is a legislative election, a village head election, or a *bupati* or gubernatorial election—he is always part of the action. During the 2014 legislative election he acted as a success team member for six candidates simultaneously: two from Gerindra, one from Hanura, two from PKS and one from Partai Demokrat (the Demokrat candidate was the only one running for a provincial seat; the other five were competing against each other at the district level). As voting day approached, he had Rp 2,800,000 to carry out vote buying for five different candidates. He distributed only about Rp 1 million. In my meetings with him, he repeatedly laughingly referred to the election as a *pesta rakyat*—a people's festival, or party: "Time for the people to party" ("*Saatnya rakyat berpesta*"). By attending various success team meetings for five candidates (one of the Gerindra candidates did not use a success team, but instead had contacted Dwipa directly) he reckoned he had made an additional Rp 1 million in "petrol money" fees. Add the money he skimmed from his vote-buying responsibilities, and he had enough to put down a deposit and pay the first two instalments on a new motorcycle (it was parked in the corner of his front room when I visited him after the election).

---

[26] Confidential interview, 26 Mar. 2014.

[27] Ibid.

Of course, there were also brokers who worked honestly for their candidates. These were typically those who were tied to the candidate through a party or personal relationship. One PDI-P *kader* I met not only did not skim off money from vote buying but he also returned envelopes if he could not locate the recipient: "And if from the 15 [I was targeting] there were some who didn't seem convincing, well, I wouldn't give them the money either. I'd return it. Or I'd find someone else I could give it to."[28]

Overall, then, we can conclude that vote-buying success depended on brokers. With profit-oriented brokers, vote buying often failed, because cash simply did not go beyond their own hands. But in the hands of loyal and honest brokers, it could be successfully conducted.

CONCLUSION

Electoral dynamics in Madiun show that an open-list PR system such as that practised in Indonesia, especially in conditions of social inequality where prominent individuals are expected to show charitable concern for others, can give rise to highly personalised and patronage-based political competition. However, although most candidates in the district stressed their personal connection with voters, in the end they depended on brokers: people who could connect them with voters and ensure that their patronage did not go to waste. If candidates wanted to win over voters from within a certain social network—such as in one of Madiun's famous *pencak silat* schools—then they needed to first win over some of its leaders prior to delivering "donations" to the school. If they wanted to dominate a particular location, they needed to obtain the support of influential local figures, or their pork barrel spending there would be wasted. If they wanted to deliver cash payments to individual voters, they had to distribute it via brokers who knew the recipients personally.

As a result, candidates were at the mercy of brokers. In a climate of general cynicism about elected representatives, not a few brokers

---

[28] Confidential interview, 7 Apr. 2014.

felt it was reasonable to deceive their candidates, work for more than one simultaneously, or keep most of their money for themselves. They often justified such actions by saying they were engaging in rough social justice, redistributing wealth from rich or corrupt politicians—even if the beneficiaries were primarily themselves rather than the poor. In this way, Indonesian democracy has given rise to a new parasitical layer at the heart of the body politic.

Map of South Kalimantan

Province boundary
District boundary

EAST
KALIMANTAN

TABALONG

CENTRAL
KALIMANTAN

BALANGAN

NORTH
HULU SUNGAI

CENTRAL
HULU SUNGAI

SOUTH
HULU
SUNGAI

KOTABARU

*Macassar
Strait*

TAPIN

SOUTH
KALIMANTAN

BARITO
KUALA

BANJAR
MASIN

BANJAR

BANJAR
BARU

TANAH
BUMBU

KOTA-
BARU

Sebuku

Laut

TANAH
LAUT

0   kilometres   125

*Java
Sea*

chapter **18**

South Kalimantan: Islamic Party Candidates Who Refuse to Buy the Vote

Ahmad Muhajir

Other chapters make it clear that candidates in the 2014 election used varied patronage-based strategies. Many distributed club goods to community groups, or gifts or cash payments to individuals. In this context, finding serious candidates who did *not* employ money politics was like searching for needles in a haystack. It was even more challenging to identify candidates who did not use it and then actually won their seats. But conventional wisdom suggests there will always be exceptions. In this chapter, I discuss several candidates who refused to "play the money game" (*main uang*). I focus on candidates from two Islamist parties competing in the province of South Kalimantan, showing that, although general attitudes are permissive toward vote buying, candidates holding onto religious and ethical ideals have by no means disappeared from Indonesia's political landscape.

The Islamist parties I focus on are the Partai Persatuan Pembangunan (PPP, United Development Party) and the Partai Keadilan Sejahtera (PKS, Prosperous Justice Party). Different from other Islamic parties that adopt the state ideology Pancasila as their party basis, PPP and PKS are decidedly Islam-based. They are labelled Islamist because they seek to formalise Islam in law, and generally support the top-down Islamisation of public life.[1]

---

[1] Greg Fealy, "Indonesia's Islamic Parties in Decline", *Inside Story*, 11 May 2009, available at: http://inside.org.au/indonesia%E2%80%99s-islamic-parties-in-decline/.

At the national level, PPP takes symbolic credit from having struggled—
though unsuccessfully—in 2000–02 to re-insert into the constitution the
Djakarta Charter, a seven-word-clause that obligates Muslims to observe
the shariah. PKS proposes a similar idea which it calls the "Madinah
Charter", referring to a historical document regulating the coexistence
of the multi-religious inhabitants of the city of Madinah in the era of the
Prophet Muhammad.

Historically, South Kalimantan is a province with strong support
for Islamist parties and movements. In Indonesia's first elections in
1955, 80 per cent of the vote went to two Islamic parties, Nahdlatul
Ulama (NU) and Masjumi.[2] This province was also a site of the Darul
Islam rebellion, which aimed to establish an Islamic state in the 1950s.
Even during the New Order, Golkar was unable to beat PPP in the
provincial capital Banjarmasin until 1982.[3] In post-Suharto elections,
South Kalimantan voters have consistently handed victory to Golkar,
however, though Islamist parties still command a sizeable vote. In the
next section, I briefly introduce South Kalimantan and the strength of
PKS and PPP in the province. After that, I explore the dilemmas PPP and
PKS candidates competing in South Kalimantan faced in 2014: whether
to adapt to the dominant culture of money politics, justifying this as a
necessary response to an emergency situation, or to keep their values
intact and avoid temptation.

BACKGROUND: PPP AND PKS IN SOUTH KALIMANTAN

Formed in 1956, South Kalimantan is a multi-ethnic province. The
Banjarese, who now comprise three-quarters of the population, are the
largest ethnic group, followed by the Javanese at 14.5 per cent, Bugis
(3 per cent), Dayak (1.9 per cent), Madurese (1.5 per cent) and some

---

[2] Data courtesy of Kevin Evans, personal communication, 4 Dec. 2013; Herbert Feith, *The Indonesian Elections of 1955*, Interim Report Series (Ithaca: Cornell Modern Indonesian Project, Cornell University, 1957), p. 69.

[3] Kevin Evans, *Sejarah Pemilu dan Partai Politik di Indonesia* [History of Elections and Political Parties in Indonesia] (Jakarta: Arise Consultancies, 2003), p. 92.

other local and migrant groups.[4] The Banjarese dominate political and public office, especially since the post-Suharto decentralisation, though a few Javanese also occupy senior bureaucratic positions in some of the province's 11 districts and 2 municipalities, and in the provincial government.

Most of the province's population of 3.6 million people live in rural areas (58 per cent), according to the population census of 2010. They mostly reside in the province's *kabupaten*, which are also home to 47 per cent of the total urban population of over 1.5 million. The capital city of Banjarmasin has the largest population in the province, with 17.3 per cent of the province's inhabitants.

South Kalimantan is a strongly Muslim province, with only a little over 3 per cent of the population being non-Muslims. It is mostly traditionalist, with 55 to 59 per cent of the Muslims in the province identifying themselves as members of NU, and only 3 per cent claiming affiliation to the modernist Muhammadiyah.[5] Even so, the role of Muhammadiyah in religious, social and political affairs in the province is greater than this figure suggests, with its members running numerous orphanages, schools, campuses and health facilities, and being represented on many official bodies. The Banjarese have identified strongly with Islam since the Sultanate of Banjar, and local politicians, regardless of their party or ethnic backgrounds, still accommodate Islamic sentiments and show respect to Islamic teachers (*ulama*). Even so, Islamic political parties have been unable to overshadow Golkar, an officially nationalist party which has consistently come first in legislative elections in the province. Popular support for Islamic parties in this province has also been declining, from 54 per cent in 2004, to 42 per

---

[4] The ethnicity figures are based on the 2010 population census data, quoted in Edward Aspinall, "Ethnicity, Ethnic Conflict and Ethnic Politics in Kalimantan", in *Cutting and Digging: Development, Environment and the People of Kalimantan*, ed. Budy P. Resosudarmo, Ida Aju Pradnja Resosudarmo, Lydia M. Napitupulu and M. Handry Imansyah, Table 7.1 (forthcoming).

[5] Data courtesy of Lembaga Survei Indonesia (LSI), personal communication, Burhanuddin Muhtadi, 11 Feb. 2010 and based on surveys conducted in South Kalimantan in October 2009 and January 2010.

cent in 2009, to another low of 37 per cent in 2014. Yet the province
is still a centre of Islamic politics, with these figures being higher than
the national averages.[6]

The two Islamic parties discussed in this chapter, PPP and PKS, are
both significant in South Kalimantan. In 1999, PPP secured the largest
Islamic vote (16.9 per cent). The predecessor of PKS, namely PK, was
still in its early stage then, gaining only 1.2 per cent, well behind PAN,
PKB and PBB. However, since 2004, PPP and PKS have taken turns in
assuming the lead position among Islamic parties. In 2004, PPP gained
14.2 per cent in South Kalimantan, coming in second to Golkar. In
2009, PKS overtook PPP by a slim margin of just under 5,000 votes,
securing 10.7 per cent, ranking third in the province after Golkar and
Partai Demokrat. In 2014, PPP regained its lead position among the
Islamic parties, with 11.7 per cent, finishing second to Golkar. PKS, on
the other hand, was in 2014 beaten by PKB, and it was placed third
among Islamic parties.[7]

With these results, PPP has sent two candidates from South
Kalimantan to the national parliament in three consecutive elections
since 2004. PKS only managed to get two national seats in 2009, and
only one in both 2004 and 2014. The electoral achievements of PPP and
PKS at the provincial level are similar.[8] PPP has gained the most seats

---

[6] Islamic parties received 38.3 per cent of the vote in 2004, 29.2 per cent in 2009, and 31.4 per cent in 2014.

[7] Figures in this paragraph are based on DPR results in South Kalimantan: Pemi Apriyanto, *Database Pemilu 2004: Peta Daerah Pemilihan, Perolehan Suara dan Kursi untuk DPR RI, DPRD Propinsi, dan DPRD Kabupaten/Kota se-Indonesia* [2004 General Election Database: Maps of Electoral Districts, Votes and Seats for the DPR, Provincial DPRDs and District DPRDs Throughout Indonesia] (Jakarta: Spirit Research and Database, 2007); Komisi Pemilihan Umum Kalsel [South Kalimantan General Elections Commission], *Buku Saku Pemilu Kalimantan Selatan* [South Kalimantan General Election Pocketbook] (Banjarmasin: Sekretariat KPU Kalimantan Selatan, 2011); Komisi Pemilihan Umum Kalsel, *Hasil Pemilu Legislatif Tahun 2014 di Kalimantan Selatan* [Results of 2014 General Legislative Election in South Kalimantan] (Banjarmasin: KPU Kalsel, 2014).

[8] Badan Pusat Statistik Kalimantan Selatan, *Komposisi Anggota DPRD Tingkat I Kalimantan Selatan menurut Fraksi Hasil PEMILU Tahun 1997–2009* [Composition

among Islamic parties, with PKS closely following in 2004, matching it in 2009, but dropping behind PPP and PKB in 2014. The shares of the two parties combined comprised about a quarter of the seats in the South Kalimantan DPRD in 2004 and 2009, and over one-fifth in 2014. These results have made the parties serious contenders in provincial politics, including in gubernatorial elections: PKS has twice fielded deputy governor candidates, and PPP's Rudy Ariffin was elected governor in 2005 and 2010.

At the district level, PPP and PKS have also controlled a considerable share of parliamentary seats and a few executive offices. In the provincial capital Banjarmasin, the Islamist parties were the 2 strongest parties after the 2004 election, controlling 13 of 45 seats in the municipal representative assembly. In that year also, PPP alone gained 20 per cent of the seats in Banjar district, an achievement equalled only by Golkar. In 2009, PPP was the first-placed party in North Hulu Sungai district. Overall, in the last 3 elections, PPP peaked in 2004 when it won almost 15 per cent of parliamentary seats in 13 South Kalimantan districts; in the 2009 and 2014 elections the figure levelled off at about 10 per cent. And PPP cadres twice attained deputy *bupati* positions in North Hulu Sungai.

For PKS, the districts of South Hulu Sungai and Central Hulu Sungai have been strongholds since 2004. These areas in the 1950s were bases of the modernist Islamic party Masjumi, which in 1955 won 55 per cent of the vote there. Since the collapse of the New Order regime, the heirs of Masjumi, such as PAN, PBB and PKS, have competed to regain the support of older generation of voters who are still sympathetic to Masjumi. PKS, won the largest number of seats in both district parliaments in 2004 and 2009, and in South Hulu Sungai in 2014. The party faltered in 2014 in Central Hulu Sungai, falling to the fourth place behind Golkar, Gerindra and PPP. My informants cite differing attitudes

of South Kalimantan Provincial DPRD Based on Party Representation following General Elections, 1997–2009], available at: http://kalsel.bps.go.id/?set=viewDataDetail2&flag_template2=1&id_sektor=37&id=733; KPU Kalsel, *Buku Saku Pemilu Kalimantan Selatan* (2011); Sekretariat KPU Kalimantan Selatan; Komisi Pemilihan Umum Kalsel, *Hasil Pemilu Legislatif Tahun 2014.*

toward the dawn attack strategy as the most important explanation for
the fall, which I explore below. PKS has also succeeded in getting its
local elites elected as deputy *bupati*: twice in South Hulu Sungai and
once in Central Hulu Sungai.

More than 50 per cent of PPP and PKS South Kalimantan votes
come from rural villages.[9] Despite PKS's image as an urban party, in
fact a slightly higher proportion of its votes come from rural areas
than do PPP voters in this province: 56.6 per cent and 50.1 per cent
respectively. In urban precincts, they fare similarly, while PPP tends
to do better in semi-urban subdistricts. Geographically, PKS and PPP
election results are mirror images of each other in the province: when
one gains higher votes in rural districts, the other goes up in cities,
and vice versa, suggesting that they compete for the same voters. The
district DPRD results in 2014 indicate that PKS generally achieved higher
votes in rural areas, while PPP generally did better in cities, while the
pattern was the opposite in 2009.

The educational background of PKS leaders in South Kalimantan
varies. Some have studied in the Middle East, others in non-Islamic
campuses in Indonesia and a few in Institut Agama Islam Negara
(IAIN, State Islamic Institutes). Still others are graduates of traditionalist
Islamic boarding schools in South Kalimantan and do not have college
educations. Such leaders have typically been party cadres for a long
time, reaching senior positions after going through various "cadreisation"
steps. As far as devotional matters are concerned, they generally practice
mainstream traditionalist Muslim rituals, as they themselves were raised
and taught that way. PPP officials in the province are predominantly
products of the Indonesian education system. Most were activists in
Pergerakan Mahasiswa Islam Indonesia (PMII, Indonesian Islamic
Student Movement, the NU-aligned student group), during college,

---

[9] Here, I separate the 2014 district DPRD results according to urban and rural
villages whose lists are available in BPS, *Peraturan Kepala Badan Pusat Statistik
Indonesia Nomor 37 Tahun 2010 tentang Klasifikasi Perkotaan dan Pedesaan di
Indonesia, Buku 3: Bali, Nusa Tenggara, Kalimantan, Maluku dan Papua* [Central
Bureau of Statistics Regulation No. 37 2010 on the Classification of Towns and
Rural Villages in Indonesia] (Jakarta: BPS, 2010), pp. 260–316.

usually at IAIN Banjarmasin, or they were recruited to the party through family connections. They are heavily traditionalist in their ritual practice and religious thinking, sometimes condemning "wahhabism" to win over traditionalist voters.

PPP: RESISTING TEMPTATION

In this section, I discuss three PPP candidates to illustrate that this party (presumably, like all parties) had its share of idealists. They ran in three different elections: one for a provincial parliament seat in Banjarmasin city, and two for district seats, one in Banjarmasin and another in Banua Enam district. All were first-time candidates in 2014, but only one succeeded. Their stories suggest that the sources of emotional strength candidates draw on when resisting temptations to engage in vote buying vary, but Islamic teachings play a significant role.

The first idealist candidate was Rusdiansyah Asnawi (known as Rusdi), a *kyai* or Islamic scholar running for the provincial assembly in the electoral district comprising the city of Banjarmasin. He was a retired judge in a religious court and also an ex-chairperson of the provincial NU branch. The governor of South Kalimantan entrusts him with the day-to-day management of the great mosque of Sabilal Muhtadin, one of the province's major Islamic symbols. In accordance with normal practice, as the person in charge of the great mosque, he also holds a position in the local ulama council, Majelis Ulama Indonesia (MUI, Indonesian Ulama Council); in his case, in its legal ruling (fatwa) commission. The most relevant MUI fatwa for our purposes is one released just prior to the April 2014 legislative election which prohibited money politics, declaring it to be a form of *risywah* (bribe) condemned by Allah and His Messenger.

Rusdi's main appeal as a candidate was his position at the Sabilal Muhtadin mosque. When I asked people about Rusdi, they typically described him in relation to the mosque, and he himself exploited the opportunities his position gave him to reach out to voters. Sabilal Muhtadin runs a weekly Islamic course (*pengajian*) attended by around 5,000 people from all over Banjarmasin. As head of the mosque's management, Rusdi was well placed to let them know that he was a candidate. Electoral rules, however, prohibit campaigning in houses of worship. Candidates can generally ignore this rule without serious consequences in small prayer houses whose congregations come from a single precinct. But whatever happens in the great mosque is public and would be noticed by electoral authorities and Rusdi's competitors. To promote his candidacy without breaking the rules, Rusdi ordered his staff to distribute his campaign leaflets "just outside the fence of the mosque".[10]

Rusdi was a serious candidate. He competed to win a seat, not just to get votes for his party. He ordered 85,000 copies of calendars with his picture and profile printed on them, around 1,500 banners, 200 wall clocks and a few thousand stickers, and had them distributed to voters.[11] In the three months leading up to voting day, he visited hundreds of communities, mostly with other PPP candidates running for seats in higher and lower representative assemblies. With two to three gatherings every day, he "travelled around the city of Banjarmasin and reached its remote spots".[12] Sometimes, he attended meetings in venues with terrain that was hard on his old body, with muddy or slippery footpaths; a couple of times he sustained minor injuries. Rusdi used every connection he had, be it with other mosque managers or with former subordinates in the religious court, to organise these meetings and reach out to voters. In short, he did everything other serious candidates did, except distribute cash to voters.

Rusdi is an orator. In the early days of the New Order, he had delivered speeches at PPP mass campaign rallies. Thus, in 2014 he gave religious talks when he promoted his candidacy, appealing to the audience to vote for him, in part with religious arguments. One important element of his talks was explaining the MUI fatwa prohibiting money politics. Rusdi argued against vote buying because, according to a sound *hadith*, acts of bribery condemn perpetrators to hellfire. He typically continued by linking money politics to political corruption, something he promised to fight. When audience members sometimes asked what they should do if they were given money to vote for other candidates,

---

[10] Interview, Rusdiansyah Asnawi (Rusdi), 3 May 2014.
[11] Ibid.
[12] Ibid.

he would jokingly say: "Take the money, but vote for me. God Willing, you will not get the wrong candidate."[13]

In a typical meeting, Rusdi would give the host money to provide snacks for the audience and he often received requests from the host community, usually for fairly humble objects, such as a modest sound system to be used at religious and social events or drums to accompany the recitation of praises for the Prophet. If he was collaborating with two other candidates in a "tandem" arrangement, the three usually evenly divided the cost of such gifts. But if the national DPR candidate was physically present, rather than being represented by a team member, "he would take care of the community request and we are freed from making a contribution".[14] In any case, such community gifts did not, according to Rusdi, count as money politics.

In Rusdi's mind, the term money politics (*politik uang*) referred only to vote buying with cash, a practice also known as the dawn attack. His is not a unique view. According to Aspinall, "[a]lmost all of the opprobrium directed toward 'money politics' in Indonesia is reserved for this phenomenon: the provision of individual cash payments, or goods, to voters in the immediate lead up to the election."[15] While giving collective goods to communities was fine for Rusdi, he firmly believed that distributing money in envelopes to individuals was not. The latter practice was the very subject of the fatwa he always cited in his campaign speeches. Thus, he did not launch any dawn attacks, hoping instead that his hard work over three months would get him into the provincial parliament. Other candidates confirmed that Rusdi did not engage in individual vote buying.[16]

In the end, Rusdi did win a seat, coming first in his electoral district among PPP candidates. He defeated an incumbent who had been a provincial parliamentary leader, and who hence had access to government "social assistance funds" to support local projects and generate support. A fellow PPP candidate for the city legislature was

---

[13] Ibid.

[14] Ibid.

[15] Edward Aspinall, "Money Politics", *Inside Indonesia* 116, Apr.–June 2014, available at http://www.insideindonesia.org/weekly-articles/money-politics.

[16] Interviews, 22 May 2014; 30 May 2014.

impressed with Rusdi's consistent refusal to distribute money, and shared a personal experience:

> Two days before the election, *Pak Kyai* [Rusdi] and I were summoned by a figure from Muslimat [a women's organisation affiliated to NU] who offered to bring in 100 votes for both of us. But to get the votes, money was needed: Rp 50,000 per vote for two tickets. She said that without money it was very difficult to secure votes. We knew that she was trustworthy, but *Pak Kyai* did not take the opportunity and so neither did I.[17]

This informant explained that he knew of no other PPP leader who was like Rusdi. According to him, all other leading PPP candidates distributed money in envelopes. Rusdi was the only one of the party's winning candidates who, in his observation, had passed the moral test.

Rusdi cemented his personal brand by openly declaring that he disagreed with vote buying. Instead he relied on name recognition, Islamic sentiment and tireless campaigning to win. In one respect, by taking this approach he helped to protect his reputation as a religious and moral leader of the community. At the same time, this was a stance that came with serious personal risks: Rusdi spent hundreds of millions of rupiah on his campaign, a large part of his retirement fund.[18] A loss would have meant him spending the rest of his life depending on the generosity of his children and others. From a purely economic point of view, the temptation to protect his investment by buying votes must have been very great. Many other candidates from Islamic parties took this path, distributing cash but labelling it "alms-giving" (*sedekah*).

Personal idealism also played a part in a second candidate, whom we will call Rahmad, deciding not to buy the vote; in his case the decision was backed by his sociological reading of the electorate, metaphysical advice, and the persuasion of his family. His reading of voter preferences, however, proved to be inaccurate, leaving him astonished and disappointed with his own people when he was defeated by an internal party rival, an incumbent whom he says bought votes.

---

[17] Confidential interview, 30 May 2014.
[18] Interview, Rusdi, 3 May 2014.

Rahmad is a holder of a master's degree, and a young lecturer in a private tertiary educational institution in Banjarmasin. He runs a successful car rental business and has a few assets in the form of land and property. He works for his party at the local parliament, mainly preparing responses to draft regulations, and holds a significant party post. With this background, he was able to secure the top position on the PPP ticket in his electoral district. Like Rusdi, Rahmad was serious about getting out the vote. His campaign was clientelistic in nature. He distributed cards that promised that "the holder of the card will benefit from a free ambulance service and the family will get 'grief money' [*uang duka*] of about Rp 500,000 should the holder pass away".[19] He printed 11,000 cards and distributed most of them to members of *kelompok pengajian* (Islamic study groups) and individuals contacted through other connections. He also hired 15 electricity meter-readers to deliver the cards to voters in residential areas; each handed out 200 cards. In addition, he contacted RT (sub-neighbourhood) heads and the local committees who organise funeral processions (*pengurus rukun kematian*); these individuals would be the first points of contact for community members who wanted to claim the benefits. He explained this plan with pride, saying "no one before had the nerve to make such a big commitment".[20] He claimed he had done the calculations and was optimistic about the programme's feasibility. The idea was not entirely new, with similar programmes having been carried out by the city administration and sporadically by previous elected candidates. But Rahmad was right in that previous members of parliament had never specified the amount of "grief money" they would pay.

Rahmad did not stop there. He also gave out various keepsakes and community gifts. He paid for the food served at his campaign events, also giving those present promotional packs containing the *Yasin* (a chapter of the Quran, often printed independently for regular use), headscarves, and key rings with his name. He also accommodated specific requests from groups of voters, one of the most expensive being for a new fire engine hose (made in Germany, it cost him Rp 8 million, though he split

---

[19] Interview, Rahmad, 30 May 2014.
[20] Ibid.

the cost with another candidate).[21] Like many other candidates, Rahmad viewed such expenses as legitimate spending, not as illicit money politics.

Having worked hard during his campaign, Rahmad felt confident. He roughly calculated that if a third of the recipients of his cards voted for him, he would win a seat. However, he also realised that his chances could fall if other candidates distributed cash to voters. He not only felt this instinctively, but also pointed to a study by a Yogyakarta university that showed that the two things voters most wanted from candidates were cash and foodstuffs. Little wonder, then, that he was tempted to engage in vote buying. Several people offered to get votes for him. For instance, one head of a neighbourhood (RW) offered him 400 votes. In one *kelurahan* (precinct), a vote canvasser offered to work on voters in 49 polling stations. In another area, a friend proposed getting him ten voters per polling booth. All of these operations required per head cash payments.

Three things held Rahmad back from following his peers and launching a "dawn attack". The first was his sociological analysis of the voters in his city: he thought most would be too scared to sell their votes. This was partly because, accepting the conventional wisdom about South Kalimantan's strong religious traditions, he believed that people would follow the advice of a revered religious scholar (*tuan guru*). Not long before voting day, he explained, a famous charismatic *tuan guru* whose *pengajian* were regularly attended by 4,000 to 5,000 people and broadcast by radio, told his congregation loudly three times: "Those who bribe or take bribes all will end up in hellfire." Rahmad reasoned that since Muslims in his city usually listened to religious figures, especially charismatic ones, he would not need to distribute envelopes. Another event strengthened his conviction. He personally heard a national parliamentarian warn an audience of hundreds in a neighbouring district that police officers and military personnel would be in disguise on election day, dressed up as vegetable or meatball soup vendors, with the goal of "catching the perpetrators of money politics, those who distribute cash as well as the recipients".[22] Rahmad thought that the information must be valid because it came from a national politician, close to policymakers.

---

[21] Ibid.
[22] Ibid.

In Rahmad's understanding, voters had thus received both worldly and otherworldly warnings. He concluded that they would be too afraid to take money from candidates.

A second source of his resistance was spiritual. Rahmad visited several Islamic shamans believed to have the ability to foresee the future. They gave him happy news. As he explained, "I have asked the *habib* (Prophet Muhammad's descendants) and *muallim* (Islamic teachers) in Martapura, Gambut and Alalak and they say: 'You will be a parliamentarian.'"[23] He also asked the shamans and his mother to do *salat hajat* [special prayers asking for a blessing for an endeavour] for his success.

Ultimately, however, it was a third factor, persuasion by his family that made him steer clear of retail vote buying. His wife told him that if he gained a parliamentary seat by using illegitimate means, the income he generated from the position would not receive heavenly blessings (*berkah*). Also, he would be forced to accumulate wealth as quickly as possible to replenish the savings he would have expended, and in doing so, likely engage in illegal and corrupt activities. As Muslims who believed in the ill effects of financing one's family with the proceeds of unlawful activities, his wife asserted that neither of them wanted to raise immoral children or lead a life full of misfortune and distress: "Even if we get richer, we will not have peace of mind," he said, repeating his wife's words.[24] His brother, too, begged him not to distribute envelopes, saying, "If the seat belongs to you [in the knowledge of God], then you will get it."[25] His family asked him to be strong in facing down temptation, and he complied.

When the vote count showed he had lost, the friend who had proposed vote buying told him it was his own fault. Rahmad was shaken and began to question his decision, though he had reconciled with himself by the time I interviewed him seven weeks later. He told me that in a recent party meeting, he had badly wanted to express his distaste for his fellow PPP candidates:

---

[23] Ibid.

[24] Ibid.

[25] Ibid.

> I wanted to state that I have chosen PPP as a political vehicle so that I will not see practices like bribing people in order to vote. We are an Islamic party, for God's sake. I joined PPP, not any other party, so I will not become a ghost when I die [for bad deeds during one's lifetime].[26]

The only thing that stopped him speaking out was the fact that he had received funding from the party leadership. The funding was supposed to partially finance his campaign and, when necessary, to pay voters. Several loyalists of the party leader were beneficiaries of such funds, although they did not receive the same amounts.[27] Rahmad told me that one provincial candidate "got 100 million [rupiah], but I got less than that", though he did not specify the sum.[28] The justification leaders gave for paying individual voters was that even eating pork was permissible for Muslims in an emergency. Rahmad did not want to upset the leadership with his criticism, as he still wants a political career. He also wanted to avoid a mocking reply which he imagined as: "Did we not also give you money? Where did you spend it?"[29] In this case, it was basically the candidate's personal religious beliefs—plus an element of miscalculation—that stopped him from being wooed by vote canvassers. He did not win, however, because unlike Rusdi he lacked a strong public reputation to attract voters without having to pay them.

The last PPP candidate I include in this category of idealists ran in Banua Enam district. Let us call him Taufik. He was a married man in his thirties, highly educated, and a qualified lecturer. A student activist during his college days, he experienced first-hand in Yogyakarta the 1998 mass movement that brought down the New Order regime. His impetus for involvement in politics was also awakened by his father, a loyal PPP supporter since the New Order. He became acquainted with PPP elites in his district when his elderly father was chosen by the party to serve as a member of the local representative assembly (2004–09). He accompanied his father to party meetings and got involved in discussions

---

[26] Ibid.

[27] Interviews, Saleh, 18 May 2014; Jenah, 22 May 2014.

[28] Interview, Rahmad, 30 May 2014.

[29] Ibid.

of local politics in PPP circles. But his family was also well known in the village for running a successful home-based beverage industry and for its commitment to education. His father had established an Islamic elementary school several decades ago, and Taufik is now its principal. In the 2014 election, the party put him at the top of its candidate list in his electoral district. His strongest internal rival was an incumbent previously holding an important position in the district assembly.

The test of his convictions came when a politically powerful relative presented him with an opportunity to defeat his rival. The circumstances were unusual: the local election commission had decided to conduct a re-vote in ten polling stations where voters had been sent the wrong ballot papers on voting day. The result of the initial count in the remainder of the electoral district had shown that the incumbent candidate led the race, but so narrowly that Taufik had a chance to overtake him through the re-vote.

A day before the re-vote took place, Taufik was summoned by his powerful relative. The relative belonged to a different party, not PPP, but apparently believed it would be advantageous to have a relative in the district parliament. Besides, it would not look good if he let his relative lose. According to a confidant, Taufik was not enthusiastic about being summoned: "He did not pick up his mobile phone when it rang and it was only after he was visited three times in that day by different messengers that he finally responded to the call."[30] When Taufik eventually went to his relative, he found many people were already present. It turned out that it was a meeting to monitor the moves of candidates and their success team members in the field around the ten polling stations. Again, it was not a meeting of PPP, but a rival party: those present were primarily concerned with internal competition in their own party, but the powerful relative had also seen an opportunity to benefit Taufik.

The relative proposed to help Taufik defeat his PPP rival and asked his field operators to brief them about the latest activity of the front-runner. They reported that the man had already distributed envelopes containing Rp 100,000. The relative ordered them to pay a higher sum,

---

[30] Confidential interview, 22 Aug. 2014.

Rp 150,000, to reverse the direction of support. He also asked a candidate from his own party who was present—and for whose benefit the meeting was primarily being held—to "surrender" some "secured" votes for Taufik. The person asked to make this sacrifice did some quick calculations and explained that he could not give up more than 100 votes without jeopardising his own chance of winning a seat.

After a little more talk, it was clear that this powerful patron was offering Taufik both the funds and the field operators necessary to launch the dawn attack. All Taufik had to do was say "yes". The powerful figure remarked to Taufik that he would be pleased to see him in the parliament where they could "work together".[31] It was almost midnight, on the eve of the re-vote. Taufik sat quietly, expressing neither agreement nor disagreement. After some moments without a clear answer, the host let Taufik leave the meeting, asking him to immediately give him a call should he decide to take up the offer. But Taufik never did. In the end, the result of the second vote count was no different than the initial one: Taufik's internal PPP rival won the seat. Victory had been there for the taking, but Taufik had let it pass him by.

An old friend of Taufik attributes his defeat to his personality, saying that the candidate "has too much pride".[32] Another friend regretted his attitude. In his opinion, realpolitik necessitates manoeuvres and former student activists should leave their idealism behind. "He would have won. He was shown the way. But it seems to me that he himself *does not want to win*."[33] His brother saw it differently. He explained that Taufik has a reputation and values to protect. He teaches at an Islamic school and a local campus. "He is an educator. What would people think of him if he accepted the proposal? People would say he is no different from others, also willing to practise money politics!"[34] Moreover, he would have tarnished the good name of his family, otherwise respected for its piety and continuing support for religious education. He stressed that their

---

[31] Confidential interview, 22 Aug. 2014.
[32] Confidential interview, 1 Aug. 2014.
[33] Confidential interview, 2 Aug. 2014.
[34] Ibid.

father "never taught us to betray our friends and our party".[35] In the end, the candidate and his relatives were able to look on the bright side of the episode. It is true that he was defeated, but he came out with an elevated reputation. Previously, he was just a regular candidate. Now, local political players know that he was the man who was able to face down temptation and spurn victory when it was offered to him on a platter.

PKS: LOCALISED VOTE-BUYING POLICIES

After discussing how some individual candidates decided personally to spurn vote buying, in this section I focus on the party level, using the case study of the PKS in two districts: South Hulu Sungai (Hulu Sungai Selatan, HSS) and Central Hulu Sungai (Hulu Sungai Tengah, HST). In the former district, local party elites were lenient toward money politics; in the latter, they were firmly against it. As with the preceding candidate, rejecting vote buying seemed to be a costly decision for the party in electoral terms, because the party's vote declined in HST.

The districts of HSS and HST are good examples of PKS's success in penetrating rural areas while staying strong in urban areas. Support for PKS has grown in both districts, neither typical PKS territory, with the party normally seen as representing the urban and well educated. The districts are predominantly rural, with urbanisation rates of 25 per cent for HSS and 19 per cent for HST. Yet in South Kalimantan since 2004, PKS has consistently won a bigger share of parliamentary seats in these districts than in urban centres like Banjarmasin and Banjarbaru. At the same time, PKS has kept its urban disposition in the two districts. The 2014 DPRD results indicate that 20.6 per cent of HSS's urban voters supported PKS, compared to only 16.8 per cent in rural areas. In HST the figures were 14.9 per cent and 9.6 per cent respectively.

PKS cadres in the areas ascribe their success to the effectiveness of their community-level campaigning, primarily involving regular visits to the houses of voters and community leaders, and the endorsement of descendants of Prophet Muhammad (*habib*) who are deeply respected in

---

[35] Interview, 2 Aug. 2014.

the area.[36] The districts' PKS activists also go to the sites of fires, accidents and floods to collect and distribute donations and offer physical support to those affected; and they provide free education in remote areas.[37] The most revered *tuan guru* in the area, whose regular *pengajian* attracts thousands of people, is publicly sympathetic to the PKS.

In 2014, PKS candidates did better in HSS than in HST. In HSS, PKS came first, gaining six parliamentary seats, an improvement on its five seats in 2009. This result continued the party's tradition of being the largest party in the district assembly since 2004 and made HSS (according to party sources) one of only three districts throughout Indonesia where PKS came in first, a result that generated pride among its local cadres. In contrast, the party lost two seats in HST, down from five in 2009, also losing its position as the largest party in the district parliament. This result was in line with wider provincial results, with the PKS vote in eight districts declining in 2014. Party elites in HST pointed the finger at massive vote buying by rival parties.

The two branches carried out similar preparatory work before the election. The national board of PKS had decreed that the party's strategy in 2014 would be polling-station based. The key was to recruit as many voters as possible in each station, recording their names, addresses and contact numbers and reporting them upward to party boards. The South Kalimantan chairperson of PKS explained that the HSS branch had presented the most orderly work in this regard, but the HST branch closely followed it.[38] The composition of candidates running for the party in both districts was also similar. Long-time cadres occupied the top two positions on both candidate lists, with recently recruited members placed in middle or lower positions. These newcomers were often individuals with relatively strong financial resources they could use for their campaigns. Thus, both branches of PKS diversified their candidate pools, although those winning seats were primarily leading cadres.

Various informants also testified that vote buying occurred in both districts. Indeed it was so common in HST that Rosyadi, a

---

[36] Interviews, Faqih Jurjani, 3 Aug. 2014; Ardiansyah, 5 Aug. 2014.

[37] Interview, Gazali, 5 Aug. 2014.

[38] Interview, Ibnu Sina, 30 April 2014.

re-elected PKS candidate, recounted that "one person broke a record for collecting 18 envelopes from different candidates".[39] A local election commissioner in HSS explained that no party was innocent of money politics in that district, including the Islamic ones: "They are all the same!"[40] According to him, voters were eagerly awaiting the dawn attack: "When I drove around on the evening before 9 April and stopped at one point, some citizens approached, asking if I was bringing money on behalf of particular candidates."[41] There were many such stories in both districts.

However, the two PKS branches differed in their attitudes toward vote buying. One candidate running for the provincial DPRD whose constituency crossed the boundaries of three districts, including HSS and HST, explained:

> In HST, *ustaz* [preacher] Faqih [the PKS chairperson in HST] did not allow the dawn attack strategy. In HSS, in contrast, PKS fought back when candidates from other parties distributed cash. They let them finish [their attack]. Then, they distributed Muslim prayer clothing [Malay-style shirts or *baju koko*, *sarung* and women's prayer robes, *mukena*] to voters who had previously committed to support PKS candidates.[42]

This informant explained that no cash was distributed; some other sources, however, said that PKS cadres also distributed money in HSS, though I was unable to confirm these reports from anybody from the party there.

Ustaz Faqih himself told me that "here in HST, we do not use money", stating that it was simply unacceptable to distribute cash to gain political office.[43] He explained that, during the campaign, village-level PKS officials often said they should give money to persuade voters, arguing that this was what other candidates were doing. In reply, he softly rejected the idea by pointing out the risks: "If there will really

[39] Interview, 3 Aug. 2014.
[40] Interview, Imron, 5 Aug. 2014.
[41] Ibid.
[42] Interview, Riswandi, 25 May 2014.
[43] Interview, Ustaz Faqih, 3 Aug. 2014.

be arrests for money politics, and at that time, we follow the others in distributing envelopes, God forbid, we may get caught."[44] More deeply, he personally believed that giving money to individual voters was bribery (menyogok). Indeed, some of Ustaz Faqih's relatives describe him as "too straight" to be a politician.[45]

The situation in HSS was different. One PKS ideologue in HSS said that Ustaz Faqih was old fashioned, and did not follow the latest political developments.[46] For this informant, elections were exactly like war. "You cannot expect to win if you fight a tank or automatic weapons with sharpened bamboo. The realistic thing to do if you want an equal chance of winning is to at least use similar weapons."[47] When everybody uses money, doing so was not only justifiable but also necessary. According to him, he had expressed this idea in front of local party cadres, some of them running as candidates. Judging from his story, the cadres were glad to have his backing. Indeed, one PKS leader-cum-candidate in HSS agreed, comparing what corrupt politicians were prepared to do to win with what good people with virtuous goals should countenance. In his opinion, virtuous candidates should have the same courage to make financial sacrifices: "If those robbers of public funds have spent to the utmost, why don't we, people with a religious cause, do the same?"[48] For this candidate, the moral superiority of PKS candidates would be proven by their behaviour once in power, rather than by the distinctiveness of their electioneering strategies. Accordingly, the HSS branch took an ends-will-justify-the-means approach, while the HST branch believed that moral virtue should be reflected in electoral strategy too. Nonetheless, people from both branches were convinced that what they did was justified, politically if not religiously.

In the context of our discussion, however, it was the HST branch of PKS that was more interesting, in that it sought to hold on to its anti-corruption ideals despite considerable internal and external pressure to

---

[44] Ibid.
[45] Confidential interview, 1 Aug. 2014.
[46] Confidential interview, 5 Aug. 2014.
[47] Ibid.
[48] Ibid.

use cash to sway voters. Its attitude was simple and essentially religious. However, its policy did not bring about electoral victory, but in fact reduced PKS candidates' competitiveness in the district. The branch leader was willing to accept this electoral cost, saying it made it easier for him to face God in the Hereafter.

CONCLUSION

The idealists discussed in this chapter were not frivolous candidates, uncommitted to getting elected. They all ran serious campaigns, through such means like engaging in hundreds of face-to-face meetings with voters, or by placing hundreds of their banners along roadsides. They also accommodated common practices of gift giving and making donations to communities. But they refused to offer cash to individual voters.

These candidates did not view money politics as representing a broad continuum in which a range of patronage-based practices can be included. Rather, they saw it as a straightforward, even black-and-white category, identifying cash payments to individuals days or hours prior to a vote as the primary, even the only, form of money politics. One may argue that these so called "idealists" were therefore practically in the same category as most candidates, who also approached voters using many types of patronage, or at least that the difference between them and the others was merely a matter of degree, rather than type.

To appreciate these idealists, however, one must take into account the common view of the 2014 election in South Kalimantan—which was perhaps not far different from that in most parts of Indonesia. Most of my informants who were candidates contended that if they offered only words, name cards or brochures—and nothing more—to voters, then the slice of the electorate they could realistically target would be too narrow to allow them to win a seat. Success team members out in the community often told candidates straight up that they needed to make cash payments in order to ensure that the voters they had been cultivating would not turn their backs and run to cashed-up rivals. In this context, the choices made by the candidates in this chapter seem not only morally upright, but also politically bold. And most of them paid for it—at least that is what they think—by losing.

Map of Sulawesi

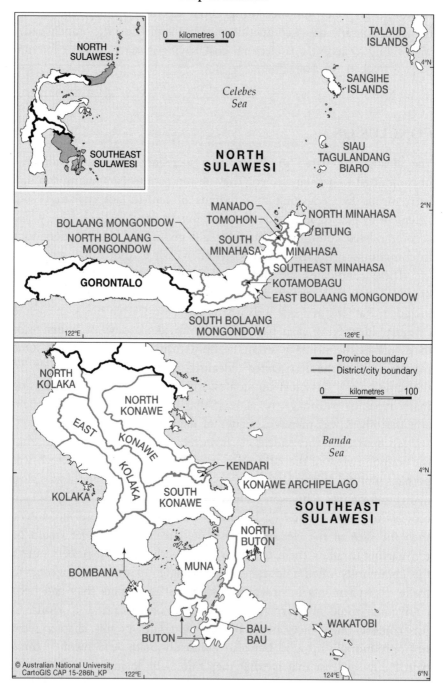

NORTH SULAWESI

SOUTHEAST SULAWESI

0   kilometres   100

TALAUD ISLANDS

4°N

Celebes Sea

SANGIHE ISLANDS

NORTH SULAWESI

SIAU TAGULANDANG BIARO

2°N

MANADO
TOMOHON

NORTH MINAHASA

BITUNG

BOLAANG MONGONDOW

NORTH BOLAANG MONGONDOW

SOUTH MINAHASA

MINAHASA

SOUTHEAST MINAHASA

GORONTALO

KOTAMOBAGU

EAST BOLAANG MONGONDOW

SOUTH BOLAANG MONGONDOW

122°E

126°E

Province boundary
District/city boundary

0   kilometres   100

NORTH KOLAKA

NORTH KONAWE

EAST KONAWE

KONAWE

Banda Sea

4°N

KENDARI

KONAWE ARCHIPELAGO

KOLAKA

KOLAKA

SOUTH KONAWE

SOUTHEAST SULAWESI

NORTH BUTON

BOMBANA

MUNA

WAKATOBI

BUTON

BAU-BAU

© Australian National University
CartoGIS CAP 15-286h_KP

122°E

124°E

6°N

chapter **19**

North Sulawesi: Clan, Church and State

Nono S.A. Sumampouw

North Sulawesi is a relatively prosperous part of Indonesia. It has the third highest Human Development Index score in the country, after Jakarta. Yet this does not mean that politics here are highly programmatic or take place only through formal institutions like parties. On the contrary, during the 2014 election in the province, the majority of candidates drew on their personalist networks in order to campaign. In particular, almost all candidates used kinship and religious networks, drawing on two of the most deeply entrenched informal social institutions in North Sulawesi. To some extent these informal networks substituted for patronage delivery—candidates could often call upon kin to deliver political support without rewarding them materially—but just as often the affective ties forged between candidates and supporters through these networks were backed by delivery of material benefits, especially club goods. While family and religious networks were available to all candidates, the most powerful and successful candidates typically also drew upon a formal institution to provide them with support: the government bureaucracy.

Though politicians are formally proscribed from using public office for political campaigning, this was a common practice in the province. Mobilisation of bureaucratic support was key to the success of many candidates, especially those with relatives holding senior government office. In this regard, of course, North Sulawesi is hardly unique in

Indonesia, with the local bureaucracy often dominating local economies and representing a powerful source of political influence in local communities. The contemporary prestige of the bureaucracy also has historical roots in North Sulawesi, with scholars such as Maria J.C. Schouten and David Henley noting the important role that white-collar employment as *ambtenaar* (bureaucrats) had in constituting a new elite during the colonial period.[1] Whatever its social roots, as we shall see, the bureaucracy is a formidable mobilisational tool and mechanism of patronage delivery in contemporary North Sulawesi.

BACKGROUND: GEOGRAPHIC, DEMOGRAPHIC AND POLITICAL CHARACTERISTICS

Located at the tip of the northeast peninsula of Sulawesi island, North Sulawesi province is about 2,000 km from Jakarta, three days and nights by passenger ferry. To the north, the province directly borders the southern Philippines. Its population of about 2.3 million is roughly 65 per cent Protestant, with most of these Christians concentrated in the Minahasa region around the capital, Manado (altogether consisting of four rural districts, *kabupaten*, and three urban municipalities or *kota*), and the northern islands of the Sangihe, Talaud and Sitaro archipelagos (three districts). The Bolaang Mongondow region (four *kabupaten* and one *kota*) in the south, bordering Gorontalo province, is majority Muslim.

Each of these three subregions—Minahasa, Sangihe-Talaud and Bolaang Mongondow (often abbreviated as Bolmong) has its own distinctive history and sociocultural features. The archipelago and Bolaang Mongondow had long histories of being ruled by kingdoms, with the result that cultures of paternalism are still influential in

---

[1] Maria J.C. Schouten, *Leadership and Social Mobility in a Southeast Asia Society: Minahasa, 1677–1983* (Leiden: KITLV Press, 1998); David Henley, *Nationalism and Regionalism in a Colonial Context: Minahasa in the Dutch East Indies* (Leiden: KITLV Press, 1996).

these two areas.[2] The Minahasa region, in contrast, was never ruled by a kingdom and was instead divided into various self-governing communities, with a largely egalitarian culture.[3] Since the colonial period, the territory's political and bureaucratic elite has largely been drawn from the Minahasans, who adopted Western education early and were close to the Dutch through their shared Protestant religion. Minahasan dominance continued into the independence period; except for a brief time after the Permesta (Piagam Perjuangan Semesta, the Universal Struggle Charter) revolt of the 1950s, which was strong in North Sulawesi, all of the province's governors have been Minahasan. One product of this dominance has been the tendency for other groups to segregate themselves politically along geo-ethnic lines, such as when Gorontalo, a Muslim-majority region, split away from North Sulawesi in 2001 to become a province of its own. There has since been repeated geo-ethnic splitting and formation of new districts and municipalities within the province, as well as movements favouring the creation of new provinces of Bolaang Mongondow Raya (Greater Bolaang Mongondow) and Nusa Utara (Northern Islands).[4]

This ethnic and cultural diversity means that great care must be taken in making generalisations about the province's politics. This was obvious, for example, in the first Indonesian election in 1955. At that time, the nationalist PNI (Partai Nasional Indonesia) and the Protestant party, Parkindo (Partai Kristen Indonesia) did very well in predominantly Christian areas (respectively 23.4 and 51.7 per cent in Sangihe-Talaud; 21.1 and 26.0 per cent in Minahasa) while the Islamic parties, Masjumi and PSII (Partai Syarikat Islam Indonesia) swept the results in Bolaang

---

[2] A. Wendyatarka, "Dua Kultur di Tiga Kawasan" [Two Cultures in Three Districts], *Kompas*, 20 Feb. 2009, available at: http://nasional.kompas.com/read/2009/02/20/08483467/dua.kultur.di.tiga.kawasan.

[3] Henley, *Nationalism and Regionalism*; David Henley, *Jealousy and Justice: The Indigenous Roots of Colonial Rule in Northern Sulawesi* (Amsterdam: VU University Press/CASA-Asia, 2002); Schouten, *Leadership and Social Mobility*.

[4] Alex J. Ulaen, *Pemekaran Wilayah: Haruskah ke Akar Etnis?* [Should Regional Development be Ethnically Based?] (Manado: MarIn-CRC, 2010).

Mongondow (35.3 and 31.8 per cent).[5] But these parties were unevenly distributed: Parkindo won in Minahasa and Sangihe-Talaud, while PSII was strong among the Muslims of Bolaang Mongondow and the PNI vote was evenly distributed. Such local variation was blurred by Golkar's dominance in the New Order years, and in fact Golkar has remained the largest party in post-Suharto North Sulawesi as well (though in 2014 it dropped behind PDI-P in the provincial elections). Even so, religious and ethnic factors have been significant in electoral politics over the last decade. For instance, in the 2004 and 2009 elections the Protestant-based Partai Damai Sejahtera (PDS, Peace and Justice Party) did well in both 2004 and 2009 (in 2014 PDS was unable to compete because it had failed to reach the national electoral threshold of 2.5 per cent in the 2009).

Though Golkar has remained a major player in the province, its dominance has eroded: it received 49 per cent of the North Sulawesi DPR vote in 1999, 32 per cent in 2004, 24.5 per cent in 2009, and 15.4 per cent in 2014, by which time PDI-P placed first with 31.9 per cent. In 2014, though Golkar was still the largest party in most district and municipal parliaments, its cadres held only two district-head positions: in South Minahasa and Tomohon. Six districts were headed by PDI-P members, two by PAN and the remainder by candidates supported by Partai Demokrat, PPP, PKPI or party coalitions. Going into the 2014 elections, therefore, though Golkar was strong in local parliaments throughout the province, it was also vulnerable, given that local government leaders from rival parties not only had considerable cultural capital as local "strongmen", but also controlled the levers of the bureaucracy. The governorship had been lost in 2005 when Sinyo Harry Sarundajang, a former bureaucrat nominated by PDI-P won the post; he was re-elected in 2010 under the Partai Demokrat banner, and in 2014 was enrolled as a candidate in that party's ultimately abortive presidential "convention" process. In 2014, two of his children stood for parliamentary seats for PDI-P, one stood for the non-partisan DPD and another was a deputy *bupati* (district head). In short, by 2014 North

[5] Barbara S. Harvey, *Permesta: Half a Rebellion* (Ithaca, NY: Cornell Modern Indonesia Project Monograph Series 57, 1977), p. 27.

Sulawesi had ceased being a Golkar bastion and was now a battleground for most of Indonesia's major parties, especially the nationalist ones, and for politicians' family and other personal networks.

FAMILIAL AND FRIENDSHIP RELATIONS

In North Sulawesi, as in other parts of eastern Indonesia, the term for a clan is *fam*, adopted from the Dutch *familienaam*, and equivalent to *marga* used in other parts of the country. A *fam* follows the father's line, with children adopting their father's *fam* name, but this does not mean that kinship relationships are strictly patrilineal; on the contrary they are bilateral, with strong relationships maintained with the mother's kin. *Fam* size can vary greatly, but a *fam* name is a widely used marker of social identity, and is especially useful in asserting a family connection with persons of higher status, such as government officials.

Fam ties can be readily mobilised for political purposes. Politicians often draw their relatives in as the core of their success teams, and they see doing so as both cheap and effective. Normally, a relative will feel reluctant to ask for any sort of material reward for doing this sort of work, which might be considered *mapalus* (a traditional Minahasan term for freely rendered and reciprocal collective labour to achieve a common goal in a village setting). Only a few people encountered during my fieldwork received payment for their political work on behalf of a candidate who was a relative; they were typically students, the jobless, or youths with non-permanent work who were given only small sums of "transport money" or "cigarette money".[6] If the campaign succeeds, however, even distant relatives will be able to ask for financial assistance from the successful candidate for church or mosque activities, family events and organisational or student fees or similar needs, although they will rarely get access to major or continuing economic opportunities.[7] Many people who work politically on behalf of a family member are not too concerned about the economic rewards or

---

[6] Interviews, 10, 11 Mar. 2014.

[7] Interviews, 10, 30, 31 Mar. 2014; 8 Apr. 2014.

access to public services they might gain if the relative is elected. Instead, they receive psychological rewards in the form of shared family pride when a relative succeeds politically and acquires status as an important person in local society. Accordingly, many contribute financially to their relatives' campaigns without expecting a direct material benefit.

From my field interviews, it was obvious that all candidates and their success teams tried to maximise family support in their political campaigning. At the very least, candidates drew in their spouses, children and siblings, and often parents and in-laws, as "free" success team members. Most then extended from this core to the wider family by drawing on bilateral kinship links from both parental lines, following the various branches of the family tree as far as they go. One candidate using this strategy was Aditya Moha, a Golkar DPR incumbent, who in his base area of Bolaang Mongondow built support by following his father's family line, which was Gorontalo, that of his mother, who was of mixed Batak–Mongondow heritage and that of his wife, who was Bugis.[8] Jerry Sambuaga, a Golkar DPR candidate likewise used all available family relationships in his base area of Minahasa.[9]

The forum most often used to maximise family ties was the meeting of the extended family. These were in turn typically organised by *rukun*, informal social organisations that brought together members of a particular *fam*, or members or descendants of a particular village, region or descent group. Examples include the Polii *rukun* (Polii is a *fam*); the Sonder *rukun*, where Sonder is a region in Minahasa (*rukun* that use place names are usually set up for people from a particular area who now live elsewhere); the Borgo *rukun*, where Borgo is a local term for people of mixed local and European descent; or the *rukun* for Talaud people that is active in Manado. *Rukun* meetings are informal get-togethers where members can renew their bonds, usually involving plenty of food and drink, prayers and other religious activities, and paid for by whoever is hosting the meeting.

In the lead-up to election season, candidates usually increase the tempo of their interactions with whatever *rukun* they might be linked

---

[8] Interview, Aditya Moha, 15 Mar. 2014.
[9] Interview, Jerry Sambuaga, 10 Mar. 2014.

to, including by making contact with *rukun* they have never visited before. Locals call this *stor muka*—"showing your face"—a term that can have negative connotations, depending on how it is expressed. Indeed, candidates often hosted *rukun* meetings, paying for the food, drinks, entertainment, equipment hire and the like. *Rukun* meetings enabled them to promote their candidacy, gauge the strength of their support in a particular network, and sometimes get financial support. Candidates also contributed donations to their *rukun* at other times, to pay for collective events such as religious festivities, including Christmas services, pilgrimages and cleaning up gravesites.

Many candidates produced publicity material that explicitly mentioned their *fam* relationships, place of origin and other social networks that would be useful in mobilising votes. For example, Jhon Albert Octavianus Dumais, a provincial DPRD candidate for the Partai Demokrat in Bitung, listed not only the names and places of origin of both major branches of the Dumais clan on his campaign leaflets, but also listed those of his mother and in-laws. A similar phenomenon was visible with some Talaud voters who lived in Manado and who went back to their home islands and villages in order to vote, with their transport and consumption costs covered by candidates from their home villages.[10]

This style of familial clientelism extended not only to true kin, but also to close friends. An example was a man who was a member of the success teams of both Lili Binti, a Manado DPRD candidate, and Olivia Manoppo, a provincial candidate, because he was a close friend of Lili's brother, as well as being a friend of Olivia herself:

> I've been good friends with Lili's brother since school right to the present time, so I would feel uncomfortable saying no to her invitation [to join his sister's team]. It was lucky that Olivia was standing in level I [that is, the province] because we are good friends too. If not, we might have ended up fighting, just because of the election.[11]

In such cases, the clients receive a psychological reward for acting loyally to a friend, but material considerations often also feature. Take

---

[10] Confidential interviews, 14, 15 Apr. 2014.
[11] Confidential interview, 31 Mar. 2014.

the example of Ramli (not his real name), a member of the success team of Sisca Mangindaan, a Demokrat candidate for the provincial parliament. Ramli set up a team to work for Sisca on his own initiative and used some of his own money to design campaign material and hold campaign events for her, using staff of his own event-organising company to make the arrangements.[12] But friendship was not all there was to this relationship; Ramli was also entrusted to run Sisca's company, called "I ♥ M Production" (with the M standing for "Mangindaan"). Ramli had previously managed some big events sponsored by Sisca such as a major boxing competition, and Sisca, plus Steven Makenly Suwuh, a Manado city DPRD Demokrat candidate, were known to frequently help Ramli out by providing him with funds for events when sponsorship money had not yet been paid. When I interviewed him, Ramli's facial expressions certainly suggested he expected compensation for the money he was putting into Sisca's campaign.

RELIGIOUS NETWORKS

As well as drawing on family and friendship ties, many candidates mobilised religious networks. This happened with every religious denomination, but let us focus our attention on Gereja Masehi Injili di Minahasa (GMIM, Christian Evangelical Church in Minahasa), the largest Protestant denomination in the province. GMIM's political credibility has been considerable, especially since the organisation played an important role in steering the province away from communal conflict in the early post-Suharto period, in part by refusing to engage in formal political life.[13] Church leaders explain that the organisation is not formally

---

[12] Confidential interview, 4 Apr. 2014.
[13] David Henley, Maria J.C. Schouten and Alex J. Ulaen, "Preserving the Peace in Post-New Order Minahasa", in *Renegotiating Boundaries: Local Politics in Post-Suharto Indonesia*, ed. Henk Schulte Nordholt and Gerry van Klinken (Leiden: KITLV Press, 2007), pp. 307–26; Fadjar I. Thufail, "Ketika Perdamaian Terwujud di Bukit Kasih: Pencegahan Konflik, Lembaga Gereja dan Politik Adat di Minahasa" [When Peace Came to Love Hill: Conflict Prevention, the Church and *Adat* Politics

involved in partisan politics and that its officials are urged not to involve themselves in practical politics.[14]

However, GMIM congregations are potentially important vote banks, and many candidates are not only affiliated to GMIM but are active in the church's governing bodies and/or within church-affiliated organisations of students, graduates and the like. Many candidates in 2014 likewise bore important church titles such as *Penatua* (Pnt., church elder, chosen by the congregation from among its own members). Several important incumbent legislators had backgrounds as GMIM pastors, including the speaker of the provincial parliament from 2009 to 2014, Meiva Salindeho-Lintang (Golkar) and Tonny Kaunang, the former head of the Golkar faction in the provincial parliament (he stood as a PAN DPR candidate in 2014).

In practice, therefore, the official distance between the Church and political life counts for little. This first became obvious in 2004 when Marhany Pua, the Youth Chairperson of the GMIM Synod, stood for election to the DPD, and won the seat with the highest vote in the province and with minimal costs, precisely because church networks helped his campaign. Then, in 2005, A.O. Supit, the Synod chairperson, openly backed the re-election of Governor A.J. Sondakh, praising him as a GMIM cadre.[15] (Sondakh's poor track record resulted in him losing to S.H. Sarundajang.)[16]

---

in Minahasa], in *Kegalauan Identitas: Agama Etnisitas dan Kewarganegaraan Pada Masa Pasca Orde-Baru* [Identity in Crisis: Religion, Ethnicity and Citizenship in the Post-New Order Period], ed. Martin Ramstedt and Fadjar Ibnu Thufail (Jakarta: PSDR-LIPI, Max Plank Institute for Social Anthropology and Grasindo, 2011), pp. 149–66.

[14] Interviews, Ferry Liando, 7 Mar. 2014; Richard A.D. Siwu, 17 Mar. 2014.

[15] Interview, Richard A.D. Siwu, 17 Mar. 2014.

[16] David T. Hill, "Media and Politics in Regional Indonesia: The Case of Manado", in *Political Regimes and Media in Asia*, ed. Krishna Sen and Terence Lee (London and New York: Routledge, 2008), pp. 188–207; Marcus Mietzner, "Indonesia and the Pitfalls of Low Quality Democracy: A Case Study of the Gubernatorial Elections in North Sulawesi", in *Democratization in Post-Suharto Indonesia*, ed. Marco Bunte and Andreas Ufen (London: Routledge, 2009), pp. 124–49.

Since that time, politicians, bureaucrats and their relatives have rushed to take up church positions open to laypeople. This is visible in the composition of the 2010–14 governing board of BIPRA (Bapak, Ibu, Pemuda, Remaja, Anak), the church's organisation for Fathers, Mothers, Youths, Teenagers and Children, which is dominated by politicians and their relatives. An example is Jefferson Rumajar, the Golkar chairperson and mayor of Tomohon who was elected to head the Men's/Father's Commission and, when he fell afoul of corruption charges, was replaced by Djendri Keintjem, the head of the PDI-P faction in the provincial parliament.

Elections for the BIPRA chair and the Synod board were held between January and March 2014. Many politicians viewed these elections as a sort of pre-legislative election test with which to assess and solidify their networks,[17] and many took positions in both bodies (see Table 19.1). Many politicians also erected banners and billboards, or took out advertisements in local newspapers, expressing support for the Synod. Then, during the legislative election campaign period, candidates with GMIM backgrounds made use of them whenever they could, for example, by ensuring that any church titles they had, such as Pdt. (for *Pendeta*, or pastor) or Pnt. were included in their publicity material. Some candidates with prominent church positions, such as Pdt. Johan Nicolaas Gara, a charismatic preacher and Nasdem DPR candidate, and Pnt. Stefanus Liow, elected as chairperson of the Fathers unit within BIPRA in 2014, were especially advantaged (I am unsure of the extent to which these two used their church networks for their political campaigns, but they were at least highly advantaged by the free media publicity they gained through their church activities).

The North Sulawesi provincial electoral district V, incorporating the districts of South Minahasa and Southeast Minahasa, provides a good site to observe the use of church networks for campaigning. Billy Lombok, who had just ended his second term as the chairperson of Pemuda GMIM (Youth Fellowship Commission) here, stood for Partai Demokrat, with the highest position on that party's list. He recruited most of his success team from church networks and provided motor vehicles to the Youth Leader of Elim Congregation in Pangu village and

---

[17] Interview, Ferry Liando, 7 Mar. 2014.

Table 19.1

Legislative Candidates Elected to GMIM BIPRA Positions, 2014

No.	Name	BIPRA position	Background
1	Stefanus Liow	Chair of Synod P/ KB Fellowship Commission	DPD candidate
2	Edyson Masengi	Deputy Chair of Synod P/KB Fellowship Commission	Golkar incumbent & candidate N. Sulawesi DPRD
3	Hanny Joost Pajouw	Deputy Treasurer of Synod P/KB Fellowship Commission	Golkar candidate, N. Sulawesi DPRD
4	Maurits Mantiri	Member of Synod P/KB Fellowship Commission	PDI-P incumbent and candidate, Bitung DPRD
5	James Karinda	Member of Synod P/KB Fellowship Commission	Demokrat candidate, N. Sulawesi DPRD
6	James A. Kojongian	Member of Synod P/KB Fellowship Commission	Golkar candidate, Minahasa DPRD
7	Miky Wenur	Secretary of Synod W/KI Fellowship Commission	Golkar candidate, Tomohon DPRD
8	Fransisca Tuwaidan	Member of Synod W/KI Fellowship Commission	Demokrat candidate, N. Sulawesi DPRD
9	Inggrid Sondakh	Member of Synod W/KI Fellowship Commission	Golkar candidate, N. Sulawesi DPRD
10	Iwan Frederik	Secretary of Synod Teenager Fellowship Commission	Hanura candidate, N. Sulawesi DPRD
11	Santy Luntungan	Deputy Treasurer of Synod Teenager Fellowship Commission	PKPI candidate, Bitung DPRD

the Youth leader for the Ratahan region. They used it to campaign for him, including by visiting youth prayer services before the election and enlisting support from first-time voters in attendance.[18] In this case, we see clear hierarchical mobilisation: from the head of the Synod Youth, to the regional head, down to the level of the *jemaat* or congregation. We can assume that other candidates in the same electoral district used similar methods: for instance, Herlina Siwu, a Gerindra candidate, had powerful church connections; she had just ended her term as head of the Women's Commission in the Synod and was the wife of the deputy head of North Sulawesi district, Jeremia Damongilala, who was himself a former head of the GMIM Synod Youth Commission.

Though GMIM is the largest organised religious group, North Sulawesi is religiously plural. GMIM credentials are therefore not always a guarantee of political success. On the contrary, there is a sort of informal power-sharing between religious groups in the province: for example, everybody knows the governor has a KGPM (Kerapatan Gereja Protestan Minahasa, Union of Protestant Churches in Minahasa) background, that the deputy governor represents GMIM, and that people like Sompie Singal, the *bupati* of North Minasaha, are Catholics. Well-known public officials with backgrounds outside GMIM are commonly seen as representing "their" communities. Meanwhile, in multi-member constituencies, it is feasible for members of minority denominations to try to achieve electoral success by mobilising coreligionists. One candidate who did so in 2014 was Jackson Kumaat, a Demokrat candidate for the DPR, who organised a major event—a "Spiritual Awakening Service" (Kebaktian Kebangunan Rohani) in Manado involving thousands of worshippers in the final days of the campaign under the banner of Gereja Pantekosta di Indonesia (GPdI, Pentecostal Church in Indonesia), one of the biggest Protestant denominations in North Sulawesi, and often seen as GMIM's main rival. A member of a charismatic church himself, Kumaat focused his campaigning on this segment, having failed to publicly support GMIM during its Synod elections, unlike other candidates.

---

[18] Confidential interview, 6 Apr. 2014.

Some candidates tried to maximise their number of supporters by appealing to several religious communities simultaneously. Jerry Sambuaga, a Golkar DPR candidate, for example, stated that religion was a private matter.[19] In practice, however, he was one of the most enthusiastic public supporters of the Synod meeting, taking out repeated media advertisements celebrating the event and being publicly prayed for as a GMIM candidate by the Synod head. At the same time, his mother's family were Catholics, and he was endorsed by Pastor Yong Ohoitimur, a prominent Catholic figure, in an informal meeting of students and others at the seminary in Pineleng near the border of Manado and Tomohon.[20]

In Bolaang Mongondow, meanwhile, candidates used their Muslim, non-Minahasan identity to appeal to voters. The DPR members Aditya Moha (Golkar) and Yasti Mokogouw (PAN) were represented by their supporters as sources of pride and representation for the Mongondow people. Aditya Moha himself explained:

> It's clear that religion and ethnicity are some of my main political advantages. As a region with our own ethnicity and religion, we need representation at the centre. As a result of this demand, it's now not too bad, there are two people representing Mongondow at the centre: Yasti and I.[21]

Both of these candidates were re-elected in 2014, alongside four DPR members of Minahasa descent.

Dropping in scale, in Muslim-majority areas of the province such as Bolaang Mongondow, Christian politicians who were elected equally presented themselves—and were seen by their supporters—as symbols of minority success and representation.[22] In Christian areas such as Minahasa, Islamic parties likewise struggled to win seats and some Muslim candidates targeted pockets of Muslim residents. In the Sario-Malalayang neighbourhood in Manado, for example, a PKS candidate campaigned on the basis that the community should "make history" by making 2014 the first time that its 6,000 or so Muslim residents

---

[19] Interview, Jerry Sambuaga, 10 Mar. 2014.
[20] Interview, Maria Heny Pratiknjo, 2 Apr. 2014.
[21] Interview, Aditya Moha, 15 Mar. 2014.
[22] Interview, Pitres Sombowadile, 15 Mar. 2014.

elected a representative in the city parliament.[23] (He was not elected, but the electoral district did elect a Muslim PAN candidate for the first time in 2014.)

As well as using religious networks, many candidates also based their strategies at least in part on providing patronage to them. A dramatic example here is Olly Dondokambey, the PDI-P major figure in the province, as the chair of the North Sulawesi board of the party, national party treasurer and the deputy chair of the DPR's Budget Body (Banggar) and Chair of its Commission XI, which covers finances and banking. He was a major GMIM patron in Minahasa, using his strategic positions in the national parliament to direct considerable *bansos* (social assistance) funds to assist church activities and building projects. Many other Christian candidates gave generously out of personal funds to support church construction, or to support choirs, Bible training, training events and so on. Muslim candidates were equally likely to donate to *kelompok pengajian* (Islamic study groups) or mosque repairs.

Candidates had varied approaches to such matters. For example, Sisca Mangindaan did not give cash donations, but instead provided building materials such as roofing and bricks.[24] Candidates who had bureaucratic links could pay for the club goods they delivered by accessing government social assistance (*bansos*) funds; incumbents could access "recess" funds or "Asmara" funds (the North Sulawesi version of aspiration funds). Overall, the distribution of patronage to religious networks and institutions in such ways was not only normalised, but also considered praiseworthy by most segments of North Sulawesi society.

BUREAUCRATIC MOBILISATION

One of the distinguishing features of the 2014 election in North Sulawesi was that many of the strongest candidates had family ties with established players in the province's politics and bureaucracy. Indeed, North Sulawesi rivalled only Banten province for attracting national media attention to

---

[23] Confidential interview, 2 Apr. 2104.
[24] Confidential interview, 4 Apr. 2014.

the role of political dynasties.[25] But whereas in Banten dynastic politics were concentrated around a single family—that of governor Ratu Atut Chosiyah—in North Sulawesi the dynastic map was more complex.

This phenomenon first became visible during the governorship of local Golkar chief A.J. Sondakh (2000–05).[26] Officials say that all of his immediate family members attained public office: two children were in the city and provincial legislature, his wife was elected to the DPD, his younger brother, who was initially made head of the local Development Planning Agency, then became rector of Sam Ratulangi University, the main state university in Manado. A local wordplay described his power dynamics as AMPG—the initials of the Golkar youth organisation Angkatan Muda Partai Golkar (Golkar Party Young Generation), but in the new version Anak, Mama, Papa Golojo (Children, Mum, Dad are Greedy).

In the 2014 elections, I was able to identify 29 prominent legislative candidates across the province who were the close family members of former or serving local government heads or prominent legislators, though this figure probably significantly understates the phenomenon. The 29 included 2 of former Governor Sondakh's children who were re-elected to legislative seats in the Manado and provincial parliaments, as well as Vanda, Fabian and Eva Sarundajang, the children of S.H. Sarundajang, the North Sulawesi governor and former mayor of Bitung, and siblings of Ivan Sarundajang, the deputy *bupati* of Minahasa. Cindy and Erwin Wurangian, elected as Golkar members of the provincial and Bitung parliaments, respectively, were children of the late Vanny Wurangian, the former Bitung DPRD Deputy Speaker and Golkar chairperson, and Baby Palar, the current Bitung deputy speaker and Golkar chair. Kristovorous Decky Palinggi, elected through Golkar to the provincial DPRD, was the son-in-law of the late Jopie Paruntu (a former provincial legislator) and Jenny Tumbuan (South Minahasa parliament

---

[25] See, for example, "Demokrasi Tak Hapus Nepotisme: Jabatan Dibagikan pada Kerabat" [Democracy Does Not Eradicate Nepotism: Positions Given to Relatives], *Kompas*, 14 Apr. 2014, available at:http://print.kompas.com/baca/KOMPAS_ART0000000000000000006062426.

[26] Interviews, Ferry Liando, 7 Mar. 2014; Maria Heny Pratiknjo, 2 Apr. 2014.

speaker and Golkar chairperson); Kristovorous's wife is Christiany E. Paruntu, the *bupati* of South Minahasa. In Bolaang Mongondow Raya, Raski Mokodompit (Golkar) was elected to the provincial parliament; Raski was the son of Djelantik Mokodompit, the former mayor of Kotamobagu (Golkar) who was also elected to the city DPRD. Elected to represent the electoral district of Bolaang Mongondow Raya in the provincial parliament were two PDI-P members, one of whom was the wife of Herson Mayulu, the South Bolaang Mongondow *bupati* and PDI-P chair; another was the brother of Yanny Tuuk, the deputy *bupati* of Bolaang Mongondow and PDI-P chair (whose wife, for good measure, was also elected to the Bolaang Mongondow DPRD under the same party banner). Such intermeshing of family, bureaucratic and political power was a complex—but frequent—feature of electoral politics in North Sulawesi.

The basic assumption is simple: if one member of the *fam* takes an important public position, then close relatives will be advantaged in accessing the bureaucracy and political opportunities. Candidates whose family members held important positions in local power structures were advantaged in several ways. If the relative is dominant in a party and/or holds an important legislative post, it is likely that he or she will be able to mobilise the party structure in support. If he or she holds a leadership position in a local executive government—either one of the senior elected posts or as a senior appointed official—then it is likely he or she will be able to access public resources for the campaign, and to mobilise civil servants behind the candidate. Civil servants are often the wealthiest and most influential persons in their local communities, so their word carries great weight at election time. The following quotations from informants, all of whom were themselves relatives of influential bureaucrat-politicians, help introduce us to how the system works:

> Everybody knows that province officials are playing the game. Official cars here all have black number plates [in contrast to the red number plates government vehicles are supposed to use] so they can [be used for campaigning and] avoid the Election Supervisory Agency.[27]

---

[27] Confidential interview, 2 Apr. 2014.

The governor isn't involved directly, so he can stay clean. It's the deputy governor who is coordinating all the heads of bureaus. For example they are using sports equipment, bought by the government, and distributing it to schools as campaign material.[28]

During the campaign period, the most recent example was during the election of the *bupati* of Minahasa, when all the bureau heads were told to go home to their villages every week to campaign and to use their office money to do so.[29]

According to several sources, in the 2014 election when three of Governor Sarundajang's children were contesting legislative posts, the deputy governor played the main role in ensuring that bureaucrats returned to their villages every weekend in order to support their campaigns, including by using their office budgets and preparing campaign materials for them.[30] Another example was the city of Manado, where the mayor, Vicky Lumentut, was also the provincial head of Partai Demokrat. Regular training meetings (known as *bimbingan teknis*, technical guidance) for *pala*, the local term for neighbourhood heads, were used to direct these officials—located at the lowest run of the city government—to campaign for Demokrat candidates.[31] These *pala* were directed to support different candidates at different levels: in the Manado electoral district, Jackson Kumaat for the DPR and James Karinda for the provincial DPRD, Stela Pakaja for the city DPRD in Tikala electoral district, Nortje Van Bone in Sario-Malalayang, and Sicilia Longdong in Singkil Mapange.[32] The *lurah* (the heads of urban precincts one step higher in the bureaucratic structure than the *pala*) were charged with coordinating the effort and were threatened with being transferred to less lucrative posts or distant locations—or even to be relieved of their duties but kept on the payroll (*non-job* is the Indonesian term)—if they did not achieve significant results for the candidates supported by the mayor in their territory.

---

[28] Confidential interview, 2 Apr. 2014.
[29] Confidential interview, 14 Mar. 2014.
[30] Confidential interview, 2 Apr. 2014.
[31] Confidential interview with participant, 15 Apr. 2014.
[32] Confidential interviews, 2, 3, 9 Apr. 2014.

Such mobilisation reflected an attitude that public servants need to be loyal to their superiors, even if that involves campaigning on their behalf (even though doing so is prohibited by Indonesian law). This attitude was visible across all three of North Sulawesi's major cultural areas. About a month before the election, the *bupati* of Minahasa, Jantje Sajouw (also the deputy provincial head of PDI-P), in a speech made when distributing social assistance packages, pointedly stated that citizens and public servants alike needed to be loyal to their leaders. Likewise, Herson Mayulu, the *bupati* of South Bolaang Mongondow was cited by a local newspaper as explaining that civil servants should "stand behind me", and were not allowed to be politically neutral because, unlike members of the armed forces and police, they had voting rights.[33] The unspoken link was to his wife, who was standing as a provincial PDI-P candidate.

One widespread phenomenon was a rash of bureaucratic transfers, promotions and incentives in the lead-up to the campaign period. Though government heads never admitted this, it was widely reported in the local press that these transfers related to the perceived loyalty of the officials concerned, and were aimed at electoral mobilisation. Certainly the posts where most transfers occurred were those with the greatest power over both budgets and territory, such as heads of government bureaus, *camat* (subdistrict heads) and *lurah* (heads of urban precincts). Waves of transfers about a month before the election occurred in, among other districts, Manado city, Minahasa and Sangihe. Also in the lead-up to the election, civil servants received various incentives, presumably in order to secure their loyalty and motivate their mobilisational efforts. These included wage rises for the *pala* in Manado city, and motorcycles and social assistance funds to *hukum tua* (village heads) in Minahasa.

At the same time, as was elsewhere in Indonesia, incumbent legislators also had direct access to the state budget and could direct

---

[33] David Manewus, "Mayulu Ingin PNS Ada di Tempat Tepat" [Mayulu Wants Public Servants to Be in the Right Place], *Tribun Manado*, 20 Mar. 2014, available at: http://manado.tribunnews.com/2014/03/20/mayulu-ingin-pns-ada-di-tempat-tepat.

various programmes to their constituencies, though this depended on what leadership positions they occupied in the legislature and on what legislative commission they were part of. As already noted, district and provincial parliamentarians had access to aspiration or recess funds they could direct toward favoured constituents, including when they made constituency visits. Members of the national DPR made much of their ability to bring home "programmes" from the central government. For instance, Yasti Mokogouw, the former national general treasurer of PAN and former head of DPR Commission V, which has responsibility for development issues, claimed that he had successfully obtained approximately Rp 5 trillion in national budget funds for his base area in Bolaang Mongondow.[34] He played a significant role in challenging Golkar hegemony in Bolmong to PAN's advantage, partly by helping PAN candidates access PPIP (Proyek Perbaikan Infrastrukur Pedesaan—Village Infrastructure Improvement Projects) funds and direct them toward favoured locations.[35] He also claimed to be responsible for bringing substantial RTLH (Rumah Tidak Layak Huni, Unliveable Housing) funds to the area. Olly Dondokambey, the provincial PDI-P boss mentioned above, was also able to mobilise enough funds through his strategic positions within the national legislature—and through the support of PDI-P *bupati*—to subsidise the campaigns of many of the party's lower-level candidates.

CONCLUSION

The North Sulawesi case confirms the observation that clientelism can adapt to a wide range of social, economic and cultural structures.[36] As we have seen, candidates in the province made particular use of three kinds of networks: those based on kinship, religion and the bureaucracy. Each in its own way represented an important local social structure.

---

[34] Confidential interview, 15 Mar. 2014.
[35] Ibid.
[36] Allen D. Hicken, "Clientelism", *Annual Review of Political Science* 14, 1 (2011): 290, 300–1.

Indeed, a determinant of political success in the 2014 election in North Sulawesi was a candidate's ability to draw on all three sets of resources. Those who relied on just one or two networks often failed. Given that virtually all candidates could access family and religious networks, the deciding factor was often influence in the bureaucracy. For example, all three of the governor's children who stood for office were elected: they certainly had strong family and church networks behind them, but the civil service was also massively mobilised for their benefit. Many other successful candidates had personal, including familial, ties in the bureaucracy, even if their backing was not as high-level as that enjoyed by the Sarundajang clan. In contrast, many seemingly promising candidates from influential families and with leadership positions in religious organisations failed to be elected because they lacked bureaucratic support.

Distribution of patronage through such networks was central in most campaigns, despite North Sulawesi's relative prosperity and the assumption of many scholars that clientelism is most common in poorer populations.[37] In fact, though I have not focused on it in this article, retail vote buying (the dawn attack) was also common in all areas of the province, with cash payments varying between Rp 50,000 and Rp 500,000 per vote. Even so, patronage was far from being the only factor, and sometimes cultural or psychological rewards related to family pride or prestige, religious solidarity or similar factors were enough to motivate many political supporters, substituting material rewards or even outweighing them. In other words, a spirit of voluntarism—not just clientelism—was sustained through these family and religious networks. Yet the trump card remained bureaucratic mobilisation, and this had everything to do with hierarchy. Of the 29 candidates identified in this research as having close family members in the bureaucracy, 25 (86 per cent) were elected. Despite civil servants representing little more than 3 per cent of the province's population, their social weight and political influence in North Sulawesi is tremendous.

---

[37] Hicken, "Clientelism", p. 299; Edward Aspinall, "Money Politics: Patronage and Clientelism in Southeast Asia", in *Handbook of Southeast Asian Democratisation*, ed. William Case (London: Routledge, 2015), pp. 299–313.

chapter **20**

Southeast Sulawesi: Money Politics in Indonesia's Nickel Belt

*Eve Warburton**

Southeast Sulawesi (Sulawesi Tenggara) is a remote province in Eastern Indonesia, with a population of 2.8 million. Until recently, the province's main economic drivers were cassava and maize crops, and its growth and development indicators lagged behind much of the country. Over the past decade, however, this rural backwater became a hub for the country's nickel mining industry. Driven by demand generated from China's industrialisation, nickel production increased from 700,000 tons in 2001 to over 29 million tons in 2013.[1] China's economic boom has had a dramatic impact on the province. Kendari, the once sleepy capital of Southeast Sulawesi, now boasts a Lippo Group mall, several large hotels and an abundance of karaoke bars, all built to service the expanding extractive industry.

---

* During fieldwork in Southeast Sulawesi, I was helped immensely by local researchers, especially Kiki Andi Pati, Yasril Rhilone, the late Aliem Nur, and Abdi Rachmy.
[1] Badan Pusat Statistik Sulawesi Tenggara, "Production and Production Value of Nickel Mining, 2001–2013", in *Sulawesi Tenggara dalam Angka 2014* [Southeast Sulawesi in Figures], available at: http://sultra.bps.go.id/images/pub/06perindustrian_2014.pdf.

This chapter examines electoral dynamics in one of Indonesia's resource regions. Political and fiscal decentralisation began in 2001 and coincided with the global commodities boom, which peaked around 2003–09. Resource-rich districts throughout this period have, therefore, experienced a huge increase in investment. Plantation and mining licences in particular are a major source of capital for the regions' political elites, and the impact of resource rents on local political institutions has drawn increasing attention from analysts.[2]

A central question that drove this research was whether campaign strategies, patterns of patronage, and vote buying in Southeast Sulawesi were distinctive by virtue of the province's resource-based political economy. I also asked whether campaign strategies differed from district to district within the province, depending on how much districts relied on extractive sectors. These questions became especially relevant in January 2014, when the central government introduced a ban on the export of nickel ore in an effort to compel companies to process raw minerals domestically and export them at higher value. At the time of writing, piles of nickel ore lined the province's now-abandoned ports, and the hotels, restaurants and karaoke bars were empty. Southeast Sulawesi has effectively gone from resource boom to bust.

In fact, and despite this dramatic backdrop, a major finding of the research is that resource politics was not a feature of the 2014 legislative campaign. In that regard, the Southeast Sulawesi experience demonstrates just how little legislative elections engage with pressing economic and social issues. Moreover, mining rents did not play a decisive role in the election results. A handful of successful mining businessmen entered the legislative race, and companies provided donations to prospective parliamentarians. But the sector's overall impact on the election was peripheral.

---

[2] See, for example, Budy P. Resosudarmo, ed., *The Politics and Economics of Indonesia's Natural Resources* (Singapore: ISEAS, 2005); Erwiza Erman, "Deregulation of Tin and the Making of a Local Shadow State: Case Study of Bangka", in *Renegotiating Boundaries; Local Politics in Post-Suharto Indonesia*, ed. Henk Schulte Nordholt and Gerry van Klinken (Leiden: KITLV Press, 2007), pp. 171–202; John F. McCarthy, "The Limits of Legality: Governance, Extra-legality and Resource Control in Indonesia", in *The State and Illegality in Indonesia*, ed. Edward Aspinall and Gerry van Klinken (Leiden: KITLV Press, 2011), pp. 89–106.

Instead, as was the case around the country, candidates in Southeast Sulawesi ran highly personal campaigns, without reference to broader socioeconomic issues, and with little support from their parties. They spent copious amounts of their private wealth on campaign paraphernalia, political consultants, campaign teams, community associations and development projects, and in most cases, they distributed cash straight to voters. Each candidate drew upon his or her own savings, borrowed from family, friends and banks, and sought sponsorship from local businesses. While money from the mining sector contributed to some candidates' campaign war chests, mining money did not determine results. This was the case whether candidates competed in a mining district or an agricultural area.

To deliver patronage, candidates needed strong, effective networks that could reach down into the electorate. People in Southeast Sulawesi consistently emphasised the importance of a candidate's *figur* (an adaptation of the English term "figure"), which refers to a candidate's combination of wealth, reputation and politico-business networks. Strong *figur* were often those with influence over government structures, so former *bupati* (district heads) and government administrators were significantly advantaged. *Figur* also had command over community-based organisations—ethnic and religious groups, business networks, women's organisations and youth groups, for example—and used these networks to channel patronage to voters.

Candidates always claimed their most important assets to be a large family network and a loyal social base, made up of the organisations described above. Yet social networks were also up for sale. Consultants and vote brokers marketed themselves to candidates as having leverage in a particular subdistrict or village, within an ethnic organisation, or in some other social network. Intense competition between candidates, and the proliferation of professional vote brokers and campaign consultants, contributed to the fragmentation of social networks. Candidates at all levels also engaged modern tools and strategies such as opinion polls, surveys and text messaging technology to target voters outside their established support bases. This chapter, therefore, attempts to analytically reconcile the centrality of personal and particularistic community networks and the penetrating commercialisation of electoral politics.

The chapter begins with a background to Southeast Sulawesi's political economy, explaining how the resource sector has become important in direct elections for regional heads, yet played only a limited role in the legislative election. The chapter then moves through each level of electoral competition—district, provincial and national—dissecting what made some candidates more successful than others, and how candidates cultivated networks for delivering patronage efficiently and effectively. The final section looks at a single candidate, whose story illustrates the ways candidates supplemented their communal ties and personal networks with commercial tools like opinion surveys and professional vote brokers. This candidate patronised a group of villages for months, believing this demonstrated his capacity to care and provide for the community, rather than being a form of unacceptable money politics.

The story that emerges from Southeast Sulawesi shows that, in order to be successful, candidates could not simply buy votes and offer material rewards or even rely solely on existing personal and social networks. To win a seat in a legislature, candidates had to build robust and loyal networks of brokers and local leaders who could help them establish relationships with residents in targeted areas. Most candidates said success depended upon the cultivation of long-term relationships with voters, based on the provision of goods and all manner of financial and social assistance. In short, candidates drew a moral distinction between "dirty" money politics and more socially grounded acts of patronage.

BACKGROUND: NUR ALAM AND THE NICKEL BOOM

Governor Nur Alam—a successful businessman and PAN cadre—is the most influential member of the province's politico-business elite. His success and style of patronage politics forms an important backdrop to the 2014 legislative elections. Nur Alam has overseen a period of prosperity for Southeast Sulawesi. Growth rates have been consistently above the national average, at 7–10 per cent since 2001; the poverty head count has decreased faster as well, from almost 20 per cent in 2008 down to 14 per cent in 2014.[3] The mining industry has driven recent

---

[3] Badan Pusat Statistik, "Jumlah dan Persentase Penduduk Miskin, Garis Kemiskinan, Indeks Kedalaman Kemiskinan (P1), Indeks Keparahan Kemiskinan (P2) Menurut

growth, with spillover effects into the hotel, restaurant and construction sectors. Since coming to power in 2008, the Governor has used part of the proceeds of the boom to fund free health and education programmes, and to provide block grants for village governments.

During his reign, Nur Alam has also managed to remake the province's political map. Every local political observer, including Nur Alam himself, is quick to point out that the governor has *memenangkan* (brought to victory) eight district heads from his party, PAN, and has secured PAN deputy district heads in two of the four remaining districts.[4] This makes Southeast Sulawesi one of only a few PAN strongholds in the country. It is common to hear local observers refer to Nur Alam as a political *dukun* (shaman), or to comment that "everything Nur Alam wants, Nur Alam gets"—usually said with cynicism rather than admiration. He is also an avid supporter of the central government's mineral export ban and plans to build a local smelting industry, which is one reason locals say there has been little public opposition to the central government's policy.

For years, Nur Alam has contracted the services of Jaringan Suara Indonesia (JSI, Indonesia Voting Network), one of the country's dubious survey institutes that was embroiled in a false quick-count scandal during Indonesia's presidential elections in July 2014.[5] JSI's director, Widdi Aswindi, runs all manner of surveys for Nur Alam and other party members. For example, when it comes to district elections, Widdi surveys the electability of several potential candidates from the party and beyond. A candidate who polls well will then attain the governor's blessing and, according to local political observers, his financial support.[6]

Provinsi" [Total Number and Percentages of Poor People, the Poverty Line, Poverty Gap Index (P1), Poverty Severity Index (P2) by Province], 2014, available at: http://www.bps.go.id/linkTabelStatis/view/id/1488.

[4] Interview, Governor Nur Alam, 29 Apr. 2014.

[5] "Walau Hitung Cepatnya Sama dengan KPU, Persepsi Tak Jamin JSI dan Puskaptis Kredibel" [Although Their Quick Counts are the Same as the KPU, Persepsi Does Not Guarantee that JSI and Puskaptis are Credible], *Kompas*, 16 July 2014, available at: http://nasional.kompas.com/read/2014/07/16/17202661/Walau.Hitung. Cepatnya.Sama.dengan.KPU.Persepi.Tak.Jamin.JSI.dan.Puskaptis.Kredibel.

[6] Interviews, lecturer at Haluoleo University, 26 Mar. 2014; local journalist, 26 Mar.

This system locks the PAN district head into a patron–client bond (if one didn't already exist) with Nur Alam, and sets the scene for exchange of further political favours. For example, when Nur Alam came up for re-election in 2012, he called upon his PAN district heads to mobilise their government machinery to support him: "I used the government structures, and involved the district governments … because, remember, by my second election, I'd already helped many PAN district heads win their district elections."[7]

Given the influence that Nur Alam wields over the provincial bureaucracy, and his far-reaching politico-business networks, it was no surprise to anyone that Nur Alam's wife, Tina Nur Alam, won the largest popular vote by far in competition for the DPR in 2014 with 131,520 votes. The mobilisation of bureaucratic networks for political campaigns is not unique to Southeast Sulawesi, being a well-documented feature of elections for local executive leaders around the country. There has, however, been less focus on the impact and consequences of bureaucratic partiality in legislative elections—a prominent feature of Southeast Sulawesi's election that will be discussed later.

It is important to note that there remain a handful of districts where Nur Alam's candidate for district head was unable to secure victory—Kolaka, North Konawe, South Konawe and Wakatobi. In Wakatobi and South Kolaka, Nur Alam was able to negotiate a PAN deputy district head, whereas Kolaka and North Konawe have been elusive and PAN remains outside the local ruling coalition in each

---

2014; Partai Demokrat candidate, 16 Mar. 2014. The use of surveys for regional election campaigns is now common throughout the country (Marcus Mietzner, "Indonesia and the Pitfalls of Low Quality Democracy: A Case Study of the Gubernatorial Elections in North Sulawesi", in *Democratization in Post-Suharto Indonesia*, ed. Marco Bunte and Andreas Ufen [London: Routledge, 2009], pp. 124–49). However, the close personal and business relationship between Widdi and Nur Alam is unique. See: Anton Septian et al., "Putar-putar Duit Nikel" [Circulating Nickel Money], *Majalah Tempo*, 8 Sept. 2014, available at: http://majalah.tempo.co/konten/2014/09/08/NAS/146237/Putarputar-Duit-Nikel/28/43. Local observers also consistently describe JSI as playing an intimate role in Nur Alam's political success.

[7] Interview, Governor Nur Alam, 29 Mar. 2014.

district. These two districts are highly strategic mining areas: there are over 80 official mining licences in North Konawe, and Kolaka hosts one of the country's largest nickel mines, operated by state-owned company PT Aneka Tambang.

In Southeast Sulawesi, as in other resource-rich provinces, extractive sectors have become a source of funding for local political elites. Indonesia decentralised its mineral and coal mining sectors as part of its political and fiscal decentralisation in 2001, giving local politicians significant access to resource rents. District leaders distribute mining permits, introduce local taxes, and can mandate non-tax contributions from mining companies as well. Permits, in particular, have provided district leaders with easy access to sizeable funds, which are often used to finance *bupati*'s political campaigns.[8]

In Southeast Sulawesi, local analysts and politicians believe that mining rents have effectively insulated district leaders in Kolaka and North Konawe from Nur Alam's allies. In North Konawe, the incumbent Partai Demokrat district head came to power fortuitously around the time of Indonesia's nickel boom; while in Kolaka, the 2013 election pitted Nur Alam's candidate against a Golkar candidate, Ahmad Safei, who in his previous position as Regional Secretary had cultivated strong relationships with local nickel investors.[9] Haerul Saleh, the district's most successful mining businessman (whom we learn more about later) became a key member of Ahmad Safei's campaign team in 2013.[10]

The question we posed for this research was whether politico-business networks and lucrative rents from the mining sector influenced Southeast Sulawesi's legislative elections, both within mining districts, as well as in the province more generally. The answer was, surprisingly, not so much. While mining money certainly circulated throughout

---

[8] Robin Burgess et al., "The Political Economy of Deforestation in the Tropics", *Quarterly Journal of Economics* 127, 4 (2012): 1707–54; Danang Widoyoko, "Deforestation, Rent Seeking and Local Elections in West Kalimantan", *Inside Indonesia* 117, July–Sept. 2014, available at: http://www.insideindonesia.org/ deforestation-rent-seeking-and-local-elections-in-west-kalimantan.

[9] Confidential interviews, 16 Mar. 2014; 13 Sept. 2014.

[10] Interview, *Kompas* journalist, 13 Sept. 2014.

the "campaign economy", the sector was not important in determining results. And while there were some differences in the nature of money politics between mining and non-mining districts, these were attributable to other contextual factors. The next section explains why.

MONEY POLITICS AND MINING

The mining sector had little noticeable impact on the nature of money politics in Southeast Sulawesi. At first glance, it appeared as though inflationary pressures in the province's mining districts had significantly driven up the price paid during vote buying. In North Konawe, for example, the price paid per vote was at least Rp 500,000, and often around Rp 750,000,[11] compared with the average price elsewhere in the province of Rp 300,000. But in fact, by all accounts, expensive votes were a product of smaller populations. For example, in North Buton, with a registered voting population of just 42,006 but no significant mining, journalists told stories of how votes reached a price of Rp 1 million. The logic is that, where there are fewer votes to buy, candidate pay higher prices per vote. Residents also knew that their votes were dearly sought and took advantage of this competition. The residents of one village in North Buton even set a minimum price for their votes, and respectfully declined offers that fell below Rp 500,000 per resident.[12] Such rejections were rare, and most villagers gladly accepted cash from multiple candidates.

Mining companies themselves played only a peripheral role in Southeast Sulawesi's legislative elections. Members of parliament do not have the power to issue or deny mining licences, or collect taxes, which makes them a less direct concern for the industry. Candidates also did not politicise the closure of the province's nickel mines due to the central government regulation banning ore exports. Nor did industry folk appear to lobby candidates for the national parliament, with the goal of cultivating local opposition to the nickel export ban.

---

[11] Interview, PDI-P district candidate, 10 Aug. 2014.
[12] Interview, local journalists, 29 July 2014.

It was widely seen as an issue beyond the jurisdiction and capacity of the province's parliamentarians.

But the mining sector was not entirely absent from these elections. First, local mining men are emerging as part of the province's political elite. While most investors come from China and Jakarta, a handful of local entrepreneurs have invested significant capital in nickel mines and contracting companies; some have diversified into hotels as well. Some now fancy a political career. For example, Anton Timbang and Haerul Saleh, both from Gerindra, ran expensive and high-profile campaigns for DPR seats. They are young, relatively new faces on Southeast Sulawesi's political scene; their successful nickel investments gave them the resources to challenge the province's old stock of political elites for seats in the national parliament.

Second, mining companies in Southeast Sulawesi (as in other mineral-rich provinces), typically provide donations to the most promising candidates in electorates where they operate. They do so because they fear disruption; for example, mining companies feel vulnerable to extortion by local parliamentarians who can mobilise local villagers against mine projects (for example, to oppose real or exaggerated environmental problems).[13] Hence, both foreign and local companies watch legislative elections carefully, and cultivate relationships with candidates.

In Kolaka, for example, it is public knowledge that mining companies provide donations to political candidates, whether for gubernatorial, district or legislative elections.[14] One manager for an Indonesian gold mining company operating elsewhere in Sulawesi explained how his company contracted a national survey institute to conduct polling of candidates for the provincial legislature.[15] The company then made donations to the top 140 candidates, with the expectation that every member of the new parliament would come from that pool. The company would then have established a financial bond with each and every member of the local parliament.

---

[13] Interviews, mining company executives and staff, 7 May 2014, 23 Aug. 2014, 28 Aug. 2014.

[14] Interview, local journalist, 13 Sept. 2014.

[15] Interview, company external relations manager, 28 Aug. 2014.

By all accounts, this corporate insurance policy was common in Southeast Sulawesi; but it was not a decisive factor in the outcome of the province's legislative elections. Mining rents financed some candidates' campaigns. It was the strength of networks rather than the size of war chests, however, that decided who won. Starting with the contest for national parliament, the next section explains how established elites used long-standing patronage networks to dominate their competitions.

FIGUR IN SOUTHEAST SULAWESI

The refrain amongst candidates, local political analysts and party leaders alike was that in competition for the national legislature the most successful candidates were those who were strong *figur*. A *figur* has much more than charisma or personal appeal; they have the capacity to draw upon substantial material resources and mobilise strong networks of community leaders and government officials. These networks were often built while holding previous government leadership positions. Successful candidates for the national legislature, therefore, generally came from the old stock of Southeast Sulawesi's political elite—former district heads, governors or, in the case of Tina Nur Alam, the wife of the sitting governor.

Ridwan Bae, the provincial Golkar chairperson and former district head of Muna, won the second-largest personal vote in the DPR competition, with 91,747 votes. His largest block of 40,000 votes came from Muna district where he maintains a strong network of community leaders—Muslim scholars and clerics, *adat* leaders, and members of the district bureaucracy—who campaigned on his behalf regardless of party affiliation.[16] When he was *bupati*, Bae proved able both to deliver on programmatic promises and to provide opportunities and material rewards to bureaucrats, community leaders, business contractors and the like.[17]

---

[16] Interview, Ridwan Bae, 1 July 2014.
[17] Interview, lecturer, Haluoleo University, 26 Apr. 2014.

Putra daerah (son of the region) and ethnic appeals also often counted in building personal networks. Bae attributes his victory in equal parts to his political networks and ethnic loyalty. He believes Muna people wanted to back a prominent figure from their own ethnic group.[18] Similar patterns of voter support can be observed for the other successful DPR candidates. Ali Mazi, for example, is Butonese and also a former governor. He won decisively in Buton with over 22,000 votes. The former mayor of Bau Bau, Amirul Tamim of PPP, won a seat by dominating in his home town where he pulled in over 31,000 votes. What separated these popular men from other candidates were their long-established political networks, histories of patronage delivery, and loyalty from *tokoh masyarakat* (community leaders). Ethnic loyalty and patronage are difficult to disentangle when explaining who won DPR seats.

DPR candidates who lacked records of patronage delivery, in contrast, went about furiously cultivating new patronage networks in the months, and sometimes the entire year, leading to the April 2014 election. The best example is Anton Timbang, a Gerindra candidate, who entered politics in 2013 after making a personal fortune in the nickel industry. Timbang is the director of several mining companies and the head of the Indonesian Nickel Miners Association in Southeast Sulawesi. In 2013 he won the bid to become provincial head of Gerindra, a point of controversy within the party, partly because he had few ties with party elites and because he is Christian.[19] Despite the controversy, Timbang won the leadership ballot unanimously; something he puts down to dedicated prayer; others put it down to his deep pockets.

Timbang's strategy was to cultivate the province's Christian and Catholic communities, which consist of around 53,000 residents, plus the (predominantly Christian) ethnic Toraja community. Timbang is himself both Torajan and Christian, but was not considered a *tokoh* (leader) in the Christian population. The strategy, as he described it, was to provide club goods like places of worship, new roads or improved water facilities for communities. In offering goods rather than money, Timbang said he could prove his capacity to provide for the community:

---

[18] Interview, Ridwan Bae, 1 July 2014.
[19] Interview, Anton Timbang, 18 Mar. 2014.

These [gifts] are not just momentary [*sebentar saja*] like money politics
… these projects demonstrate that I can look after the community for
the long term, for the next five years if I get a seat in the DPR.[20]

Timbang hired a team of professional political consultants. They
identified 2,500 polling booths with a high proportion of Christian
and Torajan voters. His campaign focused entirely on these areas. To
reach these voters, Timbang hired subdistrict coordinators (*koordinator
kecamatan*) and polling booth coordinators (*koordinator TPS*) who
had lists of all residents in their areas. The non-Muslim voters
were approached and "socialised" with information about Timbang's
campaign.[21] "Socialisation" in this context is what Aspinall calls the
distribution of "getting-to-know-you" gifts, like campaign paraphernalia,
and foodstuffs at candidate-subsidised village meetings.[22] The majority
of Sulawesi's Christian and Catholic communities reside in Kendari and
Kolaka, each with around 15,000 such people. Timbang had calculated
that, if he received most of the non-Muslim vote in these and other
pockets around the province, he would be assured a seat.

In Kendari, Timbang pulled in over 7,000 votes; but in Kolaka he
received only 4,528. One of his consultants described how many of the
local leaders, brokers and volunteers they recruited (and were paying)
were not committed and had not been spreading Timbang's message or
rallying support for him. The consultant performed an evaluation, and
suggested that not even half of the 800 volunteers were "active", and
he suspected many were being paid by other candidates at the same
time.[23] Thus, despite running a well-resourced campaign, Timbang was
unable to compel loyalty from his sprawling network of coordinators
and volunteers.

Timbang was beaten narrowly by fellow Gerindra candidate, Haerul
Saleh, another successful miner. Haerul had two assets that gave him

---

[20] Ibid.
[21] Ibid.
[22] Edward Aspinall, "Parliament and Patronage", *Journal of Democracy* 25, 4 (2014): 104.
[23] Confidential interview, 8 July 2014.

an edge over Timbang: a set of loyal and committed personal and professional networks in his home town of Kolaka; and the support of Kolaka's district head. In other words, like senior *figur* who won DPR seats, Haerul had a popular base (*basis*) plus access to bureaucratic networks. Haerul Saleh became a household name from around 2009, when his investments in Kolaka's nickel sector began to bear fruit. In Kolaka, Haerul has a reputation of being a successful but generous businessman who offers opportunities in the form of jobs or capital to people within his personal networks. His private wealth and reputation gave him obvious political potential, and in 2012 Ridwan Bae (the Golkar head and DPR candidate discussed above) recruited Haerul to run with him as deputy in the gubernatorial elections on a Golkar ticket. While the pair could not defeat the incumbent governor, Nur Alam, Haerul boosted his political profile substantially.

Then in Kolaka's 2013 district election, Haerul became a central force in the campaign team for Golkar's successful candidate, Ahmed Safei. When it came to the time for Haerul to run for the national parliament, according to local observers, *Bupati* Ahmed returned the favour and gave Haerul institutional support. Haerul decided to run on a Gerindra ticket, based on the sound expectation that if Golkar won a seat it would go to Ridwan Bae, one of the strongest political notables in the province. But the bond between Ahmed and Safai trumped party loyalty, as is often the case in legislative elections.

Bupati Ahmad's support was critical; but Haerul also mobilised his old networks, calling on leaders of various youth associations, providing them with funds and programmes, setting up new community groups and generally organising Kolaka's youth to be his volunteers and campaign members. Haerul had always been active in youth associations "and he never forgot these old friends; he continued to socialise and associate with his old networks and offer them opportunities and support, even after he became a very successful businessman".[24] In other words, Saleh had a strong "*basis*", while Timbang only had money.

---

[24] Interview, Kolaka journalist, 12 Aug. 2014.

SUPPORT FROM THE TOP

Bureaucratic networks and *bupati* support played an even more significant role in competition for the provincial legislature. Backing from the governor or a district head typically gave a DPRD candidate an insurmountable advantage over competitors. In Southeast Sulawesi, executive government wields significant control over the civilian bureaucracy, and this power is leveraged for political ends during election season. The manipulation of the bureaucracy is a prominent feature of regional politics more generally in Indonesia.[25]

It was virtually always a candidate from the party with which the district head was affiliated who won the highest personal vote in a given district. This was not because voters were driven by party loyalty, but because these candidates had close personal ties to the district head and benefitted from their political backing. Thus, one candidate for the provincial legislature and senior Partai Demokrat member in Southeast Sulawesi frankly admitted that his party expected big wins in North Konawe, where the *bupati* was a fellow Demokrat. He explained that district heads can "mobilise" the government administration.[26] "Mobilisation" in this context means compelling lower-level government officials—the heads of villages, hamlets and various district government departments—to solicit votes for favoured candidates. Mobilisation requires some form of incentive, like cash for the government officials themselves, or cash for distributing to voters. The district head of North Konawe, for example, was caught on video handing out envelopes containing money to district employees during a "quiz". The quiz invited staff to name the "correct" details of legislative candidates, for which they received a cash prize.[27]

---

[25] See Maribeth Erb and Priyambudi Sulistiyanto, eds., *Deepening Democracy in Indonesia?: Direct Elections for Local Leaders (Pilkada)* (Singapore: ISEAS, 2008).

[26] Confidential interview, 19 Mar. 2014.

[27] "Bagi-bagi Duit Saat Kampanye, Bupati Asal Partai Demokrat Ini Terancam Bui 1 Tahun" [This Demokrat *Bupati* Threatened with One Year's Jail for Handing Out Cash during a Campaign], *Kompas*, 16 July 2014, available at: http://regional.kompas.com/read/2014/04/16/0916378/Bagi-bagi.Duit.Saat.Kampanye.Bupati.Asal.Partai.Demokrat.Ini.Terancam.Bui.1.Tahun.

Such incentives were sometimes supplemented with threats: if the desired outcome was not achieved in a particular village or neighbourhood, this could jeopardise the career of the government official responsible (or those of relatives). A local academic and long-time observer of Southeast Sulawesi's politics joked that the entire district government was the success team for incumbent district leaders and their preferred candidates, and that the local budget was used to fund their campaigns.[28]

District leaders often directed their support toward a family member. The wives of four sitting district heads won seats in the provincial parliament: Suryani Imran (South Konawe); Waode Farida (Muna); Murniaty M. Ridwan (North Buton); and Isyatin Syam (North Konawe). The wife of the provincial secretary, an important government position, Yati Lukman Abunawas, also won a seat. The wives of two former district heads (of Muna and Buton) did the same. Kendari's Mayor Asrun ensured that his two sons each won a seat in the city and provincial assembly. And the daughter of South Konawe's *bupati* also gained a seat.

A similar pattern of nepotism and bureaucratic patronage occurred in district legislative races, with many reports circulating of children, cousins and business partners being sponsored by regional leaders for contests in their district legislatures. One incumbent legislator in North Konawe described how the *bupati* was paying village officials in each village a wage of Rp 100,000 per week in order to lobby for one of his family members, Jefri Prananda, who was running for the district legislature.[29]

Bupati seek close allies in the DPRD in part because a friendly legislature is more likely to approve budget plans and regulations proposed by his or her government. But regional legislatures are also sites of business transactions. Legislators oversee regional budgets, in consultation with the executive. They can organise, or simply agree to, budget allocations for large development projects, and in return they are awarded project contracts, kickbacks or other sorts of fees.[30] For a

---

[28] Confidential interview, 26 Mar. 2014.
[29] Confidential interview, 20 Mar. 2014.
[30] See John F. McCarthy, "Sold Down the River: Renegotiating Public Power over

bupati, it makes sense to have allies participating in and monitoring such transactions, and collecting the lucrative kickbacks. Finally, putting business partners, wives, children and cousins in the DPRD expands the *bupati*'s personal control over government institutions, and facilitates dynastic occupation of government.[31]

The most brazen example of nepotism emerged in the capital, Kendari, where PAN-affiliated Mayor Asrun ensured the victory of both his sons. Adriamata Dwi Putra (known as ADP) was elected to the provincial legislature and Asrizal Pratama Putra to Kendari's city legislature. ADP collected 25,387 votes, giving him the highest personal vote of any provincial candidate. Yet ADP had virtually no public profile. Even during the campaign, he made few public appearances, rarely spoke to the media, and gave no public address. One local political consultant working with a national survey institute described how Mayor Asrun leveraged his powers for his son's campaign:

> At any *musrenbang* [a public consultation between residents and local government to organise local development planning] held by the City Government in the lead-up to legislative election there was always a kind of "gift" [*titipan*] for those who attended—a promise at least, if not some kind of gift.[32]

The consultant gave an example of how at one community meeting Asrun offered street vendors in one part of Kendari a grace period of three months on their licence payments if they agreed to vote for his son.

There were far more serious allegations levelled at Kendari's mayor. Local journalists, consultants and other candidates (including fellow PAN candidates) all believed that Asrun had promised to transfer large amounts of money, in the vicinity of Rp 100 million, to precinct and village heads on the condition that they returned 100 per cent support

Nature in Central Kalimantan", in *Renegotiating Boundaries*, ed. Schulte Nordholt and van Klinken, pp. 151–76.

[31] Michael Buehler, "Married with Children", *Inside Indonesia* 112, Apr.–June 2013, available at: http://www.insideindonesia.org/feature-editions/married-with-children.

[32] Confidential interview, 8 July 2014.

for his sons at their polling booths. While an impossible target, the bribe was intended to motivate serious action by these community leaders. Asrun and ADP were never available for interview to confirm or deny these accusations, either for this research or for local journalists. But the story was repeated regularly, and there was a consensus that Asrun's strategy was to bribe the city's voters into submission.

Most candidates and political commentators felt that Asrun's blatant support of his sons' political careers was arrogant and excessive. Yet similar strategies occurred throughout the province with impunity. It was well known that district heads were mobilising government staff in favour of family and friends—all with the goal of extending their grip on power. Rather than outrage, Sulawesi residents and even legislative candidates displayed a marked sense of defeatism, accepting that this was how elections were run.

Obviously, many candidates did not have bureaucratic networks at their disposal, and most spoke of how they relied on their family and social networks to cultivate votes and deliver patronage. Their success teams and campaign volunteers typically came from community-based organisations where the candidate had roots—religious institutions, prayer groups, women's organisations, NGO networks and the like. In order to reach voters outside their existing networks, candidates sought the services of vote brokers.

CONSULTANTS, BROKERS AND SURVEYS

Well-resourced candidates (incumbents, party elites or prominent businesspeople) at all levels of the competition used surveys to get an indication of the polling booth locations where they were already popular, those that were dominated by other candidates, and others that were *abu-abu* (grey). Some surveys even offered details on precisely what kind of material benefits a given community would prefer. Candidates often quoted the same figure: over 60 per cent of Southeast Sulawesi's residents were "transactional", meaning that they would vote for candidates in return for cash and material goods, rather than making choices based on candidates' programmes, personal reputations or ethnic or religious identity. One provincial Partai Demokrat candidate explained that surveys helped him identify precisely what kind of goods different voters wanted, and then, "whatever they request, we provide".[33]

Even in Southeast Sulawesi's poorest and most isolated villages, candidates for the district legislature worked closely with success teams and political consultants in identifying the urban precincts and villages where they could get the largest return on their investments. The story of Anwar (not his real name), a Golkar candidate in one district DPRD, is illustrative. Anwar was prominent in Komite Nasional Pemuda Indonesia (KNPI, Indonesian National Youth Committee), a nationwide youth association initially affiliated with Golkar and that has its roots in the New Order period. This position gave him a large network in his district. He said that the various organisations that fell under KNPI's umbrella all lobbied for his candidacy.[34] He was also a successful businessman, and was regarded as having significant personal wealth with which to fund his campaign.[35]

But survey data also played an important part in Anwar's campaign. Golkar's provincial party branch funded a survey which candidates used in planning their campaigns. The results showed that 70 per cent of the residents of Anwar's district wanted direct cash rewards for their votes; more specifically, they wanted Rp 300,000 each.[36] Anwar said the survey helped him establish which communities to target. After mapping out his electorate, he decided Kolaka's fishing communities held the most potential, so he and his team members forged a relationship with relevant village heads and spent one year cultivating trust, bringing *sembako* (staple foods), and providing them with "donations", like fishing equipment. Anwar won 1 of the 8 seats in his electoral district in the face of tough competition from the other 96 candidates.

Anwar used the word *melayani* (to serve or provide services) to describe what might otherwise be identified as a patronage relationship; many candidates (particularly at the district level) used this word when explaining how they delivered material benefits to constituents. It implies

---

[33] Confidential interview, 19 Mar. 2014.

[34] Interview, Anwar, 11 Aug. 2014

[35] Interview, journalists, 12 Aug. 2014.

[36] Interview, Anwar, 11 Aug. 2014.

an ongoing relationship rather than a one-time transaction, usually cultivated for at least a few months or, in Anwar's case, an entire year prior to polling day. A Gerindra candidate in North Konawe said that caring for the needs of their community, by way of *melayani*, was precisely what a leader should be doing, and what the community expected: "We [candidates] have to have compassion for our poor constituents ... we have to show real proof that we can look after them, not just give empty promises."[37]

Candidates often distinguished between *melayani*, as the more morally and culturally grounded political transaction, and the *kasar* (crude) money politics involving direct purchase of votes. Yet, there is strong anecdotal evidence that virtually every candidate distributed cash close to or on the day of the election.

CONCLUSION

The elections in Southeast Sulawesi involved over 4,000 candidates, each running personalised campaigns, drawing upon their own funds, and adopting varied strategies for eliciting votes. In this context, it is difficult to identify patterns and make generalisations about why some people won, and thousands lost. What most people are entirely convinced of, however, is that not a single poor candidate won a seat. La Ode Ota, a senior environmental activist in the province and a PDI-P DPR candidate, was highlighted by *Tempo* magazine as one of the country's cleanest candidates.[38] His methods included door knocking and texting random people with information about his programmatic promises. Not at any stage of his campaign did La Ode Ota pay voters or channel patronage to sections of the electorate. In the end, he received only 5,604 votes, far short of a winning margin.

---

[37] Confidential interview, 20 Mar. 2014.

[38] Knik Kusuma Rein, "La Ode Ota: Populer di Darat dan Laut" [La Ode Ote: Popular on the Land and the Sea], *Tempo*, 30 Mar. 2014, available at: http://majalah.tempo. co/konten/2014/03/24/LK/144971/Populer-di-Darat-dan-Laut/04/43.

Of course, rich candidates failed as well, as illustrated by the story of Anton Timbang, who hired 800 volunteers, solicited the services of consultants from Jakarta, and by his own estimate had spent over Rp 2 billion by the week before the election. Respondents' consistent emphasis on the importance of a candidate's *figur* means many successful candidates had qualities that went beyond wealth. Ridwan Bae, the Golkar candidate with the second-highest personal vote, is rich and has powerful patronage networks—but he also has a reputation for being outspoken, and for getting things done when he was head of Muna district.

Even so, the patronage system that characterises legislative elections makes it hard for new blood to enter the local political scene. The DPR seats are stacked with a cast of former district leaders; even the new, rich and charismatic Haerul Saleh needed the extra boost of a *bupati's* support; of the eight women who won seats in the provincial parliament, most are wives or daughters of district leaders and administrators. It is no wonder that local political observers and activists comment cynically on the state of democracy in Southeast Sulawesi, lamenting the rise of money politics, the impunity of corrupt elites and the weakness of electoral monitoring.

But for all the vices that plague Indonesian elections, legislative campaigns engage large segments of the public and inject a huge amount of capital into the local economy via printing companies, survey institutes, local consultants and vote brokers, not to mention cash payments and other forms of patronage. Studies show that elections have a positive impact on household income, especially for the poorest Indonesians.[39] Despite the many complaints that voters and candidates share about the rise of money politics, patronage democracy provides distributional benefits which satisfy Indonesian citizens as well.

One head of an urban precinct (*kelurahan*) in the subdistrict of Molawe, North Konawe, expressed this sentiment well. He lamented that vote buying was rampant in his neighbourhood, and that only

---

[39] Budy P. Resosudarmo and A.A. Yusuf, "Survey of Recent Developments", *Bulletin of Indonesian Economic Studies* 45, 3 (2009): 287–316.

wealthy people could afford to run for office; but he saw legislative campaigns as a valuable and socially engaging exercise:

> Candidates have to meet with [the community] often and find out what they want; they come door to door and sit with people like me as the *Pak Lurah* and smoke, and eat, and talk about what the people need. This didn't used to happen. Here, to be successful you need to start socialising your message around one year prior to the election and begin looking after people; you have to be the one that villagers call if they need help.[40]

Whether we call it patronage or *melayani*, the way candidates attempted to engage the support of their constituents could have immediate and positive impact on some of the province's poorest citizens. The fishing villages that Anwar patronised, for example, were deeply impoverished. The question, of course, is whether elected officials will continue to demonstrate such care throughout their terms in office. When asked this question, Southeast Sulawesi's residents responded, overwhelmingly, with scepticism.

---

[40] Confidential interview, 11 Aug. 2014.

Map of East Nusa Tenggara

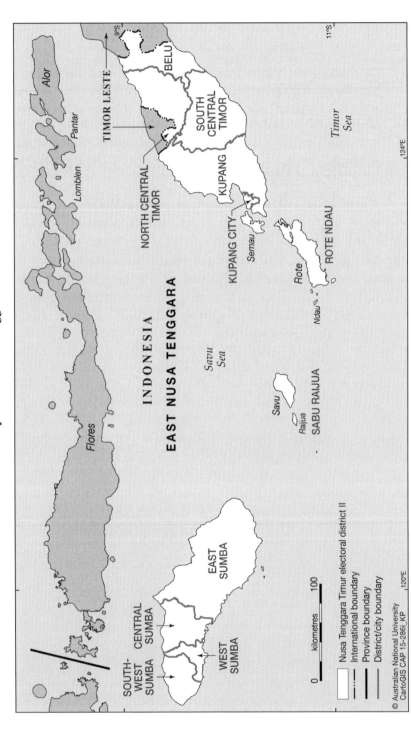

© Australian National University
CartoGIS CAP 15-286i_KP

Nusa Tenggara Timur electoral district II
International boundary
Province boundary
District/city boundary

kilometres
0   100

East Nusa Tenggara: Patronage Politics, Clientelism and the Hijacking of Social Trust

Rudi Rohi

Patronage and clientelism were ubiquitous features of electioneering in the 2014 legislative poll in Nusa Tenggara Timur (NTT, East Nusa Tenggara) province. Candidates at all levels distributed money, goods and services to constituents, or made promises to do so. Meanwhile, they built campaign machines using clientelistic patterns of political organisation and penetrating all sorts of social institutions and relationships: family and kinship networks, ethnic ties, religious networks, relations founded on *adat* (custom) and so on.

In this chapter I explore the patterns of election campaigning used by candidates at all levels in national electoral district NTT II, a constituency which covers about half of the province, including West Timor and the islands of Sumba, Sabu and Rote. It incorporates 5 of the 8 electoral districts for the provincial parliament, and 46 of the province's 86 *kabupaten* and *kota* electoral districts.

My basic argument is that clientelistic politics proliferates in this region as a response to the failures of formal political institutions. The state's inability to deliver welfare and social justice to citizens generates low levels of social trust in state institutions and formal politics. Politicians respond by hijacking existing social institutions and networks for campaigning purposes. They do so precisely because such institutions and networks can provide the crucial ingredient that they otherwise lack: the trust of their constituents. A few candidates also try to borrow symbols from the worlds of law and the economy to convince voters to have confidence in them.

BACKGROUND: A PLURAL SOCIETY

NTT is one of the most diverse provinces of a diverse country. It is also one of the poorest, with the population spread through a sprawling archipelago with generally poor transportation infrastructure, especially roads. With a total population of 4.6 million according to the 2010 census, the major population centres are the largely Catholic island of Flores (around 2 million people), and the Protestant-majority West Timor (about 1.6 million) and Sumba (about 600,000). Much of the election action in electoral district NTT II was concentrated in West Timor, with a little over a million voters, or about 65 per cent of the constituency, followed by Sumba (27 per cent), Rote (5 per cent) and Sabu (3 per cent).

Educational levels in NTT are among Indonesia's lowest: 37 per cent of people over the age of ten have not finished elementary school, with one implication being high levels of informal sector employment, with 65 per cent of the workforce employed in agriculture and fisheries in 2012.[1] NTT is ranked as the third lowest Indonesian province in Human Development Index terms. Poverty rates are among the highest in the country, never having dropped below 20 per cent. Such extensive poverty could be expected to make NTT's voters particularly amenable to patronage-based appeals.

Ethnic and religious structures are also a very important political factor. In NTT II the Timorese are the dominant group, constituting about 53 per cent of the total, but they are in turn broken down into various subethnic and linguistic groups including the Antoni Meto,

---

[1] Badan Pusat Statistik Nusa Tenggara Timur, *Nusa Tenggara Timur dalam Angka 2013* [NTT in Figures 2013] (Kupang: BPS NTT, 2013).

Dawan, Bunak, Kemak, Tetun and Helong. Other significant groups in the electoral district are from Sumba (24 per cent), who are mostly confined to their own island, Rote (9 per cent) and Sabu (6 per cent). There are also various migrant groups, including people from Flores (2 per cent), Java and Alor (each about 1 per cent) and others (4 per cent), with the biggest concentration of migrants living in and around the provincial capital, Kupang, in the south of Timor. As in other parts of Indonesia, *putra daerah* ("local son") sentiment can have an important impact on electoral preferences. At the same time, kinship structures are critical in social life, and follow both lines of descent and marriage relationships, so that all persons are located in potentially vast interlocking familial networks that can be turned to political use, and which often cross boundaries between ethnic groups.

Though Catholics make up a majority of the province as a whole, with 55 per cent, they are mostly concentrated in Flores. In electoral district II, the largest religious groups are Protestants (59 per cent), Catholics (36 per cent) and Muslims (just under 5 per cent). The big religions are themselves, however, divided along regional lines. The major protestant churches are the Gereja Masehi Injili di Timor (GMIT, Evangelical Christian Church in Timor) and Gereja Kristen Sumba (GKS, Christian Church of Sumba), though there are also many small denominations. There is a major concentration of Catholics around the districts of Belu and North Central Timor. There are also divisions, without extreme segregation, between local and migrant Muslim communities.

Politically, the region is marked by the domination of nationalist parties, and micro parties have played a role they often lack in Java. Between 2009 and 2014, in the 46 district and municipal parliaments in NTT II, Golkar held 16.9 per cent of the seats, PDI-P 13.5 per cent, Gerindra 11.1 per cent and Hanura 7.1 per cent, followed by parties that in the 2009 election failed to meet the national parliamentary threshold of 2.5 per cent and so were not represented in the national DPR, such as Partai Demokrasi Kebangsaan (PDK, Nationalism Democracy Party), 5.2 per cent, Prosperous Peace Party (PDS, a Christian outfit), 3.4 per cent, and Partai Keadilan dan Persatuan Indonesia (PKPI, Indonesian Justice and Unity Party), 3.1 per cent, as well as others with a total of 2.5 per cent.[2] Islamic parties are much less significant than in other parts of Indonesia. In 2014, the provincial DPRD result still had Golkar in first place (18 per cent) followed by PDI-P (15 per cent), Gerindra, Demokrat and Nasdem (each at 12 per cent), PKB, PAN and Hanura (each at 8 per cent), PKPI (5 per cent) and PKS (3 per cent). The Islamic parties PPP and PBB gained no seats at the provincial level. The main parties represented in the provincial parliaments also dominate executive governments: thus the governor and district head of North Central Timor are from PDI-P; the heads of South Central Timor and Central Sumba are from Gerindra; the heads of Sabu Raijua and East Sumba are from Golkar, and so on.

One feature of the 2014 election here was a low rate of incumbency turnover. At the national level, 46 per cent of DPR members lost their seats in 2014. In NTT II only one of seven did so: Anita Yakoba Gah, a Partai Demokrat member who lost to Viktor Bungtiulu Laiskodat from the new party, Nasdem, but who had sat in the DPR between 2004 and 2009 representing Golkar. Of the 65 members of the provincial DPRD elected in 2014, 23 (35 per cent) were incumbents, but another 5 (8 per cent) were moving from positions as district heads (*bupati*) or members of district-level DPRDs. As we shall see, one reason for this relative stability was the particular effectiveness of patronage-based strategies in this part of Indonesia.

POLITICS OF PATRONAGE AND CLIENTELISM: WHAT, WHO AND HOW?

The vast majority of candidates at all levels in NTT II formed personal teams to help them campaign. These teams were known by various names: *tim sukses* (success teams), *tim keluarga* (family teams), *tim kerja* (working teams), *relawan* (volunteers), *laskar* (troops) and so on. Though they varied greatly in their scope and roles, minimally they included people whose role it was to coordinate campaigning at

---

[2] Author's calculation based on district data.

the level of the *kelurahan* (urban precinct) or village. Well-resourced candidates could establish teams that went down to the polling booth level. Candidates built these teams by drawing in family members, relatives, friends and trusted colleagues, and then asking them to mobilise their own ties to expand the team. One distinguishing feature of these teams in NTT was that they were all typically founded on family and kinship ties. As a member of the "family team" of a Partai Demokrat incumbent in the DPR explained:

> Of course, we will definitely ask for support from the family, starting with the core family, and then going through relations by marriage [*kawin mawin*], then the Sabu and Rote ethnic groups, because we [the informant and the candidate] are from Sabu and his wife is from Rote.[3]

The costs of running a team were usually borne by the candidates themselves, either individually or through cost-sharing, if candidates were part of "tandems" with other candidates. When tandem arrangements applied, the biggest expenses were handled by the DPR candidate. As in most parts of Indonesia tandem cooperation usually occurred within a single party, but it sometimes crossed party lines, with some DPRD candidates effectively becoming part of the success teams of national candidates from rival parties, in order to save costs. Such cross-party collaboration usually reflected the strength of kinship ties, because it typically involved candidates who were related. For instance, a PDI-P candidate for the East Sumba DPRD became the secretary for a DPR candidate from Partai Demokrat; a PPP DPRD candidate in Kupang city helped the team of a PDI-P DPR candidate, and so on, all because of family ties. In NTT, kinship often trumps party.

Our research team did not identify significant differences in team structures across Sumba, Timor, Rote and Sabu. But we did identify some differences in the methods used. Though patronage distribution was everywhere, sometimes it was provided to voters using persuasive methods, sometimes it was accompanied by threats. Persuasive methods were especially common in or near urban areas. A Partai Demokrat

---

[3] Interview, Nixtau, 13 Apr. 2014.

candidate for the North Central Timor DPRD explained what was involved:

> At times like this I have to make sure I never run out of credit on my handphone so I can always communicate with people, even if it's just to tell them to have a good Sunday or to send out SMS containing wise words from the Holy Book.[4]

As well as being able to communicate in a free and friendly manner with one's constituents, a "persuasive" approach also involved gift-giving. A Nasdem candidate in the same legislature explained: "At election times like this, there's no way you can go out to the community without money in your pocket, at least if you want to approach people in the right way."[5] A success team member supporting a Gerindra DPR incumbent agreed: "You always have to take cigarettes and *sirih pinang* [betel] every day when you go out to meet the people. If you don't it will be hard to open communication with the people."[6]

Cigarettes and *sirih pinang* are a basic part of social etiquette when visiting people in this part of Indonesia. The tradition is that a guest visiting a community will provide *sirih pinang* in a box made from woven palm leaves, alongside a cash gift and at least a packet of cigarettes. In more formal and sacred versions of the ceremony a bottle of a local alcoholic beverage called *sopi* and a white rooster will be included. These gifts are presented to a village elder or whoever is particularly respected among the hosts. Discussion, interaction and agreement occur only after the *sirih* and all its contents have been received and enjoyed by those present, especially by the respected elders, as a sign that the guest has been welcomed.

But it was a different story with several teams in parts of Sumba distant from the towns. Here, as well as gift-giving, some teams also used threats. A Hanura candidate for the West Sumba DPRD, concurrently a member of the success team of an incumbent in Jakarta, explained:

---

[4] Interview, Alrman, 29 Mar. 2014.
[5] Ibid.
[6] Interview, Natber, 17 Apr. 2014.

Money politics and assistance alone are of course not enough. You've got to follow it up with threats and if necessary some proof of violence. There was one person whose horse was slaughtered and just left lying there as a message to its owner that you had better vote for a certain candidate.[7]

In parts of Sumba, too, the slogan "Take the money but don't vote for the candidate", widely used among activists and candidates trying to discourage money politics, led to the following response passing from mouth to mouth: "Go ahead and take the money and don't vote for the candidate, but then a machete and matches will follow." Machetes and matches are local symbols for murder and arson.

Central to the strategy of virtually all candidates and team members were face-to-face meetings with voters. These meetings could take the form of house-to-house visits or, more commonly, small-scale community meetings where voters would gather together, often in a community hall or a private home, to meet with the candidate or his or her team members. The first step would be to identify the people and places to visit. Usually candidates would start by locating a local contact who could organise the meeting. This was usually a relative, and/or someone who was locally influential, such as a civil servant, a village head, an RW (neighbourhood) or RT (subneighbourhood) head, a youth, religious, *adat* or ethnic leader, or the head of a large clan. Candidates frequently spent much of their campaign time travelling to and from such meetings, often speaking of daily visits to remote villages and kinsmen; one Gerindra DPR candidate, for example, spoke of his main strategy as consisting of "carrying out a face-to-face approach with family, relatives, ethnic groups, tribal leaders, religious leaders and *adat* leaders".[8] Many candidates stressed that their first priority was meeting with both close and distant relatives, this being not surprising in a society where kinship structures figure so strongly.

Typically on house-to-house visits the candidate, or his or her team members, would bring betel, cigarettes, coffee and sugar. A Hanura candidate, for example, said that such gifts were an important

---

[7] Interview, Triad, 18 Apr. 2014.
[8] Interview, Aloma, 2 Apr. 2014.

campaign instrument because they allowed him to then sit down and chat with recipients while chewing betel, smoking and drinking coffee.[9] Typically, he said, the topics of such conversations would be working out their family connections, talking about distant relatives or old friends, reminiscing about days gone by, and whatever else would help create a pleasant social connection.

Larger meetings could take place at several scales: small (10–50 persons), medium (50–100) and, less often, large (100–400). It was insufficient to provide just *sirih pinang*, cigarettes and coffee at such meetings; candidates also had to provide drinks, snacks and sometimes more substantial meals. Indeed, because so many candidates held such gatherings, they often became a sort of competition of prestige between them. They often cost from Rp 2.5 million to Rp 15 million, with this money mostly going towards the purchase of livestock for the meal. A Gerindra DPR candidate said he spent on average Rp 4 million on meals at every meeting.[10] A Nasdem DPR candidate spent a similar amount, according to a team member: "In every meeting in the main *adat* building with relatives and kinsmen we will eat at least one entire cow."[11] A campaigner for a national Nasdem candidate explained: "Meetings … cost Rp 5 million for buying a pig, rice, cigarettes, betel and *sopi*."[12]

Third, almost all serious candidates distributed what they thought of as "assistance" (*bantuan*), either to individual voters, to communities or to groups. The provision of such assistance is such a deeply ingrained part of local political tradition that candidates say they cannot create genuine emotional connections with voters without it. Assistance can take the form of money, goods, services and promises of future aid. The same Nasdem DPR candidate explained, for example, that he always provided donations of varied amounts, but usually no less than Rp 20 million whenever he met with Church leaders.[13] He also distributed 1,000 pigs to communities throughout the city of Kupang, claiming that this was a

---

[9] Interview, Serman, 2 Apr. 2014
[10] Interview, Aloma, 2 Apr. 2014.
[11] Interview, Itang, 17 Apr. 2014.
[12] Interview, Tayos, 29 Mar. 2014.
[13] Ibid.

way of building the grassroots economy.[14] A Partai Demokrat candidate and incumbent DPR member was famous for using his success team to hand out Bantuan Siswa Miskin (BSM, Poor Student Assistance) grants to families in his own name, though they actually were a national government programme. A team member explained frankly:

> We use the strategy of persuade, entice, embrace and threaten. We persuade and entice by giving them BSM, and if they receive it we embrace them to ensure that they don't shift to any other candidate. And we threaten them by reminding them that they need to vote for him, and if they don't they won't get BSM.[15]

A similar explanation was given by a member of the team supporting a Golkar incumbent in the Belu DPRD, who was also helping a Golkar DPR incumbent. In this case, the assistance distributed came both from the private funds of the DPR candidate and from the district and national budgets. The candidates used their own money to pay for small projects or donations, but drew on their access to the budget for costlier gestures:

> She usually gives out things like, well, for example, five water pumps for five groups, and next year she will help with six hand tractors. That's all from the district budget. She also uses her own money to help churches by donating keyboards, guitars, metal sheeting, cement, timber and such like. She's helped at least six churches like that.[16]

Of course, it was typically only incumbents who could use the state budget in this way. Control over information about what sort of government projects were available, and who could access them, itself was an important patronage resource.

Fourth, in terms of discursive strategies, almost no candidates emphasised ideology, national issues or programmes with general applicability. Only a few referred to national leaders in their campaign speeches (mostly PDI-P candidates who promoted Jokowi, and Gerindra candidates who spoke about Prabowo). Instead, most candidates were

---

[14] Interview, Vilubas, 25 Feb. 2014.
[15] Interview, Nixtau, 13 Apr. 2014.
[16] Interview, Malmel, 1 Apr. 2014.

determinedly local in their focus, emphasising their local roots and the attention they had paid, or would pay, to the region. Though many stressed ethnic and religious themes, they did so in a moderate manner, without implying conflict with other groups. One Golkar candidate for the national DPR was described by a team member as using the following appeals:

> Vote for a candidate who will pay attention to the interests of the church. As well as that, he always tells people in his campaigns that there has got to be someone from Sumba sitting in Senayan [the location of the national parliament building] so that, when it comes to dividing up the "meat" of development, they will be able to get part of it and bring it home to Sumba.[17]

In making this appeal the candidate was making an analogy that would have been immediately recognisable to voters in Sumba where, at the end of traditional festivities, the host calls out the name of each person in attendance and gives them meat to take home. Only those present have the right to take their share. Thus, we can see that even the identity appeals that candidates mobilised were mostly closely linked to patronage.

HIJACKING THE SOCIAL INFRASTRUCTURE

By the hijacking of social infrastructure, I mean the utilisation of social networks—mostly family and kinship networks, but also those based on religion, friendship, place of origin, ethnicity and the like—for campaign purposes. There are two basic reasons that this phenomenon is all but ubiquitous in NTT; one is a pull factor, the other a push factor.

The pull factor is the strength and characteristics of such informal networks, which make them very attractive to politicians. In particular, the family and wider kinship group is considered by most NTT residents to be the basic foundation of social life. With people facing significant poverty, inequality and uncertainty in their lives, family networks are

---

[17] Interview, Jupot, 19 Apr. 2014.

often a means for them to cope with both daily difficulties and major life crises. As a result, these networks are typically imbued with trust— people feel they can rely on family members more than on others, and will turn to them first if they need help. This trust can be turned to political purposes. Many politicians told me that they believed that "if my own family doesn't support me, then why would other people vote for me?". Indeed, as Francis Fukuyama has observed, societies with very powerful family and kinship relationships can sometimes find it hard to develop strong associational life based on other ties.[18]

The push factor, accordingly, is the weakness of political parties in the province. Many candidates, though all nominated by parties, were not long-term party cadres, and many of them lived outside their electoral districts (they typically lived in the district capital if they were district candidates, in Kupang if provincial candidates, and in Jakarta if national candidates) and therefore lacked strong links with the party organisation in the region where they were standing. Competition between candidates within the same party was also intense, given the open-list PR system that Indonesia employs. As one Golkar candidate for a seat in the national parliament put it, "Becoming a candidate is like heading straight into the wild woods."[19] Only the strong survive intra-party competition, and there are few permanent friendships or alliances to be had within a party where you may end up competing for positions. Poor recruitment, coordination, cadre training and communication strategies make it all the more harder for candidates to rely on party structures.

These two factors prompted candidates to use informal social networks to build their campaign teams. Moreover, when they talked about how they built their campaigns, candidates often barely mentioned political parties. As one explained: "Networks we use, in addition to the family, are networks or structures such as those based on *adat*, ethnicity, religion, the bureaucracy, civil society organisations or other social structures."[20]

---

[18] Francis Fukuyama, *Trust: The Social Virtues and the Creation of Prosperity* (New York: Free Press, 1995), p. 308.
[19] Interview, Silanga, 17 Apr. 2014.
[20] Interview, Imbleg, 7 Apr. 2014.

Perhaps the most extreme form of such networking occurred when candidates used family or other connections, not simply to bypass parties, but also to influence the vote-counting process itself. During our research, we found many examples of "wholesale" vote buying, where candidates paid election officials to manipulate the count. For example, one success team member recounted how he paid Rp 12 million to election committees at three polling booths to boost the numbers for Golkar candidates in Kupang.[21] This form of electoral manipulation was facilitated because the voting booth committee (KPPS, Komite Penyelenggara Pemungutan Suara) personnel were themselves drawn from the ranks of local residents, with the RT or RW heads often ex officio becoming their coordinators, and then appointing the members. As a result, recruitment into these committees itself often followed social networks—family, kinship, ethnicity and so on. These ties connected committee members, not only to one another, but also to community leaders in nearby neighbourhoods, to officials higher up in the government bureaucracy, and therefore to political candidates and their teams.

It should be noted, however, that no candidate put all their eggs in one basket and relied on just one social network. Instead, they relied on multiple networks, adapting to local circumstances. Though family and kinship ties were almost always primary, candidates also typically relied on kampung of origin, ethnicity, religion and so on. Usually, the bigger the electoral district (with of course the DPR candidates operating in the biggest such districts) the greater the number of social ties and relations the candidate would bring together.

As already touched upon, it was the success teams which brought these disparate webs of social connection together. We found two basic forms of teams. The first form was unstructured and was more common among district-level DPRD candidates, where the social distance separating candidates from voters was not great. In such cases, campaign volunteers—who had widely varying institutional, social, economic, party and cultural backgrounds—interacted directly with the candidate. The second form were centralised teams, with a coordination

---

[21] Confidential interview, 12 Apr. 2014.

hub in Kupang (if the candidate was running for the DPR) with a team structure then going down through the levels of district, subdistrict, urban precinct or village, and then to the polling booth. Typically, there was a single coordinator in each subdistrict whose job was to recruit village coordinators and act as the hub connecting their work. It was then the role of team members in the villages to coordinate the polling booth workers who directly interacted with voters. Payments came in one of two methods: routine payments to village and polling booth coordinators (sums of Rp 500,000 per month, rising to Rp 1 million nearing the election, were common) or incidental payments to cover activities. A critical role of team members was to identify requests for assistance—both cash and goods—being made by community members, and then pass them upward to the campaign centre. This sort of team structure was costly, however, so only well-resourced candidates, such as Partai Demokrat and Golkar incumbents, could use it.

This sort of structure was used by the Partai Demokrat DPR incumbent mentioned above who distributed scholarships. He formed a "centre" in each district capital in NTT II, drawing on his family, kin and ethnic network in each location, but with a campaign headquarters in Kupang. These centres, however, did not systematically recruit brokers at the subdistrict, village and polling booth levels. Instead, they mostly used people who worked to distribute and process application forms for the BSM student assistance programme, asking them to ensure that recipients then repaid the candidate with their votes. According to a campaign coordinator, between 2010 and early 2014 the team had received more than a million application forms, with 433,000 of the applicants receiving BSM assistance.[22]

PATRONAGE POLITICS AND SOCIAL TRUST

It should be stressed that the crisis of trust goes deeper than popular attitudes to political parties. More generally, in NTT there is deep distrust in the state in general, and its ability to deliver welfare and

---

[22] Confidential interview, 12 Apr. 2014.

social justice in an equitable way to the population. A survey carried out by the Power, Welfare and Democracy project coordinated by Gadjah Mada University showed very low levels of confidence in the capacity of state institutions to provide people in NTT with justice.[23] Community members prefer to seek welfare protection and redistribution through informal social institutions like the family, kinship ties, churches and the like, though these institutions, too, cannot possibly satisfy all social needs.

This is where patronage politics come in. Politicians present themselves as filling the gap between social and state provision by providing communities and individuals with much-needed goods and services, either personally or by facilitating their access to government assistance (as with the Partai Demokrat incumbent mentioned above). But how do they avoid being tainted by the suspicion that characterises popular attitudes toward other formal institutions? After all, we know from many parts of Indonesia that politicians who rely on patronage face great difficulty in ensuring that voters repay their munificence with political support; often even their brokers cheat and deceive them.[24] Candidates in NTT II respond to this problem in several ways, but let me highlight two.

The first method should be obvious from the discussion so far: most candidates made use of socially embedded institutions and networks for their campaigns and thus tried to bind voters to them by hijacking the trust that infuses those institutions and networks. To elaborate, let us focus on a case study: our candidate, "Ibu Yum", was standing for the Golkar party for a seat in the parliament of Belu, a district of Timor that runs along the border with Timor-Leste.

Ibu Yum was one of the few women who already held a seat in the district parliament, and was again running in 2014. Her main strategy consisted of providing assistance to various people, families, ethnic associations and religious institutions. Her "family team"

---

[23] Olle Törnquist et al., "Power, Welfare, and Democracy" (draft report, Universities of Oslo/Gadjah Mada, 2013).

[24] Edward Aspinall, "When Brokers Betray: Clientelism, Social Networks, and Electoral Politics in Indonesia", *Critical Asian Studies* 46, 4 (2014): 545–70.

distributed assistance to some families in the form of wedding outfits and decorations, assistance with marriage registrations, flower bouquets at funerals, and the like. For this purpose, and for financial reasons, the candidate even started up two small businesses: one specialising in hiring out wedding gear, the other a small florist shop. In addition the candidate was very active in *kumpul keluarga* (family gatherings), the local informal institution by which kin members—and often close friends, neighbours and others thought to be like kin—would gather together to help celebrate major family gatherings, notably funerals and weddings, and to provide cash or other gifts to help fund these events, with the gifts recorded in a family ledger.

Ibu Yum also helped connect 213 households to the electricity grid and paid for the purchase and installation of their meters, and she led a 200-member church youth group which met weekly at her house for worship and choir practice.[25] Beyond her family and other close social connections, she also distributed goods to other groups, such as water pumps to farming communities, and uniforms, guitars, keyboards and other equipment to choral groups. She helped religious groups, notably the local Protestant church, by assisting it to get a land certificate to build on and by donating building materials—cement, stones, sand, electric cables and plywood—and she promised to help build two chapels for local Catholics. She provided assistance to ethnic associations (*paguyuban*) representing people from Alor, Rote and Sabu, as well as former East Timorese, in the district. In these cases she gave cash, goods and services, and she had already obtained special funding for teachers along the border, and promised to do more if re-elected.[26]

Ibu Yum was from a migrant ethnic group in this district—she was from Alor—and she was a Protestant. In Belu, which is dominated by Catholic Timorese, it is unusual for outsiders to enter into such intimate social interaction with locals. It is even more unusual for such a person to achieve a strong vote in a community that is known for valuing local ethnic traditions and its own religious identity. Yet she was able to become part of local social relations and so attained a level of trust.

---

[25] Confidential interview, 1 Apr. 2014.
[26] Interview, Mamel, 1 Apr. 2014.

For example, her role in getting the land certificate for the church was extremely time consuming, and meant that she became a part of the congregation, which consisted mostly of locals. The long process she went through in securing the certificate involved an equally long process of social interaction with her fellow churchgoers, who eventually saw her as a part of their congregation and as standing up for their shared standards, norms and rules of behaviour—all of which Fukuyama sees as the basis of trust.[27] Now, she is seen by these members of the local community as an integral part of their own identity group, and thus as deserving of their trust.[28]

Ibu Yum also provided patronage in a more munificent form: her assistance in building six Protestant churches. The local Protestant communities saw this as her stepping into meeting a need that was not being fulfilled by the state. Her help, when they needed it in meeting what they saw as a basic community need and a focal point of community identity, meant that they viewed her as a key player in their own community, prompting a broadly shared consensus in the local Protestant community that Protestants should vote for her. The key point is that this strong political support arose, not from any political interaction between Ibu Yum as a candidate and the community, but purely from social interactions.

Patronage was important in forging this relationship of trust, by helping to create a sense of "solidarity, meaning and participation"[29] in the social relationship Ibu Yum was part of. It was not necessarily the size of the gifts that counted, but rather their appropriateness, the intensity of the social interactions in which they were embedded, and the networks through which they were distributed. Perhaps this helps explain why so many candidates—in NTT as in other parts of Indonesia— distribute large amounts of cash, goods and services to voters, yet fail to get elected. In contrast, some candidates whose patronage resources are limited do succeed.

---

[27] Fukuyama, *Trust*, p. 26.

[28] Diego Gambetta, "Can We Trust Trust?", in *Trust: Making and Breaking Cooperative Relations*, ed. Diego Gambetta (Oxford: Basil Blackwell, 1988), pp. 217–8.

[29] Niklas Luhmann, "Familiarity, Confidence, Trust: Problems and Alternatives", in Gambetta, *Trust*, p. 94.

A second method that candidates sometimes used to convince voters to trust them, their promises and the material exchanges they offered was to borrow symbols from the fields of law and the economy. In particular, they often offered voters quasi-legal documents, such as "political contracts", receipts and other proofs of transaction, instruments that can be understood as a form of "symbolic representation" to convince voters of their trustworthiness.[30] Here our case study is another candidate in the Belu DPRD, this time an ethnic Arab incumbent from the Islamic party, PPP.

Pak Alatmi was a Muslim in a district where Muslims were only 2 per cent of the population. He built a strategy that was based on getting enough voters to sign "political contracts". To do this he built a special team, consisting of a general coordinator and then five coordinators in each village and *kelurahan* in his electoral district. Each of those village-level coordinators was charged with finding 15 people who were prepared to sign a political contract. These coordinators were then charged with acting for the following five years as contact points between the candidate and the voters, including in communicating their requests for patronage to him, and helping him to distribute it.[31] Contracts were prepared for that purpose by the village coordinators and were signed at meetings between the candidate and community members. As well as the core promise, the documents contained the name, photograph and signature of the candidate, the name and signature of the subdistrict and village coordinator, the name of the *dusun* (hamlet), the PPP logo, and then a table with the names, ages, employment status and signatures of recipients.

The contract was essentially a written agreement that the candidate, should he be re-elected, would provide ongoing patronage support to the signatories for his five years in office. This support would come in two forms. First, funds derived from him personally would be distributed to participating villages via a foundation that the candidate had established, with the support of other donors, in 2009. So as to ensure an impression of political neutrality, the chair of the foundation was another person,

---

[30] Ibid., pp. 96–7.
[31] Interview, Alatmi, 31 Mar. 2014.

not the candidate himself. Assistance distributed by the foundation took various forms, depending on the requests submitted by the contract signatories: assistance with electrification, financial assistance for the sick or when somebody died, financial help for livelihood programmes and so on. Each gift would be accompanied by a receipt noting the identity of the recipient and the purpose and size of the gift, and including the recipient's signature. The second form of support Pak Alatmi provided was derived from the government budget. In this case, the candidate promised to deliver projects to recipient communities, for example, outboard motors for their boats, market construction projects, street lighting and the like. The candidate promised to prioritise the communities which supported him for these programmes.

This was an unusually elaborate scheme; part of the reason was doubtless that the candidate was a Muslim Arab in a majority Christian Timorese district, and he therefore lacked access to both kinship and church networks. Even so, many candidates issued political contracts and quasi-formal agreements with individual voters and communities, which both they and future beneficiaries signed. At the simplest level, these documents reinforce my earlier observations that candidates were aware that voters did not trust them and their promises, and they needed to use special efforts to overcome this problem. In this case, they borrowed the symbols of legal procedure and financial transactions— contracts—to convince voters that they would fulfil their promises and, most importantly, get them to deliver their votes.[32]

This form of trust building was obviously not as socially embedded and therefore perhaps not as substantive as working through social networks to which the candidate was organically connected.[33] It was also more short-term, not requiring the long-term process of convincing a community through social interaction. Yet both methods could be effective, and in Belu both Ibu Yum and Pak Alatmi had been elected in 2009, and in 2014 they both received more than 700 individual votes, a significant total that exceeded the totals of many candidates who were

---

[32] See Charles Tilly, *Trust and Rule* (New York: Cambridge University Press, 2005), p. 36; Fukuyuma, *Trust*, pp. 25–6.

[33] See Gambetta, "Can We Trust Trust?", p. 235.

elected. However, in their cases their party colleagues did poorly and their party totals were insufficient to deliver them seats.

CONCLUSION

Patronage distribution was central to the campaigning of virtually all candidates in the 2014 legislative election in NTT II. The main argument proposed in this essay is that patronage politics worked through a hijacking of social infrastructure and social trust. Candidates needed networks through which they could reach down to voters in order to construct mutually beneficial patron–client relations. The candidates used these networks to deliver patronage. But they also needed to be able to build trust in this interaction: they wanted to convince the voters to believe in them, and they wanted to be able to trust that voters would deliver on their side of the bargain.

Existing political institutions, including parties, were inadequate to this task. Accordingly, candidates turned to informal institutions, notably those based on kinship, but also ethnicity, religion, place of origin, friendship and *adat*, precisely because voters were more likely to have faith in such relationships. The fact that we see less individualised vote buying (the notorious dawn attack) in NTT than in some parts of Indonesia (though I should stress that this form of patronage was also present) probably also reflects the deeply socially-embedded form of patronage politics we see here: many more candidates relied on kinship ties than distributed individual cash payments. A few candidates also created legalistic "political contracts", though this method tended to be more financially costly. The former method was exhausting and time consuming, but it was also most common, because most candidates had connections to kinship and other networks, and were already habituated—as members of local societies—to meeting their social needs through them. Accordingly, electoral competition in NTT involved an extraordinary fusion of patronage and informal social networks.

Map of Papua

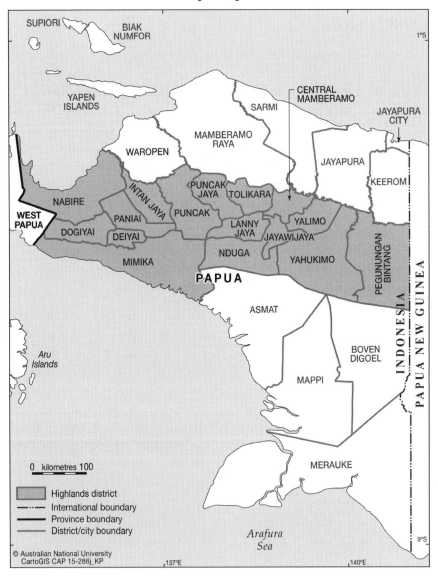

chapter **22**

North Jayapura, Papua: Buying the Voters and Buying the Administrators

Ridwan

The district of North Jayapura is located at the heart of Jayapura, the capital of Papua province. As the easternmost major town of Indonesia, and as the capital of a region with a history of ethnic politics—indeed, with a long-running campaign for independence—that marks it out from other parts of Indonesia, we might expect to find distinctive patterns of electoral mobilisation in Jayapura. In fact, as the following study shows, the pattern of electioneering in the town would be immediately familiar to people from many other locations around the country, especially the multi-ethnic migrant towns of Eastern Indonesia.

The analysis in this chapter focuses on candidates competing in North Jayapura, which is not only a district (*distrik*, but equivalent to a subdistrict, or *kecamatan*, in other parts of Indonesia) but also one of four electoral districts in Jayapura in which candidates competed for seats in the Jayapura city DPRD. The analysis details a pattern of success team formation and patronage distribution that is fundamentally similar to patterns elsewhere in Indonesia. Aspiring candidates in North Jayapura, as elsewhere in the country, tried to draw influential local community leaders into their success teams as a way to attract the votes of those leaders' clienteles. Candidates also relied on patronage distribution as a major part of their campaign strategies, distributing small mementoes at face-to-face meetings with voters, making larger donations of collective goods to communities, and also engaging in retail vote buying in the days leading to the poll.

However, the analysis also draws attention to one aspect of electoral dynamics that is particularly prominent in Papua: the bribery of electoral officials in order to facilitate manipulation of voting and vote-counting processes. Though this phenomenon is not unique to Papua, problems of electoral administration do seem particularly marked in this province. Put simply, candidates running for elected office in Papua had a choice: did they direct their patronage funds toward voters and brokers, or did they go straight to the election officials and try to buy, not the vote, but the count. As we shall see, very often candidates did both, paying voters, but also buying electoral officials in order to "safeguard" or expand their base vote.

BACKGROUND: PAPUA'S METROPOLIS

The city of Jayapura, as the capital of Papua province, is both remote and metropolitan. A five-hour direct flight from Jakarta, it is in fact closer geographically to the Melanesian world, and to Australia, than to the major population centres of western Indonesia. The city itself has a highly mixed population of about 280,000, consisting predominantly of migrants from other parts of Indonesia, as well as indigenous Papuans, most of whom have moved here from elsewhere in the province. As the province's major administrative centre, it has the usual range of government buildings and a high population of civil servants, as well as major commercial buildings.

North Jayapura is one of the five districts that make up the city. Located at the northern tip of Yos Sudarso bay and facing northwards toward the Pacific Ocean, the district includes a wide range of physical terrains, including striking 700-metre mountains and hills set back just a few kilometres from the bay, and the iconic Base-G beach. Importantly, it also includes the major commercial centre of Jayapura and thus of Papua, hosting the Central Papua Bank building in Imbi *kelurahan* (urban precinct) along with the Matahari shopping mall and Jayapura's best hotels, such as the Swissbell, Aston and Horison. Most of the residential areas, however, are filled with crowded lower-middle-class and poor housing, though there is also luxurious middle-class housing in the Angkasa *kelurahan*.

Though some of the district's population of 65,000 are middle-class office workers, most are employed in the informal sector, notably trade and services—selling foodstuffs or clothing, running foodstalls or mobile telephone kiosks, washing laundry, working in vehicle workshops, and the like.[1] There are also fishing communities along the coast. About 60 per cent of the population are migrants from other parts of Indonesia, while others are from elsewhere in Papua, making North Jayapura something like a "mini Indonesia", especially given that most residential areas are themselves mixed.

As with other migrant cities in Indonesia, this multi-ethnicity is reflected in associational life, with many community organisations coordinating cultural and social activities for the relevant communities. These include the Kerukunan Keluarga Sulawesi Selatan (KKSS, South Sulawesi Family Association), the Ikatan Keluarga Flobamora (Flobamora Family Network) for people from East Nusa Tenggara, as well as similar associations representing people from Java, Madura, West Nusa Tenggara, Sumatra (Bataks), and so on.[2] Indigenous Papuans in the town have many similar organisations, such as the Ikatan Keluarga Pegunungan Tengah (Central Highlands Family Network), Ikatan Keluarga Serui (Serui Family Network) and Ikatan Keluarga Biak (Biak Family Network). North Jayapura has a religiously plural population: various Protestant denominations are the largest group at 45 per cent, followed by Muslims (31 per cent), and Catholics (23 per cent).[3]

Party representation has generally been fragmented in Papua's parliaments.[4] Thus, in 2009, Jayapura's 30-member parliament had

---

[1] 2010 figures provided by BPS (Badan Pusat Statistik) Jayapura.

[2] For the political roles that these associations play in Eastern Indonesian towns, see Gerry van Klinken, "The Limits of Ethnic Clientelism in Indonesia", *Review of Indonesian and Malaysian Affairs* 42, 2 (2008): 35–65.

[3] Badan Pusat Statistik Jayapura, *Jayapura dalam Angka 2013* [Jayapura in Figures 2013] (Jayapura: BPS, 2014), p. 75.

[4] Richard Chauvel, "Electoral Politics and Democratic Freedoms in Papua", in *Problems of Democratisation in Indonesia: Elections, Institutions and Society*, ed. Edward Aspinall and Marcus Mietzner (Singapore: ISEAS, 2010), pp. 307–29.

representatives of 12 parties. As in most of Papua, however, PDI-P, Golkar and Partai Demokrat (at least since 2009) have consistently represented the "big three". In 2014, a mixture of newcomers and incumbents took the ten seats on offer in North Jayapura: two from Golkar and one each from Nasdem, PKB, PDI-P, Gerindra, Demokrat, PAN, Hanura and PKPI. Of these, six were indigenous Papuans and four were members of ethnic groups originating in other parts of Indonesia; seven were women. Of those elected, the candidate with the highest personal vote was Junaedi Rahim of PKPI, with 3,646 votes, while Nasdem's Inis Kogoya was the lowest, at only 1,305. All the winning candidates were relatively well-resourced compared to the candidates they defeated.

CLIENTELIST POLITICS AND SUCCESS TEAMS

As in most parts of Indonesia, personal success teams rather than parties played the key role in organising campaigns. As Aspinall has argued, success teams "are essentially networks of political brokers, involving a wide range of community leaders, fixers, businesspeople, activists, religious leaders and the like".[5] In fact, in North Jayapura, most candidates used terms such as "family network", "small team" and "volunteer team", rather than "success team", because they believed the latter term implied professionalism and, hence, wages. As one candidate put it: "If you are professional, then you start talking numbers."[6] But the basic function was the same: collecting data from voters on their preferences, introducing and promoting the candidate, and influencing voters to give their support.

Collecting data typically involved dividing locales into "base areas" (*daerah basis*), non-base areas, and locations of swing voters (*massa mengambang* or "floating mass"). A base area could be the place where a candidate lived, had strong ethnic or religious ties, or had provided

---

[5] Edward Aspinall, "When Brokers Betray: Clientelism, Social Networks, and Electoral Politics in Indonesia", *Critical Asian Studies* 46, 4 (2014): 548.

[6] Confidential interview, 17 Mar. 2014.

goods and services. This analysis would then typically be used to help the candidate and the team in distributing patronage—usually in the form of cash and/or basic foodstuffs—with base areas getting priority. In non-base areas, candidates typically tried to reach out first to community leaders and ensure they were onside before distributing material. Many avoided doing so altogether in such places, feeling that there was no way to be sure that swing voters would reciprocate with a vote for any kind of gift.

Candidates used a variety of methods to recruit team members. Some relied on family, friendship and ethnic ties. Often, core team members were close family members of the candidate, such as children or siblings. Such people were especially likely to be loyal, and to work hard on the campaign. Otherwise, candidates use varied approaches: some tried to recruit better-educated people as team members, others did not care about this factor; some avoided recruiting poor volunteers, thinking they would become a financial burden, others did not discriminate on this basis. The size of teams also varied. Most candidates had a core group—"ring one" was a frequently used term—of advisors and planners whom they provided with direct personal access. But in "ring two" and wider circles the numbers could be in the single digits, the dozens or even the hundreds. In the larger teams, success team members working in the same neighbourhood would not always know one other personally.

To maximise their votes, many candidates recruited community leaders, including religious leaders, heads of social organisations and leaders of ethnic associations, to their success teams. Some candidates did not care about recruiting individuals with formal positions, but just looked for informal leaders who "possessed masses" (*punya massa*), such as influential motorcycle taxi drivers or even local street toughs, *preman*, as team members. One thing was clear, however: recruiting respected community leaders generally cost money. As one candidate put it, encouraging such persons to support one's campaign always involved "stimulation first, so we can talk easily"[7]—in other words, community

---

[7] Confidential interview, 1 Apr. 2014.

leaders typically first had to be provided with cash payments or other forms of "assistance" before candidates could hope for their support.

Candidates were generally aware that disloyalty among success team members could be a major problem.[8] Some tried to tie their team members to them by paying them, though many also made promises of future assistance, saying that team members would be paid bonuses or taken on as staff in the event of victory. There was even one candidate who checked the loyalty of his team members by "testing them through hunger". By this he meant he would get them involved in the campaign, and get them to come to the first couple of meetings without providing them with transport money at all. "If they pass, only then do we make a commitment, or offer them a political contract."[9] Poorer candidates had little choice but to try to ensure their team members' ongoing support by "continually keeping up the communication and face-to-face meetings with them".[10] Even so, there were some success team members who played a double game: one admitted to simultaneously campaigning for two candidates (one was his adopted father, another was a work colleague), admitting that he was struggling with how to "divide up the votes between them both".[11]

Despite the great ethnic diversity of the setting, relatively few candidates relied on ethnic networking for their success teams and campaigning. To be sure, there were a few who appointed co-ethnics to head their success teams, but even these candidates also drew members of other ethnicities, including indigenous Papuans, into their teams. In short, most candidates deliberately tried to build cross-ethnic and cross-religious teams, and consequently did not focus their patronage on just one group. The fluidity of ethnic and religious ties in this metropolitan, plural city made exclusive reliance on a single group a hazardous enterprise.

---

[8] Aspinall, "When Brokers Betray".
[9] Interview, Triwibono, PKB candidate, 19 Mar. 2014.
[10] Interview, Apner Siang, Nasdem candidate, 24 Mar. 2014.
[11] Confidential interview, 15 Apr. 2014.

MONEY POLITICS: BRIBING THE VOTERS

What factor was critical in ensuring electoral victory in North Jayapura? Almost all informants agreed that, in the words of one candidate, "it's the figure [of the candidate] that is most important in affecting constituents' votes".[12] But when people talked about the "figure" (*figur*), they were not simply talking about a candidate's personality traits. Often, they were also referring to his or her reputation for generosity or largesse. The informant continued:

> Take, for example, religious festivals. Often religious groups have trouble paying for such events, well, so we can participate in that [that is, help out financially]. I think that the figures who can work out what the people need will be known and remembered by the people … So we just need to work out what the community needs. That doesn't mean we have to squeeze out our salary, no, we just share it a bit so these events can take place. Most candidates I see are like that.[13]

Similarly, one PKB candidate explained that *ketokohan*—reputation as a leader—was important, but was not sufficient, because many popular candidates were not elected if they did not distribute cash to voters. As he put it: "In Papua there's an addition, after popularity, acceptability, electability, the last thing is what's in your bag [cash]."[14] A PKPI candidate confirmed that "the *ketokohan* factor has to be accompanied by a direct 'touch' in the form of cash".[15]

In fact, the distribution of money to voters was a relatively new phenomenon in North Jayapura. In the post-Suharto period, both the 1999 and 2004 elections were relatively free of vote buying. Vote buying began after the introduction of the open-list PR system in 2009, but intensified dramatically in 2014. As one local politician recalled:

> In 2004 it was purely community based. We would just need to ask the RT [sub-neighbourhood] head to get the residents together, he would prepare the tent, food, and whatever chairs he had, and we'd

---

[12] Confidential interview, 15 Mar. 2014.
[13] Ibid.
[14] Confidential interview, 19 Mar. 2014.
[15] Confidential interview, 1 Mar. 2014.

meet with them there and promote our campaign, introduce ourselves, introduce our mission for the community and then open a dialogue, hold a question-and-answer session about what we should do as council members. *Alhamdullilah*, the people would vote for us. That was 2004, they voted for us![16]

In 2009, however, he recalled, the election was already marked by money politics. Things got even worse in subsequent years during elections for local government heads (governor and mayor) when success teams flagrantly distributed cash. In the end, he lamented, "there occurred a change in community attitudes. It's as though they now approve of the money politics game."[17]

By 2014, patronage had been normalised. In my research interviews, most candidates admitted to practising money politics, though some were embarrassed about it and acknowledged their involvement only indirectly. Others were blunt: as one PKPI candidate put it, "Whatever the community needs, that's what we give them."[18] Candidates often talked of gifts as establishing—or tightening—a bond (*pengikat*) between themselves and voters. However, the modus operandi varied greatly. Some candidates said they gave mostly in response to requests, and that they gave to individual voters:

> If we want to meet with people, we have to bring drinks and light snacks. Not a major meal. But if they ask for help [sending their children to school], or want us to help in paying for something, we help them![19]

In a similar vein one candidate explained that "giving 'vegetable money' [*uang sayur*] or 'betel money' [*uang pinang*] is important as a sign that we care for them."[20] In such cases, candidates were talking about small gifts that they were distributing in direct interactions during the campaign period.

---

[16] Confidential interview, 31 Mar. 2014.
[17] Ibid.
[18] Confidential interview, 31 Mar. 2014.
[19] Confidential interview, 15 Mar. 2014.
[20] Confidential interview, 18 Mar. 2014.

As in many other parts of Indonesia, however, there was also significant individual vote buying in the form of the so-called dawn attack—distribution of cash or food in the few days leading to the election. Though it is hard to be sure about such figures, I estimate that around 85 per cent of competitive candidates (those who won or came close) in this electoral district engaged in the practice (about 60 per cent of those I interviewed openly discussed their vote-buying strategies with me). The figures would be somewhat lower for provincial candidates, and lower still for DPR candidates (probably about 50 per cent of the competitive candidates engaged at this level). The average price paid for a vote was Rp 50,000, which as one candidate explained, "is a reasonable figure if we think of it as compensating them for transport expenses".[21] The price could run as high as Rp 200,000, but this was usually *uang nindih* (top-up money), or "dawn attack on top of a dawn attack", to quote one candidate, who was referring to the practice when candidates would try to outdo each other at the last moment—if they found a competitor was giving Rp 50,000, they would give Rp 100,000, for example.[22]

A few candidates experimented with methods for ensuring that recipients truly reciprocated with votes. For example, some directed voters to tear the candidate's number out of the ballot paper (in Indonesia voters mark their vote for a candidate by punching a hole through his or her image or name on the ballot paper), and show it to the success team in order to receive payment. Some instructed voters to take their mobile telephones into the booth, photograph their punched ballot, and only then receive payment. This method was difficult to apply, however, given that voters were expressly prohibited from taking telephones into the polling booth in 2014, and also because most booths were only partially obscured from the outside. As a result, most candidates and their teams had difficulty in knowing exactly which voters cast ballots in accordance with the money they received.

Some candidates, however, said they refused to provide money to individuals: "If somebody comes to me and asks for assistance to help

---

[21] Confidential interview, 1 Apr. 2014.
[22] Confidential interview, 18 Mar. 2014.

with some personal matter, no matter how much money he or she asks for, I will refuse to pay."[23] Such candidates typically preferred to provide collective gifts (club goods) to community groups. One explained that he would "give communication equipment to fishers and prayer groups, as well as giving regular donations to mosques and churches".[24] When I interviewed him at his home, several people were visiting him with written proposals, seeking funds for, among other things, mosque construction. He promised to pay.

There was of course, socioeconomic targeting in money politics. A PKPI candidate explained, "There are three layers in the community when it comes to money politics: the middle-to-upper layer, the middle-to-lower layer, and the bottom-most layer."[25] He explained that money politics played a role in the middle group, but was "massive" among the poorest community members. More prosperous residents of Jayapura, he explained, did not need the money, tended to be uninterested in politics, and often did not bother to vote. PKS cadres, meanwhile, who were amongst the most assiduous door-to-door campaigners, even carried out a sort of informal survey of voter preferences as they leafleted households, with a majority of people they met receptive to cash gifts.[26] With a large section of the voters so inclined, and with many candidates participating, it is unsurprising that most serious candidates decided to distribute cash or gifts, even if it was only—to borrow a term used by one PKB candidate—to "balance" other candidates. Those who did not participate in vote buying sometimes regretted it afterwards. One candidate complained bitterly about his experience in 2009:

> I half killed myself promoting my campaign, and it was all taken by others on voting day. It hurt! I spent a lot of money on assistance to the community. But it didn't count. On voting day, [my rival] wiped me clean. With some voters, all you have to do is just give them rice and they will change.[27]

---

[23] Confidential interview, 31 Mar. 2014.
[24] Confidential interview, 15 Mar. 2014.
[25] Confidential interview, 1 Apr. 2014.
[26] Confidential interview, 20 Mar. 2014.
[27] Confidential interview, 31 Mar. 2014.

Though this candidate won in 2009, he did so only narrowly. He apparently learned from this experience and was one of the more active vote buyers in North Jayapura in 2014, and recorded a much higher vote than in 2009.

MONEY POLITICS: BRIBING THE OFFICIALS

Candidates with resources could choose whether to distribute cash or goods to voters, or use them to influence election administrators. One technique that was very widespread in 2014 in North Jayapura was the purchase by candidates or their success team members of voter registration cards from members of voting booth committees (KPPS, Komite Penyelenggara Pemungutan Suara). In one case I learned of, a candidate purchased 50 such cards at a total price of Rp 15 million, or equivalent to Rp 300,000 each. In another case, the same number of cards was purchased for Rp 10 million, or Rp 200,000 each. Thus, the cost per ballot was several times the market price paid to individual voters. When the cards were purchased, however, the candidate could be certain of how many votes were being bought, whereas when giving money to voters it was generally impossible to be sure about how many of them would deliver. The certainty was of course possible because the booth officials were in on the deal. When cards were bought wholesale like this, the committee members themselves typically marked the ballots in the candidate's favour, but it was also possible to buy cards in smaller amounts, in which case the operation still required one more step: the buyer had to pay people to take the cards and use them to cast additional votes. The cost was Rp 50,000 per vote for the persons performing this service, who typically voted multiple times.[28]

---

[28] My source for this information was a success team member who helped two candidates win in this way, but I also learned of a candidate for the provincial parliament who told me that he had paid for voter cards at a price of Rp 30,000 each in several places, including Serui and Jayapura. Confidential interview, 15 Apr. 2014.

Part of the reason why this method was reliable was that there was little effective monitoring of the voting process by official election supervisory bodies. In my own observations in polling booths on voting day in Jayapura, residents came to booths, surrendered their cards, and got their ballot papers without having to show any further papers to verify their identity. This made it possible for some voters to make multiple trips to booths, and some I met made between Rp 500,000 and 800,000 by voting several times. Of course, this mostly happened where polling booth officials were in on the deal, and was also facilitated by the fact that, in my observation, the ink used to stain voters' fingers could easily be removed with cleaning fluids.

The buying of voter cards in this way was only the crudest form of intervention in electoral management. Over the last decade, it has become clear that electoral administration in Papua is rife with collusion between candidates and election officials. It has become common for candidates in both executive government head elections and legislative elections to pay officials to manipulate the count in their favour. The head of the provincial chapter of PKB, and an unsuccessful DPR candidate in 2014, Triwibono, calls collusion between candidates and electoral bodies a form of "system attack", in contrast to the "dawn attack" which targets only voters.

In North Jayapura in 2014, manipulation was not as blatant as in highland areas, but there were plenty of signs that some candidates paid for their vote numbers to be boosted during the count in several precincts. This "vote inflation" (*penggelembungan suara*), as it is usually known, typically occurred at the subdistrict level, where candidates could bribe those tabulating the results. As a result, the polling booth results recorded on voting day sometimes differed from those compiled at higher levels, leading to major disputes between candidates and officials. The final meeting of the North Jayapura electoral commission was quite chaotic as a result, with the sessions being suspended several times, and some candidates still alleging that cheating had occurred after the results were finalised. Several candidates also spoke about "vote trading", which occurs when unsuccessful candidates "sell" some of their individual votes—with a cut paid to relevant election officials—to candidates who needed to boost their own votes in order to defeat other candidates on their party list.

THE PRICE OF A SEAT

Winning a seat, even in a district parliament, is an expensive business in Papua. A candidate has to expend considerable sums at every stage: when seeking nomination, early promotion efforts, the official campaign period, paying for polling booth witnesses, and preparing for a court challenge. Lots of candidates used up their personal wealth on such expenses. Some depended on support from their families, or took loans from friends or business partners.

Not all candidates I interviewed had to pay their parties for obtaining a nomination. But some, including those from PAN, PKB and PKPI, were charged an "administrative" or "operational" fee by their nominating parties. For example, candidates running with PKPI had to pay Rp 25 million for the candidate with the top position on the party list, Rp 15 million for number two, Rp 10 million for number three, and the remainder, Rp 5 million each. Other parties, perhaps because they were larger and more serious about winning, did not charge their candidates in this way.[29]

Next was expenditure for "socialisation" (*sosialisasi*): promoting one's candidacy through stickers, name cards, T-shirts, calendars, posters, billboards and advertisements in the print or electronic media. Candidates' capacity to pay for such things varied greatly. Some campaigns were promoted lavishly and visibly on the streets, while some were all but invisible. In addition, serious candidates paid for meetings with constituents, hiring tents or meeting places, paying for snacks and drinks, and typically also providing small "souvenirs", which could be Rp 50,000 notes in envelopes, calendars, T-shirts, prayer mats and the like.

At the end of the campaign period were yet more expenses. Candidates paying for the dawn attack generally found this the single greatest item of expenditure, though few were willing to discuss the details. Another major cost was paying for polling booth witnesses, generally considered a critical expenditure item if candidates wanted to "secure" (*mengamankan*) their vote from the sort of "system attack" discussed above. The going rate for a witness in Jayapura was Rp 300,000,

---

[29] Confidential interviews, 21 and 27 Mar. 2014.

plus transport, communication and food money. Poor candidates were thus unable to pay for witnesses, with the consequence that many of them lost votes as they were counted and tabulated. Most DPR candidates also felt they had to set aside cash (up to Rp 1 billion) in the eventuality of a Constitutional Court challenge to the results (only a few DPRD candidates did this).

Candidates' total expenditure varied widely, but those who won seats tended to spend a lot. Several candidates for DPR seats spoke of total expenditure of Rp 1.5 to Rp 7 billion (one DPR candidate who scraped through to victory admitted that he spent Rp 7 billion; but a party colleague said that his actual expenditure had been closer to Rp 30 billion). Winning candidates for the provincial DPRD mostly spent in the range of Rp 500 million to Rp 1 billion, with a few exceeding this amount. For seats in Jayapura's city council, candidates tended to spend between Rp 25 million and Rp 500 million. It should be noted, however, that these estimates cover only expenditures from the beginning of the nomination process in 2013: many candidates had also expended great sums earlier on social expenditure in their constituencies, such as building bridges, assisting mosques or churches, and so on. For many candidates, it was thus not surprising that, as one of them jokingly put it, "All our money is gone!"[30]

CONCLUSION

Money politics is rampant in Papua. As Triwibono, the Papua head of PKB, put it: "If you put money politics on a scale of one to ten, then in Papua it's a ten."[31] Yet in many respects this is a question of degree, not a distinctive pattern. The analysis of electoral dynamics in North Jayapura in the preceding pages suggests patterns of money politics similar to those found in other Indonesian provinces and towns. Success teams, brokerage, club goods, vote buying, even bribery of election officials: all this is widespread across much of Indonesia.

---

[30] Confidential interview, 27 Mar. 2014.

[31] Ibid.

Why should patterns of patronage politics in North Jayapura be so familiar, when we often think of Papuan politics as very different from that elsewhere in Indonesia? One reason, of course, is that Jayapura itself is largely a migrant town, in a part of the country that has long been a magnet for internal migration. Many of the candidates and voters discussed in this chapter were themselves migrants, who brought their own forms of social and political organisation with them from other parts of Indonesia. Though ethnic Papuans are a major part of the population of Jayapura, in other respects the ethnic mix in the town is similar to many of the polyglot settlements found in eastern Indonesia. It is not surprising, then, that the electoral patterns should be similar.

Yet another factor is also important: the electoral rules and structures that shape electoral competition in Jayapura are the same as those found throughout the country. It is not surprising that the same open-list PR system, with the same political parties, should produce similar patterns of electoral competition, even if those patterns adapt to the particularities of local societies. It should be noted, however, that not all of Papua is like this. In many parts of Papua province, there is a system of collective community voting entirely unlike anything found elsewhere in the country. As we shall see in the next chapter, this distinctive electoral institution *does* shape dynamics of electoral competition in the parts of Papua where it operates.

chapter **23**

Papua's Central Highlands: The *Noken* System, Brokers and Fraud

Cillian Nolan

This chapter looks at the 2014 legislative election in Papua province, which was in many ways an exception to national trends.[1] The province forms a single electoral district for the DPR competition, but this chapter focuses on the 16 *kabupaten* (districts) that make up the central highlands, along a mountain chain that bisects the province from east to west. It was the 2.11 million registered voters in the highlands (66 per cent of the provincial total) who were the determining factor in the DPR race, and who elected 34 of the 55 seats in the provincial assembly (which in Papua is called the Dewan Perwakilan Rakyat Papua, or DPRP). Across these highlands *kabupaten*, many communities use a form of bloc-voting called the *noken* system, in which community leaders are permitted to vote on behalf of all registered voters. This style of voting makes the strategies used by candidates running for local or provincial office in the highlands, as well as by nearly all candidates running for national office, unique in Indonesia.

---

[1] Unlike the other authors of chapters in this book who were present during the elections, for this chapter I largely draw on interviews with candidates and success team members conducted after the elections, and on the wealth of testimony produced during election disputes.

Noken voting is entirely unregulated, and because it entails broad disregard for electoral regulations applied nationally, it creates a permissive environment for fraud. By many measures, Papua is home to Indonesia's worst-administered elections. In 2014, the province generated the largest number of disputes at the Constitutional Court (over 100) and of ethics cases before the Dewan Kehormatan Penyelenggara Pemilu (DKPP, General Election Honour Council). Also, at least 25 KPU (Komisi Pemilihan Umum, General Elections Commission) members were sanctioned in Papua in 2014; 14 were fired, and there were criminal investigations into misconduct by at least 25 elections officials. Papua was also the province with minimal independent monitoring.

The kind of bloc-voting that *noken* permits sets up a system of brokerage in truncated form, where community leaders do not act to mobilise or influence voters on behalf of a candidate, but instead make binding decisions on behalf of all the registered voters in a given area. This system might be expected to eliminate the investment risk associated with patronage politics elsewhere, where the secret ballot makes it hard to know exactly which voters are voting for what candidates and, therefore, which brokers are delivering or failing to do so. In the highlands, it is easy to determine whether brokers have delivered the blocs they promised simply by looking at the results. In many areas, there is no need for voters to turn up to polls—turnout was registered as being 100 per cent across the highlands, meaning all the votes were arranged beforehand and few people actually voted. The net effect of this system is thus to strengthen the influence of a narrow elite—the candidates and the brokers—at the expense of giving eligible voters a democratic voice.

Nevertheless, for two main reasons, *noken* voting in Papua produced results that were difficult to predict, even for the candidates, brokers and election officials involved. First, the unregulated nature of *noken* meant that a variety of competing figures claimed to serve as community- level brokers representing the same voters and thus ultimately creating uncertainty in the electoral process. Second, because there were so few controls on how *noken* voting works, and because it occurred within an election system more vulnerable to fraud than elsewhere in the country, intervention by polling officials at various levels provided another vehicle for winning blocs of votes.

After setting elections in Papua within the national context and exploring how and why the Papuan highlands are distinct, this chapter provides an explanation of how *noken* voting has developed and what this diverse, unregulated system of voting generally entails. It presents examples of the competing brokerage mechanisms that offered access to votes and then examines how pay-offs by some candidates to election officials further affected the results.

BACKGROUND: POLITICS IN PAPUA

Papua's central highlands have long been a distinct region, marked off from the rest of the province by both geography and demographics. The height of these mountains (home to Mt Carstenz, Indonesia's highest peak) and difficulty of access have long separated the area from the coastal plains to the north and south. The Dutch colonial state arrived very late to this area, making little contact with highland settlements before the early 1950s. Even since the 1969 integration of Papua (then Irian Barat) into the Indonesian republic, the presence of the state is limited in many areas. A Law on Special Autonomy enacted in 2001 brought devolution of some central government powers and increased budget transfers to Papua, to help accelerate development and quell separatist sentiment in the province but, while the province's income has increased, development indicators continue to lag. The highland districts are home to some of the country's highest poverty rates, and many communities can only be accessed by plane.[2]

The isolation of the highlands has made them home to far fewer migrants than other parts of Papua. While migrants make up 41 per cent of the population in the coastal districts, according to 2010 census figures, they are just 12 per cent of those in the highlands. If we exclude the districts of Nabire and Mimika, at the northwestern and southwestern fringes of the highlands respectively, the figure falls to

---

[2] Tim Nasional Percepatan Penanggulangan Kemiskinan (TNP2K), "Indikator Kesejahteraan Daerah Provinsi Papua" [Prosperity Indicator Papua Province], Nov. 2011, available at: http://data.tnp2k.go.id/file_data/Data/IKD/94_Papua.pdf.

2.5 per cent. Papua is heavily Christian—in the 2010 census, 83 per cent of the province-wide population identified as either Catholic or Protestant. Most of the Muslim population is concentrated in the lowlands, in the urban centres of Jayapura and Merauke, or areas that have a history of transmigration resettlement.

The indigenous communities of the highlands are nevertheless not ethnically homogeneous, but instead consist of a broad variety of clans and language groups. This diversity is particularly striking in some of the district capitals, where groups from several neighbouring districts often live together. Elsewhere, highlanders live in isolated, homogeneous villages. This fragmentation has been one contributor to the rapid rate of administrative division (*pemekaran*) in the highlands, as new villages, districts and subdistricts are created along clan and subclan lines.[3]

The challenges of mountainous terrain, low literacy rates and isolated communities mean that two major obstacles to administering elections in the highlands are distributing and collecting ballots and finding literate and independent polling officials. Literacy rates here are low (they average just 46 per cent), which makes staffing polling stations with competent staff difficult, particularly outside the urban centres.

The province has traditionally been a stronghold of the Golkar party, but in 2009 Partai Demokrat made significant inroads, picking up 3 of 10 seats in the DPR and 9 seats in the DPRP (second only to Golkar, which held 12). Partai Demokrat's power base is largely in the highlands. One man is responsible more than any other for the party's success here: the current governor, Lukas Enembe. The former *bupati* of Puncak Jaya, he was elected governor in January 2013 after campaigning on the message that "now is the time for the highlanders".

The province elects ten members to the DPR from one province-wide electoral district. At the provincial level, voters elect 55 members to the DPRP from 7 electoral districts. Prior to the 2014 polls, the

---

[3] "Carving Up Papua: More Districts, More Trouble", Institute for Policy Analysis of Conflict (IPAC), 9 Oct. 2013, available at: www.understandingconflict.org/conflict/read/8/Carving-Up-Papua-More-Districts-More-Problems.

electoral districts at provincial level were reconfigured to adjust for the rise in recorded population in the highlands. An additional electoral district was added so that 4 of the 7 are now in the highlands—together they elect 34 of the 55 DPRP members.

The last element of voting in Papua that requires explanation is the systematic inflation of population statistics and voter rolls. Voter rolls expanded rapidly here in the five years leading to the 2014 election, with the number of registered voters rising from just over 2 million in the 2009 parliamentary elections to 3.2 million in 2014, a rise that far exceeds any reasonable estimate of population growth.[4] A disproportionate amount of this growth has been in the highland districts, explaining why they are now home to two-thirds of the province's registered voters.

THE *NOKEN* SYSTEM

Before examining how voting worked in the parliamentary election, it is necessary to review the mechanics of voting under what is called the *noken* system. This method of voting has never been defined in law and there is no common definition of what it involves—it is best understood as a set of deviations from standard electoral practice that has been upheld by the Constitutional Court in the name of acknowledging customary practice. Because it is unregulated, and in the absence of effective monitoring or observation, it is difficult to know exactly where it is applied, but it is broadly accepted that the practice may be used across the 16 highland districts that make up the La Pago and Mee Pago *wilayah adat*, or regions of common *adat* (customary) practice in Papua.

Noken is a traditional bag made from bark; the phrase "*noken* system" may have originally described a process through which community members gathered on election day and placed their votes in *noken* bags, one hung on a stake for each of the candidates. Little

---

[4] "Open to Manipulation: The 2014 Elections in Papua Province", Institute for Policy Analysis of Conflict (IPAC), 10 Dec. 2014, available at: http://www. understandingconflict.org/conflict/read/32/Open-to-Manipulation-The-2014-Elections-in-Papua.

appears to have been written about its history, but defenders of the practice claim it has been used in Indonesian elections in Papua since 1971, following the 1969 integration of the former Dutch colony into the Indonesian republic. They say that it classically entailed visits by prospective candidates to a community, cash payments and promises of future investment, consultation between community leaders (especially the clan chief) and the community at large, and finally the closing of a deal through a ceremony, often in the form of a traditional feast known as *batu bakar*. The practice was therefore defended as according with local ideals of community consultation and communal (notably, clan) interests. As a technical exercise, it was always partly designed to help ensure that these community decisions were respected by all involved, because it took away the element of secrecy: any member of the community who decided to deviate from the "consensus" view and vote for another candidate would quickly be identified. But at a minimum, this version of the *noken* system preserved the physical act of going to a polling station and voting, even if it meant doing so in public.

In more recent practice, both the element of consultation and the physical act of voting seem to have disappeared from *noken* voting. In five separate decisions since 2009, the Constitutional Court has upheld the practice while progressively expanding the interpretation of what *noken* voting might entail. By March 2013, in a ruling on the disputed results of the January 2013 governor's election, the Court appeared to accept at face value the testimony of the Majelis Rakyat Papua (MRP, Papuan People's Council)—a sort of consultative assembly that was established as part of Special Autonomy arrangements—that the element of community consultation was not crucial. The man called before the Court to offer this testimony was Timotius Murib, the MRP chair and a political ally of the governor, whose election was at stake. It is worth quoting the Court's summary of Murib's testimony because it has repeatedly returned to it in subsequent decisions:

> One aspect of the traditional political structures of indigenous Papuans is the leadership of *Pria Berwibawa* or "The Big Man", which exists in the [La Pago and Mee Pago *adat* areas]. For this reason, decisions on matters of shared interests may be made through consultation but may also be made through decisions based on the authority of the

clan chief (*kepala suku*), who is also the political representative of the community.[5]

In that decision, the Court once again argued that *noken* voting had to be allowed because the customary practice of *adat* communities was constitutionally protected, even if there was no provision anywhere in the law for the kind of bloc-voting or proxy voting that the practice usually requires.

Despite these decisions, neither the national parliament, the DPRP nor the electoral commission has made any effort to regulate the practice. They fear that writing *noken* voting into law would create a precedent that would lead other regions in the country—Aceh and Yogyakarta, for example, which both have special autonomy arrangements of their own—to demand similar accommodations.[6] The only regulation to date that mentions *noken* is a hastily issued decision by the provincial election commission in January 2013, before the governor's poll, that permits the replacement of ballot boxes with *noken* bags. It makes no mention of consultative decisions, proxy voting or the like. The effect of this legal vacuum, plus the accumulated Constitutional Court decisions, is very permissive: as long as officials can claim that voting procedures follow established customary practice, they can interpret *noken* as they wish.

The impact of this permissiveness on the 2014 legislative election was striking. In the 14 highland districts where *noken* is broadly applied—Nabire and Mimika are the partial exceptions—turnout was recorded in the official results as being 100 per cent. In coastal areas, turnout rates remained above the national average of 75 per cent, but largely stayed between 80 and 90 per cent.[7] These made Papua the

[5] Mahkamah Konstitusi [MK, Constitutional Court], Decision in case No. 14/PHPU.D-XI/2013, 11 Mar. 2013, pp. 165–9.

[6] Interview, Jimly Asshiddiqie, former MK chief justice, 18 Sept. 2014.

[7] I calculate the turnout rate by dividing the total number of votes cast by the number of registered voters in the Daftar Pemilih Tetap (DPT, Fixed Voters List). The DPT does not include voters who registered late, who registered at polling stations other than their permanent place of residence or who simply showed up on voting day with proper identification. The total number of votes cast by those not on the DPT in Papua province was 21,774, or 0.7 per cent of the total. Only

national electoral district with more votes than any other in the country, and made the number of accumulated party and personal votes a party needed to win to attain a seat very high, at 289,667.[8] Ballot spoilage rates (*suara tidak sah*) tell a similar story. There were no spoiled ballots in 13 of the highland districts; elsewhere in Papua the rate was 8.6 per cent.

Together, these factors made Papua an outlier nationally. It had the highest turnout rate (95 per cent) and the lowest rate of spoiled ballots (3 per cent). While support for Partai Demokrat fizzled nationally, in Papua—where a Partai Demokrat politician was governor—the party produced its strongest showing ever, and received among the highest votes of any party in any electoral district nationally (700,150).

BROKERS AND VOTE INFLATION IN THE *NOKEN* SYSTEM

Noken voting creates a system of brokerage in an extreme sense, in that community leaders assume the right to vote on behalf of all the registered voters in a given community. But what defines a community and who qualifies as a community leader? Because there are no regulations, these critical issues have largely been left to the candidates and voting officials to define, though the courts have provided some guidance.

The Constitutional Court's working definition in the 2013 case, cited above, named the clan chief (*kepala suku*) as one figure with authority to make voting decisions on behalf of a community, while also leaving the category vague and open to the possibility that other "political representatives" could qualify. *Kepala suku* have no definition in law; they are not elected and are not formally recognised by the state.[9] Nor

---

four districts in the highlands had any such voters, another indication that normal procedures were not applied in this province.

[8] Some parties won seats with less than this figure, by receiving the largest remainders once the full party quotas were distributed.

[9] Several of those interviewed noted that decrees issued by the *bupati* in the distribution of social support funds (*dana bansos*) were documents in which the role of *kepala suku* were officially recognised.

is the post always a hereditary one—Indonesian anthropologists have generally adopted the term "big man" from English to describe a system in which the position of clan chief is open to competition. Moreover, the distinction between clans and subclans is not always clear and remains dynamic, meaning the level at which representative political decisions are made may not be clear.

One candidate who tried to leverage the positions of *kepala suku* as brokers was Helina Murib, who was running for one of Papua's four DPD (Regional Representative Council) seats. To support her complaint to the Constitutional Court, she called as a witness a Damal clan chief from Puncak district, Asen Murib. In the hearings, he explained that, as the daughter of the deceased clan chief, Helina had "a right" to all the votes in the district, but that those votes had been lost during manipulation of the counting process.[10] That claim would seem to fit well with former Constitutional Court decisions recognising the role of *kepala suku* in *noken* voting. But this term is a slippery one. Asen Murib presented himself simply as a *kepala suku* from the district, but the judges later refer to him as *kepala suku* of the entire district. This makes little sense, as Puncak is home to several clans and competition between two leading Damal and Dani political figures led to violence in a protracted local election process in 2011–12; some 40 people died as a result of clashes between the two clans. The example points to a broader difficulty in permitting customary structures to make decisions on behalf of blocs of voters who are grouped by state administrative boundaries: the two overlap, but are by no means identical. The judges appear to have missed this distinction, but they nevertheless threw out Helina Murib's appeal on the grounds that the testimony was poorly supported by legally significant documentation. No candidate has successfully challenged the KPU's results by appealing to the proof of a clan chief's support.

Another class of institutions whose members jockeyed for brokerage roles in some parts of the highlands were the Lembaga Masyarakat Adat (LMA, Adat Community Institution), formal institutions set up

---

[10] Mahkamah Konstitusi, Decision in case No. 06-32/PHPU-DPD/XII/2014 (Provinsi Papua), 25 June 2014.

in many parts of Papua with government support in order to regulate customary affairs. Their structures mirror those of government, with a main body at district level and representatives in subdistricts and villages. Many of these LMA are seen as lacking local legitimacy; they were set up largely to counter the influence of another *adat* institution, the Dewan Adat Papua (Papuan Adat Council), an unregistered network that the government views with hostility, suspecting it of providing an umbrella for separatist sentiment. In Paniai, in the western highlands, a district leader argued that the LMA had agreed that all the district's votes would be given to native son Yulianus Yogi, who was running for a DPR seat for Nasdem. Representatives of the LMA signed a letter that read:

> These 90,632 votes we bind together using the *noken* method for the native son of Paniai named Father Yulianus Yogi, S.Th., M.A., on the condition that the future development of Paniai will be discussed with the central government.[11]

As the members of the LMA understood it, they were trading electoral support for efforts to increase government investment in Paniai. According to this leader's testimony, no ballots were punched on election day; the LMA sent its representatives to all subdistricts to generate a tally that fulfilled the terms of the agreement. The KPU later claimed that three different candidates had received votes in Paniai, but that Yogi had received no votes. The Constitutional Court threw out his case, questioning the authenticity of the letter and finding no reason to distrust the KPU's count.

Though Yogi failed in his efforts, one effect of the *noken* system was that candidates' votes tended to be highly geographically concentrated. Candidates often successfully captured a substantial share of all the votes in a particular district. The most striking example was a DPR candidate, Tony Wardoyo. A Christian Javanese businessman, he had served before as a DPR member from Papua, from 2004 to 2009 (representing PKB). In the DPR he sat on Commission II, which among other things approves

---

[11] Mahkamah Konstitusi, Decision in case No. 01-01-32/PHPU-DPR-DPRD/XII/2014 (Provinsi Papua), 27 June 2014.

the creation of new districts and provinces. In 2007, he supported the creation of Puncak district, carved out of Puncak Jaya the following year. In 2014, running on the PDI-P ticket, he won 86 per cent of the votes in Puncak, where the *bupati* is also a leading PDI-P supporter. Elsewhere he picked up only a handful of votes; Puncak provided him with 98.9 per cent of his total votes. Results like this suggests that the district heads were often the critical behind-the-scenes brokers in the *noken* system.

In fact, *all* candidates who succeeded in the DPR race drew the bulk of their votes from only one, or at most two, highland districts. This suggests that successful DPR candidates focused their investments in one particular area rather than trying to pick up a smaller number of votes in a broad number of areas. Elion Numberi, a Protestant preacher who had served in the DPD from 2009 to 2014 but joined Golkar to run for the DPR in 2014, moved to Yahukimo for the two months before the race, apparently motivated partly by the presence of a Golkar-aligned district head there. He picked up 50,000 votes in the district, the bulk of the 85,374 that saw him elected. In the DPR race, this kind of dedicated focus was necessary in part because the number of votes necessary to win a seat was so high. Of the ten candidates elected, Numberi received the fewest. In 2009, when the role of *noken* was far less clear, Peggi Pattipi, for example, was elected with just over 20,000 votes; in 2014, she won over 100,000 votes (98 per cent from Mimika).

A similar effect occurred in the DPRP race in the highland electoral districts, where successful candidates needed far more votes than their colleagues in coastal electoral districts. Yakoba Lokbere received more votes than anyone else in the DPRP race and was elected from Papua VI electoral district, comprised of Nduga, Jayawijaya and two smaller districts. Lokbere is originally from Nduga and her husband is John Wetipo, the Jayawijaya *bupati* who heads the local chapter of the PDI-P and is a leading contender for the post of provincial party chair. She won over 100,000 personal votes, while the runner-up in the district was Partai Demokrat candidate John Rouw, the brother of Wetipo's deputy, who won half that amount, but was still elected. In the electoral district around Merauke and Jayapura on the coast, by contrast, candidates needed only between 8,000 and 18,000 personal votes.

The need to obtain so many votes made appeals to brokers with district-wide influence an important strategy, and this was one reason why *bupati* played such an important role in brokering votes. Their influence rested on distribution of cash payments; control over district budgets (which fund much of the district KPU's operations); and promises of forward-looking patronage, such as future investment in roads and buildings in return for votes. These resources meant that it was often relatively easy for the district head to exert pressure on *kepala suku*, LMA leaders and others who had control over how subdistrict tallies were reported, in order to sway them to direct *noken* votes toward favoured candidates. It also meant that *bupati* were often able to intervene during the vote counting and tabulation process as new aggregate tallies were created at district and provincial level.

District heads had many reasons for favouring certain candidates. Often it was simply a matter of wanting to reward political supporters or relatives. But they also had personal incentives for seeing certain candidates elected, especially given that in 2014 there were strong signs that policy changes at national level would be introduced to shift the election of *bupati* from direct polls to indirect elections by the DPRDs.[12] That meant that many *bupati* had a personal interest in ensuring that the district councils were comprised of sympathisers. It also meant that *bupati* with strong party links had an incentive to ensure that party colleagues or other associates were elected to the provincial council, to support the election of the next governor.

One aspect of the *noken* system that makes it attractive for politicians is that it eliminates the reciprocity problem observed elsewhere. By producing results in blocs, it makes it obvious who should be rewarded with patronage. The centralised distribution of ballots, which in the

---

[12] In addition to national legislation under consideration at the time, there was separate legislation that would have made amendments to Papua's Special Autonomy law to make the same change in Papua, irrespective of national policy ("Otsus Plus: The Debate over Enhanced Special Autonomy for Papua", Institute for Policy Analysis of Conflict (IPAC), 25 Nov. 2013, available at: http://www.understandingconflict.org/conflict/read/20/Otsus-Plus-The-Debate-over-Enhanced-Special-Autonomy-for-Papua). Ultimately, the proposals at both national and provincial level were discarded in late 2014.

highlands generally meant that they had to be sent out by plane from the district capital, also helped cement the influence of the *bupati*. For example, under Bupati Wetipo's eye in Jayawijaya district, ballots were loaded onto planes with the instruction "make sure they all come back red!", a reference to the colour of Wetipo's PDI-P party. Subdistrict polling officials say that they nevertheless often reserved one-third to one-half of votes to sell off themselves for private ends.[13]

The *bupati*'s influence over the KPU budget could also affect the outcome. The distinction between budgetary support for election activities and personal payments to officials in exchange for intervention to ensure specific candidates won was sometimes blurred. In Tolikara, for example, one polling official alleged that the *bupati* made payments of Rp 5 million to all 45 subdistrict-level polling officials to ensure Partai Demokrat candidates were successful. In a separate incident, the DKPP found that he had made a payment of Rp 25 million to the district KPU with the same aim, although he claimed the payment was part of the district's budget for the election. The DKPP gave the KPU members only a stern warning (*peringatan keras*). The head of the DKPP, Jimly Asshiddiqie, explained they could not apply the same ethical standards in Papua as they did elsewhere because it would almost certainly lead to the firing of a disproportionately high number of election officials.[14]

THE *NOKEN* SYSTEM AND ELECTORAL FRAUD

If candidates elsewhere faced choices between either investing heavily in buying votes or buying off the election officials, in the highlands of Papua, the *noken* system eliminated the distinction: in many areas, no voting took place, and the polling officials often performed the job of voting themselves. Polling stations did not open in many parts, and where they did, voting was sometimes a sideshow. One observer from Jayapura told of showing up at a polling station in Dekai, Yahukimo

---

[13] Confidential interview, 30 Oct. 2014.

[14] Interview, 18 Sept. 2014.

district, planning to vote using just his identity card, a practice allowed nationwide during the last hour of polling. What he found was a building with two rooms, in which a crowd of locals were all gathered in one room, where a large spread of food had been made available by a handful of candidates. In the other room, polling officials were punching ballots on behalf of the community. No one was allowed into the room to cast a vote.[15]

In the rest of Indonesia, voting takes place in the morning, and counting starts in the early afternoon. *Noken* voting, by largely eliminating actual voters from the process, allowed the negotiation of voting results to continue over several weeks. Thus even scenes like the previous one, in which officials punched ballot papers on behalf of a community on voting day, were not actually necessary to deliver a community's vote, or were not necessarily binding. Instead, candidates could negotiate with community leaders or, more likely, election officials at a later date. This made it difficult for candidates to estimate the final price of any seat, because there was always the risk of being outbid later. Papua was one of the very last provinces to report results at national level; the provincial "recapitulation" (*rekapitulasi*) of the count was so late that it had to be adjourned without a final agreement in Jayapura and was finalised in Jakarta, without most witnesses present.

One unsuccessful DPR candidate from the Nasdem party described the atmosphere in the capital of Jayawijaya district, Wamena, which is a transport hub for the highlands and thus became a gathering place for election officials on their way to Jayapura. All the ATMs in town had run out of money three days before voting day. On voting day itself, polling stations closed at 9 a.m. or never opened. The real decisions were made in the lobby of a local hotel, where candidates or their representatives bargained with election officials, usually from the subdistrict level committees. The starting price was 5,000 votes for Rp 50 million; in some highly contested areas, the price was higher. These officials conducted negotiations with a photocopy of the official tally form in hand; that meant if they later received a higher offer, they

---

[15] Confidential interview, 30 Oct. 2014.

could simply alter the tally.[16] It also meant that none of the candidates who were buying results had any proof of the new results that would be accepted in a legal dispute.

One member of the provincial KPU explained the variation in the counting process that made this kind of auction possible. In much of the highlands, "there were no C forms, only D", he explained, referring to the forms on which polling officials across the country record polling-station tallies, and subdistrict aggregates, respectively. That meant that polling-station committees were often never convened and counting was not officially recorded at the polling-station level. Instead, adherence to the standard counting procedures observed nationwide began only at subdistrict level, and in some cases polling-station tallies were then produced retroactively.[17] It was difficult to determine to what extent this represented a consensus decision on the part of voting officials or simply how things worked out as a product of the bargaining processes. If there was an agreement to this effect, it was unwritten.

In many cases, the subdistrict became the unit of bargaining or brokerage in the determination of results. That sometimes meant that the entire bloc of votes available in a particular subdistrict would be sold to one candidate. This was particularly pronounced in the July 2014 presidential elections where, for example, in Yahukimo district, the largest of the highland districts by number of registered voters, 33 of 51 subdistricts awarded *all* their votes to one candidate.

As a result, it was at these subdistrict *rekapitulasi* meetings that negotiations often ensued about who should receive the votes available. These discussions did not always involve money, goods or other material rewards. There are several examples of election officials interrupting the regular process in order to ensure that at least some native sons were elected. As an example, in Tolikara, one subdistrict election committee member told the DKPP how he had stopped counting when he became

---

[16] Confidential interview, 10 June 2014.

[17] Confidential interview, 20 Sept. 2014. This may explain why very few polling records from Papua were available on the KPU website. While 82 per cent of C-1 forms were nationally scanned and uploaded to the KPU site (pemilu2014.kpu. go.id), for Papua the figure was only 16 per cent.

aware that no locals were going to be elected to the DPRD. He suggested that three local candidates negotiate among themselves on which one would pool the votes of all three, to ensure that he was elected.[18]

The many changes that appear to have been introduced in the results by the KPU as the tally moved between subdistrict, district and provincial levels show that no matter how effectively candidates made use of brokers through *noken* voting, intervention by election officials could trump results agreed at lower levels. The case of Golkar DPR candidate Samsudin Mandja provides an example. The *bupati* of Nduga, Yarius Gwijangge, is also the district chair of Golkar. In testimony to the Constitutional Court, he explained how he had brokered an agreement between district representatives of all the political parties that the DPR vote in his district would be split between Mandja, his party colleague, and Diaz Gwijangge, an incumbent from Partai Demokrat and a fellow clan member. This agreement worked out by giving Mandja all the votes from 21 of 32 subdistricts (or roughly 96,000 votes), and splitting the balance between Gwijangge and one other candidate. Mandja presented letters from three different *kepala suku* attesting to agreements of support for this arrangement. In its final tally, however, the KPU awarded Mandja just 20,583 votes. The judges rejected all the claims put forward by Mandja, arguing that a letter between political party representatives does not a democratic election make.[19] While the Court accepted such decisions as a theoretical basis for how voting might proceed, it was not willing to accept that evidence of such decisions meant that contrary tallies held by the elections commission were necessarily fraudulent.

A final point worth noting is that some candidates interviewed alleged that the confusion around *noken* voting provided space for the intervention of the police or other security services (including the state intelligence agency, Badan Intelijen Negara) to ensure that candidates

---

[18] Dewan Kehormatan Penyelenggara Pemilu (DKPP), Decision in No. 119/DKPP-PKE-III/2014, 120/DKPP-PKE-III/2014, 229/DKPP-PKE-III/2014, 319/DKPP-PKE-III/2014, 5 Nov. 2014.

[19] Mahkamah Konstitusi, Decision in case No. 03-05-32/PHPU-DPR-DPRD/XII/2014 (Provinsi Papua), 27 June 2014.

viewed as supportive of independence were blocked from succeeding.[20]
They suggested that this helped explain the very low rate of incumbency
in the DPR race, in which only the two candidates from Muslim parties
were successful (Peggi Pattipi, from PKB, and Jamaluddin Jafar, from
PAN). Both are from outside the province, although Pattipi is from
neighbouring West Papua province. In contrast, while nearly everyone
interviewed lamented the passive role that police played while serving as
witnesses to obvious fraud (for example, standing in the Wamena hotel
lobby as candidates and officials traded cash for votes), none presented
solid evidence of police intervention in the results.

CONCLUSION

As it is ideally imagined by its advocates, the *noken* system is a practice
in which clan chiefs or other leaders make voting decisions on behalf of
the communities that they represent. Defenders of this system argue that
individuals cede their voting rights to community leaders in exchange
for the patronage that is their due as clan members. In turn, these
community leaders negotiate for cash payments and promises of future
investment from the candidates they agree to support. In its ideal form,
therefore, *noken* voting is a clientelistic practice fusing traditional clan
governance structures with the modern apparatus of electoral politics.

But this is only the ideal form. Across the highlands, the 2014
elections provided examples of how these brokerage agreements were
disrupted at various levels. Unregulated *noken* voting offered no clarity
on who is allowed to make representative voting decisions or at what
level they occur (village, clan, subdistrict, district). This uncertainty
provided space for figures from other institutions, notably from various
levels of the state administration, such as village chiefs or *bupati*, to
offer competing claims of representation. Ultimately, the *bupati* appear
to have been most influential, drawing not on traditional authority
but on far greater budgetary resources, including control over the
elections commission budget and future development projects. Because

---

[20] Confidential interviews, 10 June 2014; 18 June 2014.

the regulatory uncertainty over *noken* voting also meant that there was little clarity on the paper trail required to justify tallies by the elections commission at successive levels, in some areas *noken* voting simply provided a smokescreen for fraud by election officials.

One effect of this system was to create significant uncertainty around what candidates making investments in this form of patronage could expect the results to be. This was ironic, given that communal voting such as that practised through the *noken* system might be assumed to be more predictable than alternatives such as individualised vote buying. In fact, electoral outcomes in Papua were just as uncertain—and, it seems, just as costly—as in other parts of Indonesia.

Bibliography

Adelina, Shelly and Ani Soetjipto. "Kepentingan Politik Perempuan dalam Partai: Strategi Gender" [The Importance of Women's Politics in Parties: A Gender Strategy], special issue, "Perempuan Politisi", *Jurnal Perempuan* 81, 19, 2 (2014): 47–71.

Ali, Sjafri. "ICW: Politik Uang Harus Diundangkan sebagai Tindak Pidana Korupsi" [ICW: Legislation Should Treat Money Politics as Part of the Crime of Corruption], *Pikiran Rakyat*, 14 May 2014. Available at: http://www.pikiran-rakyat.com/nasional/2014/05/14/281428/icw-politik-uang-harus-diundangkan-sebagai-tindak-pidana-korupsi.

Allen, Nathan W. "Diversity, Patronage, and Parties: Parties and Party System Change in Indonesia". PhD diss., University of British Columbia, 2012.

———, "From Patronage Machine to Partisan Melee: Subnational Corruption and the Evolution of the Indonesian Party System", *Pacific Affairs* 87, 1 (2014): 221–45.

Alwi, Hasan. *Kamus Besar Bahasa Indonesia* [Dictionary of Indonesian]. Jakarta: Departemen Pendidikan Nasional Balai Pustaka, 2001.

Ambardi, Kuskridho. *Mengungkap Politik Kartel: Studi tentang Sistem Kepartaian di Indonesia Era Reformasi* [Uncovering the Politics of Cartels: A Study of Indonesia's Party System in the Reform Era]. Jakarta: Kepustakaan Populer Gramedia, 2009.

Amin, Muriyanto. "Kekuasaan dan Politik Lokal: Studi Tentang Peran Pemuda Pancasila dalam Mendukung Syamsul Arifin dan Gatot Pujo Nugroho sebagai Gubernur dan Wakil Gubernur Sumatera Utara Periode 2008–2013" [Power and Local Politics: A Study of the Role of Pancasila Youth's Support for Syamsul Arifin and Gatot Pujo Nugroho as Governor and Deputy Governor of North Sumatra, 2008–2013]. PhD diss., Universitas Indonesia, Jakarta, 2013.

Ananta, Aris, Evi Nurvidya Arifin and Leo Suryadinata. *Indonesian Electoral Behaviour: A Statistical Perspective*. Singapore: Institute of Southeast Asian Studies (ISEAS), 2004.

Anyarat Chattharakul. "Thai Electoral Campaigning: Vote-Canvassing Networks and Hybrid Voting", *Journal of Current Southeast Asian Affairs* 29, 4 (2010): 67–95.

Apriyanto, Pemi. *Database Pemilu 2004: Peta Daerah Pemilihan, Perolehan Suara dan Kursi untuk DPR RI, DPRD Propinsi, dan DPRD Kabupaten/Kota se-Indonesia* [2004 General Election Database: Maps of Electoral Districts, Votes and Seats for the DPR, Provincial DPRDs and District DPRDs Throughout Indonesia] (Jakarta: Spirit Research and Database, 2007).

Aspinall, Edward. "Elections and the Normalization of Politics in Indonesia", *South East Asia Research* 13, 2 (2005): 117–56.

———. *The Helsinki Peace Agreement: A More Promising Basis for Peace in Aceh?.* East-West Center Policy Studies No. 20, Washington, DC, 2005.

———. *Islam and Nation: Separatist Rebellion in Aceh, Indonesia*. Stanford, CA: Stanford University Press, 2009.

———. "Combatants to Contractors: The Political Economy of Peace in Aceh", *Indonesia* 87 (2009): 1–34.

———. "Democratization and Ethnic Politics in Indonesia: Nine Theses", *Journal of East Asian Studies* 11, 2 (2011): 289–319.

———. "A Nation in Fragments: Patronage and Neoliberalism in Contemporary Indonesia", *Critical Asian Studies* 45, 1 (2013): 27–54.

———. "Popular Agency and Interests in Indonesia's Democratic Transition and Consolidation", *Indonesia* 96 (2013): 101–21.

———. "Parliament and Patronage", *Journal of Democracy* 25, 4 (2014): 96–110.

———. "When Brokers Betray: Clientelism, Social Networks, and Electoral Politics in Indonesia", *Critical Asian Studies* 46, 4 (2014): 545–70.

———. "Health Care and Democratization in Indonesia", *Democratization* 21, 5 (2014): 803–23.

———. "Money Politics", *Inside Indonesia* 116, Apr.–June 2014. Available at: http://insideindonesia.org/weekly-articles/money-politics-2.

———. "Oligarchic Populism: Prabowo Subianto's Challenge to Indonesian Democracy", *Indonesia* 99 (2015): 1–28.

———. "Money Politics: Patronage and Clientelism in Southeast Asia", in *Handbook of Southeast Asian Democratization*, ed. William Case. London: Routledge, 2015, pp. 299–313.

———. "Ethnicity, Ethnic Conflict and Ethnic Politics in Kalimantan", in *Cutting and Digging: Development, Environment and the People of Kalimantan*, ed. Budy P. Resosudarmo, Ida Aju Pradnja Resosudarmo, Lydia M. Napitupulu and M. Handry Imansyah (forthcoming).

Aspinall, Edward and Marcus Mietzner, eds. *Problems of Democratisation in Indonesia: Elections, Institutions and Society*. Singapore: ISEAS, 2010.

Aspinall, Edward and Muhammad Uhaib As'ad. "The Patronage Patchwork: Village Brokerage Networks and the Power of the State in an Indonesian

Election", *Bijdragen tot de Taal-, Land- en Volkenkunde* 171, 2–3 (2015): 165–95.

Aspinall, Edward and Mada Sukmajati, eds. *Politik Uang di Indonesia: Patronase dan Klientelisme pada Pemilu Legislatif 2014* [Money Politics in Indonesia: Patronage and Clientelism in the 2014 Legislative Elections]. Yogyakarta: PolGov, Universitas Gadjah Mada (UGM), 2014.

Aspinall, Edward, Eve Warburton and Sebastian Dettman. "When Religion Trumps Ethnicity: Local Elections in Medan, Indonesia", *South East Asia Research* 19, 1 (2011): 27–58.

Aspinall, Edward and Gerry van Klinken, eds. *The State and Illegality in Indonesia.* Leiden: KITLV Press, 2011.

Azra, Azyumardi. *Paradigma Baru Pendidikan Nasional: Rekonstruksi dan Demokratisasi* [New National Education Paradigm: Reconstruction and Democracy]. Jakarta: Kompas, 2002.

––––––. "Dana Aspirasi: Anomali Politik" [Aspiration Funds: A Political Anomaly], *Kompas*, 17 June 2010.

Badan Pusat Statistik (BPS). *Peraturan Kepala Badan Pusat Statistik Indonesia Nomor 37 Tahun 2010 tentang Klasifikasi Perkotaan dan Pedesaan di Indonesia, Buku 3: Bali, Nusa Tenggara, Kalimantan, Maluku dan Papua* [Central Bureau of Statistics Regulation No. 37 2010 on the Classification of Towns and Rural Villages in Indonesia]. Jakarta: BPS, 2010.

––––––. "Jumlah dan Persentase Penduduk Miskin, Garis Kemiskinan, Indeks Kedalaman Kemiskinan (P1), Indeks Keparahan Kemiskinan (P2) Menurut Provinsi" [Total Number and Percentages of Poor People, the Poverty Line, Poverty Gap Index [P1], Poverty Severity Index [P2] by Province], 2014. Available at: http://www.bps.go.id/linkTabelStatis/view/id/1488.

Badan Pusat Statistik Aceh. *Aceh dalam Angka 2013* [Aceh in Figures 2013]. Banda Aceh: BPS Aceh, 2013.

Badan Pusat Statistik Provinsi Banten. *Banten dalam Angka 2012* [Banten in Figures 2012]. Banten: BPS Banten, 2012.

Badan Pusat Statistik Bekasi. *Bekasi dalam Angka 2012* [Bekasi in Figures 2012]. Bekasi: BPS Bekasi, 2013.

Badan Pusat Statistik Jayapura. *Jayapura dalam Angka 2013* [Jayapura in Figures 2013]. Jayapura: BPS Jayapura, 2014.

Badan Pusat Statistik Kalimantan Selatan. *Komposisi Anggota DPRD Tingkat I Kalimantan Selatan menurut Fraksi Hasil PEMILU Tahun 1997–2009* [Composition of South Kalimantan Provincial DPRD based on Party Representation following General Elections, 1997–2009]. Available at: http://kalsel.bps.go.id/?set=viewDataDetail2&flag_template2=1&id_sektor=37&id=733.

Badan Pusat Statistik Kabupaten Madiun. *Kabupaten Madiun dalam Angka 2011* [Madiun District in Figures 2011]. Madiun: BPS, 2012.

———. *Kabupaten Madiun dalam Angka 2014* [Madiun District in Figures 2014]. Madiun: BPS, 2015.

Badan Pusat Statistik Nusa Tenggara Timur (NTT). *Nusa Tenggara Timur dalam Angka 2013* [NTT in Figures 2013]. Kupang: BPS NTT, 2013.

Badan Pusat Statistik Palembang. *Palembang dalam Angka* 2012 [Palembang in Figures]. Palembang: BPS Palembang, 2013.

Badan Pusat Statistik Sulawesi Tenggara. "Production and Production Value of Nickel Mining, 2001–2013", in *Sulawesi Tenggara dalam Angka 2014*. Kendari: BPS Sulawesi Tenggara, 2015. Available at: http://sultra.bps.go.id/images/pub/06perindustrian_2014.pdf.

"Bagi-bagi Duit Saat Kampanye, *Bupati* Asal Partai Demokrat Ini Terancam Bui 1 Tahun" [This Demokrat Bupati Threatened with One Year's Jail for Handing Out Cash during a Campaign], *Kompas*, 16 July 2014. Available at: http://regional.kompas.com/read/2014/04/16/0916378/Bagi-bagi.Duit.Saat.Kampanye.Bupati.Asal.Partai.Demokrat.Ini.Terancam.Bui.1.Tahun.

Barter, Shane J. "The Free Aceh Elections? The 2009 Legislative Contests in Aceh", *Indonesia* 91 (2011): 113–30.

Baswedan, Anies Rasyid. "Political Islam in Indonesia: Present and Future Trajectory", *Asian Survey* 44, 5 (2004): 669–90.

Bessell, Sharon. "Increasing the Proportion of Women in the National Parliament: Opportunities, Barriers and Challenges", in *Problems of Democratisation in Indonesia*, ed. Aspinall and Mietzner, pp. 219–42.

Björkman, Lisa. "'You Can't Buy a Vote': Meanings of Money in a Mumbai Election", *American Ethnologist* 41, 4 (2014): 617–34.

Bowen, John R. *Sumatran Politics and Poetics: Gayo History, 1900–1989*. New Haven, CT: Yale University Press, 1991.

———. *Muslims through Discourse: Religion and Ritual in Gayo Society*. Princeton, NJ: Princeton University Press, 1993.

Buehler, Michael. "The Rising Importance of Personal Networks in Indonesian Local Politics: An Analysis of the District Government Head Elections in South Sulawesi in 2005", in *Deepening Democracy in Indonesia*, ed. Erb and Sulistiyanto, pp. 267–85.

———. "Revisiting the Inclusion–Moderation Thesis in the Context of Decentralized Institutions: The Behavior of Indonesia's Prosperous Justice Party in National and Local Politics", *Party Politics* 19, 2 (2012): 210–29.

———. "Married with Children", *Inside Indonesia* 112, Apr.–June 2013. Available at: http://www.insideindonesia.org/feature-editions/married-with-children.

Burgess, Robin, Matthew Hansen, Benjamin A. Olken, Peter Potapov and Stefanie Sieber. "The Political Economy of Deforestation in the Tropics", *Quarterly Journal of Economics* 127, 4 (2012): 1707–54.

Callahan, William A. and Duncan McCargo. "Vote-Buying in Thailand's Northeast: The July 1995 General Elections", *Asian Survey* 36, 4 (1996): 376–92.

Caraway, Teri and Michele Ford. "Labor and Politics under Oligarchy", in *Beyond Oligarchy: Wealth, Power, and Contemporary Indonesian Politics*, ed. Michele Ford and Thomas Pepinsky. Ithaca: Southeast Asia Program, Cornell University, 2014, pp. 139–56.

"Carving Up Papua: More Districts, More Trouble", Institute for Policy Analysis of Conflict (IPAC), 9 Oct. 2013. Available at: http://www.understandingconflict. org/conflict/read/8/Carving-Up-Papua-More-Districts-More-Problems.

Chandra, Kanchan. *Why Ethnic Parties Succeed: Patronage and Ethnic Head Counts in India*. Cambridge: Cambridge University Press, 2004.

Chauvel, Richard. "Electoral Politics and Democratic Freedoms in Papua", in *Problems of Democratisation in Indonesia*, ed. Aspinall and Mietzner, pp. 307–29.

Choi, Nankyung. "Local Elections and Party Politics in Post-Reformasi Indonesia: A View from Yogyakarta", *Contemporary Southeast Asia* 26, 2 (2004): 280–301.

———. "Democracy and Patrimonial Politics in Local Indonesia", *Indonesia* 88 (2009): 131–64.

———. *Local Politics in Indonesia: Pathways to Power*. London: Routledge, 2011.

Clark, Samuel and Blair Palmer. Peaceful Pilkada, Dubious Democracy: Aceh's Post-Conflict Elections and their Implications. Indonesian Social Development Paper no. 11, World Bank, Jakarta, 2008.

Collins, Elizabeth Fuller. *Indonesia Betrayed: How Development Fails*. Honolulu: University of Hawai'i Press, 2007.

Cox, Gary W. *The Efficient Secret: The Cabinet and the Development of Political Parties in Victorian England*. New York: Cambridge University Press, 1987.

"Dana Aspirasi DPRA Bertambah" [DPRA Aspiration Funds Increased], *Serambi Indonesia*, 17 Jan. 2015. Available at: http://aceh.tribunnews.com/2015/01/17/ dana-aspirasi-dpra-bertambah.

Danadibrata, R. *Kamus Basa Sunda* [Dictionary of Sundanese]. Bandung: P.T. Kiblat Buku Utama, 1984.

"Demokrasi Tak Hapus Nepotisme: Jabatan Dibagikan pada Kerabat" [Democracy Does Not Eradicate Nepotism: Positions Given to Relatives], *Kompas*, 14 Apr. 2014. Available at: http://print.kompas.com/baca/KOMPAS_ ART00000000000000000006062426.

Dewi, Sita W. "RI Tycoons Lend City a Hand", *Jakarta Post*, 27 Feb. 2013. Available at: http://www.thejakartapost.com/news/2013/02/27/ri-tycoons-lend- city-a-hand.html.

Ehrentraut, Stefan. "Dividing Aceh? Minorities, Partition Movements and State-Reform in Aceh Province". ARI Working Paper Series 137, Asia Research Institute, National University of Singapore, 2010.

Erb, Maribeth and Priyambudi Sulistiyanto, eds. *Deepening Democracy in Indonesia?: Direct Elections for Local Leaders (Pilkada)*. Singapore: ISEAS, 2009.

Erman, Erwiza. "Deregulation of Tin and the Making of Local Shadow State: Case Study of Bangka", in *Renegotiating Boundaries*, ed. Schulte Nordholt and van Klinken, pp. 171–202.

Evans, Kevin. *Sejarah Pemilu dan Partai Politik di Indonesia* [History of Elections and Political Parties in Indonesia]. Jakarta: Arise Consultancies, 2003.

Fauzan, Achmad Uzair. "Winning the Villages", *Inside Indonesia* 97 (July–Sept. 2009). Available at: http://www.insideindonesia.org/feature-editions/winning-the-villages.

Fealy, Greg. "Indonesia's Islamic Parties in Decline", *Inside Story*, 11 May 2009. Available at: http://inside.org.au/indonesia%E2%80%99s-islamic-parties-in-decline.

Feith, Herbert. *The Indonesian Elections of 1955*. Interim Report Series. Ithaca, NY: Modern Indonesian Project, Cornell University, 1957.

Fionna, Ulla. "Vote-buying in Indonesia's 2014 Elections: The Other Side of the Coin", *ISEAS Perspective* no. 35, 2014. Available at: http://www.iseas.edu.sg/documents/publication/ISEAS_Perspective_2014_35-Vote-buying_in_Indonesia%27s_2014_Elections.pdf.

Ford, Michele. "Learning by Doing: Trade Unions and Electoral Politics in Batam, 2004–2009", *South East Asia Research* 22, 3 (2014): 341–57.

Ford, Michele and T. Pepinsky. *Beyond Oligarchy: Wealth, Power, and Contemporary Indonesian Politics*. Ithaca, NY: Southeast Asia Program, Cornell University, 2014.

Ford, Michelle, Teri L. Caraway and T. Nugroho. "Translating Membership into Power at the Ballot Box? Trade Union Candidates and Worker Voting Patterns in Indonesia's National Election", *Democratization* 22, 7 (2015): 1296–1316. doi: 10.1080/13510347.2014.930130.

Fukuyama, Francis. *Trust: The Social Virtues and the Creation of Prosperity*. New York: Free Press, 1995.

Gambetta, Diego. "Can We Trust Trust?", in *Trust: Making and Breaking Cooperative Relations*, ed. Diego Gambetta. Oxford: Basil Blackwell, 1988, pp. 213–38.

Geertz, Clifford. *The Religion of Java*. New York: Free Press, 1960.

Good, Byron J., Mary-Jo DelVecchio Good, Jesse Grayman and Matthew Lakoma. *Psychosocial Needs Assessment of Communities Affected by the Conflict in the Districts of Pidie, Bireuen and Aceh Utara*. Jakarta: Ministry of Health, 2006.

Guillot, Claude. *Banten: Sejarah dan Peradaban Abad X–XVII* [Banten: History and Civilisation from the 10th to 17th Centuries]. Jakarta: Kepustakaan Populer Gramedia, 2008.

Hadiz, Vedi R. "Power and Politics in North Sumatra: The Uncompleted *Reformasi*", in *Local Power and Politics in Indonesia: Democratisation and Decentralisation*, ed. Edward Aspinall and Greg Fealy. Singapore: ISEAS, 2003, pp. 119–31.

———. *Dinamika Kekuasaan: Ekonomi Politik Indonesia Pasca Orde Baru* [The Dynamics of Power: The Post-New Order Indonesian Political Economy]. Jakarta: LP3ES, 2005.

———. *Localising Power in Post-Authoritarian Indonesia: A Southeast Asia Perspective*. Stanford, CA: Stanford University Press, 2010.

Hamid, Abdul. "Jokowi's Populism in the 2012 Jakarta Gubernatorial Election", *Journal of Current Southeast Asian Affairs* 33, 1 (2014): 85–109.

Harvey, Barbara S. *Permesta: Half a Rebellion*. Ithaca, NY: Cornell Modern Indonesia Project Monograph Series 57, 1977.

Heidhues, Mary F. Somers. "Company Island: A Note on the History of Belitung", *Indonesia* 51 (1991): 1–20.

Helmke, Gretchen and Steven Levitsky, eds. *Informal Institutions and Democracy: Lessons from Latin America*. Baltimore, MD: Johns Hopkins University Press, 2006.

Henley, David. *Nationalism and Regionalism in a Colonial Context: Minahasa in the Dutch East Indies*. Leiden: KITLV Press, 1996.

———. *Jealousy and Justice: The Indigenous Roots of Colonial Rule in Northern Sulawesi*. Amsterdam: VU University Press/CASA-Asia, 2002.

Henley, David, Maria J.C. Schouten. Alex J. Ulaen. "Preserving the Peace in Post-New Order Minahasa", in *Renegotiating Boundaries*, ed. Schulte Nordholt and van Klinken, pp. 307–26.

Hicken, Allen D. "How Do Rules and Institutions Encourage Vote Buying?", in *Elections for Sale: The Causes and Consequences of Vote Buying*, ed. Frederic C. Schaffer. Boulder, CO: Lynne Reinner, 2008, pp. 47–60.

———. "Clientelism", *Annual Review of Political Science* 14, 1 (2011): 289–310.

Hidayat, Syarif. "Shadow State? Business and politics in the province of Banten", in *Renegotiating Boundaries*, ed. Schulte Nordholt and van Klinken, pp. 203–24.

———. "*Pilkada*, Money Politics and the Dangers of 'Informal Governance' Practices", in *Deepening Democracy in Indonesia*, ed. Erb and Sulistiyanto. Singapore, pp. 125–46.

Hill, David T. "Media and Politics in Regional Indonesia: The Case of Manado", in *Political Regimes and Media in Asia*, ed. Krishna Sen and Terence Lee. London and New York: Routledge, 2008, pp. 188–207.

Hoban, Kirsty. "Workers Go Politics!", *Inside Indonesia*, 116, Apr.–Jun 2014. Available at: http://www.inside.indonesia.org/current-edition/workers-go-politics.

Hopkin, Jonathan. "Conceptualizing Political Clientelism: Political Exchange and Democratic Theory". Paper presented at the American Political Science Association Annual Meeting, Philadelphia, 31 Aug.–3 Sept. 2006.

Hutchcroft Paul. "Linking Capital and Countryside: Patronage and Clientelism in Japan, Thailand and the Philippines", in *Clientelism, Social Policy and the Quality of Democracy*, ed. Diego Abente Brun and Larry Diamond. Baltimore, MD: Johns Hopkins University Press, 2014, pp. 174–203.

Ibrahim. "Bisnis, Kekuasaan, dan Identitas: Studi terhadap Politik Identitas Etnis Tionghoa di Bangka Belitung Pasca Orde Baru" [Business, Power and Identity: A Study of the Post-New Order Identity Politics of the Chinese in Bangka Belitung]. PhD diss., Gadjah Mada University, Yogyakarta, 2014.

Ibrahim et al. "Pakaian Adat, Rumah Adat, dan Upacara Adat Melayu di Provinsi Kepulauan Bangka Belitung" [Traditional Dress, Traditional Houses and Malay Traditional Ceremonies in Bangka Belitung Province]. Report of joint research project with Disbudpar Bangka Belitung Province, unpublished (2013).

Ihromi, T.O. *Sosiologi Keluarga* [The Sociology of Families]. Jakarta: Yayasan Obor Indonesia, 2008.

International Crisis Group (ICG). "Indonesia: How GAM won in Aceh". Asia Briefing 61, Jakarta/Brussels: ICG, 2007.

———. "Indonesia: Averting Election Violence in Aceh". Asia Program Briefing 135, Jakarta/Brussels: ICG, 2012.

"Jimly: Politik Uang Terjadi Masif, Pemilu 2014 Bisa Lebih Buruk" [Jimly: Money Politics Massive, 2014 Election Might Be Worst Yet], *Detiknews*, 17 Apr. 2014. Available at: http://news.detik.com/berita/2558272/jimly-politik-uang-terjadi-masif-pemilu-2014-bisa-lebih-buruk.

Joewono, Benny N. "Perebutan Ruang Hidup di Lahan Sawit" [Struggle for Living Space in Oil Palm Areas], *Kompas*, 17 June 2011. Available at: http://regional.kompas.com/read/2011/07/17/18415991/Perebutan.Ruang.Hidup.di.Lahan. Sawit.

"Kapitalistik, Kanibal, dan Korupsi Hiasi Pemilu 2014" [Capitalism, Cannibalism, and Corruption Decorate the 2014 Election], *Waspada*, 7 May 2014.

Kawanaka, Takeshi. "Who Eats the Most? Qualitative Analysis of Pork Barrel Distribution in the Philippines". Institute of Developing Economies (IDE) Discussion Paper 26, IDE-JETRO, Tokyo, 2007.

King, Dwight Y. *Half-hearted Reform: Electoral Institutions and the Struggle for Democracy in Indonesia*. Westport, CT: Praeger, 2003.

Kitschelt, Herbert. "Linkages between Citizens and Politicians in Democratic Politics", *Comparative Political Studies* 33, 6–7 (2000): 845–79.

Kitschelt, Herbert and Steven I. Wilkinson, eds. *Patrons, Clients, and Policies: Patterns of Democratic Accountability and Political Competition*. Cambridge: Cambridge University Press, 2007.

Komisi Pemilihan Umum Kalsel [South Kalimantan General Elections Commission]. *Buku Saku Pemilu Kalimantan Selatan* [South Kalimantan General Election Pocketbook]. Banjarmasin: Sekretariat KPU Kalsel, 2011.

————. *Hasil Pemilu Legislatif Tahun 2014 di Kalimantan Selatan* [Results of 2014 General Legislative Election in South Kalimantan]. Banjarmasin: KPU Kalsel, 2014.

"Konflik Lahan Bahaya terpendam di Muba" [Dangerous Land Conflict Hidden in Muba], *Palembang Today*, 1 Feb. 2012. Available at: http://palday.wordpress.com/2012/02/01/konflik-lahan-bahaya-terpendam-di-muba/.

"KontraS: Ratusan Anggota DPR Miliki Rekam Jejak Buruk" [KontraS: Hundreds of DPR Members Have a Bad Record], *Detiknews*, 14 Oct. 2014. Available at: http://news.detik.com/berita/2718402/kontras-ratusan-anggota-dpr-miliki-rekam-jejak-buruk.

Lauth, Hans-Joachim. "The Impact of Informal Institutions on Democratic Performance: Theoretical Reflections and Empirical Findings". Paper presented at the American Political Science Association Annual Meeting, 1–4 Sept. 2005. Available at: http://www.allacademic.com//meta/p_mla_apa_research_citation/0/4/2/5/7/pages42574/p42574-1.php.

Lehoucq, Fabrice. "When Does a Market for Votes Emerge?", in *Elections for Sale*, ed. Schaffer, pp. 33–45.

Luhmann, Niklas, "Familiarity, Confidence, Trust: Problems and Alternatives", in *Trust: Making and Breaking Cooperative Relations*, ed. Diego Gambetta. Cambridge, MA: Basil Blackwell, 1988, pp. 94–107.

McCarthy, John F., "Sold Down the River: Renegotiating Public Power over Nature in Central Kalimantan", in *Renegotiating Boundaries*, ed. Schulte Nordholt and van Klinken, pp. 151–76.

————. "The Limits of Legality: Governance, Extra-legality and Resource Control in Indonesia", in *The State and Illegality in Indonesia*, ed. Edward Aspinall and Gerry van Klinken. Leiden: KITLV Press, 2011, pp. 89–106.

Machmudi, Yon. *Islamising Indonesia: The Rise of Jemaah Tarbiyah and the Prosperous Justice Party (PKS)*. Canberra: ANU ePress, 2008.

Mahsun, Muhammad. "Local Predatory Elite? Potret Relasi Politisi–Pengusaha dengan Penguasa" [A Local Predatory Elite? A Portrait of Relations between Politician-Entrepreneurs and Power-holders]. MA thesis, Gadjah Mada University, Yogyakarta, 2013.

Manewus, David. "Mayulu Ingin PNS Ada di Tempat Tepat" [Mayulu Wants Public Servants to Be in The right Place], *Tribun Manado*, 20 Mar. 2014. Available at:

http://manado.tribunnews.com/2014/03/20/mayulu-ingin-pns-ada-di-tempat-tepat.

Mariana, Anna and Milah Nurmilah. *Inilah Pesan Penting di Balik Berkah dan Manfaat Silaturahmi* [This is the Important Message Behind the Blessing and the Benefit of Friendship]. Jakarta: Ruang Kata, 2013.

Mietzner, Marcus. "Party Financing in Post-Soeharto Indonesia: Between State Subsidies and Political Corruption", *Contemporary Southeast Asia* 29, 2 (2007): 238–63.

———. "Indonesia and the Pitfalls of Low Quality Democracy: A Case Study of the Gubernatorial Elections in North Sulawesi", in *Democratization in Post-Suharto Indonesia*, ed. Marco Bunte and Andreas Ufen. London: Routledge, 2009, pp. 124–49.

———. "Ideology, Money and Dynastic Leadership: The Indonesian Democratic Party of Struggle, 1998–2012", *South East Asia Research* 20, 4 (2012): 511–31.

———. *Money, Power, and Ideology: Political Parties in Post-Authoritarian Indonesia.* Honolulu: University of Hawai'i Press; Singapore: NUS Press; Copenhagen: NIAS Press, 2013.

———. "How Jokowi Won and Democracy Survived", *Journal of Democracy* 25, 4 (2014): 111–26.

Milligan, Kevin and Michael Smart. "Regional Grants as Pork Barrel Politics". CESifo Working Paper 1453, CESifo Group, Munich, 2005.

Muhyiddin, Muhammad. "Nurul Arifin Menyesal Tak Sebar Duit Saat Pemilu" [Nurul Arifin Regrets Not Distributing Cash during the Election], *Tempo*, 8 Nov. 2014. Available at: http://nasional.tempo.co/read/news/2014/11/08/078620560/nurul-arifin-menyesal-tak-sebar-duit-saat-pemilu.

Mujani, Saiful, R. William Liddle and Kuskridho Ambardi. *Kuasa Rakyat: Analisis Tentang Perilaku Memilih dalam Pemilihan Legislatif dan Presiden Indonesia pasca-Orde Baru* [People Power: An Analysis of Voting Behaviour in Post-New Order Indonesia's Legislative and Presidential Elections]. Jakarta: Mizan, 2012.

Murodi. "Tutty Alawiyah: Pengembang Masyarakat Lewat Majlis Taklim" [Tutty Alawiyah: Developing the Community through *Majelis Taklim*], in *Ulama Perempuan Indonesia* [Female Islamic Scholars of Indonesia], ed. Jajat Burhanuddin. Jakarta: Gramedia and PPIM IAIN Jakarta, 2002, pp. 205–15.

Najib, Mohammad. "Keterlibatan Penyelenggara Pemilu dalam *Vote Trading*" [The Involvement of Election Organisers in Vote Trading], in *Politik Uang di Indonesia*, ed. Aspinall and Sukmajati, pp. 511–36.

Nichter, Simeon. "Vote Buying or Turnout Buying? Machine Politics and the Secret Ballot", *American Political Science Review* 102, 1 (2008): 19–31.

Noda, Kohei. "Politicization of Philippine Budget System: Institutional and Economic Analysis on 'Pork Barrel'". Policy Research Institute Discussion Paper 11A–04, Ministry of Finance, Tokyo, 2011.

North, Douglass C. *Institutions, Institutional Change and Economic Performance.* Cambridge: Cambridge University Press, 1990.

"Otsus Plus: The Debate over Enhanced Special Autonomy for Papua", Institute for Policy Analysis of Conflict (IPAC), 25 Nov. 2013. Available at: http://www.understandingconflict.org/conflict/read/20/Otsus-Plus-The-Debate-over-Enhanced-Special-Autonomy-for-Papua.

"Open to Manipulation: The 2014 Elections in Papua Province", Institute for Policy Analysis of Conflict (IPAC), 10 Dec. 2014. Available at: http://www.understandingconflict.org/conflict/read/32/Open-to-Manipulation-The-2014-Elections-in-Papua.

Palmer, Blair. "Services Rendered: Peace, Patronage and Post-Conflict Elections in Aceh", in *Problems of Democratisation in Indonesia*, ed. Aspinall and Mietzner, pp. 206–306.

Priyono, A.E., Willy Purna Samadhi and Olle Törnquist. *Menjadikan Demokrasi Bermakna: Masalah dan Pilihan di Indonesia* [Developing a Meaningful Democracy: Issues and Options in Indonesia]. Jakarta: Demos, 2005.

Putra, Heddy Shri Ahimsa. *Patron dan Klien di Sulawesi Selatan: Sebuah Kajian Fungsional-Struktural* [Patrons and Clients in South Sulawesi: A Structural-Functional Analysis]. Yogyakarta: Kepel Press, 2007, pp. 15–17.

Rahayu, Eka. *Bentuk Komunikasi Badan Kontak Majelis Taklim (BKMT) Kecamatan Pamulang dalam Mengkoordinir Majelis Taklim* [Forms of Communication in BKMT Pamulang District for Coordinating the Majelis Taklim]. Jakarta: Universitas Islam Negeri Jakarta, 2006.

Reid, Anthony. "Chinese on the Mining Frontier in Southeast Asia", in *Chinese Circulations, Capital, Commodities, and Networks in Southeast Asia*, ed. Eric Tagliacozzo and Wen-Chin Chang. Durham, NC: Duke University Press, 2011, pp. 21–36.

Rein, Knik Kusuma. "La Ode Ota: Populer di Darat dan Laut" [La Ode Ote: Popular on the Land and the Sea], *Tempo*, 30 Mar. 2014. Available at: http://majalah.tempo.co/konten/2014/03/24/LK/144971/Populer-di-Darat-dan-Laut/04/43.

Resosudarmo, Budy P., ed. *The Politics and Economics of Indonesia's Natural Resources*. Singapore: ISEAS, 2005.

Resosudarmo, Budy P. and A.A. Yusuf. "Survey of Recent Developments", *Bulletin of Indonesian Economic Studies* 45, 3 (2009): 287–316.

Robison, Richard, and Vedi R. Hadiz. *Reorganising Power in Indonesia: The Politics of Oligarchy in an Age of Markets*. London: RoutledgeCurzon, 2004.

————. "The Political Economy of Oligarchy and the Reorganisation of Power in Indonesia", *Indonesia* 96 (2013): 35–57.

Sakai, Minako, "Resisting the Mainland: The Formation of the Province of the Bangka-Belitung (Babel)", in *Autonomy and Disintegration in Indonesia*, ed. Damien Kingsbury and Harry Aveling. London: RoutledgeCurzon, 2003, pp. 189–200.

Samirin, W. "Blusukan", *Kompas Online*, 12 Jan. 2013. Available at: http://nasional. kompas.com/read/2013/01/12/11232457.

Santoso, Purwo. "Merajut Kohesi Nasional: Etno Nasionalisme dan Otonomi Daerah dalam Proses Demokratisasi" [Knitting National Cohesion: Ethnonationalism and Regional Autonomy under Democratisation], *Jurnal Ilmu Sosial dan Ilmu Politik* 4, 3 (2001): 265–88.

Schaffer, Frederic C. "Why Study Vote Buying", in *Elections for Sale: The Causes and Consequences of Vote Buying*, ed. Frederic C. Schaffer. Boulder, CO: Lynne Reinner; Quezon City: Ateneo de Manila University Press, 2007, pp. 1–16.

Schaffer, Frederic C. and Andreas Schedler. "What is Vote Buying?", in *Elections for Sale*, ed. Schaffer, pp. 17–30.

Schouten, Maria J.C. *Leadership and Social Mobility in a Southeast Asian Society: Minahasa, 1677–1983*. Leiden: KITLV Press, 1998.

Schulte Nordholt, Henk and Gerry van Klinken, eds. *Renegotiating Boundaries: Local Politics in Post-Suharto Indonesia*. Leiden: KITLV Press, 2007.

Scott, James C. "Patron–Client Politics and Political Change in Southeast Asia", *American Political Science Review* 66, 1 (1972): 91–113.

"Sebagian Ketua PAC PDI-P Pati Diapelkan" [Several PDI-P Sub-branch Chairs Required to Parade], *Suara Merdeka*, 29 Apr. 2004. Available at: http://www. suaramerdeka.com/harian/0404/29/mur3.htm.

Sebastian, Leonard, ed. "Special Focus: Political Parties and Democracy in Indonesia", *South East Asia Research* 20, 4 (2012): 463–568.

Septian, Anton, et al. "Putar-putar Duit Nikel" [Circulating Nickel Money], *Majalah Tempo*, 8 Sept. 2014. Available at: http://majalah.tempo.co/konten/2014/09/08/ NAS/146237/Putarputar-Duit-Nikel/28/43.

Shefter, Martin. *Political Parties and the State: The American Historical Experience*. Princeton, NJ: Princeton University Press, 1994.

Sherlock, Stephen. "The Parliament in Indonesia's Decade of Democracy: People's Forum or Chamber of Cronies?", in *Problems of Democratisation in Indonesia*, ed. Aspinall and Mietzner, pp. 160–78.

Slater, Dan. "Indonesia's Accountability Trap: Party Cartels and Presidential Power after Democratic Transition", *Indonesia* 78 (2004): 61–92.

————. "Unbuilding Blocs: Indonesia's Accountability Deficit in Historical Perspective", *Critical Asian Studies* 46, 2 (2014): 287–315.

Stokes, Susan C. "Is Vote Buying Undemocratic?", in *Elections for Sale*, ed. Schaffer, pp. 81–99.

————. "Pork, by Any Other Name ... Building a Conceptual Scheme of Distributive Politics". Paper presented at the American Political Science Association Annual Meeting, Toronto, 3–6 Sept. 2009, p. 10. Available at: http://ssrn.com/abstract=1449057.

Stokes, Susan C., Thad Dunning, Marcelo Nazareno and Valeria Brusco. *Brokers, Voters, and Clientelism: The Puzzle of Distributive Politics*. New York: Cambridge University Press, 2013.

Sumarto, Mulyadi. *Perlindungan Sosial dan Klientelisme: Makna Politik Bantuan Sosial dalam Pemilihan Umum* [Social Protection and Clientelism: The Meaning and Politics of Social Assistance during General Elections]. Yogyakarta: UGM Press, 2014.

Sunarto, Ahmad. *Kamus al-Fikr* [Dictionary of Fikih]. Surabaya: Halimjay, 2002.

Suryakusuma, Julia. *Agama, Seks, dan Kekuasaan* [Religion, Sex, and Power]. Depok: Komunitas Bambu, 2012.

Tadjoeddin, Mohammad Zulfan. *Explaining Collective Violence in Contemporary Indonesia: From Conflict to Cooperation*. Houndmills: Palgrave Macmillan, 2014.

Taqwa, M. Ridhah. Pola Segregasi Ekologis: Kelompok Etnis-Suku Vs Kelas Sosial di Kota Palembang [Ecological Segregation: Ethnic Group vs Social Class in Palembang City], 2014. Available at: http://sosiologi.fisip.unsri.ac.id/userfiles/Segergasi%20Ekologis%20Komunitas%20Kota%20Plbg.pdf.

Tans, Ryan. *Mobilizing Resources, Building Coalitions: Local Power in Indonesia*. East-West Center Policy Studies No. 64, Honolulu, 2012.

Tanuwidjaja, Sunny. "Political Islam and Islamic Parties in Indonesia: Critically Assessing the Evidence of Islam's Political Decline", *Contemporary Southeast Asia* 32, 1 (2010): 29–49.

Thufail, Fadjar I. "Ketika Perdamaian Terwujud di Bukit Kasih: Pencegahan Konflik, Lembaga Gereja dan Politik Adat di Minahasa" [When Peace Came to Love Hill: Conflict Prevention, the Church and *Adat* Politics in Minahasa], in *Kegalauan Identitas: Agama Etnisitas dan Kewarganegaraan Pada Masa Pasca Orde-Baru*, ed. Martin Ramstedt and Fadjar Ibnu Thufail. Jakarta: PSDR-LIPI, Max Plank Institute for Social Anthropology and Grasindo, 2011, pp. 149–66.

Tilly, Charles. *Trust and Rule*. New York: Cambridge University Press, 2005.

Tim Nasional Percepatan Penanggulangan Kemiskinan (TNP2K). "Indikator Kesejahteraan Daerah Provinsi Papua" [Prosperity Indicator Papua Province], Nov. 2011. Available at: http://data.tnp2k.go.id/file_data/Data/IKD/94_Papua.pdf.

Tomsa, Dirk. *Party Politics and Democratization in Indonesia: Golkar in the Post-Suharto Era*. London and New York: Routledge, 2008.

————, "Party System Fragmentation in Indonesia: The Subnational Dimension", *Journal of East Asian Studies*: 14, 2 (2014): 249–78.

Törnquist, Olle. "Dynamics of Indonesian Democratization", *Third World Quarterly* 21, 3 (2000): 383–423.

Törnquist, Olle et al. "Power, Welfare, and Democracy". Draft report, Universities of Oslo/Gadjah Mada, 2013.

Ufen, Andreas. "Political Parties in Post-Suharto Indonesia: Between Politik Aliran and 'Philippinisation'". GIGA Working Paper No. 37, GIGA Institute of Asian Studies, Hamburg, 2006.

————. "From *Aliran* to Dealignment: Political Parties in Post-Suharto Indonesia", *South East Asia Research* 16, 1 (2008): 5–41.

Ulaen, Alex J. *Pemekaran Wilayah: Haruskah ke Akar Etnis?* [Should Regional Development be Ethnically Based?]. Manado: MarIn-CRC, 2010.

United Nations Development Program (UNDP) Indonesia. *Partisipasi Perempuan dalam Politik dan Pemerintahan* [Women's Participation in Politics and Government]. Jakarta: UNDP, 2010.

van Klinken, Gerry. "The Limits of Ethnic Clientelism in Indonesia", *Review of Indonesian and Malaysian Affairs* 42, 2 (2008): 35–65.

van Zyl, Albert. "What is Wrong with Constituency Development Funds?". International Budget Partnership, Budget Brief 10, 2010. Available at: http://www.internationalbudget.org/publications/brief10/.

Wang Chin-Sou and Charles Kurzman, "The Logistics: How to Buy Votes", in *Elections for Sale*, ed. Schaffer, pp. 61–78.

Wasno. *Misteri Bulan Suro: Studi tentang Konflik antara Perguruan Silat PSH Terate dengan PSH Tunas Muda Winongo di Madiun* [The Mystery of the Month of Suro: A Study of the Conflict between the SH Terate and SH Winongo Silat Schools in Madiun]. Malang: PPS Universitas Muhammadiyah Malang, 2004.

"Walau Hitung Cepatnya Sama dengan KPU, Persepi Tak Jamin JSI dan Puskaptis Kredibel" [Although Their Quick Counts are the Same as the KPU, Persepi Does Not Guarantee that JSI and Puskaptis are Credible], *Kompas*, 16 July 2014. Available at: http://nasional.kompas.com/read/2014/07/16/17202661/Walau.Hitung.Cepatnya.Sama.dengan.KPU.Persepi.Tak.Jamin.JSI.dan.Puskaptis.Kredibel.

Weiss, Meredith, ed. *Electoral Dynamics in Malaysia: Findings from the Grassroots*. Singapore: ISEAS, 2013.

Wendyatarka, A. "Dua Kultur di Tiga Kawasan" [Two Cultures in Three Districts], *Kompas*, 20 Feb. 2009. Available at: http://nasional.kompas.com/read/2009/02/20/08483467/dua.kultur.di.tiga.kawasan.

Widoyoko, Danang. "Deforestation, Rent Seeking and Local Elections in West Kalimantan", *Inside Indonesia*, 117, July–Sept. 2014. Available at: http://www.

insideindonesia.org/deforestation-rent-seeking-and-local-elections-in-west-kalimantan.

Wilson, Ian. *The Politics of Protection Rackets in Post-New Order Indonesia: Coercive Capital, Authority and Street Politics*. London: Routledge, 2015.

Winters, Jeffrey. *Oligarchy*. Cambridge: Cambridge University Press, 2011.

———, "Oligarchy and Democracy in Indonesia", *Indonesia* 96 (2013): 11–33.

Laws and Decisions Cited

Dewan Kehormatan Penyelenggara Pemilu (DKPP) [General Election Honour Council]. Decision in No. 119/DKPP-PKE-III/2014, 120/DKPP-PKE-III/2014, 229/DKPP-PKE-III/2014, 319/DKPP-PKE-III/2014, 5 Nov. 2014.

Mahkamah Konstitusi [Constitutional Court]. Decision in case No. 14/PHPU.D-XI/2013, 11 Mar. 2013, pp. 165–9.

———. Decision in case No. 01-01-32/PHPU-DPR-DPRD/XII/2014 (Provinsi Papua), 27 June 2014.

———. Decision in case No. 06-32/PHPU-DPD/XII/2014 (Provinsi Papua), 25 June 2014.

———. Decision in case No. 03-05-32/PHPU-DPR-DPRD/XII/2014 (Provinsi Papua), 27 June 2014.

Undang-Undang Republik Indonesia Nomor 8 Tahun 2012 Tentang Pemilihan Umum Anggota Dewan Perwakilan Rakyat, Dewan Perwakilan Daerah, Dan Dewan Perwakilan Rakyat Daerah. [Law No. 8 of 2012 on General Elections of Members of the People's Representative Council, Regional Representative Council, and Regional People's Representative Councils].

Peraturan Komisi Pemilihan Umum Nomor 15 Tahun 2013 Tentang Perubahaan Atas Peraturan Komisi Pemilihan Umum Nomor 01 Tahun 2013 Tentang Pedoman Pelaksanaan Kampanye Pemilihan Umum Anggota Dewan Perwakilan Rakyat, Dewan Perwakilan Daerah dan Dewan Perwakilan Rakyat Daerah. [General Elections Commission Regulation No. 15 of 2013 on Amendments to General Election Commission No. 1 of 2013 on Guidelines for the Implementation of Campaigns for the General Elections of Members of the People's Representative Council, Regional Representative Council and Regional People's Representative Councils].

Undang-Undang Republik Indonesia Nomor 11 Tahun 2006 Tentang Pemerintahan Aceh [Law No. 11 of 2006 on the Government of Aceh].

Contributors

Ahmad Muhajir is a PhD candidate at the Coral Bell School of Asia Pacific Affairs, The Australian National University, Canberra, and lecturer in the Faculty of Islamic Law, Antasari State Islamic Institute, Banjarmasin.

Ahmad Taufan Damanik is a lecturer in the Department of Political Science, University of North Sumatra, Medan.

Ahmad Zainul Hamdi is a lecturer in the Faculty of Islamic Studies and Philosophy, Sunan Ampel State Islamic University, Surabaya.

Alamsyah is a lecturer in the Department of Public Administration, Sriwijaya University, Palembang.

Amalinda Savirani is a lecturer in the Department of Government and Political Science, Gadjah Mada University, Yogyakarta.

Argoposo Cahyo Nugroho is a graduate of the Masters programme in Anthropology at Gadjah Mada University and an analyst with the Indonesian Ministry of Research, Technology, and Higher Education.

Caroline Paskarina is a lecturer in the Political Science Study Program at Padjadjaran University, Bandung.

Cillian Nolan is a researcher with the Institute for the Policy Analysis of Conflict, Jakarta.

Edward Aspinall is a researcher at the Coral Bell School of Asia Pacific Affairs, The Australian National University, Canberra.

Eve Warburton is a PhD candidate at the Coral Bell School of Asia Pacific Affairs, The Australian National University, Canberra.

Gandung Ismanto is a lecturer in the Faculty of Social and Political Sciences, Sultan Ageng Tirtayasa University, Serang.

Ibrahim is a lecturer in the Faculty of Social and Political Sciences, Bangka Belitung University, Pangkal Pinang.

Idris Thaha is a researcher in the Center for the Study of Islam and Society, and lecturer in the Faculty of Social and Political Sciences, Syarif Hidayatullah State Islamic University, Jakarta.

Mada Sukmajati is a lecturer in the Department of Government and Political Science, Gadjah Mada University, Yogyakarta.

Marzuki Wahid is a lecturer in the Syekh Nurjati State Institute for Islamic Studies, Cirebon.

Muhammad Mahsun is a graduate of the Masters programme in Government and Political Science, Gadjah Mada University, Yogyakarta.

Nono S.A. Sumampouw is a lecturer in the Department of Anthropology, Faculty of Social and Political Science, Sam Ratulangi University, Manado.

Noor Rohman is a lecturer in the Faculty of Social and Political Science, Sunan Ampel State Islamic University, Surabaya.

Olivia D. Purba is a student in the Masters of Environmental Management and Development programme at The Australian National University, Canberra.

Ridwan is a lecturer in the International Relations Program at the Papua University of Science and Technology, Jayapura.

Rizkika Lhena Darwin is a lecturer in the Political Science Program at Syiah Kuala University, Banda Aceh.

Rubaidi is a lecturer in the Faculty of Education and Teaching, Sunan Ampel State Islamic University, Surabaya.

Rudi Rohi is a lecturer in the Political Science Department, Nusa Cendana University, Kupang.

Sita Winawati Dewi is a journalist with *The Jakarta Post*.

S.L. Harjanto is a lecturer in Public Administration at the 45 Islamic University, Bekasi, and a journalist for *Radar Bekasi*.

Teuku Muhammad Jafar Sulaiman is a researcher with the Aceh Institute, Banda Aceh.

Zusiana Elly Triantini is a lecturer in the Syari'ah and Law Department, Sunan Kalijaga State Islamic University, Yogyakarta.

Index